A Coffee Frontier

PITT LATIN AMERICAN SERIES

University of Pittsburgh Press

A Coffee Frontier

LAND,
SOCIETY,
AND
POLITICS
IN DUACA,
VENEZUELA,
1830–1936

Doug Yarrington

Published by the University of Pittsburgh Press, Pittsburgh, Pa., 15261
Copyright © 1997, University of Pittsburgh Press
All rights reserved
Manufactured in the United States of America
Printed on acid-free paper
10 9 8 7 6 5 4 3 2 1

Library of Congress Cataloging-in-Publication Data
Yarrington, Doug, 1961–
     A coffee frontier : land, society, and politics in Duaca,
Venezuela, 1830–1936 / Doug Yarrington.
          p. cm. — (Pitt Latin American series)
     Includes bibliographical references and index.
     ISBN 0-8229-3983-5 (acid-free paper). — ISBN 0-8229-5632-2 (pbk.
: acid-free paper)
     1. Coffee industry—Venezuela—Crespo—History. 2. Coffee
industry—Venezuela—Duaca—History. 3. Crespo (Venezuela)—
government. I. Title. II. Series.
HD9199.V43C748 1997
338.1'7373'098725—dc21   97-4791
                                                                  CIP

A CIP catalog record for this book is available from the British Library.

FOR MARIA AND BEN

Contents

List of Maps, Figures, and Tables

Preface

BETWEEN THE MIDDLE of the nineteenth century and the Great Depression, two interrelated processes—an export boom and the consolidation of national states—fundamentally reshaped Latin American society. Taken together, the transformations of this era constituted the most profound changes in the region since the European conquest. In seeking to comprehend this critical period, historians have often turned to local studies, for it has become clear that no two areas experienced the developments of these years in exactly the same way. The present book contributes to this scholarly process by examining the changes that accompanied the coffee boom and state building in Duaca, a district in the state of Lara, in west-central Venezuela.

Even Venezuelanists may be surprised at the notion of a book-length study of coffee and politics in Duaca. Regarding coffee, the nation's leading export during most of this period, it is true that some Venezuelan districts produced more than Duaca. A few districts in the Andes, in the far west of the nation, produced considerably more. But as one examines the fragmented statistics on local coffee production in Venezuela, it becomes apparent that a great deal of the nation's annual crop—probably a majority—came from districts all across northern Venezuela with yields in the general range of Duaca's, which is to say up to 3 million kilograms at the height of the boom. A search for the "typical" coffee district would be fruitless, but Duaca was, by this one standard, clearly more typical of Venezuelan coffee zones than the few districts that became famous for their unusually large harvests.

In the political realm, Duaca acquired considerable importance around the turn of the century, as the construction of a railroad through the region added to its strategic significance, and as some members of the local elite gained a reputation as skilled guerrilla leaders capable of controlling the railroad during times of civil conflict. As a result, Duaca's local elite found itself able to bargain with the men who consolidated the national state in Venezuela in the early twentieth century. The experience of Duaca allows us to explore the nature of the new political order from a local perspective, and thus to make an original contribution to historical studies of Venezuela.

In addition, Duaca merits attention for the richness and variety of its historical documentation. Notary records, including sales, mortgages, and wills, are virtually complete for the period since the early 1870s. Because no agricultural census was conducted in Venezuela until the late 1930s, these documents are indispensable for understanding the structure of land tenure in the period under study and also offer detailed information on topics such as credit relationships and the economy of peasant households. Judicial documents from Duaca recount dozens of conflicts between landlords and peasants, providing insight into changing systems of land tenure and peasants' perception of these changes. Sources for the analysis of local politics, though sparse for much of the nineteenth century, are unusually plentiful for the period beginning in the late 1890s. They shed light on topics such as the relationship between the local elite and the central state, the interplay between politics and changing agrarian structures, and the peasant protests that exploded following a change of political regime in late 1935. Few regions in the entire republic offer such a range of sources for the study of social and political transformations during this critical period.

Finally, readers should be aware that the region I refer to as Duaca has been officially known as Distrito Crespo since 1899, when its administrative status was elevated from that of a municipality to that of a district. But most people in the vicinity continue to refer to the entire jurisdiction simply as Duaca, after the town of Duaca, which has been the local administrative center ever since its creation by the Spaniards in the early seventeenth century. By adopting this local usage and referring to the entire area as Duaca throughout the book, I avoid the confusion of using different names in different time periods for the same region.

MANY PEOPLE HAVE contributed to my work on this project, and it is a pleasure to acknowledge their assistance. Indeed, as I near the completion of this book, I see more clearly than ever how much I owe to those who helped me along the way. I would never have undertaken this project at all if not for Judy Ewell, who first encouraged me to study Venezuela during my undergraduate days at the College of William and Mary. In graduate school at the University of Texas, I had the good fortune to study with Jonathan Brown, Susan Deans-Smith, Richard Graham, and Alan Knight, all of whom commented on the dissertation that served as the basis for the present study. One could not ask for a better group of mentors. I owe a particular debt to Alan Knight for graciously agreeing to supervise a dissertation outside his primary area of interest, and for his perceptive comments and questions. While at Texas, I also benefited greatly from conversations with Peter Linder, who generously shared with me insights from his own research in the state of Zulia, and who convinced me that Venezuelan archives were an underutilized treasure trove for those wishing to pursue regional history.

In Venezuela, I met a number of scholars who assisted me as I went about my research. In Caracas, Susan Berglund, Marie Price, and Mark Zelmer oriented me to various libraries and archives. Early conversations with Marie, who was engaged in a ground-breaking study of Andean coffee zones, helped me to interpret the information I found regarding peasants, land tenure, and migration. In Barquisimeto and Duaca, I received vital assistance and counsel from Octavio Galíndez, Carlos Giménez, Luisa Rodríguez Marrufo, Taylor Rodríguez, and Reinaldo Rojas. I am especially grateful to Reinaldo and Luisa for sharing with me their research on colonial Duaca and on peasant protest in the state of Lara during the 1930s (respectively), which contributed greatly to my understanding of the region. I also wish to thank the staff of the Registro Principal del Estado Lara, in Barquisimeto, where I carried out most of my research, for their patience and good humor when confronted with the unaccustomed requests of a foreign scholar. My stay in Barquisimeto was greatly enriched by the hospitality and friendship of the Rodríguez Lugo family —Cecilia, Iraida, Luis Alberto, Ghysnil, Edilio, and Francisco—who welcomed my wife and me into their home for a year and a half.

As I began to prepare material for publication, a number of scholars took the time to respond to my ideas and offer their encouragement, including Susan Berglund, Elizabeth Dore, Steve Ellner, Judy Ewell, Mary Floyd, Peter Linder, John Lombardi, and Winthrop Wright. I am especially grateful to two anonymous reviewers for the University of Pittsburgh Press, for comments and suggestions that greatly improved the final draft.

I also wish to acknowledge my debt to William Roseberry for his pioneering studies of frontier peasantries. Readers will notice that I do not always agree with Roseberry's ideas, but his influence has marked my thinking nonetheless. The questions we choose to address as we write history are often more important than the answers we propose, and in this regard my debt to him is a large one. Of course, I alone am responsible for the use that I have made of the suggestions and ideas provided by others, and thus I bear sole responsibility for any errors of interpretation or fact in the pages that follow.

Acknowledgment is due also to the Institute for International Education, for a research grant provided under the auspices of the Fulbright Program; to the University of Texas at Austin for a graduate fellowship that supported a year of work after my return from Venezuela; to the interlibrary loan staff at Adams State College in Alamosa, Colorado; and to Duke University Press for permission to reprint material that originally appeared in "Public Land Settlement, Privatization, and Peasant Protest in Duaca, Venezuela, 1870–1936," *Hispanic American Historical Review* 74.1 (1994): 33–62.

Turning to debts of a more personal nature, it is difficult to know where to begin or end. I cannot put into words what I have received from those closest to me, who offered their love and support during the years of research and writing. I can only offer heartfelt thanks to my parents, Roger and Lynda Yarrington, to Forrest and Donna Swall, and most of all to my wife, Maria Swall-Yarrington, and our son, Ben.

A Coffee Frontier

1 Introduction

THIS STUDY EXAMINES agrarian change and politics in Duaca during the years when Venezuela was a major producer of coffee for the world market. I argue that the expansion of Venezuela's export economy in the middle of the nineteenth century led to the emergence of a prosperous and relatively autonomous peasantry in Duaca. Peasant families continued to flourish into the early twentieth century largely because of the availability of land on Duaca's extensive frontier of public lands (*terrenos baldíos*) and Indian community lands (*resguardos*), which they could freely occupy and cultivate. These advantageous conditions, I contend, came to an abrupt end in the 1910s and 1920s, when Duaca's elite restructured local society in their own interest, seizing control of public and Indian lands, and imposing on the peasantry a more exploitative set of relationships than had existed in the early decades of the coffee economy. Moreover, I argue that the fundamental impetus behind this process of social transformation came from alterations in the structure of political power, both nationally and locally, for the new agrarian order imposed by Duaca's elite was made possible by their alliance with the centralized state created by two national strongmen, Cipriano Castro (in power 1899–1908) and Juan Vicente Gómez (in power 1908–1935).

Such an argument touches upon a number of broader issues embedded in Venezuelan history, the history of Latin American coffee zones, and more general theoretical debates regarding social and political transformations. To place Duaca's peasantry in these larger contexts, I have found William Roseberry's concept of "precipitate" peasantries to be a useful category of analysis. Roseberry uses this term to refer to peasant populations composed of migrants who colonized frontiers of previously vacant land to produce commercial crops for the expanding global market of the nineteenth and early twentieth centuries.[1] Precipitate peasantries, unlike peasants who resided in villages that could trace their history hundreds of years into the past, only came into being during the great expansion of world demand for tropical and subtropical products that began in the latter half of the nineteenth century. As migrants from different locales, they shared neither a common ethnic identity nor a long-established network of community institutions—traits generally associated with village peasantries. Thus precipitate peasantries (or, as I also refer to them, frontier peasantries) constitute a distinct group within the broader field of peasant studies.

Coffee, Latin America's leading agricultural export in the century between independence and the Great Depression, was often produced in frontier regions and thus is intertwined with the history of precipitate peasantries in several areas of Latin America. To be sure, some coffee frontiers, such as São Paulo, Brazil, came to be dominated by a planter class that succeeded in monopolizing land, creating a dependent labor force, and preventing the rise of an independent peasantry. But in other settings, such as Costa Rica, Puerto Rico, and parts of Colombia, peasant migrants to the frontier enjoyed relatively free access to land and became the backbone of the coffee economy during its early decades. In these regions, as in Duaca and other areas of western Venezuela, the creation of an export economy based on coffee involved the creation of a peasantry in areas hitherto unoccupied or only lightly populated.[2] Moreover, the precipitate peasantries who came into being on these coffee frontiers (unlike peasants in some parts of Latin America) participated in the export economy because they chose to do so, and on the whole they seemed to benefit from coffee as long as they had relatively unfettered access to land.

In the long run, however, peasant prosperity based on coffee production proved impossible to sustain. For reasons that varied from one region to the next, the dynamism and autonomy that marked the formative years of frontier peasantries came to an end. In Costa Rica, peasant households that had

flourished on the frontier in the nineteenth century fell victim to land shortages and population pressure after about 1900, forcing the subdivision of family farms into smaller, uneconomical units once the frontier of good land was
occupied. In other areas, such as the Colombian frontier, the decline of the
peasantry engaged in coffee production resulted from the elite's use of political influence to appropriate lands occupied by peasant settlers. Meanwhile, in
the interior highlands of Puerto Rico, demographic trends and the coercive
power of the state each played a role in the demise of small coffee producers.[3]
In sum, the decline of frontier peasantries, like the transformation of agrarian
structures in preindustrial Europe, can be explained by reference either to demographic forces or to patterns of class conflict mediated by the state, depending on the region involved or, in some cases, the preconceptions of the
historian.[4]

Despite a growing interest in Latin American agrarian history in general
and coffee regions in particular over the past twenty years or so, and despite
Venezuela's status as a major exporter of coffee before the Great Depression,
rural Venezuela has received comparatively little attention from scholars.
This neglect almost surely results from the widely held image of Venezuela as
a nation shaped so thoroughly by petroleum that all other influences may be
relegated to secondary importance. Although few would dispute the importance of oil, the economic and political crises of the 1980s and 1990s suggest
that petroleum has not given Venezuela a society or polity as distinct from
those of other Latin American nations as was once thought. By the same
token, as the years of oil-based "prosperity" recede into the past, they appear
to have been a rather brief and exceptional period in the nation's history
rather than a time of permanent and fundamental change. Thus one may ask
whether other realities in Venezuela's history—such as a social structure divided along racial lines, a political culture dominated by an ethic of patronage, and an economy dependent on a narrow range of exports since the
seventeenth century—have molded Venezuela at least as much as oil. As these
questions acquire greater urgency, perhaps increased attention will be given
to the similarities rather than the differences between Venezuela and other
Latin American nations, especially those nations where coffee has been a critical export.

Scholars who have written about Venezuelan rural history often emphasize continuity rather than change, seeing no fundamental alteration of agrarian structure since the colonial period. Pioneering studies by Miguel Acosta
Saignes and Federico Brito Figueroa, for example, emphasize landowners'

control over a dependent rural working class throughout the period between independence and the Great Depression.[5] Although Acosta and Brito argue that the Gómez dictatorship (1908–1935) brought an intensification of Venezuela's "feudal" system of large estates and debt peonage, they identify no basic change in land tenure or rural class structure during his long rule. Likewise, these scholars devote little attention to the question of regional variation within Venezuela, or to the place of small, independent cultivators in the nation's agrarian history. On the whole, they stress a uniformly oppressive agrarian structure across regions, just as they emphasize its continuity through time.

Recent studies by younger scholars give greater attention to the importance of regional variations in Venezuelan rural history, however, and focus more directly on coffee, the nation's leading export from 1830 until 1925, when it was displaced by oil. Recent works have confirmed the prevalence of large estates and debt peonage in the central coastal zone surrounding Caracas, while they also emphasize the importance of small peasant farms in the Andean states of Táchira, Mérida, and Trujillo (see map 1). Studies by Alicia Ardao, Arturo Muñoz, Marie Price, and William Roseberry have confirmed the importance of peasant production in the Andes, which became the center of Venezuela's coffee economy in the late nineteenth century.[6] Composed primarily of thinly populated frontier areas through the mid-nineteenth century, Andean coffee zones attracted large numbers of migrants after the Federal War of 1859–1863. By the 1890s the Andes produced more than half of Venezuela's coffee, making the nation the third-largest exporter in the world. Although opportunities for peasant settlers began to fade in the early twentieth century as the supply of vacant land was exhausted, the presence of a large peasantry has continued to distinguish the Andean states from the rest of Venezuela.

Duaca, the focus of the present study, is located in west-central Venezuela, a region encompassing the states of Lara, Yaracuy, and Falcón. This region lies between the Andean states and the central coastal zone of Miranda, Aragua, Carabobo, and the Federal District. Thus the west-central region is bordered to the east by an area historically dominated by large estates, and to the west by a region characterized primarily by peasant holdings. Little research has been done on the agrarian systems of the west-central zone during the national period, but it seems clear that the region included a variety of land tenure and labor systems. Locales such as Guarico (in southwestern Lara) and Nirgua (in eastern Yaracuy)—both important centers of coffee pro-

MAP 1 VENEZUELA

Map 1. Venezuela

duction during the nineteenth and twentieth centuries—contained sizable concentrations of peasant cultivators, while large estates controlled much of the land around Carora (western Lara), Barquisimeto (eastern Lara), and San Felipe (central Yaracuy). (See map 2.)

Because Roseberry developed the concept of a precipitate peasantry in his study of the coffee-producing district of Boconó, in the state of Trujillo, my use of the concept highlights the similarities between Duaca's early history and that of the Venezuelan Andes. Like many parishes established by Spanish colonists in the Andes, Duaca was founded as a center of enforced Indian settlement, but over the course of the nineteenth century it attracted an ethnically mixed population of migrants who fanned out across the landscape, cleared new land, and planted coffee. In Duaca, as in the Andes, the peasant economy was most prosperous in the nineteenth century when the availability of land allowed the spatial expansion of peasant production.

The history of the two areas diverged in the twentieth century, however. Whereas the decline of household economies in Duaca resulted from the

MAP 2 THE STATE OF LARA

Map 2. The State of Lara

elite's sudden, wholesale appropriation of public and Indian lands, the peasantry in Boconó (and apparently in the Andes generally) experienced a more gradual decline as growing population pressure eroded the small holder economy and sharpened the differentiation between rich and poor peasant families. Thus while the decline of Duaca's precipitate peasantry suggests parallels with the expropriation of peasants on the Colombian frontier, the Andean experience is much closer to the demographically driven transition typified by Costa Rican coffee zones.

Although I agree with Roseberry's notion of precipitate peasantries as a distinct social group created in the context of an expanding global market, I should make clear at the outset that I disagree with some of his conclusions about the nature of such groups. In particular, Roseberry emphasizes merchant domination of peasants from the time that they began to produce coffee, and more broadly, he stresses the manner in which the formation of a frontier peasantry served the needs of the global economy. In short, he portrays peasant society as weakened, even doomed, from the beginning by its place in the world capitalist system. Such a conceptualization seems to me to concentrate too heavily on peasants' relationship to an all-powerful commercial system, while slighting the importance of other factors that shaped peasant life just as profoundly, and which produced variation in peasant fortunes over time.[7]

MAP 3 DISTRITO CRESPO (DUACA)

Map 3. Distrito Crespo (Duaca)

By contrast, I find it more useful to draw a sharp distinction between the favorable conditions available to frontier peasants in the nineteenth century, when land was plentiful, and the increasingly dire situation they confronted in the twentieth. To be sure, peasants in the nineteenth century were already subject to exploitation in their relationships with merchants and with hacienda owners who employed them as seasonal labor. Nevertheless, the nineteenth-century coffee frontier offered opportunities as well as risks, as peasants them-selves seemed to know. Studies of peasant migration to coffee zones in the Venezuelan Andes and in Costa Rica indicate that peasants saw the possibility of commercial production as a good thing, and this perception, rather than fading after a few years' experience with coffee, continued as long as land re-mained available for colonization.[8] At least in the nineteenth century, there seemed to be no fundamental contradiction between the prosperity of fron-tier peasantries and production for the global market.

Reasoning further along these lines, I differ with Roseberry on whether the concept of "moral economy" is useful in the study of frontier peasantries. This concept, which has dominated discussion of peasant resistance and revolt over the last two decades, highlights the conservative, backward-looking nature of peasant protest; more specifically, it emphasizes peasants' propensity to defend established, "traditional," or "noncapitalist" systems of production that served the peasantry well until they were undermined by the pressure of capitalist development or intrusion by the state. Roseberry suggests that moral economy analysis is largely irrelevant to precipitate peasantries because such groups have been enmeshed in capitalism, by virtue of their links to merchants, from the moment of their formation as a class and thus have no precapitalist traditions to defend.[9]

Although I do not wish to delve into the old question of whether a society is "capitalist" from the time it enters production for the world market or only following the proletarianization of the workforce, much less initiate a sterile debate over whether frontier peasant societies are the ethical equals of the village societies commonly featured in the moral economy literature, I do think the concept may be more relevant to frontier peasantries than Roseberry suggests. As I argue in chapter 9, the peasant protests that erupted in Duaca following the death of Juan Vicente Gómez in late 1935 (as well as the less dramatic, "everyday" resistance of the previous two decades) closely parallel the dynamics outlined in the moral economy literature. Peasants who resisted the oppressive conditions imposed during the last twenty years of the Gómez regime measured these changes against their collective memory of an earlier (perhaps romanticized) period, when most land in Duaca was public or controlled by the Indian community, when families relied on usufruct rights to guarantee their access to land, and when rents on the few private estates that existed were quite low. In short, because I believe that precipitate peasantries tended to be formed under relatively favorable conditions in the nineteenth century, I find it quite plausible that peasant rebels at a later date fought to return to those conditions that had benefited their class in the past. Whether one chooses to apply the label of moral economy or not, this argument concerning the backward-looking nature of peasant protest in Duaca seems important to our understanding of political consciousness among peasantries who trace their origins to commercial production in a frontier setting.

Because agrarian change in Duaca was driven more by political factors than by market or demographic forces, I have found myself obliged to consider theoretical questions relating to the nature of the state. Simply put, I see the Venezuelan state primarily as a clientelistic network, composed of factions of the well-to-do who participate in politics largely as a means of extending their influence within society, and especially as a means of advancing their economic interests. Moreover, I agree with those who see clientelism as an enduring feature of Latin America's politics, rather than a "stage" in political development.[10] That is, I do not see political structures characterized by clientelism as a prelude to the emergence of a more "rational" bureaucratic state that separates itself from the interests of economic elites and becomes "modern." This point is all the more important because of the significance I attach to the centralization of state power, a process often highlighted in modernization paradigms.

As it occurred in Venezuela under Castro and Gómez, political centralization merely meant that the clientelist network of the dominant elite faction became more effective at subjugating competing factions. Whereas, before Castro and Gómez, regional caudillos (that is, strongmen commanding personal armies) could make or break a national government, the two Andean leaders imposed the authority of the center and demanded the personal loyalty of all those allowed to hold positions of influence. Thus regional factions answering to regional bosses gave way to a more integrated, nationwide network of patrons and clients, all of whom recognized a single, central authority. Centralization involved a reorganization of clientelism but did not signal its demise.

By focusing so intently on clientelism in my discussion of politics, I do not claim to have an answer to the long-standing riddle of how to define "the state." I only point toward the conceptualization of politics that seems most useful for understanding the processes at the heart of Duaca's history in the early twentieth century. Other scholars seeking to illuminate other questions may be right to focus on the fiscal, ideological, or bureaucratic aspects of state power, but such approaches would throw little light on the time and place I have chosen to study.[11]

Venezuelanists will recognize my reliance on scholars who have discussed centralization under Castro and Gómez and who have argued that these two leaders fundamentally altered the national state.[12] But whereas historians such as Ramón J. Velásquez, Elías Pino Iturrieta, and Inés Quintero have looked at political change primarily on a nationwide basis, this study examines a single locality. In doing so, it modifies our understanding of the relationship between local elites and power holders at the center. The accepted view of centralization under Castro and Gómez posits the complete triumph of the center over regional and local elites. The history of Duaca, however, demonstrates that local elites could turn centralization to their own advantage. Although Duaca's elite initially resisted the centralizing impulse, they later made their peace with the center and became integrated into the new national state. Prominent Duaqueños went on to use their ties to the center to carry out the transformation of agrarian structures during the Gómez regime; their political connections proved especially important in the privatization of national lands (terrenos baldíos) between 1919 and 1923.

Thus, in Duaca, members of the local elite successfully allied themselves to the national state in a way that consolidated their power over local society. By making themselves faithful and useful clients of national leaders, Duaca's elite eventually gained more than they lost from centralization. In the bargain, peasants who had participated in the coffee economy from a relatively advantageous position found themselves reduced to dependency and greater exploitation. While the present study is revisionist in several aspects, then, it is thoroughly traditional in its presentation of the Gómez era as an especially dark chapter in the history of Venezuelan working people.

2 The Early History of Duaca

From the Spanish Conquest to the
Origins of Coffee Production, 1620–1863

IN LATE 1673, the Capuchin friar Miguel de Madrid led a group of men northward out of the city of Barquisimeto, in what is now the eastern part of the state of Lara. After some forty kilometers of travel on a hot, gradually climbing road, they entered the valley of San Juan Bautista de Duaca. The party undoubtedly proceeded with some apprehension, for their mission in the valley was to pacify the Gayones Indians who had violently resisted Spanish control since the beginning of the century. But like most travelers entering the valley from Barquisimeto, Friar Miguel and his companions probably welcomed the cool air and the vistas of green rolling mountains to the east, west, and north. They soon entered the town of Duaca, the principal focus of their mission. Created by the Spaniards over fifty years earlier as a place to congregate the local Indian population, it consisted of two or three dozen houses and a small church. No one greeted de Madrid and his companions, and as they approached the church they found that the roof had caved in and the walls were beginning to crumble. The town itself was deserted. De Madrid encountered only one adult in Duaca, Juan Berós, who informed him that some of the town's "residents" were living in the surrounding mountains, but that most had migrated to Aroa, a settlement forty kilometers to the northeast.[1]

The abandoned village discovered by de Madrid characterized the limited success of Spanish attempts to establish a colonial society in the parish of Duaca. Never an economic center of consequence during the period of Spanish rule, Duaca remained outside the booming cacao economy that developed to the east, in the mountains and valleys fanning outward from the capital city of Caracas. As a result, Duaca was still a sparsely populated frontier area when Venezuela became an independent nation in 1830. Sustained economic and demographic growth began only during the decades following independence, when the expansion of Venezuela's coffee economy began to draw migrants to Duaca's vast expanses of vacant land. Even then, the lack of transportation and commercial credit restrained the growth of the local export economy, so that the region retained large amounts of open land when the coffee boom began in earnest after the conclusion of the Federal War in 1863.

Conquest, Encomienda, *and Conflict*

Spanish settlement in what is now the state of Lara began over a century before the Capuchin mission to Duaca when, in 1545, a group of settlers from the northern port of Coro established the town of El Tocuyo. Located at the eastern edge of the Andes, El Tocuyo served as a base for expeditions into the mountains rising to the west and to the lowlands stretching eastward. One such expedition set out in 1551 to search for gold, traveling eastward until a deposit was found along the Buría River. The city that the miners founded, which came to be known as Barquisimeto, was moved no less than three times before arriving at its permanent site along the Turbio River, on the edge of a lush, fertile valley.² As the gold was soon depleted, colonists turned their attention to the development of agricultural and livestock haciendas along the Turbio and in the mountains nearby.

Spaniards established their enterprises by imposing a regime of forced labor on the region's native people, the Gayones, Jirajaras, Ayamanes, and Axaguas.³ Through this system, known as the *encomienda,* the Spanish crown authorized prominent colonists throughout the empire to exact labor and tribute from designated indigenous villages. The encomienda had a much longer life in Venezuela than in more densely populated "core" areas of the empire. Although the crown ended *encomenderos'* claim to indigenous labor and tribute in central Mexico and Peru in the mid-sixteenth century, the institution survived in poorer, outlying colonies such as Venezuela, where the crown had less reason to fear that elites might use their privileges to establish themselves as an autonomous colonial nobility. Venezuelan encomenderos retained their privileges until the late seventeenth and early eighteenth centuries, when the Spanish crown ended Indians' labor obligation and diverted their tribute payments to the government treasury.[4]

Barquisimeto's settlers received their first encomienda grants in 1552, and early in the next century the Gayones Indians to the north of the city, in the area that would become the parish of Duaca, were incorporated into the encomienda system.[5] Encomenderos who received these grants, like their counterparts elsewhere in the colony, repeatedly violated royal decrees regulating the encomienda by confining laborers to haciendas for long periods of time and compelling them to work beyond the required three days per week. To address this situation, the governor of Venezuela decreed in 1620 that a town, to be named San Juan Bautista de Duaca, should be established in the valley northeast of Barquisimeto. The town was to serve as a *pueblo de doctrina,* a permanent settlement where Indians assigned to various encomenderos would live together under the supervision—and, it was hoped, the protection —of religious and civil authorities.[6]

For the next fifty years, however, few of the Indians assigned to live in Duaca actually did so. Although the Spanish never abandoned Duaca completely, as they did some of the pueblos in the region, the town existed more in theory than in reality. The difficulty of congregating indigenous people in Duaca stemmed from several factors. First, many of the Gayones Indians tenaciously resisted the European conquest and incorporation into the encomienda. Living scattered in the mountains, they occasionally raided Spanish settlements and provided a haven for "pacified" Indians who managed to flee their colonial masters.[7] Meanwhile, Duaca's encomenderos undermined official efforts to congregate the indigenous people by continuing to confine their workers on their haciendas. This abuse, observed in detail by a visiting bishop in 1625, had the effect of separating Indians from their homes and fields near the town of Duaca.[8]

Finally, the stabilization of Duaca's population was hindered by migration to copper mines in the valley of Aroa, some forty kilometers to the northeast.[9] Due to the lack of indigenous population in Aroa, miners there hired workers from adjacent areas, including Duaca. Unknown to colonial authorities, many of Duaca's indigenous people journeyed to Aroa for religious motives as well, for while at the mines they were free to practice their preconquest religion, away from the gaze of Catholic priests. "These secret gatherings in the caves and rocky hollows of Aroa," notes historian Paul Verna, "surely held a very strong appeal for the Indians of Duaca."[10] Throughout the seventeenth century, the combination of economic and religious incentives for migration proved irresistible. Thus when Miguel de Madrid arrived in Duaca in 1673 on his mission to pacify the Gayones, he found the town all but deserted and was informed that most of the residents had gone to Aroa.

Stabilization, Growth, and the Regional Economy, 1673–1836

Nevertheless, de Madrid and other Capuchins stayed in Duaca another twenty years and succeeded in gathering many indigenous parishioners to the town of Duaca. Censuses conducted in 1691, 1758, 1779, and 1800–1801 point toward a gradual increase in population for the parish as a whole, and the definitive creation of a stable population in the town itself.[11] The unusually detailed census of 1779—carried out during the visit of Bishop Mariano Martí—merits special attention because of its breakdown of the parish's population by ethnic (caste) categories, gender, age, and marital status (see table 1).

These figures should be considered as approximations at best, and the ethnic categories must be seen as highly subjective combinations of racial, cultural, and economic class factors.[12] The census indicates that even during the late colonial period, Duaca remained a predominantly Indian parish, with well

Table 1. Population of Duaca in 1779

| | Men | | Women | | Children[a] | | |
	Married	*Single*	*Married*	*Single*	*Male*	*Female*	*Total*
Indians	52	68	52	53	27	62	314
Whites	11	24	11	31	13	8	98
Free blacks	—	4	—	4	1	1	10
Mulattos	17	23	17	31	16	9	113
Black slaves	1	1	1	8	3	2	16
Total	81	120	81	127	60	82	551

Source: Obispo Mariano Martí, "Pueblo de San Juan Bautista de Duaca," in Lino Gómez Canedo, ed., *Documentos relativos a su visita pastoral del diócesis de Caracas (1771–1784)* (Caracas: Academia Nacional de la Historia, 1969), 6:377. See also Rojas, "La encomienda en Barquisimeto colonial," 358.

a. Under twelve years of age.

over half its population (314 out of 551) falling into this category. The high number of persons listed as mulattos (113)—more than one fifth of the total population—is striking, given the low number of blacks, both slave (16) and free (10), and in view of Duaca's origin as a center of forced Indian settlement. The size of this group may have reflected migration from neighboring areas with higher black populations, such as Aroa and the sugar-growing areas to the south, as well as unions involving Duaqueños who had temporarily migrated to these areas. It is also possible, however, that the census takers did not apply the term *mulatto* in its strict sense of a person of African and European heritage but, rather, applied it to a broad spectrum of the mixed-race population.[13]

The flexibility of these caste labels almost certainly explains the substantial number of persons (98) counted as white, for a note accompanying the census figures indicates that mestizos could be counted with whites.[14] In view of the comparatively limited economic opportunities in Duaca at this time, the parish probably did not attract many of the region's elite, who invariably claimed pure European descent. Many of Duaca's "whites" were probably people of mixed indigenous and European heritage who had acquired some degree of wealth and social status, at least in the context of a provincial village.

Finally, the 1779 census reveals the very limited presence of slavery in Duaca. Despite the institution's importance within the Venezuelan economy as a whole at this time, only sixteen of the Duaqueños counted were slaves. Within this group, the high number of adult women (9) compared to adult men (2) suggests that masters in Duaca acquired slaves for use as domestic servants rather than field-workers. Slaves formed a negligible part of the agricultural labor force in Duaca.

Most Duaqueños made their living by farming small plots within the lands assigned to the parish's Indian community. Such communally owned lands, known as resguardos, were granted to Indian towns throughout Venezuela by the Spanish crown in order to assure the conquered peoples an independent base of subsistence. Families within indigenous communities enjoyed the use of specific plots within the resguardos, but neither they nor the community could sell or mortgage the land. Two portions of the resguardos were to be set aside for communal use, one portion as common grazing land and one to be farmed collectively in order to raise funds for a "community chest" used to pay for religious festivals, bureaucratic and legal fees, and other village needs. In establishing the system of village lands, the crown intended to prevent the colonial elite from converting the Indians into landless, dependent laborers, and (just as important) it sought to guarantee that the indigenous people remained able to pay taxes into the royal treasury.[15]

Duaca's resguardos, which extended approximately five kilometers from the center of town to the north, south, east, and west, encompassed a variety of ecological zones and some of the best land in the parish. All of the valley of Duaca, within which the town was located, fell inside the resguardos' boundaries. This land benefited from the Tumaque stream, which provided water for irrigation and which, unlike many streams in the area, ran throughout the year.[16] Outside the valley, the resguardos included land in three distinct ecological zones. To the south, flatlands sloped gradually downward to Barquisimeto. This section of the resguardos proved suitable for livestock and, where water could be found, the cultivation of food crops. To the west of the valley rose the mountains of Bobare, which continued into the neighboring parish of Bobare. These highlands, although somewhat dry, were farmed by many Duaqueños and provided the site for some of the parish's earliest coffee groves. The richest agricultural land in the parish lay to the north and east of the valley of Duaca, in the Aroa mountains, which stretched toward the mines. Within the boundaries of the parish of Duaca, these mountains rose to a maximum height of twelve hundred meters, although within the resguardos they did not exceed nine hundred meters. The Aroa mountains received more rainfall than the parish's other ecological zones and became the center of Duaca's coffee economy in the nineteenth century.[17] The resguardos, then, enclosed a diverse area and provided the indigenous community with sufficient land to meet its subsistence needs and to produce a range of products for sale in local markets.

Throughout colonial Venezuela, the history of Indian lands differed substantially from the ideal outlined in royal decrees. Disputes over the boundaries of community lands became commonplace, in large part because colonial officials disagreed over how much land the crown intended to grant each village.[18] Meanwhile, non-Indians regularly established haciendas within the resguardos, pushing Indians off their land and usurping their crops.[19] In Duaca, conflicts repeatedly arose between the indigenous community and owners of El Buco, a sugar hacienda located on community land along the Tumaque stream. Protests against El Buco, however, were hindered by links between the hacienda and the local church. In the 1750s, the hacienda belonged to the village priest, Juan Bernabé Canelón Lanzarote, who attached an obligation to the property to guarantee that a percentage of its yearly earnings went to the church.[20]

Ownership of El Buco later passed to Don Martín de Zidardia, a resident of Barquisimeto who also owned a large cacao plantation in Aroa, but the hacienda continued to produce funds for church institutions in Barquisimeto and Duaca.[21] Bishop Martí observed that Zidardia's sugar hacienda monopolized the Tumaque's waters so completely that some Indians could not water their plots and others were reluctant to establish farms on community lands nearby.[22] Nevertheless, colonial authorities refused to enforce community rights to land and water. By using El Buco to guarantee debts owed to the church, and thus giving the church a financial stake in the hacienda, the owners of El Buco gained the acquiescence of local officials. Denied the use of some of their best land, community members were pushed to other sections of the resguardos.

Although most Duaqueños made their living primarily from subsistence agriculture within the resguardos, their lives were also shaped by the developments in the larger regional economy. Indeed, the parish's demographic stabilization and growth from the eighteenth century onward resulted largely from its favorable geographic location between Aroa and Barquisimeto. Copper mining, having flourished in Aroa in the seventeenth century, burgeoned again in the 1790s and sporadically throughout the nineteenth century. Beginning in the 1740s, the valley of Aroa became economically important for another reason: cacao. This tropical product, the bean used to make chocolate, was Venezuela's most valuable export from the mid-seventeenth century until independence.[23] Cacao production began along the central coast and inland mountains near Caracas and eventually spread as far west as the valley of Aroa. Since slaves were expensive and not always available, cacao growers in Aroa (like the local mine owners) hired thousands of free workers, many of whom came from Duaca. But migrants to the plantations, like those who went to the mines, only worked for short periods of time in the fever-ridden lowlands of Aroa before returning home. Thus Duaca, with its cooler, much healthier climate, remained a base for the subsistence and reproduction of migratory workers.[24]

The eighteenth century also witnessed the beginning of Barquisimeto's rise as an important commercial center in western Venezuela. This development reflected the city's strategic location at the intersection of several geographic regions. To the east lay the central coastal zone and its inland mountains and valleys, containing the most concentrated population in the colony and the capital city of Caracas. The road west from Barquisimeto led to the plains of Carora, an expanding center of livestock production, and eventually to Lake

Maracaibo and its port city. Traveling southwest, one entered the prosperous agricultural valley of El Tocuyo, and beyond that, the Andes. Directly to the south stretched the llanos, Venezuela's immense grassy flatlands. Thus Barquisimeto lay at a crossroads linking several of Venezuela's principal regions. By 1810 the city's growth as a commercial center had resulted in a population of 11,300.[25]

Duaca's location midway along the road between Barquisimeto and Aroa had a critical impact on its early development. The land around the village was well suited to the production of food crops, a portion of which the Duaqueños could sell in Barquisimeto and Aroa, and local merchants and mule drivers must have participated in the commercial traffic that passed through town in both directions. Although this trade came to a virtual halt during the war for independence that raged in Venezuela between 1810 and 1821, it recovered quickly thereafter. In 1824 British entrepreneurs leased the Aroa mines from Simón Bolívar, Venezuela's liberator, who had recently inherited them. Anxious to exploit the high-quality ore, which Alexander von Humboldt had declared to be some of the finest copper in the world, the British developed the mines more aggressively than previous owners. The regional economy was reborn as some twelve hundred workers, both British and Venezuelan, were drawn to the mines and copper production boomed.[26]

John Hawkshaw, a young English engineer working in Aroa, passed through Barquisimeto and Duaca in the early 1830s and, like so many foreign travelers in Latin America, carefully observed local economic conditions. Clearly impressed with Barquisimeto's prosperity, even though much of the city still lay in ruins from an earthquake twenty years before, Hawkshaw emphasized the commercial benefits derived from the copper boom and the revival of regional trade. By contrast, the young Englishman was decidedly unimpressed by his visit to Duaca, which he described as a dull provincial village. He noted the abandoned church, which was poorly served by "a little whitish old man, who lives in the neighbourhood, comes occasionally and officiates as priest." Arriving late one afternoon, Hawkshaw was irritated to find that most of the townspeople passed the evening in their houses, leaving the streets deserted except for a few children who played naked in the dusty road. The engineer and his companions passed the night in a *pulpería,* or small general store, and left early the next morning, having concluded that there was nothing of interest in Duaca.[27]

And yet some details in Hawkshaw's account suggest that the revival of trade along the Barquisimeto-Aroa axis had brought important changes to the parish. He estimated that the village contained close to one hundred houses, a substantial increase over the forty-nine counted in the 1779 census. Most of the villagers, whom Hawkshaw considered to be predominantly Indian, dedicated themselves to raising chickens and growing maize for sale in Aroa. His observation of small plots of maize on the outskirts of town and his conversation with an Indian shop owner who planned to take a few bushels to Aroa suggest that many of those involved in the trade were peasant cultivators and petty traders. Apparently many of the parish's inhabitants participated in the supply of foodstuffs to Aroa's growing population.

The intensified commercial ties to Aroa, however, proved short-lived. Although the British purchased the mines outright in the early 1830s, tensions with native workers and the high mortality rate among European employees led to the closing of the mines in 1836. Migration to the area halted and Aroa was soon deserted.[28] As the traffic between Barquisimeto and the mines ended, another chapter in Duaca's halting development came to a close. Duaqueños, whose proximity to Aroa had introduced them to producing agricultural goods for a distant market, began to look for new ways to make a living from the land. Like many Venezuelans in the years following independence, they soon turned to the production of coffee.

The Origins of the Coffee Economy, ca. 1830–1859

A number of factors pushed Venezuela toward a growing dependence on coffee during the early decades of the republic. In the central coastal zone, the long war for independence left most cacao estates in ruins, and many planters faced the task of rebuilding their farms during the 1820s and 1830s. The Venezuelan elite were already familiar with coffee, having produced it in modest quantities during the last decades of the colony, and realized that it now offered several advantages over cacao. Coffee bushes were less expensive than cacao trees, began producing a marketable harvest in three or four years rather than six, and did not require the expensive irrigation works needed for cacao. Just as important, changes in Venezuela's relationship to the international trading system also favored coffee. Venezuelan specialization in cacao had proved logical in the context of trade within the Spanish empire, but independence opened the nation to unrestricted participation in the North Atlantic economy and allowed foreign merchants to establish import-export operations in the major port cities. Meanwhile, steadily increasing coffee consumption in Europe and the United States kept prices high for much of the 1830s, and because the Venezuelan government instituted policies that were highly favorable to creditors, merchants proved eager to loan money to planters who promised repayment in coffee. In sum, ecological and market factors came together in the years following independence to make coffee the nation's leading export by the early 1830s.[29]

This description of a systematic transition to coffee, however, is drawn primarily from Venezuela's central coastal zone and is of limited relevance for understanding the rise of coffee production in Duaca. Although Duaqueños were planting coffee by the 1830s, production grew much more gradually than in the central coastal zone; in Duaca, as in western Venezuela generally, the real boom in the coffee economy did not arrive until the 1860s and 1870s. There were fundamental differences in the social structure that accompanied coffee as well. Whereas planters in the center integrated coffee cultivation into the existing structure of large estates worked largely by slave labor, in the early decades of coffee production Duaca's agrarian structure (again, like that of western Venezuela generally) was based on small-scale peasant farms, with comparatively few private estates or large-scale farms.[30]

Of equal importance, Duaca remained outside the central zone's network of credit and marketing until the mid-1860s. The difficulty of transportation between the municipality and Puerto Cabello, the nearest export point, worked against Duaca's integration into the commercial system to the east. Instead, early coffee producers depended on an assortment of ad hoc, individually arranged credit relationships, including loans from religious institutions, an increasingly rare form of credit in the center. As late as the 1850s, coffee growers in Duaca resorted to loans from church schools and hospitals in El Tocuyo and Barquisimeto.[31] Other Duaqueños growing coffee sought out individuals with money to lend in Barquisimeto or in Duaca itself, but no large merchant houses or regularized system of credit emerged.[32] So, although the coffee grown in Duaca was ultimately exported through Puerto Cabello by the same foreign merchants who marketed coffee grown in the central zone, Duaqueños began cultivating the crop well before their locale was fully integrated into the international commercial system.

The onset of coffee production in Duaca, from the 1830s through the outbreak of the Federal War in 1859, was accompanied by a steady demographic expansion. Whereas the inhabitants of the entire parish had totaled 551 in 1779, Hawkshaw reported almost a hundred houses in the town alone in 1834. And an inspection of Duaca's public lands (located beyond the resguardo boundaries and hence over five kilometers from town) found 144 farms in 1837, which suggests significant migration to Duaca's rural hinterland. Finally, the first national census, that of 1873, reported 7,471 people in the municipality. So, between 1779 and 1873, while Venezuela's population grew by 540 percent (from 330,000 to 1,784,194), Duaca's population increased by more than 1,350 percent.[33] Duaca's 1873 population probably reflects a large influx of migrants after the end of the Federal War in 1863, but when combined with the earlier figures it also suggests ongoing demographic expansion since independence. Apparently, migrants were already arriving in significant numbers in the 1830s.

Demographic growth and the search for good coffee land led to the geographic dispersal of settlement. Some settlers moved to unoccupied areas of the Indian community lands, but others settled farther away from the town of Duaca, renting privately owned land as tenants, or establishing farms on the national lands that formed the largest portion of Duaca's territory. Most settlers were peasant families who worked small fields of food crops and often planted coffee groves as well. This structure of predominantly peasant production on the resguardos, national lands, and private estates endured until the early twentieth century, and the coexistence of these three types of land tenure is fundamental to Duaca's agrarian history. The development of each type of land tenure during the early postindependence period now merits closer attention.

The Indian Community Lands (Resguardos)

During the early national period, the new government in Caracas repeatedly called for all Indian community lands in Venezuela to be parceled out to community members. Like other Latin American elites influenced by the ideology of liberalism, Venezuelan officials endorsed the idea of creating a new class of independent, landowning, indigenous farmers, tied to the national market economy. A national law passed in 1836, for example, called on provincial legislatures to divide resguardo lands among the families of each indigenous community, with households receiving title to plots that would vary in size according to the number of family members.[34] These provisions, however, violated the interests of non-Indian elites who owned haciendas on the resguardos because the law allowed only Indians to obtain title to community lands. As a consequence, the legislation was rarely implemented. Two years later the national Congress, recognizing that the 1836 law had accomplished nothing, enacted new legislation that bypassed the provincial governments, declared Indian communities absolute owners of the resguardos, and enabled them to proceed immediately with the division and privatization of their lands.[35] Once again the law mandated that only members of indigenous communities would receive title to resguardo lands, and once again it was not carried out in most of the nation, including Duaca.

While legislative attempts at privatization of the resguardos accomplished little, local elites continually sought to usurp indigenous lands.[36] On occasion, government officials attempted to defend Indian ownership until such time as legal privatization might be carried out. In the early 1850s, for example, numerous indigenous communities petitioned the president for protection against outsiders who, under the pretext of measuring national lands (terrenos baldíos) for purchase from the government, had encroached on the resguardos. In response, federal officials ordered governors of all Venezuelan provinces to protect Indian rights to the resguardos.[37] Some provincial governments assisted a few communities in the defense of their lands.[38] These occasional efforts notwithstanding, illicit appropriation of Indian land became common in the decades following independence.[39]

In Duaca, struggles for control of indigenous lands followed the broad outlines of national developments, as provincial officials offered occasional aid to the community but stopped short of evicting non-Indians from the resguardos. In 1828 and 1840 officials in Barquisimeto responded to petitions from Duaca's indigenous community by ordering local hacendados to respect native property rights.[40] But neither order was intended to remove hacendados from community land; each order sought only to prevent further encroachment. That Duaqueños had to appeal to Barquisimeto to receive even this limited support suggests that Duaca's local government either was too weak to address the problem or was controlled by the very persons who usurped the indigenous lands.

Duaqueños' struggle for community control over the resguardos suffered an irreparable setback in the early 1850s when a large portion of community lands passed to private ownership. In 1850, fifty-one Duaca Indians gave power of attorney to Gumercindo Giménez, a Barquisimeto merchant and politician, authorizing him to supervise the demarcation, measurement, and division of the resguardos.[41] In order to pay for these procedures, Giménez received authority to collect money from the resguardo occupants and to rent or sell unspecified sections of the community lands. Although Giménez never carried out the division of all the community lands, he did use the authority granted him to sell a number of tracts of resguardo land, claiming that the proceeds were needed to pay surveying costs. In all, Gumercindo Giménez sold 2,217.5 *fanegadas* (1,549.1 hectares) of community land to fifteen individuals for a total of 2,795 pesos—a considerable sum of money and surely more than he needed to pay the costs of surveying the resguardos. Most of the land was sold off in relatively large tracts, with lots of a hundred hectares or more accounting for perhaps 75 percent of the alienated community lands.[42]

Members of the Indian community opposed the sales, and in 1865 they authorized Colonel Félix Aguilar to initiate a lawsuit to recover all community lands sold by Gumercindo Giménez.[43] Although no further documentation concerning the conflict has survived, it would seem that Giménez's prestige in Barquisimeto political circles doomed the villagers' efforts. A national congressman in the 1850s and 1860s who obtained the rank of general in the Federal War of 1859–1863, Giménez presumably had sufficient clout to defend himself against the Indians from the north.[44] Moreover, he could cite the clause in the 1838 law that made Indian communities absolute owners of their communal lands, a condition that implied the right to sell the land to whomever they (or their representatives) chose. And, since roughly eighty-five hundred hectares of the resguardos were not affected by the sales, many community members may have declined to support the struggle against Giménez.

For whatever reason, the attempt to overturn the sales ultimately failed, and the new landowners maintained control over their plots scattered throughout the resguardos.[45] The most prominent of these landowners was Gumercindo Giménez himself, for after selling community lands to his brother Sacarías Giménez, the latter soon resold much of the land to Gumercindo.[46] Gumercindo already owned a house and some coffee groves on one of the tracts, located just south of Duaca in the village of El Eneal; no doubt he originally sold the land to Sacarías with the understanding that he would later buy it back. Giménez did not plant all the land himself but leased some of it to tenants, a practice also followed by some of the other purchasers of Indian land.[47] Giménez's heirs were still collecting rent from the occupants of his land in El Eneal in the early 1900s.[48] Thus the privatization of a portion of the resguardos meant that some land that had been freely available to peasant families became accessible only through the payment of rent.

Public Lands

Beyond the boundaries of the resguardos lay the public lands (terrenos baldíos). These lands—which belonged to the Spanish crown during the colonial period and, after independence, to the national government—included all territory not owned by individuals or corporate entities such as towns or Indian communities. This included land on all sides of the Duaca resguardos but was concentrated to the north, in the fertile, well-watered Aroa mountains. As in most of Venezuela, Duaca's public lands remained sparsely populated and accessible by only a few poor roads.

Almost from its inception, the republican government viewed Venezuela's public lands as a promising source of revenue and an important resource for economic development.[49] In pursuit of these two goals, the government embarked on a program to promote the sale of baldíos to private citizens. By the outbreak of the Federal War in 1859, however, only a small fraction of the national lands had been sold and the returns to the treasury were disappointingly small. This failure resulted in part from the weakness of the new national government. Following the long wars for independence, the state lacked the resources to carry out a comprehensive survey of public lands.[50] The reformed baldío law of 1848 partially addressed this problem by requiring prospective buyers to pay the surveying costs and other bureaucratic fees.[51] These expenses, however, were beyond the means of poor squatters who farmed on the public domain; the requirement that all paperwork be carried out in the provincial capital created an additional burden that fell disproportionately on poor occupants. It is not surprising that only the wealthy and the politically influential managed to buy tracts of public land. In the 1830s they tended to be former officers of the patriot army and, between 1848 and 1858, the ruling Monagas family and their allies.[52]

Another reason that few Venezuelans bought national land was that, in practice, access to the baldíos was usually free of cost. Laws and decrees aimed at forcing squatters to pay rent on the land they occupied went unenforced throughout much of Venezuela, including the province of Barquisimeto. "In the immense national lands of this province," reported a commission in Barquisimeto in 1842, "there lives a multitude of people who make use of the land without paying the corresponding fees."[53] Consistent rent collection might have provoked more squatters to attempt to purchase their plots, but the government never implemented such a program. Moreover, farmers occupying the public domain could sell or mortgage their holdings (that is, crops, buildings, and other improvements to the land) even though they did not own the land or pay rent to the government. Finally, the state gave squatters security by granting them first option to purchase the land they occupied if a second party applied to buy it.[54] To be sure, powerful men bent on expanding their haciendas sometimes used force or subterfuge to deprive Venezuelan peasants of their farms on the baldíos, but in sparsely populated areas such as Duaca peasants presumably enjoyed a greater possibility of escaping the abuses of the elite.[55]

Peasants in Duaca, like small cultivators in other parts of Venezuela, migrated to the public lands to plant coffee soon after independence.[56] A government inspection in 1837 found 144 farms on Duaca's public lands. Only 13 farms, occupying a total of 9 hectares, used the land to graze livestock; the remaining 131 farms cultivated just over 100 hectares.[57] All of these families occupied small plots, the largest being only seven hectares and the great majority less than one hectare. In contrast to the resguardos, there were no large haciendas on the baldíos at this time. The public land occupants recorded in Duaca in 1837 all lived just beyond the southern, eastern, and western boundaries of the resguardos, near the hamlets of Pegón, Las Veras, La Puente, El Guayabo, Licua, and Naranjito. Notarial records show peasants also growing coffee on the baldíos north of the resguardos by the 1850s.[58] Despite this movement of small cultivators to the public lands during the early decades of coffee expansion, peasants occupied only a small fraction of the baldíos in the parish. Most of Duaca's public domain—especially the mountains to the north of the resguardos—remained a frontier of unclaimed virgin land.

The Estate of Los Chipas

Although the republican government did not alienate any public land in Duaca until the 1860s, in 1714 the Spanish crown had granted private title to a small tract of land east of the resguardos, in the place known as Los Chipas. The estate that developed in Los Chipas played a critical role in Duaca's history well into the twentieth century. The early owners of the estate illegally expanded its boundaries, claiming an ever larger area, and eventually enclosed a vast terrain. The most flagrant expansion occurred in the 1840s under the ownership of José María Laviera, who sold the bulk of the estate to Anselmo

Alcalá in 1846.[59] This illegal enclosure of public lands, occurring during the initial spread of coffee in the region, did not go unnoticed. In 1869 an official surveyor of national lands noted that for years rumors had circulated to the effect that most of the land claimed by owners of Los Chipas was legally part of the public domain.[60]

Despite doubts concerning the legal boundaries of Los Chipas, many settlers on the estate paid rent to the "owners" for the plots they occupied.[61] These tenants were drawn to the estate by its fertile mountains, well suited to coffee cultivation, and by its access to the year-round water of the Tumaque stream. Like occupants on the Indian lands and baldíos, tenants on Los Chipas owned all the improvements to the land they occupied and could sell or mortgage their farms as they wished. These occupants of Los Chipas were an economically diverse group, including some well-to-do hacendados as well as small cultivators. Miguel Hernández was among the latter group. Working the land himself, he planted a small patch of coffee bushes along the Tumaque, shaded them against the sun with banana trees, and interspersed them with other food crops, a practice common among the peasantry. In 1862, when he sold this small grove, Hernández declared, "I came to own the things that I sell by planting them with my own labor, with the permission of Señor Alcalá, to whom I have always paid the rent [piso] corresponding to the land where the said crops are planted."[62]

By contrast, Vicente Colmenares, who made out his will in May 1838, was clearly among the wealthiest tenants on Los Chipas.[63] His coffee farm on the estate, which also produced maize, bananas, and other foods, did not constitute his only source of income. He kept over sixty head of livestock on Los Chipas, including over thirty cattle, and owned two houses in Duaca and one in Barquisimeto. Colmenares invested in commerce as well; he ran a pulpería, or small general store, out of one of his houses in Duaca and estimated that various people owed him a total of about five hundred pesos. Colmenares's silver riding gear, sword, two female slaves, and his ability to set aside money for religious rites following his death testify to his prominence vis-à-vis the more humble tenants of Los Chipas. This range of social and economic status among the tenants on Los Chipas, and on other coffee estates established at a later date, would continue to form part of the social structure of Duaca as long as the coffee economy lasted.

The Question of Debt Peonage

Whereas peasant families relied on their own labor to clear land and plant their crops, well-to-do coffee farmers like Vicente Colmenares hired their poorer neighbors to carry out these tasks. The nature of the relationship between hacendados and their workers during this period has become the subject of considerable discussion among historians of Venezuela. Disagreement and debate has centered on the question of whether employers succeeded in imposing a coercive system of debt peonage on their workers.

There is no doubt that Venezuelan hacendados made advances of food and other supplies to their workers, and that many workers accumulated debts equivalent to several months' wages or more.[64] It is also indisputable that indebted peasants often preferred to work in their own fields, or they moved away, and hacendados often found it difficult to compel them to work when they were needed. In response, provincial legislatures throughout Venezuela enacted laws calling on the police to force indebted peons to comply with the demands of their employers.

At this point, however, the historical record becomes vague, for evidence concerning the day-to-day enforcement of debt peonage is scarce and can be used to support contradictory arguments. Federico Brito Figueroa, author of several influential works on Venezuelan social and economic history, cites examples of high peon debts, reviews the harsh police codes enacted between independence and the Federal War, and concludes that hacendados succeeded in imposing a "feudalistic" regime of forced labor on the peasantry.[65] On the other hand, John Lombardi believes that efforts to establish such a regime "failed because no police force existed to manage the laws and the planters could not restrain each other from the practice of offering bonuses to lure peons from neighboring haciendas."[66]

Both views seem extreme, and Robert Matthews makes a convincing case for a more nuanced interpretation.[67] Relying mostly on newspapers and documents from the provincial bureaucracies, he argues that enforcement of worker debts was generally lax but also varied from one locale to the next. Legislatures routinely complained that rural police forces had yet to be established, and as late as 1857 such forces existed in only about half of the districts in Venezuela's central agricultural zone, presumably the region where the state was strongest. Nevertheless, Matthews believes that the police carried out the peonage laws often enough to incur the resentment of the peasantry.

He points out that rural workers clearly attached some significance to their debts, for in some areas they searched out and destroyed records of labor contracts and debts at the outbreak of the Federal War.

Although I have found no documentation concerning the enforcement of debt peonage in Duaca before the 1860s, evidence from the province of Barquisimeto as a whole suggests that hacendados never established a rigid system of labor control. To be sure, the provincial legislature enacted police codes as harsh as any in Venezuela.[68] Local judges were to establish registries of all workers living within their jurisdiction, and give to each one a *boleta* (pamphlet) where employers would note outstanding debts. Employers could not hire new workers unless their boletas showed all previous debts had been cleared. Laborers who left the workplace without permission or repeatedly failed to carry out an employer's orders would be arrested and jailed. To travel outside their home jurisdiction, workers needed a passport issued by the local judge. Moreover, these regulations applied not only to workers who voluntarily sought employment, but to all adults who, in the police's judgment, lacked independent means of support. If the poor failed to obtain papers or remained unemployed for extended periods, they risked arrest and forced labor on public works as vagrants. Such was the elite's plan for creating a pliant labor force in the province of Barquisimeto.

But the project remained a pipe dream throughout this period and (as we shall see) during the rest of the nineteenth century. Hacendados who faced the possibility of losing their harvests if they could not find sufficient workers did not always demand solvency papers, nor did judges and police search for peasant families to register, nor did they patrol the borders of their jurisdictions. Certain articles in the Barquisimeto police codes indicate where the system broke down. For instance, clauses prohibiting peasants from settling outside the reach of the nearest judge indicate that there were geographical limits to effective state control. New clauses added in the 1850s to impose fines on officials who failed to register workers and on employers who hired them without demanding proper documentation suggest common lapses in enforcement. As late as the mid-1840s, the police commander in Yaritagua had to ask who possessed the authority to issue boletas to workers, and his counterpart in Cabudare had to remind the governor that the legislature had not appropriated money to have the boletas printed. Also, when judges did set about issuing work papers, they sometimes did so with ulterior motives. Thus Governor Jacinto Lara denounced magistrates who profited by forcing "honorable" women and minors to obtain work papers and then hired them out to unscrupulous employers.[69]

If enforcement of the provincial police codes was sporadic and arbitrary, then surely Duaca was one area where the peasantry enjoyed relative freedom from the regulations. Given the municipality's poor roads and limited government personnel, enforcement probably diminished the farther one traveled from the town of Duaca. In particular, the more than one hundred peasant families who had settled on Duaca's public lands were probably not affected by the work laws, for if the government could not force them to pay rent on the land they occupied, it must also have failed to impose the system of rigid social control envisioned in the police codes. In other instances, enforcement might have depended on the political force wielded by the hacendado. Gumercindo Giménez, for example, presumably had sufficient political influence to prod the local judge or police into action against recalcitrant workers and, since his coffee lands in El Eneal bordered the road between Duaca and Barquisimeto, his workers probably lived within officials' reach. Hacendados of lesser stature whose enterprises were more isolated must have faced greater difficulty in bringing the law to bear consistently, although even the occasional or arbitrary application of the police codes might have made a worker think twice before offending an employer. In sum, even though the police codes did not bring a pervasive system of debt peonage to Duaca, they most likely exerted some influence on the texture of relationships there, if only by reinforcing the social distance between the peasant majority and the small elite of hacendados and landowners.

Conclusion and Postscript

Duaca's early history, from the arrival of Spanish colonists to the eve of the coffee boom that began in the second half of the nineteenth century, falls into three periods. During the half century following its creation in 1620, the parish remained the scene of constant struggle among Spanish encomenderos, crown officials, and the Gayones Indians, the area's indigenous people. As a result of these struggles, the crown's attempt to congregate the indigenous population in Duaca was largely frustrated. At the same time, movement to the mines and to secret religious gatherings in Aroa reinforced the tendency toward a migratory way of life for Duaca's native people. Thus the period from 1620 until the 1670s was characterized by conflict and shifting patterns of settlement.

Between the late seventeenth century and the 1830s, the parish population stabilized and began to grow. This resulted from both the pacification of the Gayones and the development of the regional economy along the Barquisimeto-Aroa axis. Duaca's location between the mines and cacao plantations to the northeast and the growing commercial center to the southwest ensured its survival as a populated center and determined much of its economic activity during this period. Short-term migration to Aroa continued, but production of foodstuffs for regional markets became increasingly important to the village economy. Whereas the struggles of the seventeenth century revolved largely around the labor demands of encomenderos, conflict in the eighteenth century came to center on control of the resguardos, pitting the Indian community against local hacendados.

The final period in Duaca's early history began in the 1830s with the closing of the Aroa mines and the beginning of coffee production. The population of the area began a sustained increase that would extend through the end of the century, and peasant agriculture expanded beyond the resguardos to public lands and to the private estate of Los Chipas. The early expansion of the coffee economy provided the context for the appropriation of resguardo lands and for the enclosure of public lands by owners of Los Chipas and may have heightened tensions between employers and indebted workers as well. Nevertheless, poor transportation and a limited supply of commercial credit restrained the local coffee economy during its first three decades. As a result, much of Duaca's territory remained unoccupied at the close of this period, a reality that would fundamentally shape the region's development in the years that followed.

The social and economic tensions that accompanied the expansion of coffee in Venezuela contributed to the destructive power of the conflict that engulfed the nation from 1859 to 1863. The Federal War, as it came to be called, led to a greater loss of human life than any war since independence. One person out of every eight perished as the national population dropped from almost 1.79 million to 1.56 million.[70]

Factional disputes within the elite over the spoils of government, which were rationalized as a high-minded disagreement over centralism versus federalism, provided the immediate cause for the outbreak of violence. Nevertheless, the struggle's fury and duration suggest that broad segments of the population felt that they, too, had something at stake in the conflict. Government attempts to impose debt peonage and the usurpation of peasant land had accentuated social divisions during the three decades preceding the war.[71] Liberal-federalist demagogues issued a string of opportunistic appeals to the masses to overthrow their oppressors. In short, although a breakdown in elite politics led to the outbreak of the war, broadly based class grievances became entwined in the conflict and gave the Federal War its particular destructive fury.

The province of Barquisimeto became the scene of several campaigns during the struggle and produced more than its share of generals.[72] The violence extended to the countryside around Duaca, causing many inhabitants to abandon their homes and fields. Some, like Miguel Hernández, the tenant on Los Chipas, fled to the relative security of Barquisimeto. Upon selling his coffee grove in 1862, Hernández declared that he had not seen the property "since I was forced to abandon my crops by the guerrilla bands that devastate the area, where I have declared I shall not return, even though I lose part of the value of what I sell."[73] But when peace was established the following year, many people did return to Duaca. The region's population and coffee production expanded more rapidly than ever before, and the outlines of future conflicts began to take shape.

3 The Coffee Boom and
Peasant Society, 1863–1899

DURING THE THREE AND a half decades following the Federal War (1859–1863), the Venezuelan coffee economy experienced a process of increasingly rapid expansion. National coffee exports rose from 82,466 tons in 1850–1855, the highest total for any five-year period before the war, to 101,076 tons in 1870–1875, and then more than tripled, to 312,375 tons, in 1895–1900. By 1890, Venezuela had become the world's third-largest exporter of coffee, supplying 6.5 percent of the global market. Despite the warnings of Venezuelans who saw the dangers of national dependence on a single crop produced for foreign consumption, the fate of Venezuela's economy became closely tied to the world coffee market.[1]

These years also witnessed a geographic shift in coffee production within Venezuela, away from the central coastal zone to the Andean states of Trujillo, Mérida, and Táchira. Andean production, which had remained relatively insignificant in national terms before the Federal War, accounted for roughly one half of Venezuela's coffee by the end of the century. Unlike the central coastal zone, where large haciendas dominated coffee production, peasants grew most of the coffee in the Venezuelan Andes.

Anthropologist William Roseberry has examined the history of the coffee economy in the Andean district of Boconó, located some 180 kilometers southwest of Duaca, in the state of Trujillo. His work holds comparative value for the study of Duaca's peasantry in the nineteenth century because Roseberry uses the study of Boconó to develop his analytical framework for the understanding of "precipitate" peasantries, which emerged in frontier regions and engaged in production for the world market. Roseberry emphasizes that until roughly the mid-nineteenth century, Boconó remained sparsely populated and isolated from the world market. The "peasantization" of the district occurred only during the second half of the century as a network of merchant capitalists emerged to integrate Boconó into the world market and as large numbers of migrants made their way to the district and settled on previously vacant land. As a class, then, the Boconó peasantry lacked both the long history and the web of communal institutions typical of indigenous, village-based peasantries in areas such as central Mexico, Guatemala, and the Andean highlands of Bolivia and Peru. Rather, according to Roseberry, the peasantry in Boconó (and other frontier zones of Latin America) was created —or, in his words, "called up"—by the nineteenth-century expansion of commercial capitalism.[2]

The formation of a precipitate peasantry in Duaca fundamentally parallels the scenario laid out by Roseberry, though some deviations from his model deserve mention. Roseberry's emphasis on the role of capitalism in "calling up" a peasantry in Boconó, for example, suggests that the district's integration into an international commercial network provided the crucial impetus behind the creation of the peasantry. However, peasants (and a few hacendados) initiated Duaca's coffee production in the 1830s in the absence of a well-developed system of credit and marketing. Into the late 1850s, Duaqueño coffee producers continued to rely on an assortment of ad hoc arrangements to finance their operations. Similarly, substantial migration into the municipality began before the Federal War and initiated the dispersal of population and coffee as early as the late 1830s. In contrast to Roseberry's model, then, a coffee-producing peasantry appeared and grew well before a merchant network tied the municipality to the world market. To argue that capitalist expansion "called up" a peasantry in Duaca would slight the active role of the peasants themselves in creating the local coffee economy—and in creating themselves as a class—during the decades before the Federal War.[3]

Nevertheless, during the period 1863–1899, Duaca did experience many of the same processes taking place simultaneously in the Andes, and on a roughly similar scale. Without doubt, these years, rather than the decades before the

Federal War, witnessed the most dramatic increase in local coffee production. Duaca's annual harvests rose from approximately 1 million kilograms of coffee in the early 1870s to 2.5 or 3 million kilograms in the early 1890s.[4] Underlying this boom in production were the very changes that Roseberry identifies as characteristic of the creation of a "precipitate" peasantry: a continued influx of migrants, the further geographical dispersion of population as peasants occupied new lands, and the emergence of a well-defined commercial network to finance coffee production and market the crop. In short, whereas the 1830s, 1840s, and 1850s witnessed the initial emergence of Duaca's coffee economy, the years between 1863 and 1899 marked the local economy's most dynamic phase of expansion.

Migrants flocked to Duaca in the decades following the Federal War, arriving in greater numbers than ever before. The population of the municipality, which had reached 7,471 in 1873, leaped to 11,068 in 1881, an increase of 48.1 percent in only eight years. During the same period, the national population grew by only 16.3 percent, from 1,784,194 in 1873 to 2,075,245 in 1881. Much of Duaca's population growth, then, undoubtedly resulted from in-migration. According to Angel María Núñez, Duaca's chronicler, migrants came to Duaca from several locations, including the state of Yaracuy to the east and the state of Falcón to the north, and from other parts of the state of Lara. Regarding this latter group of migrants, scattered information in notarial records indicates that a number of nineteenth-century Duaqueños were born in Quibor, the district immediately west of Barquisimeto, which experienced considerable out-migration during the second half of the nineteenth century. In Duaca, as in the Andes, plentiful land, an expanding coffee economy, and a healthy climate attracted migrants throughout the second half of the nineteenth century.[5]

This steady increase in population led to a further dispersal of settlement. The Indian community lands (resguardos) continued to absorb population, but as pressure on these lands increased, peasants moved in ever greater numbers to land outside the resguardo boundaries, accelerating the trends of earlier decades. On the estate of Los Chipas, for example, the hamlets of Agua-fría and Rincón-hondo became thickly populated by tenants during the three decades following the Federal War. Other peasants migrated to public lands. Indeed, the most dramatic new development in migration patterns was the intensification of settlement on Duaca's extensive public lands north of the resguardos. Whereas migrants had barely penetrated this area in the

1860s, by the mid-1890s settlers had reached the northern boundary of the municipality. This northern tier, however, still contained areas of vacant land at the close of the nineteenth century.[6] The continual availability of unoccupied territory was a crucial aspect of Duaca's social formation in the latter part of the nineteenth century.

Migration and the spatial expansion of settlement had begun well before the Federal War, but the emergence of a well-defined commercial network linking Duaca to coastal export markets occurred only after the war's conclusion. In the 1860s, a few large merchants—most notably Serapio García, a Spanish immigrant—opened commercial establishments in Barquisimeto that specialized in coffee marketing. Receiving credit from the major British and German export houses in Puerto Cabello, García and other Barquisimeto merchants such as Isaac Chapman, another immigrant, often made loans directly to hacendados in Duaca.[7] Most peasants, however, received their loans from merchants located in the town of Duaca or in smaller rural hamlets, who in turn borrowed from García, Chapman, or other Barquisimeto traders. Other small producers secured credit from local hacendados. Whatever the source of their loans, the peasantry became integrated into the web of credit and debt that now stretched from Duaca's hinterland to North Atlantic import markets.

Improvements in regional transportation reinforced Duaca's integration into this larger commercial system. The British company that owned the Aroa copper mines had planned to build a railroad to the coast as early as the 1830s, but civil wars and problems at the mines repeatedly delayed construction. When the company finally built the railroad in 1877, the narrow-gauge line carried goods from Aroa to the port of Tucacas, whence merchandise was sent via coastal shipping to Puerto Cabello in the state of Carabobo, the region's major import-export center. In order to facilitate access to the railway, in 1877 the road from Barquisimeto to Aroa, which passed through Duaca, was upgraded to accommodate carts and wagons. In 1891 this new highway was superseded by a second railway (also built with British capital), which linked Barquisimeto to the inland terminus of the older railway at Aroa. The new line passed through Duaca, making it one of the few coffee-producing areas in Venezuela to be connected by rail to a coastal port. Improvements in transportation thus strengthened the commercial linkages between Barquisimeto, Duaca, and the world market.[8]

These years of headlong economic expansion—from the end of the Federal

War in 1863 to the outbreak of another critical war, the Revolución Restauradora of 1899—form the background against which to study Duaca's peasantry.[9] I begin by examining the economics of the peasant household, seen as the central unit of peasant life but with linkages to the larger society of creditors and seasonal employers. Initially, I shall treat the peasantry as a single class, not distinguishing between those peasants who lived on private estates as rent-paying tenants and those who occupied the public lands and resguardos. This unified treatment of peasant households is plausible because a number of their principal characteristics—such as family settlement patterns, linkages to merchants, and the seasonal employment of some household members as wage workers—were shared by all peasants, whether they lived on an estate, the resguardos, or public land.

Later, the discussion shifts to examine the three separate land tenure regimes as they developed during the late nineteenth century. Throughout the chapter, I address the question of how Duaca's peasantry maintained its existence in the midst of increasing commercialization. I argue that the peasantry benefited from certain conditions of the era, such as divisions within the elite (both locally and nationally), and the existence of large expanses of unoccupied land. At the same time, actions carried out by the peasantry themselves, such as economic cooperation among peasant households and resistance to the demands of employers and landowners, also played a part in the resilient nature of peasant society.

While focusing the peasantry, I necessarily make reference to the elite in and around Duaca. The next chapter examines the development of the local elite in detail, but a few words concerning this group are in order here. During the 1860s, Duaca's upper class was relatively small and financially dependent on Barquisimeto merchants, but by the mid-1870s prominent Duaqueños had a firm grip on the area's expanding commerce, and some eventually bypassed their Barquisimeto creditors to establish direct ties to Puerto Cabello export firms. Virtually all members of Duaca's elite owned coffee haciendas, but by the early 1870s many also engaged in commerce, and commerce claimed an increasing share of elite investment during the remainder of the nineteenth century.

Throughout this period, very few among Duaca's elite owned land. Well into the early twentieth century, the greater part of Duaca's territory was composed of public and Indian community land and thus was outside the sphere of private ownership. Whereas a handful of prominent Duaqueños held private title to land, most members of the local elite did not own the land

under their haciendas. Some occupied land belonging to the Indian community, others occupied public land without acquiring title, and still others occupied private estates as rent-paying tenants. In short, an hacendado—that is,
the owner of an agricultural enterprise worked year-round by hired labor—
was usually not a landowner.[10]

This situation, especially the longevity of Duaca's public lands and corpo-
rately owned indigenous lands, proved unusual in context of Latin America's
coffee zones. Latin American coffee growers often began production on untitled land, but they normally gained private title to the terrain within a decade
or so, whereas in Duaca privatization of most of the resguardos and baldíos
did not occur until the 1910s and 1920s, a half century after the onset of the
boom.[11] Among other Latin American coffee producers, only Honduras, a
relatively minor exporter whose surge in production began comparatively
late, continued coffee production on untitled land for a similar length of
time.[12]

This limited control over land restricted the elite's ability to exploit Duaca's
peasantry during the nineteenth century. Although the elite certainly extracted a surplus from the peasantry—by extending credit, by employing seasonal labor, and by charging rent on the few private estates that existed—the
peasantry in general did not depend on the elite for access to land. Relatively
free access to land in Duaca undoubtedly contributed to the area's attractive-
ness to migrants and sped the expansion of the local coffee economy. Ironi-
cally, this growth of the local export economy—growth fueled primarily by
peasant migration and production—helped to lay the groundwork for the
eventual consolidation of Duaca's elite in the late nineteenth and early twentieth centuries.

The Economy of Peasant Households

As they cleared and settled new land, peasants in Duaca combined customary
methods of subsistence agriculture with production of the new export crop.[13]
Peasants who grew coffee continued to produce food crops, particularly corn,
black beans, and bananas, for their own consumption. The techniques used to
work the patch of subsistence crops (known as a *conuco*) represented a continuation of traditional slash-and-burn practices. At the beginning of the dry
season, peasants establishing a conuco cut the underbrush in the area to be
cultivated, felled the trees, and later burned the debris after it had dried in the

sun. The family could then cultivate the conuco for only a few years before the deterioration of the soil forced them to clear a fresh patch. Thus subsistence agriculture was traditionally migratory and required continual access to new land.[14] Planting a coffee grove, however, represented a long-term investment in a particular plot of land. Coffee bushes generally did not yield a crop until the third or fourth year after planting, but with proper care—two annual weedings, one annual pruning, and adequate shade—they would continue to produce for twenty years or more. Peasants often combined their conucos and coffee groves, planting banana trees to shade the coffee bushes and placing corn and beans between the young, nonproducing bushes, thus reducing the amount of land that had to be cleared or weeded in a single year. Once the coffee grove reached maturity, corn and beans were often shifted to a separate plot.

As they cleared and planted new lands, peasants often settled in family clusters in order to facilitate economic cooperation among households linked by ties of kinship; indeed, collaboration among relatives proved to be a vital support to peasant society as the coffee economy grew. Many peasant farms on the resguardos, public lands, and private estates were bordered on one or more sides by fields belonging to a sibling, parents, uncle, or aunt.[15] Peasants routinely enlisted the labor of these nearby kin when establishing a new holding. For example, when children reached adulthood and formed their own households, they established their new farm with the cooperation of relatives living close by, often adjacent to the new holding. Sometimes, particularly in the case of adult siblings, the workers retained joint ownership of the new coffee grove or conuco and continued to work it together.[16] In other instances one member of the group would buy the rights earned by the other adults, in effect paying them for their labor.[17] At harvest time, when rapid gathering of crops could be critical, an abundance of nearby relatives would facilitate the cooperative practice of *días cambiados* (exchange days), a reciprocal exchange of labor among separate households.[18] In short, the desire to utilize family labor to clear, plant, and harvest new lands dictated that farms be established near one's kin. Thus newly colonized areas often included clusters of coffee groves and conucos owned largely by members of an extended kin group.

The practice of adult sons leaving home and establishing their own holdings while their parents were still alive was particularly important in perpetuating the structure of the peasant economy, for it allowed Duaqueños to avoid the contradictions that undermined some peasant societies in other parts of Latin America.[19] Certainly this practice, like the regular shifting of conucos, depended on continual access to virgin land, and throughout the nineteenth century virgin land remained available to Duaca's peasantry, most abundantly on the public land frontier north of the resguardos. In other areas of Latin America, including the Costa Rican coffee zone of Santo Domingo de Heredia analyzed by Lowell Gudmundson, land became scarce much earlier than in Duaca and peasants entering adulthood lost the opportunity to establish new holdings.[20] Instead, they continued to live and work at home. When parents died, their children faced the choice of whether to divide the family holding into a number of small plots or to leave it intact in the hands of a primary heir whose siblings would migrate and confront an uncertain future. The families of those who either inherited small plots or did not prosper from migration came to depend on wage work for an ever larger share of their income; they drifted from a peasant livelihood toward that of a proletariat. By contrast, the continuing availability of virgin land in Duaca meant that peasants entering adulthood could usually establish separate farms that were economically viable. The favorable ratio of population to land and the steady expansion of settlement allowed the household economy to reproduce itself from one generation to the next while maintaining a structural continuity.

Nevertheless, Duaqueños lived with the possibility of numerous contingencies that could threaten their self-sufficiency. The most common threat (though usually a manageable one) was debt. Credit relationships were widespread, for peasants who planted coffee usually borrowed against future harvests. Small loans might be handled on an informal basis as interest-free credit at the merchant's store.[21] Larger advances, however, drew interest charges and had to be formalized with a mortgage on the peasant's property. To be sure, peasants did not own land to mortgage, but peasants living on the resguardos, baldíos, or private estates did own the improvements—coffee groves, conucos, houses, and rights to cleared land—that they had established or purchased. In mortgaging these goods to a creditor, peasants accepted the obligation to repay principal and interest with the coming harvest. In some cases the price of the coffee was stipulated in the mortgage document, in other instances the peasant and merchant agreed to adopt the current market price (*precio de la plaza*) at the time of delivery. Mortgages clearly involved the risk that if the harvest was smaller than expected or if the world price of coffee fell, the borrower might not repay the loan on time and the creditor could exercise his right to seize the mortgaged farm.

In practice, the risk of losing a farm for unpaid debts varied according to the location of the creditor. Merchants based in Barquisimeto generally had little interest in acquiring small farms in Duaca and often continued to grant credit to peasants who failed to settle their accounts on schedule, provided they turned over each year's harvest to pay off what they could.[22] This tolerant attitude toward debt (which often prevailed in Andean coffee zones as well) meant that peasant-merchant relations could take on considerable flexibility.[23] Creditors based in Duaca, on the other hand, were sometimes keener to seize a debtor's property. Some of these local creditors were hacendados who made loans to peasants owning neighboring farms.[24] It might be argued that such loans embodied a paternalistic relationship in which the hacendado provided aid in exchange for the peasant's services and loyalty, but in some instances this was clearly not the case. Hacendados' propensity to foreclose on neighboring peasants for unpaid debts suggests that a strictly economic rationale lay behind many of these loans.[25]

Merchants based in the town of Duaca could also prove less willing than their Barquisimeto counterparts to continue the credit of peasants who failed to pay their debts on schedule. These local merchants did not restrict their operations to credit and commerce but also owned agricultural properties. Acquiring additional farms for unpaid debts simply represented an expansion of their investment in direct production. If the mortgaged farm could be integrated into a merchant's existing operations, foreclosure became attractive.

In general, however, peasants paid off their mortgages, either on time or with the aid of an extension. Entering into credit relations, then, did not usually signal the onset of increasing dependency and impoverishment.[26] But peasants carrying mortgages were vulnerable to the problems that always plague agriculturalists, such as adverse weather and fluctuations in market prices. The slump in world coffee prices between 1879 and 1883, for example, reverberated through the entire Venezuelan coffee economy, affecting merchants and producers alike, and causing many Duaqueño peasants to lose their holdings to creditors—many more than lost property for debt in normal times. The crisis also led some small producers to abandon their coffee groves and allow them to become overgrown.[27] Most, however, chose to maintain production, for they knew that prices might rise again and that reestablishing a lost coffee grove would entail a long wait for the new bushes to mature.[28] Despite the hardships brought on by price fluctuations, the peasantry remained committed to producing coffee for the world market.

The untimely death of a family member also represented a common threat to the economic fortunes of the peasant household, particularly when it was preceded by a long illness. When Felipe Días, a tenant on Los Chipas, fell ill in

1880, he and his wife, Juana Garcés, found themselves unable to pay for medical care. Perhaps because of the low coffee prices of that year, they could not raise a loan and were forced to sell their grove of six thousand coffee bushes to the owner of the neighboring hacienda. Felipe succumbed to his illness, and some of the funds from the sale went to cover burial expenses, leaving Juana and her ten children, none of whom had reached adulthood, with few resources other than their labor. In a similar case, Antonio Camacho, another tenant, had to borrow money to pay for his wife's medical care, and the debt eventually grew to include the cost of her funeral and family subsistence needs. Camacho's creditor, José de la Paz Alvarado, a neighboring hacendado, foreclosed on the loan and incorporated the Camacho family's grove into his own growing hacienda. Peasant illness, then, often led to painful calculations as to whether the benefit the patient might receive from a doctor's services warranted the imposition of additional hardships on the rest of the family, including the possible loss of property. Small wonder that Venezuelans, with dark humor, referred to a type of fever that killed its victims quickly (that is, before a doctor could be summoned or medicine bought) as "la económica" (the economical one).[29]

An illness that did not prove fatal or require expensive medical care could still prove costly if it came at the wrong time. Jesús Méndez once fell ill during the harvest season and thus gathered only seven sacks of coffee rather than the twenty-six that his grove usually produced. As a result, his creditor foreclosed and bought the grove at judicial auction. Given the persistence of endemic disease in rural Venezuela before the middle of the twentieth century, it is somewhat surprising that more peasants did not suffer a similar fate. In all probability, the labor of most peasants who were sick at crucial times could be replaced by a nearby relative or by all members of the household working harder. Thus Méndez's loss of his coffee grove resulted not only from illness, but also from an inability to mobilize the supplemental labor upon which most peasants could depend.[30]

On occasion, debt could lead to impoverishment even when it did not result in the definitive loss of property. As an alternative to foreclosure, peasants sometimes agreed to contracts surrendering their coffee groves to creditors for an extended period of time, usually from four to eight years. The peasant family reserved the right to live in their house and cultivate food crops, but clearly, while the contract was in force, they faced a considerable loss of income. In some cases debtors were obliged to do occasional wage work for the creditor who assumed control of their coffee patch, such as the arduous task of weeding the grove twice a year at the going wage for day laborers. Even when labor obligations did not appear in the contracts, the family probably found themselves obliged to perform wage work in order to compensate for the income they previously obtained from their coffee groves. Thus peasants forced to "rent" their groves to creditors found themselves sliding from self-sufficiency toward markedly greater dependence on wages.[31]

When peasants were unable to pay debts on schedule, assistance from relatives sometimes allowed them to satisfy creditors without suffering forced "rental" or foreclosure. In some cases, peasants risked their own property to come to the aid of a desperate relative. The case of Juan Eusebio Colmenares, a public land occupant, serves as an example. In 1875 Colmenares mortgaged his coffee grove to a Barquisimeto merchant, and when he failed to repay the loan the following year, the merchant took him to court, an action that often led to the seizure of the debtor's property. In this case, however, Colmenares's brother Gumercindo, who owned an adjoining grove, agreed to mortgage his property to guarantee payment of the debt, which now included forty-five pesos in court costs. The creditor agreed to the arrangement and Juan Eusebio retained his mortgaged property. In a similar instance, Miguel and Manuel Rodríguez, two brothers who had planted their groves next to their father's in the Indian lands, found that their debt to a Duaca merchant had risen above the amount they could secure. Their father, Prudencio, assisted them in satisfying the merchant by mortgaging his farm as additional security. Other examples of peasants helping their kin to fend off creditors could also be cited. So, just as peasants used cooperative labor in establishing their holdings, cooperation along kinship lines also played a role in preserving peasant property.[32]

These cases of peasants stepping forward to aid relatives by mortgaging their own property were somewhat unusual. More common were the small loans of money or produce that peasants made to one another, and which were not limited to kin. Because of its relatively informal nature, this network of peasant loans produced little documentation. It appears only in the few peasant wills that have survived from the period. José del Carmen Soto declared that he had made a dozen small loans in cash and coffee, none of which carried interest, including loans of four pesos to his nephew Francisco Soto and seven sacks of coffee to his compadre José Mariano Soto. José del Carmen's description of a loan to his son-in-law Apolinario Mendoza indicates the strong element of trust that underwrote these informal arrangements: "Apolinario also owes me [money], and I don't know how much it is, but as my son-in-law he will pay when he can." Similar assortments of small credits appear in other peasant wills.[33] In short, peasants who needed a little extra money to pay a doctor, who needed a few more bushels of corn to feed themselves until the next harvest, or whose coffee crop proved insufficient to pay a merchant or landlord, sometimes found a more prosperous relative or friend willing to advance them what they needed. These peasant-to-peasant loans meant that shortfalls in the household economy did not always lead to the loss of property or to greater dependence on the elite.

To be sure, economic relations among peasants were not always harmonious. At times cooperation gave way to conflict and sharp dealing, even between close relatives. Consider the story of the brothers Dionisio and Venancio Soto, two tenants with contiguous holdings on Los Chipas. In April 1877, Venancio recognized a debt to Dionisio and promised to repay it with the following year's coffee crop. When Venancio failed to pay the debt on time, his brother brought judicial action to force compliance, but he settled for Venancio's pledge to repay the loan, with interest of 2 percent per month, in April 1879. Venancio again failed to pay, and this time Dionisio waited only six days before seizing his brother's coffee grove to settle the debt.[34] Such action between kin was the exception rather than the rule. In a society where economic security often depended on mobilizing resources through kinship ties, self-interest if not familial affection warned against alienating one's relatives.

Household production for the market fostered economic differentiation among the peasantry in many areas of Latin America in the late nineteenth century, and Duaca was no exception. Some peasant families clearly accumulated more property than others as the coffee economy expanded. A typical household in Duaca owned a conuco and a small coffee grove, but some peasants came to own larger holdings or, more commonly, multiple small farms. The most common pattern of accumulation appears to have been for a peasant household to establish one grove and, if the family prospered, to purchase a second grove.[35] In some instances, financial assistance and cooperative labor within the extended family provided the means for acquiring multiple properties. In other cases, a large number of children surviving into adulthood apparently contributed to the household's prosperity.[36]

Such accumulation, however, usually occurred on such a small scale that it did not transform a peasant family's class position. Peasants who became relatively well-to-do employed a few of their poorer kin or neighbors as wage workers during the harvest,[37] they made loans of money and produce and on occasion charged interest, but they remained essentially family cultivators whose livelihood depended more on their own labor than on the exploitation of wage workers or on the management of credit. The available documents do not reveal any cases of peasants joining the elite. At best, upward mobility within the peasant class gave families a cushion against future contingencies. Lorenzo Sánchez, for example, came to own two coffee groves in the hamlet of Tucuragua; he lost one because of debts arising from a poor harvest and the death of his wife, but he retained ownership of the second. One suspects that the ownership of a second coffee grove, or the flexibility to loan out small sums on a regular basis, often came late in life, following years of constant toil and careful saving.[38]

Despite changes in the fortunes of individual peasant families, some of whom prospered while others slid into poverty, the overall structure of peasant society remained essentially unchanged during the latter part of the nineteenth century. The bulk of the peasantry achieved self-sufficiency, living on the production of their own farms and able to avoid constant wage work away from the family holding. At the upper end of the spectrum, the better-off households employed a few seasonal laborers to help with the harvest, while at the lower end the poorer peasantry depended heavily on seasonal employment to supplement the produce of their own holdings.

Peasant Households and Seasonal Wage Labor

The high degree of self-sufficiency achieved by many peasant households, then, placed limits on the number of peasants forced to search for wage work. Despite the waves of migrants who settled in Duaca during the late nineteenth century, hacendados regularly found that the number of peasants looking for jobs as day laborers was insufficient to cover their needs—particularly during the crucial period of the harvest, between October and January. Many peasants spent this time tending their own holdings, and some of those looking for additional work were hired by well-off peasants. Unable to find enough laborers, hacendados in Duaca complained of a "shortage of workers." Clearly they referred not to a scarcity of working people per se, but rather to the lack of workers who found it necessary or desirable to sell their labor at the going wage. Similar conditions prevailed in other parts of Latin America where hacendados attempted to recruit laborers from a peasantry with independent access to land. As Arnold Bauer has noted, "the paradox was everywhere; people thick on the ground yet the landowners constantly lamenting the *escasez de brazos* (shortage of hands)."[39]

So, hacendados continued to offer wage advances as inducements to attract scarce peasant laborers, the increase in Duaca's population notwithstanding. They similarly allowed indebted workers to increase their debts again and again by borrowing against the promise of future work. In receiving these advances, peasants became subject to the labor demands of the hacienda, which at times conflicted with the labor requirements of their own holdings, but in exchange they gained access to a source of credit they could draw upon during periods of economic hardship.[40]

Coffee haciendas in Duaca had long used wage advances to attract workers, but the practice increased as the coffee economy expanded. The amount of money that hacendados invested in loans to workers varied greatly. The Virgües family, who owned an hacienda in the resguardos valued at about 2,000 pesos, carried only 88 pesos in worker debts. By contrast, Avelino and Aurelio Giménez Méndez, large tenants on the estate of Los Chipas, had over 2,250 pesos (9,000 bolívares) loaned to their workers. Most haciendas fell somewhere between these two extremes. Elsewhere in Latin America, landowners had the option of attracting labor with offers of access to subsistence plots, but in Duaca, where few hacendados owned land and the peasantry enjoyed ready access to virgin land, wage advances to local peasant cultivators remained the rule.[41]

Some insight into this labor system can be gained from the only available list of indebted peons in nineteenth-century Duaca (though, of course, it is impossible to know how representative the data might be). When Policarpo Peralta and José Tomás Rojas Vélis dissolved their agricultural and commercial partnership in 1893, the goods they divided included 991.48 pesos in peon debts, which were distributed among twenty-seven workers (seven females and twenty males).[42] The amount of debt carried by each worker varied widely, from a high of 166.20 pesos to a low of 2.19, with an average debt of 36.68 pesos and a median debt of 22.00. The four workers with debts of at least 75 pesos apiece are particularly noteworthy, since Peralta and Rojas Vélis clearly granted them credit well beyond the point needed to establish a claim to their labor. At the going wage of two reales (that is, one-fourth of one peso) per day, these workers had received at least a year's wages in advance.[43] The largest advance of 166.20 pesos represented a prepayment for a full two years' labor, and even the median debt of 22 pesos would require more than three months of work to cancel. Workers' ability to demand such large advances reflected their bargaining power with employers in an environment of labor scarcity.[44]

Despite such large advances, hacendados often found that their extension of credit did not secure them a reliable work force. Thus Altagracia López, owner of a coffee hacienda on the baldíos, authorized Manuel Oliveros to pursue five workers who had left the area without satisfying their debts, one of whom had taken two of López's burros with him. Similarly, Cecilio Carrera sent his brother to pursue an unspecified number of indebted peons who had left the area. That Carrera and López turned to private representatives to pursue indebted workers suggests that, despite legislation regulating peonage, employers could not always count on the police to enforce worker obligations.[45]

These were not isolated incidents. Indebted workers resisted hacienda labor so often that employers constantly had to distinguish between debts that probably would be redeemed and those that were no longer recoverable. The children of Juan Manuel Palencia, for example, included worker debts of 300 pesos in the inventory of his estate but purposefully omitted another 45 pesos 1 real as "lost in peon debts." Thus about 13 percent of Palencia's loans to workers would never be recovered. Similarly, when Justiniano Herrera sold two haciendas to Carlos Carmona, he included the 1,718 bolívares (429.5 pesos) in peon debts among the assets but agreed to reimburse Carmona for the debts of any workers who failed to honor their obligation to the new owner. When Carmona in turn sold the haciendas only six months later, worker debts totaled only 400 bolívares (100 pesos), but Carmona specified that these debts had recently been "recognized" by the workers. Labor debts thus decreased by over 75 percent during the six months in which Carmona attempted to enforce compliance. Some laborers may have worked off their obligations during the intervening harvest, but it also seems probable that a number of debts had proved irrecoverable. Most hacendados simply refused to take responsibility for the enforcement of worker debts when selling their haciendas, a tacit acknowledgment of employers' frequent inability to control indebted labor.[46]

Seasonal wage workers, then, confronted employers from a position of strength. Wages usually represented a supplement to the production of their family holding rather than peasants' chief means of subsistence.[47] Moreover, peasants who accepted wage work gained a degree of security in that they could draw substantial advances from their employers. Despite the dependency implied by debt, only a handful of peasant workers became full-time resident peons on haciendas.[48] The great majority of wage workers continued to live on their holdings, making surveillance by their employers problematic. Wage labor during the nineteenth century did not draw the peasantry into ever deepening dependency on hacendados, much less signal the beginning of a process of proletarianization, but rather played a role in maintaining peasant households. Thus Duaca's peasantry reproduced itself as a class—an economically heterogeneous class, to be sure—despite the challenges of commercial credit, world market cycles, endemic illness, and a partial reliance on wage labor.

The Duaca Resguardos

Having examined the dynamics of the peasant household economy, we now turn to local systems of land tenure in the latter part of the nineteenth century, beginning with the lands claimed by Duaca's indigenous community. Although Duaca was founded by the Spaniards as an Indian parish, by the late nineteenth century most people residing in the area were not descendants of Duaca's indigenous population. By the time of the 1779 census, only 57 percent of Duaca's population (314 out of 551) was Indian, and nineteenth-century migration into the municipality inevitably produced a steady decrease in the percentage of residents who could trace their ancestry through Duaca's indigenous community. (Since post-independence censuses did not make racial distinctions, we cannot trace precisely the changing composition of Duaca's population.) Meanwhile, the fading away of a distinctive Indian way of life by the end of the colonial period, as well as the continuing process of racial mixture, undermined the cultural basis of a separate indigenous identity.[49] By the latter part of the nineteenth century, the only important distinction between Indians and non-Indians was that the Indian "community" (that is, residents of Duaca claiming descent from the area's prehispanic inhabitants) was still recognized as the legal owner of the resguardos granted to Duaca's indigenous people by the Spanish crown.

Duaca's Indian community was unusual in Venezuela in that it continued to exercise ownership over its resguardos throughout the nineteenth century. The national government after the Federal War continued to promulgate laws calling for the privatization of Indian lands, and in most regions of Venezuela, including the Andean coffee zones, the final three decades of the nineteenth century witnessed the disintegration of the Indian resguardos. In the state of Lara, several indigenous communities divided their lands under individual ownership in the late nineteenth century. By contrast, Duaca's resguardos remained under community control until 1916.[50]

The Indian community of Duaca not only remained the formal, legal owner of the resguardos (with the exception of the fifteen hundred hectares sold by Gumercindo Giménez in the 1850s) but also exercised effective control over most of its land. The collection of rent from non-Indians occupying the resguardos was the most visible sign of community control. Although no documentation has survived concerning how rents were calculated or how often they were actually collected, the community undoubtedly received payment from at least some of the non-Indians with holdings on the resguardos. Thus, when a widow rented her coffee grove in Tarana to Justiniano Herrera in 1875, she specified that while the contract was in force Herrera would assume rent payments to the Indian community for the land occupied by the grove, and she declared that she had paid her rents in full for the preceding years. Contracts concerning other holdings on the resguardos also mentioned rental payments to the community or to its legal representative.[51]

By contrast, members of the Indian community farmed on the resguardos without paying rent for the land they occupied. One member of the community, Encarnación Noguera, upon selling a coffee grove planted on the resguardos in Quemados, declared: "It should be noted that the buyer [of the grove] must come to an understanding with the Indians' representative regarding the amount of rent for the land he will occupy, for if I paid nothing, it was because, as an Indian, I also had a right in that [land]."[52] Furthermore, some Indians explained their access to plots within the increasingly crowded resguardos by referring to their status as community members or to the intervention of the community's legal representative.[53] The community's ability to give at least some of its members preferential access to the resguardos while collecting rent from the non-Indian occupants indicates that it remained a viable force in Duaca throughout the nineteenth century.

The collective power of the community was due largely to the efforts of well-to-do indigenous families who formed part of the local elite. The legal representatives of the community tended to come from these families and therefore had a personal stake in protecting the integrity of the resguardos. Aside from supervising rent collection, the representatives defended community interests before the state. When a new national law ordered that all Indian lands without sufficient documentation be reclassified as public lands, the representatives of Duaca's Indians hired a prominent Barquisimeto lawyer, Leopoldo Torres, assembled the necessary papers, and secured official recognition of community ownership of the resguardos.[54]

As during the colonial and early national periods, the principal threat to small cultivators on the resguardos came from owners of large haciendas on or near the community lands. And, as the coffee economy expanded during the second half of the nineteenth century, the number and size of haciendas increased. The largest coffee hacienda on the resguardos emerged near Tinajitas and Cerro-Gordo, to the west of the town of Duaca, under the ownership of General Juan de la Rosa Vásquez. Inheriting a modest set of coffee groves from his father, Vásquez began to purchase the groves of neighboring peasant families after the Federal War. By the time he sold the hacienda to Cipriano Bracho in 1878, it had grown to include over a hundred thousand coffee bushes and a processing center, all located on community land. Bracho continued to expand into the early 1900s, when the hacienda grew to over three hundred hectares, one of the largest in Duaca at that time. Given Bracho's combined economic and political power (he attained the rank of general in the 1870s and served as *jefe civil* [local governor] of Duaca at various times), his peasant neighbors probably had little chance of resisting Bracho's efforts to incorporate their groves into his hacienda.[55]

Bracho and Duaca's Indian community came into open conflict when, in the early 1890s, community representatives began proceedings to privatize the resguardos, an initiative intended to give Indian occupants title to their plots. The most recent law calling for the privatization of Venezuela's Indian lands, that of 1885, mandated that resguardos still under community control be divided equitably among the communities' Indian families. Although it also established complicated procedures for non-Indians living on the resguardos to receive title to the land they occupied, the 1885 law clearly gave preference to Indian community members in the distribution of community lands.[56] Rather than attempt to manipulate the division of the resguardos in his favor, Bracho (who was not a member of the Indian community) initiated rival judicial proceedings aimed at surveying supposed public lands in Cerro-Gordo in order to purchase them from the national government. The land Bracho hoped to purchase was clearly part of the resguardos, and although Bracho's hacienda occupied most of this area, part of it was farmed by neighboring indigenous families. The community representative Pantaleón Heredia, himself a member of the Indian community, again enlisted the legal assistance of Leopoldo Torres and together they successfully blocked Bracho's attempt to establish private title to the community land in Cerro-Gordo. They also resisted a similar attempt by Justiniano Herrera, a merchant who owned several coffee haciendas, to appropriate community land near Tarana.[57]

The proceedings to give community members private title to their plots, however, never resumed, presumably because of pressure from men like Bracho and Herrera who owned haciendas on community land and who objected to the conditions under which privatization would be carried out. The resguardos remained under community ownership until 1916, when they were privatized under a new law that called simply for the adjudication of the resguardos to the current occupants, regardless of whether they belonged to the Indian community and regardless of the resulting inequality in the distribution of land (see chapter 7). In short, privatization occurred only when it ceased to threaten the interests of non-Indian elites with haciendas on community land.[58]

Although the community representatives succeeded in defending the resguardos against large-scale assaults like those of Bracho and Herrera, which involved hundreds of hectares, they failed to prevent less dramatic encroachment by other members of the elite. In early 1909, Juan Bautista Cambero, a leader of the Indian community, wrote to Leopoldo Torres to inform him of encroachments by owners of two private estates bordering the resguardos and by the owner of El Buco, the large sugar hacienda within the community lands. The owners of these properties, wrote Cambero,

> as arrogant as they are unjust, are depriving others of their property by force, throwing some Indian occupants off their holdings [*propiedades de bienhechurías*], charging them rent and imposing onerous conditions in order to force them to evacuate the land that they occupy, which are Indian [lands] according to the old boundaries established by the demarcation of 1850, which you as our representative publicized in defense of the rights of this community.[59]

In a similar case the following year, Rudecindo Peralta, one of Duaca's most prominent entrepreneurs, carried out a survey of his estate, in which he expanded the boundaries to enclose a strip of community land occupied by peasant cultivators.[60] The community proved powerless to correct such abuses, in part because the vague boundaries of the resguardos made small-scale encroachments difficult to prove.

During the years between the Federal War and the privatization of 1916, then, the resguardos remained a scene of struggle between peasants, who were sometimes supported by Indian community representatives, and non-Indian hacendados and landowners who consistently attempted to appropriate community land and peasant holdings. None of the groups engaged in this ongoing contest won a clear-cut victory. The Indian community remained strong enough to defend its land against large-scale incursions and to collect rents from at least some of the non-Indian occupants. At the same time, however, the community could not force the privatization of the resguardos under the relatively favorable conditions of the nineteenth-century laws giving preference to Indians in the distribution of community land. As some members of the community fell victim to neighboring hacendados, and as their communal lands became increasingly crowded with outsiders, Duaca's indigenous minority must have sensed that their hold on the resguardos was becoming increasingly precarious as the years passed.

The Public Lands

In the decades following the Federal War, peasants in search of vacant land increasingly migrated to Duaca's public domain rather than settling on the resguardos or private estates. The factors behind migration to Duaca's baldíos were varied, but all reflected the migrants' desire to maintain their position as independent small producers in an expanding commercial economy. Access to virgin land was crucial to the reproduction of the peasant household, both within generations, because of the migratory nature of subsistence agriculture, and across generations, because it allowed children to establish their own holdings rather than divide their parents' farms into small uneconomical properties. Since virgin land was most plentiful on the baldíos, migration to the public domain continued throughout the late nineteenth and early twentieth centuries.

Some historians have suggested that peasant migration to relatively remote public lands was an attempt to escape from the commercial economy and to establish an isolated self-sufficiency, but the argument does not fit the Duaqueño peasantry. To be sure, some migrants were pushed toward the public domain by pressures and abuses linked to the export economy, such as the loss of coffee groves for debt or the appropriation of peasant farms by an hacendado bent on expanding his domain. But whatever their motives for moving, public land settlers in Duaca generally planted coffee along with their subsistence crops, demonstrating their belief that the best strategy for survival as peasants included the production of coffee for export. Public land settlers in Duaca, like their counterparts in other Latin American nations undergoing export-led expansion, migrated not to escape from the market, but to preserve their family economies as best they could within the broader commercial economy of which they were a part.[61]

The destination of Duaca's migrants shifted increasingly northward between the end of the Federal War and the turn of the century. During the 1860s, as in the years before the war, most migrants settled on lands to the west and south of the resguardos, areas made accessible by the roads spreading outward from Barquisimeto. Few settlers migrated to the rich yet relatively isolated areas north of the resguardos until the 1870s, when migration to the area of Quebrada Abajo began. Migrants traveled north at a steady pace for the rest of the century. During the 1880s, they brought land under cultivation in Piedras Lisas, Camburito, and Palo Negro, and by the mid-1890s settlers had arrived at the northern edge of Duaca's jurisdiction, at Las Casitas.[62] By the turn of the century, settlements on the northern public lands remained scattered, with stretches of vacant land still available, but Duaca's frontier of virgin land was greatly diminished.

As they brought new land under cultivation, migrants gave value to previously vacant territory, and in Duaca as in other parts of Latin America members of the elite occasionally appropriated public land farmed by peasant settlers.[63] The first public land acquisitions in nineteenth-century Duaca occurred several years after the Federal War when officers from the victorious Liberal army used military compensation bonds to purchase land from the government. The lands acquired by these officers were located just beyond the boundaries of the resguardos in areas that had already been settled to some extent. In 1867, General Santos Herrera acquired 427.5 fanegadas (298.7 hectares) of land in Cambural, on the northeastern edge of the resguardos, and four years later Coronel Félix Aguilar and Victor Escalona purchased another tract nearby.[64]

The largest purchase of national lands came in 1868, when four generals— José Luis Aguilar, Juan Eusebio Méndez, Manuel J. Chirinos, and Gumercindo Giménez (who had sold part of the resguardos in the 1850s)—acquired 11,890 fanegadas (8,307.5 hectares) along the western border of the resguardos in Tacarigüita and Tucuragua. Although much of the land purchased by these four generals was arable, they had the entire tract classified as less expensive grazing land, a common abuse in the alienation of Venezuela's national lands.[65] Referring to their military service, the generals dubbed their new estate La Recompensa (The Reward), but among the local populace it soon became known as La Posesión de los Generales (the Generals' Estate), a name that more clearly reflected the link between political power and landownership.

Peasant settlers already occupied a good deal of the land included in these sales to military officers.[66] Under Venezuelan law, public land occupants had preference in the acquisition of the land they occupied, but in practice peasants lacked the money and bureaucratic connections needed to exercise this right. On only a few occasions did public land occupants in the state of Lara manage to resist elites' acquisition of the land they farmed. In two municipalities near Duaca, well-to-do peasants blocked public land sales until the prospective buyers agreed to sell them the plots they occupied.[67] In Duaca, however, this did not occur, and none of the new estate owners sold land to the occupants. The peasants occupying the estates carved out of the baldíos became tenants, and those who did not sell their holdings began paying rent to their new landlords.[68]

Following the sales to Liberal military leaders in 1867–1871, however, only four more sales of public land in Duaca were made before the 1910s, despite heavy migration to the baldíos throughout the late nineteenth century. The four sales occurred in the early 1890s and gave members of Duaca's elite title to small tracts of land just north of the resguardos.[69] Each of the new landowners already owned a coffee hacienda on part of the land he acquired, but each of the new estates enclosed contiguous peasant holdings as well. Again, peasants already cultivating the privatized land became tenants of the new landowners.[70]

The four sales in the early 1890s, however, encompassed a total of only 379 hectares, a small fraction of Duaca's public domain, which comprised perhaps forty thousand hectares. Thus between the early 1870s and the late 1910s (when large-scale privatization of the baldíos resumed) government sales did little to impede migrants' access to public land. Virtually all the new land settled during the last three decades of the nineteenth century—including the areas around Quebrada Abajo, Camburito, Piedras Lisas, Palo Negro, and Las Casitas—remained part of the public domain until around 1920.

Continued peasant access to the baldíos during this period resulted in part from failed attempts by members of the elite to privatize additional tracts. The notary records contain references to five unsuccessful petitions for public land in Duaca between 1878 and 1901, and it seems likely that additional unsuccessful attempts were made.[71] Venezuela's long series of civil wars apparently plagued the elite's efforts to obtain private title to Duaca's baldíos. Two of the failed land petitions, those made by Rafael María Granado in 1899 and Wenseslao Parra in 1901, were doomed by the outbreak of the Revolución Restauradora (1899) and the Revolución Libertadora (1901–1903). Political factors also obstructed General Pio de Jesús Peña's attempt to purchase public land in Quebrada Abajo, where he owned several coffee haciendas. Peña attempted the purchase in 1878 but never gained title, probably because of his participation in a failed revolt led by General León Colina against President Antonio Guzmán Blanco in 1874.[72] Peña's land petition coincided with a nationwide reaction against Guzmán, but as Peña was an identified anti-Guzmancista his hopes of gaining title were dashed when Guzmán recaptured power the following year. Consequently, despite his status as a general and a prominent hacendado, Peña remained excluded from the ranks of Duaca's landowners. His name appears in the notarial records for the last time in 1893, when he ceded seven coffee farms in Quebrada Abajo to his creditors. All seven farms were located on untitled public land.[73]

The elite's inability to control land on the frontier after the early 1870s—precisely the time when large-scale migration to the northern baldíos began—is significant for two reasons. First, it indicates why so much public land remained outside the sphere of private ownership and therefore open to peasant settlers during the decades when Duaca's coffee economy expanded most rapidly. Second, it illuminates the limitations of elite power, an issue rarely addressed in the historiography of rural Venezuela.

Ultimately, the inability of Duaca's elite to assert greater control over the vast public lands settled by peasants resulted from the fragmented structure of political power in Venezuela during the late nineteenth and early twentieth centuries.[74] During this period, loose alliances of political bosses competed for dominance at the local, state, and national levels. When in power, factions used their control of government to protect their interests, expand their influence, reward their friends, and punish their enemies. Within this context, securing government favors—including title to public land—required clientelistic linkages to those in power. Such connections, however, were difficult to sustain over time because power changed hands so frequently and political alliances often proved to be short-lived. Leaders continually shifted their loyalties in an effort to strengthen their position before the next armed conflict (see chapter 5).

Factional competition was particularly fierce in the state of Lara. In the 1870s, according to historian Mary Floyd, seven caudillos competed for control of Lara's government, in contrast to most other states, where only two or three caudillos could aspire to statewide dominance.[75] Factional disputes led to the overthrow of Lara's presidents on four occasions between 1872 and 1876 alone; in all, the state presidency changed hands fifty-three times between the end of the Federal War in 1863 and the turn of the century.[76] The national state remained weak throughout this period. Unable to put an end to factional struggles at the state and local levels, the central government ruled not by subduing caudillismo, but by recognizing the legitimacy and autonomy of whichever caudillos established military supremacy in their regions of influence. Even the long rule of Guzmán Blanco (1870–1888) witnessed a seemingly endless series of revolts as local and regional strongmen vied for power.[77]

Thus members of Duaca's elite faced a daunting task when they contemplated filing a petition to purchase public lands. The petition would have to be approved by district, state, and national authorities, and at any point in the process an outbreak of armed conflict or a change in factional alignments could prevent a favorable reply. Within the highly fractured and shifting world of nineteenth-century politics, it was especially difficult (if not impossible) for local elites to establish lasting ties to the national state, which exercised final authority over public lands. The elite's appropriation of Duaca's remaining public lands occurred only in the twentieth century, following the imposition of a more centralized political structure, which bound together authorities at all levels of government in a more stable and unified system of power. As long as caudillismo and political fragmentation prevailed, then, a great deal of public land remained untitled and available to settlers.

This abundance of free land must have played a large role in attracting the peasant migrants who journeyed to Duaca in the late nineteenth century. Indeed, the location of national lands suitable for coffee shaped patterns of migration throughout western Venezuela in these years. In her finely detailed study of migration into ten coffee-producing municipalities in the Venezuelan Andes, geographer Marie Price concludes: "The fastest growing coffee townships in the Andes were ones that had public lands available to colonists."[78] In Duaca, as in the Andes, peasant migrants actively pursued free access to land and the opportunity to produce a commercial crop.

Landlord-Tenant Relations on Duaca's Private Estates

Historians of the Venezuelan landed estate have emphasized the large degree of control supposedly exercised by landlords over their tenants. According to this view, landowners imposed high rents and oppressive work obligations on tenants and, by also controlling tenants' access to outside markets, made the estate a "closed economy" reminiscent of its counterpart in European feudalism.[79] Indeed, until the 1970s, scholars tended to accept such a model of landlord-tenant relations as valid for much of Latin America. More recently, however, this closed-economy model of the Latin American estate has come under criticism for exaggerating the power of landowners and failing to recognize the bargaining power and economic choices available to tenants. The history of landed estates in Duaca during the nineteenth century, I will argue, conforms more closely to this revisionist model of Latin American estates than to the "feudal" model still influential in the literature on Venezuela.

Relationships between estate owners and tenants in Duaca were clearly molded by the agrarian structure of the region as a whole. The abundance of vacant land—especially the large expanses of public land—critically weakened landowners' hold over their tenants. Peasants had alternatives to settlement on the estates; if landlords proved too harsh, they could go elsewhere. Moreover, landowners lacked the capital and labor to cultivate more than a fraction of their land directly and were therefore anxious to attract rent-paying tenants. These factors gave peasants considerable bargaining power with their landlords into the early twentieth century.

As a consequence, the conditions that estate owners offered to their tenants were relatively mild. Estate owners and tenants in Duaca did not sign rental contracts per se; rather, each estate owner wrote a *reglamento* (set of rules) outlining the obligations and rights of his tenants, and everyone cultivating land within the estate was bound to abide by these conditions.[80] No limitations were set on the length of time tenants could remain on the estate, and as long as they complied with the reglamento their tenure could be indefinite. Moreover, as the reglamentos and the (more numerous) sale and mortgage records make clear, tenants were the absolute owners of their coffee groves, food crops, houses, and all other improvements to the land they occupied. When tenants decided to sell their holdings, they were obliged to give their landlord first option to buy, provided that he matched the highest offer from other prospective buyers. After paying rent, tenants were free to sell their crops to whomever they chose. The great majority of tenants marketed their produce to merchants outside the estate, who in turn provided them with supplies and credit. Finally, Duaqueño landlords—unlike landowners in some areas of Venezuela and Latin America—did not impose a labor obligation on their tenants. Even though almost all landowners in Duaca owned coffee groves on part of their estates, and even though they had to confront the labor shortage that occurred every year during the harvest season, no landlord demanded that his tenants work on his hacienda.

Tenants' principal obligation, then, was to pay rent, and the very low rents charged by landlords clearly reflected their loose hold over tenants. For land planted in coffee, tenants paid 5 or 6 percent of the harvest in rent.[81] Not only was the percentage low, but under this system tenants paid proportionally less in years of poor harvests. Furthermore, tenants paid no rent on newly planted coffee bushes until they reached maturity. Some landowners charged a fixed rate of one-half quintal (one quintal equals forty-six kilograms) of coffee for every hectare planted in the crop, but this system (which amounted to a charge of 5 percent of the harvest in a normal year) was the exception rather than the rule. For land planted in food crops, tenants paid one fanega of corn per hectare, the equivalent of one-tenth of a normal harvest for land planted exclusively in corn. Significantly, Duaqueño landlords did not impose the most onerous system of rental, that of fixed cash rents, which forced tenants to assume all the risks associated with poor harvests and price cycles. Duaca's system of rents-in-kind, then, cushioned tenants against the effects of price fluctuations and, in the case of coffee rents, usually provided compensation in years of substandard harvests as well.[82]

A comparison of tenant conditions in Duaca with those in Venezuela's other coffee regions confirms the thesis of a relatively mild estate system in Duaca and brings into clearer focus the historical factors in its development. The plantations along Venezuela's central coast, the center of cacao production during the colonial period, dominated national coffee production after independence and continued to utilize slave labor until emancipation in 1854. Because the central coastal zone had long been a center of settlement and production, there was little unclaimed public land for emancipated slaves or other workers to settle. Instead, they continued to live and work on private estates. Tenants paid as much as a quarter of their harvests to the landowner and were also required to work in his fields a certain number of days each week.[83]

By contrast, in areas of the Andes where public lands were especially abundant, such as the municipalities of Rubio and Santa Ana in the state of Táchira, landowners set conditions as generous as the ones that prevailed on Duaca's estates.[84] Thus, a relatively onerous system of tenantry in the central coastal zone grew out of slavery in an area where large estates monopolized access to land. The more moderate system of tenantry in Duaca and parts of Táchira developed in areas where peasants had the alternative of moving to the extensive public domain or (in the case of Duaca) to the Indian lands.

Rental conditions on estates in Duaca also compared favorably to those offered on coffee estates in São Paulo, Brazil, and Cundinamarca, Colombia, during the late nineteenth and early twentieth centuries. In both of these

important coffee-producing areas, landowners maintained exclusive ownership of all coffee groves within their estates and required tenants to perform
wage work in exchange for access to a subsistence plot within the estate. As in
the central coastal region of Venezuela, estate owners' control over access to
land in Cundinamarca and São Paulo enabled them to limit tenants' participation in the commercial economy and (especially in the Colombian case) to
impose relatively severe obligations on their tenants.[85]

There remains the question of whether landlords in Duaca managed to impose obligations on their tenants beyond those specified in the estates' formal
regulations. Given the labor shortage that prevailed in the area, the landlord
might have attempted to force his poorer tenants to work in his coffee groves
during the harvest, even though labor obligations never appeared in estate
regulations.[86] Materials from Duaca are silent on this question, but information from a coffee estate in the neighboring municipality of Bobare, where
rental conditions paralleled those of Duaca, sheds some light on the matter.

The information from Bobare comes from an inventory of the property of
Apeles Pereira, an immigrant from the Dutch island of Curaçao, who died in
1895.[87] Pereira's chief property was the estate known as El Páramo, located
just a few kilometers outside the boundary of the municipality of Duaca. At
least nineteen tenant families owned coffee farms and other crops on Pereira's
land at the time of his death. Pereira had accumulated coffee groves scattered
throughout the estate. To work these groves, Pereira relied on a large labor
force of 121 peons, whose names are listed in the estate inventory along with
their debts, which totaled 9,160.64 bolívares (2,290.16 pesos). In comparing the
list of indebted peons to the names of known tenant families, only a very
weak correlation emerges. It seems from these imperfect data that eight
tenant households may have provided a total of fourteen workers to Pereira,
although no evidence can be found regarding indebted labor from the remaining eleven tenant households.[88]

If Pereira had compelled his tenants to perform wage work on his haciendas, one would expect to find much stronger linkages between tenant households and the indebted workers. In reality, the weak correlation that emerges
probably resulted from the needs of tenants rather than from the coercive ca-
pability of their landlord. For tenant families in search of supplemental income, the landlord's hacienda undoubtedly stood out as a likely source of
employment, even in the absence of coercion. In short, these data simply suggest that some tenant households (less than half) may have sent at least one
member to earn wages on Pereira's haciendas. When he set about recruiting

laborers, Pereira clearly concentrated his efforts on the larger world outside his estate.

The commercial relations of tenants on nineteenth-century Duaca estates offer further indications of their independence from landlord domination. Notary documents record 224 mortgages of tenant property in Duaca between 1863 and 1899, virtually all of which called for repayment with coffee.[89] Only one of these cases involved a tenant mortgaging his property to his landlord.[90] By contrast, thirty-eight of the mortgage loans came from other tenants within the same estate as the mortgaged property, and the remaining 185 loans came from merchants outside the estate, almost all of whom resided in Barquisimeto or Duaca. Clearly, Duaqueño landlords did not control tenants' access to credit, nor did they control the marketing of tenants' crops.

Similarly, when tenants sold their holdings, the landlord seldom exercised his option to buy. As specified in the reglamentos, tenants were required to notify their landlord of all sales in advance and had to sell their holdings to him if he matched the highest price offered by other prospective buyers. Of the 250 tenant farms sold between 1863 and 1899, however, landlords purchased only twenty-one (8.4 percent), failing to exercise their option to buy in over 90 percent of the recorded cases. By contrast, at least eighty of the tenant properties sold in these years were purchased by other tenants. So, when a tenant decided to sell his or her property, the probability that another tenant would buy it was much greater than the probability that the landlord would. In some cases, the tenants purchasing the property were peasants buying an additional small coffee grove, but other tenant-to-tenant sales represented cases of large tenants buying out their poorer neighbors. The presence of these tenant hacendados within the estates was an important aspect of the nineteenth-century landed estate in Duaca.

By any measure, these tenant hacendados belonged to the Duaqueño elite. It was not uncommon for large tenants to own coffee groves totaling 25,000 bushes or more and to extend between 1,200 and 5,000 bolívares (from 300 to 1,250 pesos) in credit to their workers. Occasionally the holdings of elite tenants included housing for harvest workers and pulperías (small stores).[91] Aside from making loans to workers, large tenants frequently made interest-bearing loans to poorer tenants, requiring payment in coffee or, more rarely, in food crops. The political influence wielded by some tenants confirms their elite status. Three of these elite tenants—José de la Paz Alvarado, and the Giménez Méndez brothers Aurelio and Avelino—held the rank of general during the civil wars of 1899 and 1901–1903 (see chapter 5). Two other tenants

—José de la Cruz Castillo and General Isidro Giménez—served as governor of the municipality during the nineteenth century.[92] So, although most tenants were peasants, a significant minority clearly belonged to the local elite.

Relationships among tenants were thus double-edged. On the one hand, wealthier tenants clearly prospered at the expense of their poorer neighbors. Elite tenants (like hacendados elsewhere in the municipality) expanded their holdings by acquiring the groves of small cultivators, they used debt to mobilize peasant labor, and they often made interest-bearing loans. Even though these economic relationships between elite and peasant tenants might at times be carried out under a veneer of paternalism (such as when loans against future labor or the next harvest allowed peasant families to survive a lean year), the unequal status that shaped these transactions surely reminded poorer tenants of their exploitative nature.

Nevertheless, their common position as tenants at times became the basis of alliances between the poor and the well-to-do, momentarily outweighing the class divisions that separated them. The presence of members of the elite among the tenantry, and their ability to confront landlords at the head of a broad-based tenant alliance, constituted an important check on landowner power. The most important example of such an alliance between peasant and elite tenants occurred in the northeastern part of the estate of Los Chipas, where a dispute between the estate's owners and tenants simmered throughout the late nineteenth century.

Most of the land in this estate had been enclosed by illegal boundary changes made earlier in the century, and many Duaqueños knew that the estate's titles were fraudulent. Nevertheless, the various owners of Los Chipas (it changed hands every decade or so during the second half of the nineteenth century) usually had enough political pull to defend their claim to the land. For example, when, in the 1860s, a public land inspector attempted to reclassify part of Los Chipas as belonging to the public domain, the estate owners secured a judicial ruling in their favor. Similarly, a quarter-century later, José Regino Cadevilla, a tenant in the southern hamlet of Agua-fría, attempted to buy the land he occupied from the national government, again arguing that it was public land. The estate owners once more defended their claim to the land in court. In both cases the owners of Los Chipas won by simply producing recent bills of sale with the expanded boundaries and by gathering testimony concerning the successful collection of rent in some of the disputed areas. The court never probed the deeper legal history of the estate, which would have turned the proceedings against the owners. As long as they faced weak individual opponents (one bureaucrat or a single tenant acting alone), the owners of Los Chipas proceeded aggressively against those who questioned their claim to the land, and they prevailed.[93]

But the conflict in the northeastern section of the estate was a very different matter.[94] Here a broad-based coalition of tenants steadfastly refused to pay rent. When Eloy Parra, the administrator of Los Chipas during the 1880s and 1890s, attempted to collect rent in this part of the estate, which included the hamlets of Quebrada de Oro, Pajaritos, La Danta, and Los Volcanes, only two or three tenants willingly paid. The rest—elite and peasant alike—refused, saying that the land was in reality part of the public domain. Moreover, they informed Parra that they were in contact with certain persons (whom they refused to name) who could prove the true boundaries of Los Chipas.[95]

Parra conferred with the estate owners to find a method of forcing the tenants to pay rent. They considered initiating a civil lawsuit; as they were probably aware, landowners in the neighboring municipality of Bobare occasionally took such action to enforce rent collection, and they always won.[96] But in the end Parra and the estate owners decided not to initiate legal action against their tenants. As Parra himself later stated, he and the owners realized they did not have good title to the disputed area, and they feared a protracted, costly legal conflict, which they could easily lose. The principal owner of Los Chipas, José Antonio Torrealba, attempted to use his influence in Caracas to secure title to the land from the national government, but failed.[97] Meanwhile, Parra continued in his attempts to persuade those occupying the disputed area to pay rent, but without success. The multiclass alliance against rent collection held firm, and the owners never succeeded in imposing their authority over tenants in the northeastern part of Los Chipas. Although subsequent sales of the estate repeated the old boundaries, in practice the tenants in the disputed zone continued to live as public land occupants for the rest of the nineteenth century. Thus the owners of the largest estate in Duaca failed to establish their authority over many of their "tenants."

Landlord-tenant relations in nineteenth-century Duaca, then, did not conform to the widely accepted model of the Venezuelan landed estate, in which a powerful landed elite allegedly reduced the peasantry to the status of dependent laborers. Rather, the power Duaqueño landlords exercised over their tenants was decidedly limited by the widespread availability of land outside their estates on the resguardos and the public domain. Rental conditions on the estates reflected the bargaining power of tenants who could choose to settle elsewhere. Landlords never challenged their tenants' right to own coffee groves, nor did they control the marketing of tenants' crops, nor did they impose a labor obligation. Rents remained remarkably low, and the prevailing custom of calculating coffee rents as a proportion of the harvest cushioned tenants against the consequences of depressed prices and poor harvests. Moreover, the presence of elite hacendados among the tenantry provided an additional safeguard against any attempt by landlords to impose new, harsher conditions.

Conclusion

During the final third of the nineteenth century, as western Venezuela experienced the onset of the coffee boom, peasant society in Duaca entered a period of dynamic expansion and, on balance, it prospered. Peasant migration into the municipality quickened, settlers cleared and planted new lands, merchant networks connected Duaca's producers to export houses on the coast, and local harvests of coffee tripled between the early 1870s and the turn of the century. As in the Andean coffee zones further west, peasant prosperity depended to a great extent on the availability of vacant land for colonization. Unoccupied lands remained abundant in Duaca during most of this period, largely because of its location outside the central coastal zone, which formed the economic heart of Venezuela until the mid-nineteenth century.

While geography and history had made Duaca a sparsely settled frontier zone at the onset of the coffee boom, political factors allowed much of the unoccupied land to remain public and hence open to peasant settlement once the boom began. Power struggles among rival caudillos created a fragmented state and prevented the local elite from extending their control over national lands during the years when peasant migrants brought much of the public domain under cultivation. Meanwhile, Duaca's resguardos remained under the control of the indigenous community and open to peasant cultivators until 1916. Thus most peasants lived on the baldíos or resguardos, free of landlord control, throughout the late nineteenth century. The availability of national and community lands meant that peasants who did settle on private estates secured terms more generous than those available to tenants in most other Latin American coffee zones; it also meant that the elite encountered "labor shortages" and found themselves obliged to offer concessions to seasonal laborers from peasant households. As local coffee production boomed, peasants confronted the local elite from a position of strength.

But the resiliency of the peasant economy in the late nineteenth century was not merely the product of such "structural" factors as a favorable ratio of population to land, the expansion of world demand for coffee, or the fragmented structure of the Venezuelan state. The actions of peasants themselves also underpinned the continuation of a thriving peasant economy during these years; human agency as well as more impersonal structural realities shaped Duaqueño society.[98] Peasant migration to Duaca, a critical feature of local society in this period, occurred because peasants chose to move.[99] Peasants also chose to produce coffee for the world market, to settle in family clusters, to engage in labor exchanges among households, to make loans to other members of their class (especially their kinfolk), and on occasion to risk their own livelihood to come to the aid of another. When it served their interests, peasants participated in alliances with members of the elite, as when the indigenous community defended its land, and when occupants of the disputed zone of Los Chipas banded together to resist landlord authority. When obliged to seek employment on the elite's haciendas, workers sometimes negotiated for larger advances than their employers could ever hope to reclaim. It would be foolish to imply that peasant behavior transformed Duaca into a rustic utopia, of course, but human action did play a role in the peasantry's ability to meet the challenges of market fluctuations, demands by creditors, endemic disease, and the occasional loss of a harvest. Peasant families who survived the pressures of the coffee boom were not the passive beneficiaries of favorable conditions: they survived largely because of their own cooperative strategies and propensity to struggle.

Together, then, structural factors and peasant behavior placed real limits on the elite's ability to assert control over the peasantry. To be sure, members of the elite extracted profits from small cultivators, but their hold over local society could not proceed beyond a certain point. Most production continued to be carried out on peasant farms and more or less on the peasantry's own terms. If, as scholars often suggest, peasants' chief goal is simply to survive as small cultivators from year to year and generation to generation, then Duaca's peasantry continued to thrive through the turn of the century. The society that emerged from the coffee boom remained a peasant society; its fundamental dynamics favored the reproduction of peasant households and the spatial expansion of peasant cultivation. By contrast, the elite's efforts to expand control over land and labor were often frustrated.

4 Commerce and the Local Elite, 1863–1899

COFFEE DID NOT IMPOSE a single, uniform social structure on the Latin American societies that produced it in the nineteenth century. Rather, a variety of social formations emerged in the region's coffee zones. At one end of the spectrum, in areas best exemplified by São Paulo, Brazil, a powerful elite imposed their control on society by restricting access to land and creating a dependent, landless working class.[1] By contrast, in Costa Rica the coffee economy democratized access to land as peasant cultivators occupied sparsely settled areas to grow the new crop. Faced with a dynamic, expansive peasantry, the Costa Rican elite invested in credit, marketing, and processing rather than attempt to control production. Although Costa Rican peasants endured exploitation in their commercial dealings, throughout the nineteenth century they retained control over production.[2]

Duaca's elite also confronted a peasantry with access to large amounts of vacant land. As in Costa Rica, the proliferation of peasant farms in Duaca provided merchants with an ever increasing host of clients, while the predominance of household production hindered attempts to mobilize hacienda labor, and both trends led the elite to favor investment in commerce over production. As coffee expanded in the late nineteenth century, then, the wealth of

Duaca's elite came to depend more and more on control over the peasantry's commercial relations. To be sure, members of the local elite continued to own haciendas, as they had since the Spanish conquest. Beginning in the mid-1870s, however, Duaca's elite, which had traditionally derived most of its wealth from agriculture, began to invest increasingly in commerce.

This intensification of trade during the late nineteenth century steadily transformed the town of Duaca into an important commercial center. Into the 1870s, Duaca remained a relatively isolated agricultural town. Local commerce was limited to small general stores (pulperías); the road passing through town toward the coast was little more than a footpath; and the town's church remained a small stone structure, unchanged since the colonial era. By the 1890s, however, offices of coffee merchants lined the streets, a railroad connected the town to the coast, a coffee-processing plant with the latest steam-powered machinery stood near the railroad station, and an impressive new church adorned the central plaza. By the turn of the century, Duaca had become a bustling commercial town, the center of credit and marketing for the coffee growers who occupied more and more of its rural hinterland.

The Elite's Shift Toward Commerce, 1863–1879

The elite in Duaca had engaged in commerce on a modest scale before the Federal War, but most of their wealth traditionally came from agriculture. The destruction wrought by the war reinforced this agricultural orientation during the decade that followed.[3] Members of the elite needed all their resources to rebuild their haciendas and lacked sufficient capital to invest in trade. So, their participation in commerce was limited to the ownership of small shops located either in the town of Duaca or in the outlying hamlets, where they sold locally produced foodstuffs and small assortments of merchandise brought from Barquisimeto. Although pulpería owners extended small amounts of credit to their customers, they did not make the larger mortgage loans often needed to finance coffee production. In general, Duaca coffee producers in need of credit during the decade following the Federal War borrowed from Barquisimeto merchants, who in turn received loans from merchant houses in the coastal city of Puerto Cabello.

Juan Aguilar—perhaps the wealthiest individual within Duaca's Indian community and whose son-in-law Francisco Palma acted as the community's representative in the 1870s—exemplified the agricultural orientation of Duaca's elite before the mid-1870s. When he made out his will in 1870, Aguilar owned two coffee haciendas with a combined total of over 70,000 bushes and worth an estimated 10,000 pesos, as well as a sugar hacienda near the town of Duaca. All three haciendas were on Indian community lands and were worked by a labor force indebted to Aguilar for a little over 300 pesos. The only hint of merchant activity by Aguilar was an assortment of debts totaling 460 pesos and 4 reales owed to him by eight individuals, but these seem to have been simple loans of money, with no mention of interest or mortgages. Aguilar, on the other hand, owed 4,350 pesos to merchants, including 3,530 pesos to Serapio García, the prominent Spanish immigrant merchant in Barquisimeto who held the mortgages on Aguilar's two coffee haciendas. Aguilar needed all his resources to produce the crops demanded by his creditors and simply did not have the means to engage in commerce on a significant scale.[4]

Other prominent members of the indigenous community in the early 1870s shared this agricultural orientation. Another member of the Aguilar family—Coronel Félix Aguilar, who apparently won his military title in the Federal War and who served as his community's legal representative in the late 1860s—became one of the few members of the local elite to own land. In partnership with Victorino Escalona, a Barquisimeto merchant, Aguilar bought a tract of public land to the north of the resguardos in 1871, the year before his death, for twelve hundred pesos in military compensation bonds. The goods divided among his heirs the following year—the recently purchased land, a sugar hacienda, and livestock—demonstrated Aguilar's confinement to agriculture.[5] Similarly, Pantaleón Heredia, another member of the indigenous elite, limited his economic activities to coffee production and never entered commerce.[6]

Nor did the established creole families of Duaca's elite engage in commerce on a large scale during the decade following the Federal War. Two landowning families with deep roots in Duaca—the Andrades and the Ledesmas, each of which owned small estates—invested exclusively in agriculture after the war.[7] Others among Duaca's creole elite, like the Alvarado and Virgües families, owned small pulperías in the town of Duaca or the outlying hamlets, but none of them became coffee merchants during this time.[8] Even Juan de la Rosa Vásquez—whose large coffee hacienda in Cerro-Gordo and Tinajitas made him one of the wealthiest Duaqueños in these years—entered commerce in only a modest way, setting up a pulpería in El Eneal.[9] As the local elite dedicated the bulk of their resources to agriculture rather than commerce during the decade following the Federal War, the financing and the marketing of Duaca's growing coffee harvests were controlled by merchants in Barquisimeto.

Merchant activity on a significant scale in Duaca began in the mid-1870s, probably because of the rising coffee prices of the preceding years. Having rebuilt their haciendas following the war, Duaca's hacendados reaped the benefits of high coffee prices in the early 1870s and some used their new capital to begin making mortgage loans to smaller producers. Longtime residents of the area who began extending credit to coffee growers in the 1870s included Cecilio Carrera, an illiterate sugar and coffee hacendado who lived in the hamlet of Tumaque, and José Maximiniano Soteldo, a large tenant on the southern part of the estate of Los Chipas.[10] Rural merchants such as Carrera and Soteldo remained important throughout the nineteenth century, but most of the local elite who entered the coffee trade—including Evaristo Segura and Nicolás Alvarado—based their operations in the town of Duaca rather than the outlying hamlets.[11]

Wherever they operated, these men profited from their commercial operations in several ways, beginning with the manipulation of interest. Often borrowing from their Barquisimeto creditors at 1 or 1.5 percent interest per month, they charged their clients 2 percent.[12] Since merchants usually advanced credit in merchandise rather than cash, the difference between the prices at which they bought and sold goods provided another source of profit. And if borrowers failed to repay their debts on time, creditors occasionally seized the mortgaged property. As a final source of profit, merchants often received coffee from their peasant clients in a semiprocessed form and completed the processing themselves.[13] Peasant farmers began the processing by drying the harvested berries on patios made of bricks or packed earth for up to three weeks after picking. The next step, removal of the dried husk that enclosed the coffee beans, was sometimes performed by the peasant family using a large mortar and pestle. But merchants often received coffee still in the husk and carried out the final processing themselves with animal-powered mills known as *trillas*.[14] Peasants who delivered their crop with the husk intact (*café en parapara*) accepted a below-market price, in effect paying the merchant to complete the processing.[15]

Whereas some of the new coffee merchants of the mid-1870s were established Duaqueño hacendados who entered commerce, others were outsiders who migrated to Duaca, apparently with capital ready to lend. Drawn by

Duaca's expanding coffee production, these elite migrants were among the area's most active coffee merchants. Most commonly, the new merchants came to Duaca from Quibor, the district located southwest of Barquisimeto. One of them, Isidro Giménez, arrived and began operations as a coffee merchant in 1873; only two years later he was named Duaca's *jefe civil* (the municipality's chief political authority).[16] At roughly the same time, José Tomás Giménez (apparently no relation to Isidro) settled as a tenant on the estate of Los Chipas, and by 1875 no fewer than five neighboring tenants had mortgaged their coffee holdings to him.[17] Of all the Quibor migrants who came to Duaca in the 1870s, none enjoyed more success in his adopted home than Rudecindo Peralta. Operating as a merchant in Duaca as early as 1874, Peralta remained a prominent figure among Duaca's elite until his death in 1919.[18] Just as the expansion of peasant production depended on migration into the area, so the emergence of a local merchant class involved migration by aspiring entrepreneurs.

The Duaca elite's growing control over local commerce is illustrated in table 2, which summarizes the changing sources of credit to Duaqueño coffee growers between 1864 and 1880. Before examining these figures, however, I should emphasize that they offer only a partial picture of the flow of credit to Duaca's coffee growers during this period. Merchants extended a good deal of credit on an informal basis, recording their clients' debits and credits in private account books. Lenders demanded a formal, registered mortgage only when a client's debt reached a certain amount.[19] Also, the deterioration of archival records for some years—particularly the 1860s and early 1870s—means that even some registered loans can no longer be counted. Nevertheless, the figures below indicate, in a general way, the Duaca elite's growing investment in commerce beginning in the mid-1870s.

Between 1864 and 1873, Barquisimeto merchants clearly controlled the financing and marketing of Duaca's coffee. Of the thirty Duaca coffee producers who registered mortgages in this period, twenty-three were in debt to lenders residing in Barquisimeto. Only three producers registered mortgages in favor of lenders in Duaca. Beginning in the mid-1870s, however, the situation changed dramatically. Between 1874 and 1880, fifty-three mortgages were registered in favor of Duaca merchants. Whereas the loans from Duaca merchants between 1864 and 1873 totaled only 1,404.50 pesos, those registered between 1874 and 1880 totaled 43,205.99 pesos. The difference suggests a large-scale investment in commerce by the local elite around the mid-1870s, even when we take into account the limitations of the data.

Table 2. Registered Loans to Duaca Coffee Producers, 1864–1880

| | Location of Creditor | | | |
	Barquisimeto	Duaca	Puerto Cabello	Other
1864	—	364.00 (1)	—	—
1865	2,025.00 (3)	—	—	—
1866	3,858.15 (2)	—	—	—
1867	1,661.47 (4)	555.50 (1)	—	—
1868	8,489.73 (3)	—	—	—
1869	5,844.00 (5)	—	165.00 (1)	1,830.00 (2)
1870	1,464.19 (1)	—	—	—
1871	655.50 (2)	—	—	270.00 (1)
1872	460.00 (2)	—	—	—
1873	440.00 (1)	485.00 (1)	—	—
1874	18,405.50 (11)	6,878.10 (8)	—	15,100.00 (2)
1875	16,434.90 (11)	6,610.40 (8)	—	4,695.00 (4)
1876	8,034.25 (11)	12,406.75 (10)	—	5,000.00 (1)
1877	37,204.25 (17)	9,035.00 (12)	—	520.00 (2)
1878	96,804.86 (16)	1,770.92 (3)	—	—
1879	25,322.12 (14)	2,343.80 (4)	—	500.00 (1)
1880	20,801.00 (14)	4,161.12 (8)	—	1,056.00 (1)

Source: Registro Principal del Estado Lara, Protocolos del Distrito Barquisimeto (Iribarren).

Note: Values of loans are given in pesos. Numbers of loans are in parentheses.

This surge of investment during the 1870s reflected Duaca's growing commercial opportunities as peasants migrated into the area and established coffee groves, a process that often required credit. Although haciendas, the traditional basis of elite wealth in Duaca, generated profits during periods of high coffee prices, investment in commerce probably proved more profitable over the long term. Interest rates, the ability to buy cheap and sell dear, and the security provided by mortgages all made commerce a safer investment than agriculture, which was more subject to the uncertainties of weather and price fluctuations.

The relations of production on Duaca's haciendas also argued in favor of limiting investment in agriculture. No matter how the entrepreneur acquired his hacienda (whether by clearing and planting unoccupied land or by acquiring peasant holdings that could be combined to form an hacienda), sooner or later he had to confront the problem of labor recruitment and control. Hacienda owners had to attract labor through wage advances, and they often lost part of this investment when laborers evaded their employer's attempts at enforcement. Moreover, Duaca's chronic worker shortage often became critical at harvest time. As late as 1905, hacendados in Duaca and neighboring municipalities periodically failed to mobilize enough workers to pick their coffee in time and had to let some of the ripened berries fall to the ground and rot.[20] Thus, although widespread peasant access to land gave merchants a host of potential clients, it also perpetuated the problem of labor control. Both considerations led the elite to shift a portion of their capital to trade rather than attempt constant large-scale expansion of their haciendas.

A similar pattern of elite development occurred in at least some of the coffee zones of the Venezuelan Andes. According to Roseberry, during the coffee boom of the second half of the nineteenth century the Boconó elite found that "their ability to control labor was becoming more problematic with the expansion of commodity production and the existence of open land for settlement."[21] This limited control over labor, Roseberry suggests, contributed to the Boconó elite's growing commercial orientation as peasant production expanded. As in Duaca, merchants who migrated to Boconó during the coffee boom played an important part in the development of local commerce, and members of Boconó's established agricultural elite often turned to trade as peasant production expanded.[22] By investing in commerce, elites in Boconó and Duaca limited their vulnerability to the uncertainties of agricultural production and lessened their dependence on what they considered to be an undependable and immoral working class.

Most members of the elite, then, divided their capital between commerce and agriculture from the mid-1870s onward. It is therefore impossible to impose a sharp distinction between merchants and hacendados within the local elite. To be sure, when compelled to declare a profession at the notary office, individuals usually chose one over the other, but "merchants" invariably owned haciendas, and "hacendados" frequently made loans to be repaid with coffee. Some members of the elite rightly declared their double profession, "agricultor y comerciante" (agriculturalist and merchant).[23] This interpenetration of agricultural and commercial enterprise remained a central feature of Duaca's elite as long as the coffee economy lasted.

Like many of his peers, Rudecindo Peralta divided his capital between agricultural production and trade. A review of his entrepreneurial activity will illustrate the elite's diversified investments. Arriving in Duaca from Quibor in the mid-1870s, Peralta made his first two loans to coffee producers in 1874 and registered a third the following year.[24] Meanwhile, Peralta began investing in the production of coffee. Between 1875 and 1878 he purchased three coffee farms, one with twenty-five thousand trees and two with five thousand each, on the estate of Los Chipas.[25] Shortly afterward, he bought the land under his growing hacienda from the owner of Los Chipas.[26] Peralta's investment in agriculture, though, did not signal an abandonment of trade. Between 1878 and 1882 he registered four more loans to coffee growers.[27] Continuing to divide his capital between agriculture and commerce, Peralta joined together with his brothers Francisco, Gabriel, and Policarpo to form the merchant firm of Peralta Hermanos in the mid-1880s, and he continued to acquire new haciendas on his own account.[28] Peralta's combination of agricultural and commercial enterprise served him well: he remained one of Duaca's most prominent entrepreneurs until his death in 1919. His wealth may have set him above most of the local elite, but Peralta's diversified investments were typical of his class.

The structure of elite investments, however, was not dictated by economic factors alone. Calculations of profit and loss argued in favor of investment in commerce, yet members of the elite constantly invested in haciendas. In part, this reflected their need for properties that could be used as collateral for loans from Barquisimeto merchants. And, when coffee prices were high, haciendas made money. Nevertheless, owning an hacienda involved political as well as economic considerations. Throughout the nineteenth century, Venezuelan politics revolved around civil wars, which broke out every few years as rival factions vied for power. For the elite, participation in politics often involved mobilizing and outfitting bands of armed peasants. Owning an hacienda was useful, if not indispensable, in this process. Aside from providing corn, beans, and meat to the troops, an hacienda could serve as a base of operations in the countryside, a place to hide guns and munitions or to gather followers, away from the gaze of the authorities. Most critical of all, owning an hacienda created ties to the surrounding peasants who worked on the hacienda, brought their coffee beans to the hacienda's trilla to be dehusked, purchased goods at the hacienda store, or sought assistance from the hacendado when one of their family fell ill. These relationships often provided the basis for recruitment into the hacendado's armed band when politics turned violent. In short, haciendas were political assets whether they provided profits or not.

Members of Duaca's elite were undoubtedly attentive to the political advantages of hacienda ownership, for many of them acquired military titles in the civil wars of the late nineteenth century. The 1891 census found seventeen generals, thirty-one colonels, and thirty-five commandants in the municipality of Duaca.[29] Local men referred to as "General" in notary records and the press between 1863 and 1897 included Cipriano Bracho, Pio J. Peña, Juan de la Rosa Vásquez, Santos Herrera, Matías Martínez, Julian Mogollón, Rudecindo Peralta, Isidro Giménez, Blas Ortíz, Ismael Manzanarez, Julio Couput, Carlos Andrade, and Nicolás Paradas. Individuals dubbed "Coronel" by their followers included Francisco Palma, Marcelo Vásquez, Francisco Sivira, Eulogio Pérez, and Félix Aguilar. For these men and those who aspired to follow in their footsteps, owning an hacienda was a matter of political influence as well as an economic enterprise. Regardless of how involved they became in commerce, therefore, members of the local elite retained at least one hacienda, in part to produce coffee for their creditors in Barquisimeto, and in part to assure themselves a political base—and, if necessary, a refuge—in the countryside.

Although virtually all members of the elite owned at least one hacienda, and some owned several, few of them owned land. In part this was because so much of the land in the area was either public or belonged to the Indian community. Also, the two largest estates in nineteenth-century Duaca were often owned not by the local elite but by absentee landlords who resided in Barquisimeto or in Yaritagua, a city fifteen kilometers east of Barquisimeto in the state of Yaracuy. From 1877 until 1886, the largest estate in Duaca—Los Chipas —was owned jointly by José Antonio Torrealba of Barquisimeto and General Epifanio Ruíz of Yaritagua. Ruíz's heirs acquired complete ownership in 1886, and in 1899 sold it to a Barquisimeto manufacturer.[30] The other large estate in Duaca—the Generals' Estate—was composed of public land sold by the national government to four Barquisimeto generals in 1868.[31] Throughout the rest of the century, investors in Barquisimeto continued to own at least half of the shares in the Generals' Estate. Because most of the local elite did not own land, they located their haciendas on public land, the Indian lands, or rented plots on the private estates.

Eulogio Pérez briefly became the largest landowner among the Duaca elite when he bought Los Chipas in 1869. Owning the estate, however, did not assure his ascendancy within the local elite. Rents throughout Duaca were low, and on the northeastern section of Los Chipas an alliance of elite and peasant "tenants" successfully resisted any rent collection at all. Pérez, who had bought the estate on credit, lost most of Los Chipas in 1877 when he could not complete the payments. He retained only 139 hectares, the land under his sugar and coffee hacienda.[32] Shortly after losing Los Chipas, Pérez began to diversify into commerce. He made his first registered loan to a coffee grower in 1880.[33] The following year, when he made out his will, Pérez owned a general store—complete with a trilla to process his clients' coffee—on one corner of Duaca's main plaza.[34] Having failed as a landlord, Pérez followed the majority of the elite into commerce.

Cipriano Bracho, the only other large landowner among the local elite, was one of the few prominent Duaqueños who did not diversify into commerce in the 1870s or 1880s. In 1874, when other hacendados were registering their first loans to coffee growers, Bracho bought one-fourth of the shares in the Generals' Estate, where he already owned a coffee grove as a tenant.[35] During the following years, Bracho extended his coffee holdings within the estate by purchasing groves from a number of tenants.[36] In 1878, he acquired Juan de la Rosa Vásquez's large hacienda in the Indian lands.[37] Bracho's haciendas, in 1878, comprised a total of 210,000 trees and probably made him the largest coffee producer in Duaca.[38] Only relatively late in his life, in the 1890s, did Bracho begin making mortgage loans to coffee growers.[39] Bracho's largest investments in the 1890s, however, went into acquiring houses in the town of Duaca. The coming of the railroad and the town's commercial development apparently made these urban properties attractive. By the time of Bracho's death in 1916, his nineteen houses in Duaca accounted for almost one-half of his total wealth, whereas land accounted for approximately one-eighth.[40] Though more belatedly than most of the local elite, Bracho too shifted his capital toward commercial ventures.

The lands owned by other members of the local elite were much smaller than the Generals' Estate or Los Chipas. These small estates included former Indian community lands sold to private owners in 1850–1851, tracts of public lands privatized by the national government soon after the Federal War and in 1890–1891, and sections of Los Chipas that owners of the estate sold off at various times.[41] The largest of these estates appears to have been the tract of 298.7 hectares sold by the national government to General Santos Herrera in 1867.[42]

Ownership of these small estates contributed little to the local elite's accumulation of capital. Leaving aside Los Chipas and the Generals' Estate, which were generally owned by Barquisimetanos, private lands in Duaca were settled by relatively few tenants during the nineteenth century.[43] The benefits derived from these small estates were further minimized by the system of low rents. The ownership of land, then, played only a small part in the development of Duaca's elite during the second half of the nineteenth century.

The local elite's turn toward commerce in the mid-1870s coincided with the rule of Antonio Guzmán Blanco, the strongman who controlled the presidency between 1870 and 1888. Guzmán benefited politically from the expansion of the coffee market, and he in turn used the government's authority to solidify Venezuela's links to the global economy. Although Guzmán confronted numerous regional challenges to his rule, and state presidents confronted endless rebellions by their local rivals, the prosperous coffee economy of the early 1870s undoubtedly dissuaded many potential rebels during the time he was building his regime. Moreover, Venezuela's growing foreign and domestic trade led to an increase in government revenues, which he skillfully distributed among regional political leaders in an attempt to secure their loyalty. The relative peace imposed by Guzmán Blanco enabled the coffee economy to grow under the longest ruling regime that Venezuelans had known since the time of José Antonio Páez (1830–1848).[44]

Seeing Venezuelan progress largely in terms of increased participation in the North Atlantic economy, Guzmán Blanco did more than any previous ruler to improve the nation's transportation infrastructure. Several projects had important consequences for Duaca's commercial growth and accelerated the emergence of the town of Duaca as an important market center. In 1877 the British-controlled New Quebrada Railway, Land, and Copper Company constructed the railroad that linked Aroa's mines, located forty kilometers northeast of Duaca, to the coastal port of Tucacas. New Quebrada also established a shipping service from the port of Tucacas to the city of Puerto Cabello, the principal import-export center in the region. Eager to facilitate access to the new railroad, the government and private investors financed the improvement of the Barquisimeto-Aroa road, which passed through Duaca, so that it could accommodate wheeled vehicles. Guzmán Blanco budgeted twenty-five thousand pesos for the project, Puerto Cabello merchants contributed fifteen thousand pesos, the New Quebrada Company put up an undisclosed amount, and the highway opened soon after the railroad was completed.[45]

The construction of the highway hastened Duaca's transition from a marginal agricultural town to a regional commercial center. The Duaqueño elite clearly realized the benefits that they stood to gain from their improved linkages to Barquisimeto and to the coast. When a group of dignitaries traveling from Barquisimeto to Aroa to inaugurate the highway stopped for the night in Duaca, the local elite sponsored a welcoming ceremony complete with banquet and fireworks. The Duaqueños' expectations proved well grounded. A German traveler later in the century observed that the building of the Aroa-Tucacas railroad and the highway marked a turning point in Duaca's history.[46] Although the growth of peasant coffee production would have made the town a modest commercial center in any event (as we have seen, a class of coffee merchants began to emerge there in the mid-1870s, a few years ahead of the highway), the development of the region's transportation infrastructure quickened the process.

Duaca's growing commercial importance during the late nineteenth century led to periodic changes in the town itself, the first of which was the construction of a new church. The leveling of the old, dilapidated temple and the construction of an imposing new building, with a three-story bell tower and gold-colored cupolas, symbolized the town's growing economic stature and prosperity. The secular significance of the new church was not lost on the men who acted as sponsors for its dedication in December 1879. These sponsors included the presidents of the states of Lara and Yaracuy; the state and regional military commanders; two prominent coffee entrepreneurs from the neighboring municipality of Bobare; Serapio García, the Barquisimeto coffee merchant; and General Epifanio Ruíz, the Yaracuy politician who had recently purchased the estate of Los Chipas.[47] For these notables—and for the members of the local elite who sponsored the weeklong festivities after the dedication ceremony—the opening of the new church was less a religious event than an opportunity to appear as patrons of Duaca's progress, to make a public display of their wealth and beneficence by funding the celebrations. None seized the opportunity more purposefully than Serapio García, who commissioned a calligrapher to prepare an intricately decorated document that forgave a debt owed him by Duaca's priest, Virgilio Díaz, who had taken out large personal loans to support the construction of the church. García's daughter, Soledad, presented the document, complete with embellished envelope, to Díaz during the dedication ceremony. The other attending dignitaries, aside from fulfilling their obligations as sponsors, presumably contributed to the general collection that raised almost fifteen hundred pesos in aid of Duaca's impoverished cleric.[48]

Regional Commerce and the Crisis of 1879–1885

Duaca's first wave of coffee-based prosperity, however, was coming to an end even as the town celebrated this symbol of newfound wealth. World coffee production, increasingly dominated by Brazil, had grown considerably in recent years, but when the industrial nations that consumed coffee fell into an economic depression in the late 1870s, the global market quickly collapsed.

Coffee prices began to decline in late 1878, fell sharply the following year, and remained depressed through the early 1880s.[49]

This prolonged crisis shook the commercial network that had emerged so recently to link Duaca to Barquisimeto, Puerto Cabello, and the international market. Creditors large and small pressed debtors for payment, but prices were so low that few had enough coffee to cover their obligations. Some elite and peasant coffee producers lost their holdings to creditors, who often resold the properties as soon as they could. In other cases merchants chose not to foreclose, afraid that they would be left with properties they could neither sell nor operate at a profit. As a result, the structure of property ownership among Duaca's coffee producers was not radically altered by the crisis. Nevertheless, the depression did produce important changes in the local elite's linkages to the regional export economy.

Before the crisis, Duaca's elite depended almost exclusively on Barquisimeto merchants for credit. The most prominent of the Barquisimeto merchants was Serapio García, the Spanish immigrant who began making loans to coffee producers in Duaca and in other parts of the state, particularly Bobare, soon after the Federal War.[50] Relying on credit advanced by the German firm of Blöhm and Company in Puerto Cabello, by the late 1860s García had become the principal link between Duaca and the coastal export-import merchants. His connections to Duaca and Puerto Cabello had made him the logical choice to oversee work on the Barquisimeto-Aroa highway, and to solicit funds for the project from Puerto Cabello merchants.[51] When the highway opened in 1877, García established a branch office in Duaca, and the coffee price quoted in his office served as the *precio corriente* (benchmark price) for dealings between most Duaca merchants and their clients.[52] García's very success in establishing himself as the intermediary between Blöhm and Company and eastern Lara's coffee producers and merchants, however, made him particularly vulnerable to the depression. Obliged to balance his large accounts with steadily depreciating coffee, García soon found himself in a precarious position.

By early 1880, García owed Blöhm over 150,000 pesos and the firm demanded some security to cover the debt. As part of an arrangement approved by Blöhm's directors in Hamburg, García mortgaged to Blöhm most of the liens he held on his clients' coffee farms in Duaca and other municipalities around Barquisimeto.[53] Over the next year and a half, though, García's debts only increased as the depression deepened. In October 1881, unable to postpone the day of reckoning any longer, he ceded to Blöhm a combination of liens, urban real estate, and agricultural property worth 222,065 pesos (888,260 bolívares). Included in this transfer to Blöhm were the debts owed to García by many of his clients among Duaca's elite.[54] García retained some commercial and agricultural property, but his days as Barquisimeto's leading coffee merchant were over.

After the 1881–1882 harvest, García's former clients among the Duaca elite arranged their accounts with Blöhm and Company, which now held the mortgages on their properties. Despite the size of the Duaqueños' debts, Blöhm preferred not to seize their property. Instead, the firm imposed strict five-year schedules for the debtors to settle their obligations, and most members of the Duaca elite rode out the crisis with their agricultural and commercial operations intact. Cipriano Bracho, for example, owed Blöhm over 25,000 pesos (107,385.60 bolívares) in 1882—the largest debt among Blöhm's Duaca clients —but managed to make his payments on time and redeem his haciendas on schedule in 1887.[55] As a result, Bracho retained his position as one of Duaca's largest coffee producers until his death in 1916. Others among the local elite, such as Cecilio Carrera, had to take out new loans from other merchants to redeem their property from Blöhm and remained heavily indebted even after coffee prices recovered in the second half of the 1880s.[56]

The major structural change brought about by the crisis, then, was the creation of direct ties between the Duaca elite and the major Puerto Cabello import-export merchants. Aside from entering into direct relations with Blöhm and Company, in the 1880s and 1890s members of the local elite began to carry accounts with firms such as Boulton and Company and Ascher and Company.[57] At the same time, agents from Puerto Cabello merchant houses began to come to Duaca annually to buy coffee.[58] Although some of Duaca's elite continued to depend on Barquisimeto merchants for credit after the crisis, many dispensed with intermediaries and dealt directly with the major export-import capitalists on the coast.

Renewed Expansion and Crisis, 1886–1899

Duaca's development as a commercial center continued in the years following the crisis, aided in part by the more favorable coffee prices of the late 1880s and early 1890s, and also by the national government's attempts to encourage investment in the coffee economy. In the late 1880s, the Ministry of Development took a particular interest in promoting the establishment of coffee-processing centers equipped with the latest steam-powered machinery. The ministry allowed selected private investors (usually merchants) to import the machinery duty-free and granted them local monopolies on the commercial processing of coffee, provided that they opened their plants to the public within one year and charged customers rates dictated by the government. In 1887, two merchants received exclusive rights to establish a processing plant in any municipality of the state of Lara that they chose.[59] Passing over the extremely rich but relatively inaccessible municipality of Guarico in southwestern Lara they selected Duaca, and by late February 1888 the plant was dehusking coffee beans at the government-imposed rate of two bolívares (one-half peso) per forty-six kilograms.[60]

The new machinery offered considerable advantages over the old animal-powered trillas: it processed the dried berries much faster, broke fewer beans, and gave the product a polished appearance much prized by exporters.[61] The new plant had little effect on the peasantry, who rarely owned trillas and who delivered much of their crop to merchants with the husk intact. For merchants eager to improve the quality of their coffee, however, the new plant—which was acquired by the Puerto Cabello merchant firm of Leseur, Römer, and Baasch soon after it opened—represented a notable advance over the old technology.[62]

As in other coffee economies, however, those who owned the new machinery exercised considerable control over those who relied on their services.[63] The Duaca elite resented this dependency all the more because the plant was owned by distant foreigners over whom they had no influence. In one fit of irritation, touched off in part by a drop in coffee prices, Duaca's leading merchants and hacendados petitioned the owners of the plant to lower their fees—which had risen from 2 to 2.50 bolívares per 46 kilograms—and threatened to resurrect their old trillas if the owners refused.[64] Such a technological retreat was not really possible, however, given exporters' preference for the higher quality beans produced by the mechanical processor. The plant remained beyond the control of the local elite until 1908, when the Puerto Cabello firm sold the plant to two Duaca merchants.[65] Although the plant changed hands several times in the years that followed, ownership remained within the local elite after 1908.

The culmination of Duaca's development as a commercial center in the nineteenth century came in 1891, when the Aroa-Tucacas railroad was extended south to Barquisimeto, passing through Duaca, which once again benefited from its location on the Barquisimeto-Aroa trade route. Railroad construction had been and would continue to be limited in Venezuela, and few of the nation's important coffee-producing areas ever claimed a rail line directly to the coast.[66] In 1891, then, with its hinterland producing between 2.5 and 3 million kilograms of coffee annually, its processing plant in full operation, and its location on the Southwest Railroad of Venezuela, Duaca boasted a combination of economic assets that few provincial towns in the nation could match. As the Barquisimeto press observed, "Duaca, with the [construction of] the Southwest Railroad, has achieved a great importance, as no one can fail to see."[67]

The arrival of the railroad brought several changes to the local elite. Whereas before the 1890s few foreigners resided in Duaca, the years after the opening of the railroad witnessed a dramatic influx of European-born merchants. During this decade at least one German, August Lapp, settled in Duaca and entered the coffee trade in a large way, using the credit he received from the Puerto Cabello firm of Beselin and Company.[68] Most of the immigrant merchants, however, came from Italy. In this regard as in so many others, Duaca mirrored developments in the coffee zones of the Venezuelan Andes, where Italian merchants also played a large role in the coffee economy.[69] Angel María Núñez, the chronicler of Duaca, identified twenty-one Italians who came to Duaca in the late nineteenth century, nineteen of whom he listed as merchants.[70] Italian coffee dealers who registered their first loans to producers in the 1890s included Gaetano Tarrallo, Blas Lomonaco, Francisco and Domingo Potenzo, and Francisco Camarano.[71] Like other Duaca merchants, these immigrants diversified their operations to include the ownership of coffee haciendas, and the structure of their enterprises became indistinguishable from those of their creole counterparts.

Meanwhile, the high coffee prices of the early 1890s and the coming of the railroad led Duaca's elite to look for new ways to profit from favorable commercial conditions. Some combined their resources in new business partnerships. These enterprises often involved the joint ownership of agricultural properties but were primarily oriented toward buying coffee and selling imported merchandise that arrived on the railroad. Commercial partnerships were not unprecedented in Duaca, of course. In the 1880s, Rudecindo Peralta and his brothers had pooled their resources to form Peralta Hermanos, and the Andrade brothers had also established a merchant company.[72] The partnerships of the early and mid-1890s, however, were more numerous and more often represented alliances between members of different families. Some of the new companies (like that of Policarpo Peralta and José Tomás Rojas Vélis) owned haciendas and made loans to coffee growers, while others (like that of Jesús María Andrade and Juan Antonio Guillén) operated general stores in Duaca in addition to their coffee enterprises.[73]

The formation of these commercial partnerships, the arrival of the immigrant merchants, and the opening of the railroad combined to produce a significant increase in the amount of credit extended by the Duaca elite during the 1890s. Table 3 summarizes the mortgages of agricultural properties in Duaca for alternate years between 1880 and 1896.[74] Again, these figures do not reflect the entire flow of credit to Duaca coffee producers, but the pattern of the mortgages suggests the general course of commercial activity in Duaca. The depression that began in 1879 and continued into the mid-1880s dampened commerce for the remainder of the decade, and the crisis (as we have seen) compelled some within the elite to mortgage their holdings to the Puerto Cabello firm of Blöhm and Company in 1882.

The 1890s, however, brought a dramatic revival of trade. Credit may have been limited by the nationwide revolt led by Joaquín Crespo in 1892 (a year in which Duaca merchants registered only five loans), but in 1894 local merchants registered fourteen loans totaling 12,903.25 pesos (51,613 bolívares). In 1896 Duaca merchants registered forty-two loans with a combined value of 42,251.36 pesos (169,005.44 bolívares). The commercial expansion of the early and mid-1890s and the relative peace imposed by Crespo until his death in 1897 combined to produce a renewed flourishing of Duaca's coffee economy.

Table 3. Registered Loans to Duaca Coffee Producers, 1880–1898

	Location of Creditor			
	Barquisimeto	Duaca	Puerto Cabello	Other
1880	20,801.00 (14)	4,161.12 (8)	—	1,056.00 (1)
1882	9,742.75 (7)	450.00 (1)	89,196.58 (11)	11,700.00 (3)
1884	14,761.00 (5)	1,883.75 (7)	—	—
1886	3,577.50 (2)	5,394.25 (5)	—	—
1888	10,550.10 (13)	1,657.90 (3)	—	—
1890	10,600.00 (3)	8,263.50 (8)	—	4,880.00 (1)
1892	7,180.00 (5)	12,961.70 (5)	—	—
1894	26,680.00 (14)	12,903.25 (14)	—	4,064.00 (2)
1896	36,330.48 (14)	42,251.36 (42)	9,685.00 (3)	1,229.00 (2)
1898	6,294.00 (3)	1,390.00 (3)	—	—

Source: Registro Principal del Estado Lara, Protocolos del Distrito Barquisimeto (Iribarren).
Note: Values of loans are given in pesos. Numbers of loans are in parentheses.

The prosperity of the 1890s, however, was ended by another dramatic fall in the world price of coffee. The crisis of the late 1890s, like that of the late 1870s, resulted from a rapid growth in the global supply of coffee, due mostly to Brazil's booming São Paulo plantations, combined with an economic downturn in the industrial nations. Prices dropped in 1897 and remained low for almost a decade, recovering only after Brazil implemented a plan in 1906 to limit its exports and stabilize world prices. In Duaca, commerce slowed considerably in 1897 and ground to a virtual halt the following year.

An article published in a Duaca newspaper, *La Integridad,* and written by a local coffee entrepreneur, Juan Giménez Girán, reveals how at least some of the Duaqueño elite viewed the crisis in December 1897.[75] Giménez noted that everyone in Duaca seemed to have a favorite explanation for the hard economic times. While some pointed to the immediate cause (the low price of coffee), others blamed corrupt politicians, the lack of immigrant (that is, European) workers, the government's failure to establish an agricultural bank, the overly generous concessions granted to foreign businessmen in Venezuela, and the high rates charged by the Southwest Railroad and by Leseur, Römer, and Baasch, the owners of Duaca's coffee-processing plant. Giménez himself pointed especially to what he saw as the abuses of the railroads and coffee processors. In sum, Giménez and others among the local elite focused on circumstantial problems affecting Venezuela's ties to the global market system and stopped well short of searching out the contradictions inherent in the global coffee economy itself.

From their own class perspective, this position was entirely logical. Although some Venezuelans of that era called into question the nation's dependence on one crop sold on a volatile world market, the Duaca elite had good reason for their more restrained assessment of the crisis.[76] As the nineteenth century drew to a close, they could look back on three decades of generally growing wealth derived from their connection to the global market. Despite the hardships of the moment, the elite's hopes for the future rested on the continuation of a commercial economy based on coffee.

Conclusion

To summarize, the period between 1863 and 1899 witnessed an important shift in the economic basis of Duaca's elite. At the beginning of this period, the elite's wealth came almost exclusively from the ownership of haciendas. Only in the mid-1870s—following several years of high coffee prices and a decade of rebuilding their haciendas after the Federal War—did prominent Duaqueños enter commerce on a significant scale. Even then, the emergence of a local merchant class depended largely on the arrival of elite migrants from other jurisdictions, most notably from Quibor. Improvements in the transportation network linking Duaca to the coast during the late 1870s reinforced the development of the local merchant class by strengthening Duaca's position as a commercial center. The prolonged depression that began in 1879 challenged this emergent class and left it saddled with heavy debts, but the crisis also led to the first direct ties between Duaca entrepreneurs and Puerto Cabello merchants. Some of the Duaqueños maintained their direct ties to coastal merchants after the crisis, bypassing the intermediaries in Barquisimeto. The opening of the railroad through Duaca in 1891 initiated another phase of commercial growth, though the expansion was halted by the depression of the last years of the decade.

Despite the challenges produced by periodic crises in the world coffee economy, Duaca's elite had, by the close of the nineteenth century, claimed an increasing share of the commercial surplus generated by the local coffee economy. Whereas in 1870 the financing and marketing of Duaca's coffee production had been controlled by Barquisimeto merchants, by the mid-1890s a large share of these commercial operations—and the profits they produced—were controlled by the local elite in Duaca. All members of this local elite owned haciendas, and some owned land, but as a class their wealth had come to depend largely on commerce.

The local elite's growing commercial orientation resulted largely from the widespread availability of land in Duaca. As in other parts of Latin America, including Costa Rica and the Venezuelan Andes, the expansion of peasant production into previously unsettled areas created ever greater numbers of clients for merchants, even while peasant access to land limited the supply of labor to the elite's haciendas, thus adding to the rationale for investment in trade. To be sure, Duaca's elite exercised increasing control over local commerce, but their control over land and agricultural production—and, ultimately, over society itself—remained limited as the nineteenth century came to an end.

5 Rebellion and Accommodation

Duaca's Elite and the National State

IN CONTRAST TO THE nineteenth century, when a prosperous peasant society emerged in Duaca, the twentieth century witnessed the subordination of the peasantry to the local elite. In part, the elite's growing dominance over local society resulted from the wealth they garnered from Duaca's coffee economy. But the changing balance of power between elite and peasantry cannot be understood by consideration of economic factors alone. Rather, the peasantry found itself in an ever more precarious position as prominent Duaqueños succeeded in expanding their political power, which they used to advance their economic interests and particularly to extend their control over land, a goal that had proven elusive in the nineteenth century. The discussion that follows concerns the local elite's relationship to the regimes of Cipriano Castro (1899–1908) and Juan Vicente Gómez (1908–1935) and the ways local leaders built their power in Duaca by allying themselves to an increasingly powerful central state.

Historians of Venezuela agree that Cipriano Castro's capture of the presidency in 1899 represented a critical watershed in the nation's political history.[1] Before Castro, effective political power was held by regional caudillos—often Liberals who had risen to prominence during the Federal War—whose ability to mobilize armed followers guaranteed their influence. Leaders aspiring to the presidency were obliged to seek the caudillos' support and to respect their regional authority. This system of decentralized power (known as *el liberalismo amarillo* in Venezuelan historiography) ended when Castro turned on his fellow Liberals and centralized power in his own hands. By creating an effective national army under his exclusive control, and by imposing his close associates as state presidents throughout Venezuela, Castro asserted the authority of the national state over the regional caudillos.

Seizing power from Castro in 1908, Juan Vicente Gómez continued the policies of his erstwhile ally and mentor. He oversaw the ongoing professionalization of the army, which became the true base of national power and by the mid-1910s precluded the emergence of any armed rebellion capable of challenging Gómez. To an even greater degree than Castro, Gómez ruled through a cadre of close associates (often fellow Andinos) whom he rotated among key positions, especially the state presidencies and key military commands.[2] And, where Castro had continued the chaotic fiscal practices of the nineteenth century such as tax farming, decentralized financial administration, and mortgaging future revenues to satisfy creditors, the treasury under Gómez was consolidated and rationalized.[3] Thus the regime established a sound financial base and won the approval of foreign business interests even before the Venezuelan oil boom of the 1920s. Between them, Castro and Gómez carried out the centralization of the Venezuelan state, much as Porfirio Díaz consolidated state power in Mexico during the late nineteenth and early twentieth centuries.

This interpretation of the transformation of Venezuelan politics has won widespread acceptance, and deservedly so. The utility of this paradigm, however, is limited by its tendency to reduce the history of the state to relations among only those at the very top of the political hierarchy. The literature either ignores local elites or implies simply that they suffered the same fate as their patrons, the regional caudillos. This leaves an important facet of the political system unstudied. If we wish to understand how the centralization of power affected Venezuelan society, we must examine local politics, for the vast majority of this predominantly rural society came into contact with the state primarily through district officials such as the jefe civil (local governor), the district judge, and their informal local allies.

This chapter examines the political actions of Duaca's elite from the 1890s into the 1920s and seeks to enlarge our understanding of the local dynamics involved in the transformation of the Venezuelan state. The fundamental political goal of Duaca's elite during this period was to gain autonomous control over their zone of economic influence. My argument is that, by forging an alliance with Castro and Gómez, they eventually achieved their goal. Duaqueños' participation in two civil wars, the Revolución Restauradora (1899) and the Revolución Libertadora (1901–1903) proved critical in negotiating this pact with the central state. By 1906, a bargain had emerged in which members of the local elite agreed to support the central regime and to use their military skills to safeguard the railroad running through Duaca, in exchange for control over local government. This pact strengthened both the local elite and the central state, indicating that, at least in the case of Duaca, the strengthening of central power benefited local elites who controlled resources important to the center and who were willing to cast their lot with the new state. In contrast to prevailing interpretations of this period, the local elite in Duaca found themselves in a stronger position once centralization had triumphed. Most important, the political power won by Duaca's elite allowed them to exercise progressively greater control over land, over agricultural production, and over the peasantry.

Politics in the Municipality of Duaca, 1892–1899

In the late nineteenth century, the Duaca elite's prosperity and growing commercial independence from Barquisimeto led to a desire for greater political autonomy. As a municipality within the district of Barquisimeto, Duaca remained subject to the district government, which wealthy men in the city of Barquisimeto tended to control. To be sure, Duaca enjoyed the rudiments of local government—a *junta comunal* (municipal council), a jefe civil, and a municipal judge—but these offices had little real power. The *consejo municipal* (district council) in Barquisimeto could overrule Duaca's council; the jefe civil of the district exercised authority over Duaca's jefe civil; and Duaca's judge heard only minor cases and carried out directives from the district court in Barquisimeto. As their economic operations expanded, Duaca's merchants and coffee producers increasingly resented their lack of control over local political affairs.

In 1892, the year after the opening of the railroad, some members of the local elite mounted a campaign to have Duaca made a district. They established a newspaper, *El Eco del Norte,* to promote the idea. The first issue argued that only district status would allow Duaca "to attend to the considerable elements of its own prosperity."[4] Hermelindo Oberto, a member of a prominent Duaca merchant family, wrote of the project in glowing terms: "Our object could not be more laudable. We want to make a piece of our homeland shine. . . . We are apostles of a grand idea."[5]

Political authorities outside the municipality proved less enthusiastic. Opponents of the change held that it would be illegal because the state constitution did not provide for the elevation of municipalities to districts.[6] Undaunted, Duaca's council in 1893 formally petitioned the state government for district status, arguing that the municipality's economic and demographic growth justified their request. The council claimed a population of between fourteen and twenty thousand located in over twenty towns and hamlets, large municipal revenues, and annual coffee production of over sixty thousand sacks. The town of Duaca itself, with its railroad station, impressive church, and ample government offices, was in the council's opinion well suited to assume the responsibilities of district government. After some vacillation, the state president denied the petition.[7]

Throughout the 1890s, tensions between Barquisimeto and Duaca continued to fester. The district government's supervision of Duaca's financial affairs provided one source of friction, as conflicts repeatedly arose over municipal tax collection and the remission of revenues to Barquisimeto.[8] The Barquisimeto council also intervened in Duaca's age-old water dispute between the Indian community, the town residents, and the owner of the El Buco sugar hacienda, all of whom depended on the Tumaque stream. To make matters worse, rulings on the water question proved contradictory, so that the Barquisimeto council eventually managed to offend everyone involved.[9] Awarding Duaca district status would allow the local elite to decide such issues among themselves, and—given the larger, better financed apparatus of a district government—it would allow prominent Duaqueños greater access to the spoils of political office.

Despite their common desire for greater local autonomy, Duaca's elite experienced important internal divisions, reflecting nationwide political conflicts. Although Liberal caudillos continued to control Venezuelan politics, a movement opposing their rule emerged in the 1890s under the leadership of José Manuel ("El Mocho") Hernández. The Nationalist Party mounted its first serious challenge to Liberal domination in the 1897 elections, when Hernández competed for the presidency against Ignacio Andrade, the hand-picked successor of Joaquín Crespo, the reigning national caudillo. The Nationalist movement proved especially strong in the state of Lara, but Liberals remained the majority in Duaca.[10] Political competition between the Liberals and Duaca's small Nationalist faction became violent, resulting in at least two deaths near the time of the elections.[11]

Upon losing the 1897 contest, the Nationalists (also known as Hernandistas) rose in revolt against the new Andrade government. Crespo led the Liberal forces in defense of his chosen successor but was killed early in the conflict. Andrade suddenly found his rule in jeopardy, as many Liberal caudillos now refused to obey their fallen leader's protégé. The first Liberal to mount a rebellion against Andrade, however, was not one of the leading regional bosses, but Cipriano Castro, a minor politician from the western state of Táchira. By mid-1899, therefore, the Andrade government faced threats from two different quarters: the Nationalists led by Hernández and the disaffected Liberals affiliated with Castro. The ensuing civil war would become a critical episode in the Duaca elite's struggle for political autonomy.

The Revolución Restauradora in Duaca

The Revolución Restauradora of 1899, which propelled Castro to national power, augmented the political influence of Duaca's elite in two respects. First, Duaqueños' armed support for Castro resulted in the elevation of Duaca to district status following his capture of the presidency in late 1899. Thus the war allowed the local elite to achieve through military action what they had failed to achieve through other means. Second, the war highlighted the strategic importance of Duaca, derived from the railroad passing through Duaca to Barquisimeto. Military control of Barquisimeto, increasingly seen as the gateway to western Venezuela, depended on control of the railroad into the city and could be facilitated by an alliance with military leaders in Duaca. As regional and national leaders came to appreciate this fact, Duaca's elite gained a political stature they had lacked in the past.

During Castro's 1899 rebellion, as in the 1897 elections, most of Lara was strongly Hernandista. Castro's only concentrated support in the state came from Duaca. Ismael Manzanarez, a Duaca merchant and hacendado long active in Liberal politics, became the leader of the municipality's Castristas when he mobilized a guerrilla force and declared his support of Castro in late August 1899. Manzanarez (who would later write an account of his military action) began the war in Duaca by raiding trains carrying Andrade's troops and supplies from Tucacas to Barquisimeto.[12] In the weeks that followed, several bands of guerrillas led by members of the local elite joined the rebels at La Quinta, Manzanarez's hacienda in the resguardos north of town. Meanwhile, Manzanarez received instructions from Castro to strengthen his control over the railroad in preparation for an assault on Barquisimeto. By September 7, Manzanarez commanded some four hundred men deployed along the railroad.[13]

Most of the leaders of the Duaca rebels came from the middle and lower levels of the local elite. To be sure, Manzanarez himself was a prosperous merchant with important agricultural properties, but the wealthiest among the elite did not actively participate in the revolt. Generals Rudecindo Peralta and Cipriano Bracho, landowners with years of activity in Liberal politics, were over sixty years of age and may have been unable to take to the field. Some of the wealthiest members of Duaca's elite helped to feed and supply the rebels over the next several months, but most did not take up arms themselves.[14]

Thus the revolt was largely in the hands of middling hacendados, such as Eduardo Colmenares, José de la Paz Alvarado, Pedro Rondón, and José de la Cruz Castillo, and small merchants who owned agricultural properties as well, such as José Tomás Rojas Vélis and Juan Pablo Paiva. It was these men and others like them, rather than Manzanarez himself, who mobilized and outfitted most of the troops. Justo Sosa and Juan Rivero, for example, raised and equipped forty men in the far north of the municipality. In the southeast, according to Manzanarez, Juan Bautista Giménez Girán and José de la Paz Alvarado (a tenant on Los Chipas) raised "fifty men, their armed peons, completely equipped and outfitted with their own resources . . . and immediately put themselves under my command."[15] The hierarchy of the guerrilla force reflected the social and economic structure of the area, with Manzanarez, the large entrepreneur and politician in command, less wealthy members of the elite acting as subordinate officers, and the peasantry providing the mass of soldiers.

After securing the railroad, Manzanarez and his men began to plan their attack on the government garrison in Barquisimeto. In doing so, they confronted a dilemma as to whether they should actively cooperate with the Hernandistas, who were planning their own attack. In Lara and throughout Venezuela the Hernandistas and the Castristas maintained separate organizations, even though each sought the overthrow of the Andrade government. Neither Hernández nor Castro would recognize the supremacy of the other, and it was unclear whether they would be able to resolve their rivalry peacefully once their common enemy was defeated. Thus, Manzanarez and the

Hernandistas around Barquisimeto held each other at arm's length during the early days of the war. In late September, Manzanarez informed Castro that he considered the Nationalist army gathering outside Barquisimeto to be as much of a threat as the government forces inside the city.[16]

The Nationalist army included a small contingent from Duaca led by two brothers, Avelino and Aurelio Giménez Méndez. It is not altogether clear why the Giménez Méndez clan, unlike Manzanarez and his more numerous followers, adhered to the Nationalist cause. Perhaps their affiliation derived from old family allegiances. Whereas most prominent families in Duaca had long associations with the Liberal Party, Norberto Giménez, Aurelio and Avelino's father, had fought on the Conservative side during the Federal War.[17] Regardless of whether Nationalism represented a rebirth of the Conservative Party, as is sometimes suggested, Nationalism attracted many political figures who had remained outside the Liberal Party during its decades of hegemony.[18] Perhaps Avelino and Aurelio Giménez Méndez, as sons of a prominent Conservative, never made their peace with the Liberals and naturally gravitated toward Hernández. In any event, as the 1899 conflict began, they marched south to join the Hernandistas outside Barquisimeto, adding their small contingent to the army that was making Manzanarez increasingly apprehensive.

Despite the tensions between the two factions, the Nationalists invited Manzanarez to join their offensive against the city. After some hesitation, Manzanarez accepted and dispatched a force of 150 men, hoping to capture part of Barquisimeto's arsenal. The combined offensive took the city, but in the process deepened the rift between the Hernandistas and the Castristas. Manzanarez's men alleged that the Hernandista commander singled them out for the dangerous mission of attacking the most heavily defended section of Barquisimeto. Disagreement then arose concerning the division of arms captured from the government forces, and Manzanarez, fearing for the safety of his men, ordered them to withdraw. Thus the Hernandistas acquired the entire Barquisimeto arsenal and consolidated their position as the dominant military force in the state.[19]

Increasingly isolated and vulnerable, despite Castro's steady progress toward Caracas, Manzanarez sought allies among the Liberals still loyal to President Andrade. He began negotiations with the commanders of government garrisons in Tucacas (the northern terminus of the railroad passing through Duaca) and Aroa, proposing that they abandon President Andrade and join the Duaqueño Liberals in order to present a united Liberal front against the Hernandistas. As Andrade's position deteriorated and the Hernandistas in the region continued to gather strength, Manzanarez's appeal for Liberal unity became increasingly persuasive. Both garrisons abandoned Andrade and turned over their arsenals to Manzanarez, with some of the former government troops opting to join the Castrista forces. Thus the Liberals along the railroad began to close ranks against the Nationalists even though Castro and Hernández had not yet moved into armed confrontation.[20]

In the weeks that followed, tensions between Manzanarez and the Nationalists continued to intensify and eventually erupted into open warfare.[21] It was the Castristas who initiated the first armed clash with the Nationalists. Joined by his superior, General Ramón Guerra, Manzanarez took three hundred Duaqueños to inspect the area under Liberal control. When a Hernandista force obstructed their movements, Manzanarez and Guerra attacked. The Hernandistas retaliated with an assault against Manzanarez's men guarding the railroad. As the two camps moved into open conflict, Manzanarez and Guerra were joined by another two hundred men from the mountains between Bobare and Duaca, but they were still hopelessly outnumbered.[22] Manzanarez's policy of resisting Hernandista authority had placed him in a precarious position.

Soon thereafter, Manzanarez and Guerra received word that Castro, who had occupied Caracas and declared himself president, had named General Jacinto Lara state president and military commander in Lara. A son of the independence hero for whom the state was named, General Lara enjoyed considerable prestige in the region. Perhaps Castro hoped that he could restore relations with the Nationalists or loosen their hold on the state. Soon after arriving in Duaca (still the only Liberal stronghold in the region), Lara wrote to his Hernandista counterpart, Carlos Liscano, asking the Nationalists to accept his command. Liscano soon sent what must have been the expected reply, a polite refusal, reminding Lara that the Nationalist and Castrista armies had remained separate throughout the revolution, and that Hernández enjoyed greater support in the state than Castro.[23] Meanwhile, Castro and Hernández themselves moved toward war. Unwilling to recognize the Andean's claim on the presidency, Hernández stole out of Caracas on the night of October 26, joined his army to the west, and declared himself in revolt against Castro. The struggle between the armies that had toppled Andrade now began in earnest.[24]

Manzanarez and his men soon felt the full weight of the superior Hernandista forces. An expedition to escort General Guerra to Tucacas in early November was ambushed and suffered heavy casualties.[25] Manzanarez and Lara saw their forces depleted further by desertions; by mid-November food was running short and the enemy blocked their communications in almost every direction.[26] Then, on the morning of November 15, a force of six hundred Hernandistas attacked the town of Duaca. Greatly outnumbered, Lara and Manzanarez organized a hasty retreat, the former fleeing north to Siquisique and the latter toward Bobare. Only a small raiding party of Liberals, commanded by Paulo Emilio Piña, remained in the immediate vicinity of Duaca.[27]

During the following weeks Manzanarez and Lara did what they could to prevent the complete disintegration of the Castrista forces in the state. Lara repeatedly implored Diego Colina, the Castrista commander in the state of Falcón, to send a large force south to dislodge the Hernandistas from Barquisimeto.[28] Lara estimated that the Liberal Duaqueño forces had dwindled to about 120 men; the establishment of a Castrista government in the state would clearly have to await the arrival of outside assistance. As they waited, however, discipline began to erode and the Duaqueño forces splintered into small roving bands. Perhaps the "army" was simply fragmenting into its component parts—the contingents raised by individual hacendados and merchants. Too outnumbered to contemplate military action, the Duaqueño commanders began to ignore Lara's orders and turned their attention to smuggling goods into Barquisimeto.[29] Lara made no attempt to end the contraband, partly because his hold over the Duaqueño Liberals was already so weak and partly because wartime profiteering was an established prerogative for officers.[30]

This period of fragmentation among the Castristas of Lara ended in early December, when they were joined by General Colina from the north and by General Rafael Montilla from Trujillo. The two generals and their armies joined Lara and Manzanarez in Bobare, and the scattered Castrista forces regrouped. They captured Barquisimeto in late December, and by February 1900 Castristas controlled virtually the entire state.[31] The Nationalist revolt came to a definitive end in late May when Castristas in the state of Carabobo took Hernández prisoner.

Even before the war ended, Liberals in Duaca reaped the reward of their support for Castro. Four days after the capture of Barquisimeto, General Lara elevated Duaca to a district, thus implementing the change long sought by Duaca's elite. The new entity, formally named Distrito Crespo after the fallen Liberal caudillo, included two hamlets, Tacarigüita and Rincón-hondo, which formerly had belonged to other municipalities.[32] Both hamlets clearly fell within Duaca's economic orbit, and both included large tracts of land belonging to estates (Los Chipas and the Generals' Estate) located principally within the old municipality of Duaca. In his decree creating the district, Lara forthrightly declared that the measure was a reward to the Duaqueños for supporting Castro in his quest for national power.[33]

The Duaqueños and the Revolución Libertadora, 1901–1903

Once in the presidency, Castro initiated a process of political change that would modify the structure of politics in Venezuela before the Duaqueño elite could enjoy the fruits of victory. Not content to rule as his predecessors had, by recognizing the authority of regional caudillos, Castro set out to undermine the military power of the provincial strongmen and centralize power in his own hands. He attempted to collect the arms held by local potentates—including those who had fought on his own behalf—throughout Venezuela. Moreover, he announced a policy to professionalize the national army, purchased large quantities of new armaments from overseas, and began to convert the antiquated Venezuelan navy into a useful military force. Castro did away with the constitutional provision that required state presidents' approval for the national army to enter their jurisdictions. The new president clearly intended to impose his rule on the caudillos rather than respect their de facto regional power.[34]

At the same time that Castro attacked the caudillos' military supremacy, he sought to curtail their control of state governments. He appointed to the state presidencies men loyal to him who had no independent power base in the regions they were sent to govern. The new president selected several fellow Tachirenses to govern states in eastern Venezuela. Other prominent Liberals who had allied themselves with Castro were appointed to state presidencies away from their native regions. For example, General Rafael González Pacheco of Trujillo was sent to replace Jacinto Lara as state president, over the opposition of local Liberals. Castro's administrative strategy was clearly designed to separate regional caudillos from their clienteles and to assert the authority of the central government in what had long been their private domains.[35]

In Duaca, this administrative restructuring reached down to the district level. Having achieved district status at last, the local elite assumed that one of their own would inherit control of the new local government, but this was not to be. General José Garbi, a politician from Trujillo who came to Lara with González Pacheco when the latter assumed the state presidency, was named Duaca's jefe civil in 1900.[36] Thus the new regime denied prominent Duaqueños what they believed to be their rightful share of power. To be sure, Manzanarez remained on cordial terms with Castro during 1900–1901 and even carried out special missions for him, and some Duaqueño commanders occupied minor district offices, but they surely resented an outsider commanding the local government they had struggled to create.[37] Elite Duaqueños became disenchanted with Castro for the same reason as the larger, regional caudillos had done: they sought to control politics and the perquisites of office within their area of economic influence with a minimum of outside meddling.

The caudillos' only hope was to overthrow Castro before he concentrated power in his own hands. By late 1901 leaders of every political persuasion, including some who held influential positions in Castro's government, had laid plans for a nationwide revolt under the leadership of Manuel Antonio Matos, a Caracas financier. In Lara the revolt began on December 19, 1901, with an anti-Castro proclamation by Amabilis Solagnie in Cabudare, just east of Barquisimeto. Solagnie's proclamation was echoed immediately in Duaca. An armed band led by Eduardo Colmenares was already in place along the railroad in Peñas Negras, just north of the town of Duaca, when Solagnie rebelled.[38]

Colmenares, Manzanarez's most capable lieutenant in 1899, now emerged as the undisputed commander of the Duaca Liberals. In some respects, he was an unlikely leader. The illiterate owner of a small hacienda in the hamlet of Tarana, often referred to as "el negro Colmenares" because of his dark complexion, Colmenares came from the lower reaches of the local elite. Like other Venezuelans of humble status who rose to prominence through military action, he was a natural leader who enjoyed an easy camaraderie with his followers. Moreover, Colmenares was a skilled guerrilla fighter who fully shared the risks of battle with those under his command. According to Angel María Núñez, Colmenares's men felt genuine loyalty and affection toward their chief. These personal and military qualities assured Colmenares's leadership of the rebel forces in Duaca, and other Liberal generals in the district, including Manzanarez, readily accepted his command.[39]

During most of the 1901 rebellion, which came to be known as the Revolución Libertadora, Duaqueños' military activity again revolved around the railroad. Upon rising in revolt, Colmenares deployed his men along the railroad north of the town of Duaca, where the mountainous terrain and curves in the track facilitated guerrilla assaults. González Pacheco, who assumed command of the Castrista forces in Lara, desperately needed to keep the line open to receive supplies and reinforcements. In early January, he led troops north, engaged the Duaca rebels, and drove them back from the railroad, but soon had to rush south to defend Barquisimeto against the main rebel army. After defending the city, González returned to Duaca to fight the guerrillas, who had reoccupied their positions, only to find himself summoned again to the defense of Barquisimeto.[40] The Duaca rebels continued to control the railroad north of Barquisimeto through early 1902, seriously obstructing government military operations in the region.[41]

By June, González's position had become critical. The rebels controlled virtually all of Lara and most of neighboring Yaracuy, and he had only five hundred men to defend Barquisimeto and its arsenal. On June 16, Colmenares and the other rebel leaders of the state launched their assault on Barquisimeto, and a ferocious battle ensued. According to one account:

> For ten days there was severe fighting in the streets of the city. Bullets rained down from barricades in the church towers and on the very roofs of houses. They made trenches at the street corners with adobe bricks, sacks of sand, and anything they could lay their hands on. There arrived a moment at which [the main street of the city] was the dividing line between the two armies. . . . Faced with the impossibility of traveling through the streets, people made holes in the walls of their houses to establish interior communications. Anyone who so much as raised his or her face to a window might be shot and killed.[42]

González's only prospect of holding the city lay in the arrival of government troops from Trujillo under the command of Leopoldo Baptista. When, on June 24, rebels led by Rafael Montilla repulsed the government expedition, González decided to enter into negotiations; he would later say that he was also motivated by the threat of starvation and disease faced by the civilian population. The rebels, also wishing to avoid further combat, allowed the government forces to march out of the city, taking their arsenal with them. González marched east into Yaracuy, toward Caracas, leaving Lara completely in the hands of the rebels.[43]

With no government army threatening their control of the state, the rebels in Lara sent a large contingent to the east, where troops from all regions of the nation were gathering to move on Caracas. When the rebel force assembled, it totaled some sixteen thousand men, the largest military force ever gathered together in Venezuela. Rather than wait for the enemy to besiege the capital, Castro marched west to intercept them, establishing his base near the city of La Victoria. He undertook the expedition with a mere six thousand men.[44]

Eduardo Colmenares, the Duaqueño commander, led a contingent to La Victoria; the trek from Duaca may well have been the longest journey the humble hacendado had ever made. At one point early in the fighting, at Flores, a column under Colmenares became separated from the main rebel army and was in danger of being trapped by government forces. His comrades thought him lost, but Colmenares managed to lead his men to safety through a series of maneuvers that won the admiration of his followers and superiors alike. The incident was one of several episodes during the rebellion that contributed to Colmenares's growing reputation as a guerrilla commander.[45]

Despite their superior numbers, the rebels could not penetrate Castro's defenses at La Victoria. When Castro received reinforcements including one thousand men from Caracas led by Juan Vicente Gómez, the tide began to turn in favor of the government. On November 2, 1902, after three weeks of fighting and more than two thousand casualties on both sides, the rebel forces began to disperse as each contingent returned to its native region to carry on the struggle. By merely surviving the encounter at La Victoria, Castro had dealt his enemies a severe blow, and now, at least on the national stage, the rebels had lost the advantage.[46]

Castro advanced his fortunes again in late 1902 and early 1903 as he turned an international crisis to his advantage. The Venezuelan government's chronic financial difficulties during the late nineteenth century had left the nation with long-standing debts to various European creditors. The exigencies of fighting the Libertadora, combined with several years of low coffee prices, prevented Castro from meeting the creditors' mounting demands. In late 1902, Britain and Germany, the most vociferous creditors, established a naval blockade of Venezuelan ports to force payment. The United States, anxious to protect its role of supreme arbiter in the Caribbean, offered to mediate the dispute. Castro had little choice but to accept both the mediation and the eventual settlement, but in the meantime he used the foreign threat to call on the rebels to join his government in defending the fatherland against the European menace. Although most of Castro's opponents ignored these overtures, José Manuel Hernández, the ever-popular Nationalist chief now languishing in a government jail, publicly endorsed Castro in exchange for his freedom. Some Nationalist generals followed their leader's direction and began to aid government forces against the Libertadores. The reconciliation with Hernández, coming only months after the government's triumph at La Victoria, boosted Castro's prospects still further.[47]

Rebel armies, however, still controlled much of the national territory, including the state of Lara. After La Victoria, Generals González Pacheco and Leopoldo Baptista had returned to the west in hopes of reasserting government control. They fought the rebels in a bloody encounter at Caja de Agua, just outside the Barquisimeto, on December 27 and 28.[48] At one point in the battle the government troops seemed on the verge of victory, and the rebel commander asked for a volunteer to lead a counteroffensive. Colmenares stepped forward, led the charge, and, in another of his exploits that would be remembered after the war, swung the battle in favor of the rebels.[49] González and Baptista retreated to the west in hopes of replenishing their supplies in Maracaibo.[50]

When Baptista and González advanced on Barquisimeto again in mid-January, the rebels chose to retreat without a battle to the mountains north of Duaca. During the next two and a half months, the government proved unable to dislodge them from their fortified base near the railroad at Peñas Negras. This mountainous stronghold, which Colmenares and the Duaqueños had established early in the war, was now defended by artillery. By late March, after several fruitless and costly assaults, González concluded that he could not defeat Montilla, Solaigne, and Colmenares without more troops, ammunition, and artillery. He also realized, however, that rebel control of the railroad would prevent the speedy arrival of any support Castro might send him.[51] In early April the rebels marched south and recaptured Barquisimeto, pushing González west once again.[52] Colmenares and his allies had demonstrated yet again that control of Barquisimeto required control of the railroad to the north.

Only in late April, after the government had scored important victories in other parts of the country, could Castro send a force capable of defeating the rebels in Lara. Juan Vicente Gómez, who had just defeated the rebel army in northeastern Venezuela, arrived in Tucacas on April 30 at the head of a large expeditionary force and marched south. Virtually the entire rebel army assembled in Barquisimeto to make its stand against Gómez. By May 21, the government forces had laid siege to the city, with Gómez pressing in from the east and González Pacheco stationed to the north. The following afternoon the rebel leaders concluded that their situation was hopeless; that night they abandoned the city. Fleeing to the north with Gómez in pursuit, the rebels hoped to join the army of their commander in chief, Manuel Antonio Matos, who had recently landed at Coro. When, in early June, Gómez defeated Matos at Matapalo, in Falcón state, the rebellion was finished in all of western Venezuela. On June 4, Colmenares and his men surrendered to government officials.[53] By the end of July the Libertadora, which had cost some twelve thousand lives, had been defeated in all parts of the country. Although no one knew it at the time, Venezuela had experienced its last nationwide caudillo war.

The Politics of Reconciliation

In the immediate aftermath of the revolt, the Castro regime continued to deny Duaca's elite control of the government of Distrito Crespo. By 1904 the district court and council, both indispensable to the daily life of the district, were functioning under the direction of the local elite. But the office of jefe civil, the most powerful in local government, remained in the hands of an outsider. José Garbi, who had occupied the post prior to the revolt, became jefe civil again after the war. Having served loyally under González Pacheco throughout the Libertadora, the Trujillo native could be trusted to guard the regime's interests in the district. The political power sought by Duaca's elite remained out of reach.

In the long term, however, Castro could not afford to proscribe from power all local elites who had rebelled against him. Given the widespread nature of the rebellion, such a policy would have left the regime without enough prominent men to govern and denied it the support of those who still wielded informal influence at the local level. Moreover, a policy of prolonged proscription would have hindered local elites' economic activity and thus de-layed the recovery of the national economy. In short, Castro had an interest in making his rule acceptable to local elites and drawing them into cooperation with his government.

By 1905, Castro felt sufficiently secure to initiate a process of political re-laxation, beginning with the release of 130 political prisoners and an amnesty to all those who had gone into exile following the Libertadora. Confident of his power, largely because of the well-equipped army he continued to build up after the Libertadora, Castro anticipated that most of his former enemies would choose either to collaborate with him or to remain aloof from politics. Those who persisted in their struggle against the regime would, he believed, find themselves hopelessly isolated. One way or another, the former rebels would be dealt with and the position of the state strengthened.[54]

In late February, as part of this political opening, Castro instructed Leopoldo Torres, the new president of Lara, that "the arms of magnanimity shall be open to all those who wish to collaborate in good faith," while all those suspected of actively opposing the regime should be imprisoned.[55] This carrot-and-stick approach to reconciliation was in keeping with Castro's national strategy, and it responded to regional necessities as well. Rafael Montilla, the popular caudillo in the neighboring state of Trujillo, had refused to surrender to Castro at the end of the Libertadora and continued to carry out occasional raids against government forces.[56] He did not pose an immediate threat to the regime, but Montilla's strong local support allowed him to remain at large and he clearly hoped to expand his theater of operations. Having campaigned in Lara during both the Restauradora and the Libertadora, Montilla had established links to state military leaders (including Colmenares) to whom he could appeal for support. Castro's orders to show "magnanimity" to all willing collaborators in Lara, then, was also an attempt to co-opt Montilla's potential allies.

In the following months an alliance was forged between the Castro regime and the former leaders of the Libertadora in Distrito Crespo. Such a reconciliation clearly responded to the interests of both parties. To the regime, the local elite could offer their loyalty and, if need be, their military prowess in defense of the railroad, thus assuring the state's security in what had proven to be a strategic area during the recent wars. To the local elite, the regime could offer control over all local affairs that did not impinge upon the security of the government, and access to the spoils that accompanied political office. More generally, the local elite could expect that cooperation with the government would give them a claim on the influence of an increasingly stable and powerful central state.

The process of reconciliation began in 1905, soon after Leopoldo Torres became president of Lara. Upon taking office, he received a letter from Colmenares and his two principal subordinates during the Libertadora, Ramón Antonio Vásquez and Paulo E. Piña. The former rebels congratulated Torres on his appointment, declared themselves to be "elements of peace and frank supporters of the national government," and offered him their services.[57] Torres, a native of Lara with years of experience in state politics (but never a military leader himself), knew of Colmenares's military skills. González Pacheco, having fought against Colmenares in the Libertadora, had informed Torres that he was the most skillful of the rebel commanders in the state. He considered Colmenares superior even to the legendary Montilla.[58] Torres also knew that Colmenares, despite his defeat, continued to be "a very important man in Duaca, where he enjoys considerable prestige." As early as

1905, Torres began to grant Colmenares small favors in an effort to "win him over."[59]

The circumstances under which Colmenares sealed his alliance with the Castro regime in 1906 can be understood only in the context of national politics. Following the Libertadora, tensions began to develop between Castro and Gómez, as some high government officials, alienated by the president's volatile personality and erratic leadership, turned increasingly to Gómez for direction. Those who remained loyal to Castro believed that the Gomecista faction would soon attempt to seize power. Adopting a byzantine strategy, Castro announced in April 1906 that he would temporarily leave the presidency and that Gómez would occupy the office during his absence. Apparently Castro wished to tempt his erstwhile friend with the prospect of complete power in hopes that he would reveal his intentions. In early May, Gómez reorganized his cabinet, promoting his own followers and giving a position to one of Castro's fiercest enemies. To many of Castro's friends, this confirmed Gómez's ambitions. Acting on instructions from their chief, they quickly organized demonstrations and petitions throughout Venezuela imploring Castro to return to office. Gómez, perhaps surprised at the continued depth of Castro's following, wrote to him in late May to declare his loyalty and request that he relieve him of the burdens of the presidency. The process that became known as the Acclamation continued as Gomecistas joined Castristas in the wave of demonstrations and petitions, and in mid-June Castro announced that he would return to office. Castro had risked civil war to subdue the Gomecistas, and won.[60]

The political tensions surrounding Gómez's interim presidency and the Acclamation gave Colmenares and his faction the opportunity to enter into Castro's good graces. Soon after becoming interim president, Gómez shuffled the jefes civiles in Lara to fortify his position in the state. José Garbi, a committed Gomecista, was moved from Duaca to the more important post of jefe civil of Barquisimeto.[61] In late May, Colmenares and his followers—including men who had served under him in the Libertadora as well as older Liberals—organized a demonstration in Duaca in support of Castro's return to the presidency. They notified Torres that they had sent Castro a petition with over five hundred signatures.[62] Significantly, Colmenares acted in defiance of the new jefe civil of the district, General Ramiro González, a Gómez appointee who opposed the demonstration.[63]

Colmenares's enemies in the district—the small Hernandista faction, led by Avelino and Aurelio Giménez Méndez—became apprehensive at the prospect of his alliance with the Castro regime. It was apparently they who planted a rumor that Colmenares was involved in a plot *against* Castro. When the "information" reached Castro, he ordered Torres to have Colmenares watched and, if necessary, arrested.

In his reply of July 15, 1906, Torres defended Colmenares, emphasizing to Castro that he remained an influential figure in Duaca despite his defeat in the Libertadora, and that he had been "the principal factor in the Acclamation" in Duaca, despite the opposition of the jefe civil. Furthermore, Torres informed Castro that he had been trying for some time to win Colmenares's loyalty for the government. Castro accepted Torres's assessment of Colmenares and ordered his appointment as jefe civil of Duaca.[64] Colmenares thus succeeded in parlaying his extensive informal influence into a position in the government he had fought to overthrow only three years before.

Upon taking office, Colmenares began to pull his followers into line in support of Torres and Castro, thus ending any possibility that they might join Montilla's rebellion. On August 31, one of Colmenares's generals during the Libertadora, General Paulo E. Piña, wrote to Torres that he had conferred with Colmenares at length and, as a result, was offering Torres his personal support. Similarly, in early September, Colmenares informed Torres, "I have come to an understanding with General José de la Paz Alvarado, who is identified with me and who has decided to support your government and that of the nation." At the same time, General Ramón Antonio Vásquez, Colmenares's closest associate, began to carry out assignments entrusted to him by Torres, including the surveillance of Duaqueños still suspected of disloyalty to the regime.[65] Thus the appointment of Colmenares as jefe civil had the effect of swinging his followers—the other important Liberal leaders of the district—into line behind Castro. Colmenares and his faction had become integrated into the patron-client network of the Castrista state.

Nevertheless, Torres sought independent confirmation of Colmenares's loyalty, and with good reason. To depend entirely on declarations of support by Colmenares and his men would be naive, for shifting one's alliances in response to changes in the larger political scene remained a fundamental feature of Venezuelan politics. So, when Torres received word in November that Montilla had made overtures to Colmenares, he sought information from Rafael Paiva, a Duaqueño whom he trusted. Paiva's response testified not only to Colmenares's loyalty to the regime, but also to the strength of the bonds between him and his subordinates. Paiva wrote:

I believe that if the moment arrives, neither temptations nor inducements will sway [Colmenares]; and the men on whom he counts will go with him without hesitation, to whatever point proves necessary, and none of them can do anything on his own account without risking a fall [from favor] because Colmenares is the only one here with a solid base; excluding the Nationalist element, of whom I can give no report. . . . General Colmenares and his friends are loyal servants of the government.[66]

As Paiva's letter demonstrates, Colmenares's leadership among the politically important men of the district was one of his principal assets in his dealings with the national state. The Castro regime could best secure its interests in the district by maintaining its alliance with the firmly entrenched local boss.

Torres had started to win Colmenares's loyalty through the granting of small favors. By the same token, Torres maintained the alliance by allowing Colmenares to enjoy the perquisites of political power. Outright gifts of money were apparently the most common of Torres's continued favors to Colmenares. In October 1906, when some of Colmenares's friends hired a tutor to teach the new jefe civil to read and write and then found themselves unable to pay the bill, Colmenares wrote to Torres for assistance.[67] Less than three months later Colmenares again requested financial assistance, this time to pay a medical doctor. He tactfully reminded Torres that it would be unfortunate if he were forced by poor health to leave the district government while Montilla remained at large.[68] Colmenares's demands on Torres may have been unusually frequent in late 1906 because of the loss of that year's coffee crop in the district.[69]

The clientelistic relationship between Colmenares and the regime did not end when Torres left office. The new state president, General Santiago Briceño Ayestarán, a native of Táchira who had campaigned extensively in Lara during the Libertadora, worked to maintain the alliance forged by his predecessor. Soon after taking office in 1907, he wrote to José Garbi:

I have taken note of what you told me regarding the organization of Distrito Crespo. In this organization, I have not only taken into account the political interests of the state, but have also taken care to show decided favor to General Eduardo Colmenares, naming him Chief of the Guard, which is a position of great confidence and much better paid [than that of jefe civil]. Because of this, our friend Colmenares is completely satisfied.[70]

Nor did Colmenares's faction suffer when he ceased to be jefe civil (a position to which he would soon return) for he was replaced by Ramón A. Vásquez, his closest associate.[71]

As a client of state presidents, Colmenares received more than the financial benefits of office-holding; he also received protection when his opponents within the district attempted to use their own networks of influence to discredit him. We have already seen how Torres defended Colmenares in July 1906, when the Duaqueño's enemies created a rumor that he was involved in an anti-Castro plot. Torres protected Colmenares against a similar intrigue some months later. In early February 1907, Castro's minister of interior relations, Torres Cárdenas, informed Torres that Colmenares had allied himself with a group of dissidents.[72] In a deferential yet firm reply, Torres emphasized his confidence in his client's loyalty and suggested that the "information" implicating Colmenares was part of a conspiracy to divide the government.[73] When Torres Cárdenas continued to push the issue, Torres penned a long defense of Colmenares, emphasizing his utility to the regime as well as his loyalty. "He is an un-schooled and common man, but a military leader by intuition," Torres began. "Valiant even among the valiant, and a good strategist, he is the premier machete in the state." After reviewing Colmenares's military exploits during the Libertadora, Torres explained that any move against the local boss would compromise the regime's support among the elite throughout northern Lara:

> His widely applauded appointment [as jefe civil] has affirmed the support of many friends of the government and has attracted others besides; . . . his bravery and his prestige are a bulwark in the north of this state. . . . If we did not have his support, it would be necessary to make great efforts to attract him. His replacement, and even worse his imprisonment, would have a disastrous effect: we could not count on the towns in the north of the state and the Liberals, who were Libertadores and today are with the government, would become alarmed, would consider themselves insecure, and we could not have confidence in any of them.[74]

In short, Torres instructed the minister on the realities of local power. Informal webs of loyalty among important men placed constraints on the national state, for insensitivity to these linkages would weaken the state by alienating the locally powerful. Conversely, integrating these existing networks of influence into the official structure of power would bolster the state's authority.

The threat to his client and hence to his own influence impelled Torres to confide his suspicions concerning the origin of the charges against Colmenares.

An unnamed member of the government in Tucacas who aspired to become president of Lara, Torres charged, was maneuvering to build influence in the state and had made an alliance with the Giménez Méndez family of Distrito Crespo. Longtime enemies of Colmenares, the Giménez clan led the small Hernandista faction in Duaca and had fought against him during the Restauradora and in the final months of the Libertadora. Torres suspected that this faction was behind the current attempt to discredit Colmenares, just as he believed they had planted the rumor of his disloyalty the previous year. Torres warned the minister that favoring the Giménez faction over Colmenares would only weaken the regime: "their following [*contingente*] is inferior to that of Colmenares in every way. That is why they continually try to bring him down." Torres's defense of Colmenares proved successful. The local strongman's large following and proven military ability continued to make him the regime's most desirable ally in Duaca.

But soon after Torres left office, yet another maneuver to topple Colmenares was set in motion. In mid-1907, Ramiro González, who had served briefly as jefe civil of Duaca in 1905, came calling on Santiago Briceño Ayestarán, the new president of Lara, with high hopes of being reappointed to the post. No less a figure than Juan Vicente Gómez (once again Castro's righthand man) had recommended him for the post.[75] Nevertheless, Briceño declined to make the appointment, largely because it would upset the regime's alliance with Colmenares. He explained to Gómez:

> Regarding General Ramiro González, it is not possible for me to name him [jefe civil] in Duaca, since in that district it is necessary to count on men who, in times of war, can secure the railroad; and, in times of peace, guarantee order in the district. You know that our friend González gets into trouble; and in this case I would be responsible for any disaster he might cause. Besides, the authority that I have in that district is ours in every sense, and it is the person of Colmenares, the most prestigious man in those places.[76]

Having fought against Colmenares during the Libertadora, Briceño appreciated his military skill, just as he recognized the strategic importance of the railroad that the Duaqueños had proved so adroit at controlling. More fundamentally, Briceño (like Torres) believed that the alliance with Colmenares should continue because he commanded the largest following in the district. What other interpretation can be given to his assertion that Colmenares was "the most prestigious man in those places"?

It would not be necessary to continually emphasize the importance of

Colmenares's following were it not for historians' assertion that the ability to command such a clientele became increasingly irrelevant in the equation of political power after the Libertadora. This view holds that Castro separated regional leaders from their clienteles, their power base, and imposed representatives of central authority—the "proconsuls" of the president, as they are sometimes called. This argument emphasizes relations between the central government and state presidents but extends to the supposedly changing nature of political power throughout the nation. Although it is true that Venezuela's regional caudillos, the former arbiters of national politics, lost all independent power, the same should not be assumed of district-level authorities, of which the jefe civil was the most important. In Duaca the old, informal basis of power—the ability to command a following, a numerous clientele —remained an important factor in determining who ruled. Colmenares came to office largely because he mobilized over five hundred men to demonstrate support for Castro during the Acclamation, a conspicuous display of his large following. State presidents repeatedly acted to keep Colmenares in office, not simply because he was loyal to the government, but because he commanded an impressive clientele whose loyalty could be assured by their leader's alliance with the regime. The state presidents acted as patrons to the local cacique, granting him protection and perquisites in exchange for his fealty. And, like patrons elsewhere, they became, if only temporarily, the captives of their client, anxious to please and careful not to offend.[77]

Military considerations were paramount in the regime's rationale for seeking the support of local strongmen such as Colmenares, even after Gómez seized power in 1908. National leaders continued, into the 1920s, to prize their clients' ability to mobilize armed bands to combat local rebellions. Even as Gómez continued to expand and professionalize the national army, he developed networks of loyalists who, using their own influence as much as that of the central regime, could raise armed followers in strategic areas in the event of renewed uprisings.[78] Jefes civiles like Colmenares were often the linchpins in these networks.[79] Such informal military forces assumed considerable importance in Lara during the political crisis of 1913, the pivotal moment in the consolidation of the Gómez regime. This was the moment at which Colmenares and his faction sealed their alliance with Juan Vicente Gómez.

The crisis began when, in early 1913, Gómez made clear his intention to remain as national president beyond the elections scheduled for the following year. Many political figures had backed Gómez's coup in 1908 as simply the most expedient method of ousting Castro, believing that the unsophisticated and taciturn Gómez would prove incapable of holding on to the presidency for more than one term. Now they had to choose whether to aid the general in perpetuating his regime or to take up arms against him. Many of Gómez's putative allies entered a conspiracy against him, but the plot was uncovered and repressed. Purposely exaggerating the extent of the crisis, Gómez claimed that Castro was planning an invasion to coincide with an internal insurrection. He cancelled the elections, suspended constitutional guarantees, and personally led the army on campaign. Few rebels were found, but the real goal had been to separate friend from foe, and the manufactured crisis served this purpose well. Those who failed to give Gómez clear and unflinching support were now suspect; those who showed more vigorous dissident leanings were jailed or exiled. Meanwhile, those who stood firmly by Gómez in 1913 were rewarded, in some cases remaining key figures in his regime for the next two decades.[80]

Colmenares and his followers were among those who supported Gómez and became identified as staunch Gomecistas. Their loyalty must have proven all the more praiseworthy in the dictator's eyes given the attitude of many politicians in Lara. A number of Gomecistas in the state, while remaining loyal to the general, spent much of 1913 maneuvering for personal advantage and jostling for promotions. One Gómez loyalist—the future president of Zulia state, Vincencio Pérez Soto—visited Lara in July 1913 and sent his chief a grim report. In Pérez Soto's view, the state's leaders gave more attention to their personal feuds than to preserving the national regime. "They are so busy winning allies for themselves," he informed Gómez, "that no one has won allies for you."[81] Even the state's highest officials "think of petty politicking rather than administration." Most alarming, some of the army commanders had allowed their followers to retain private caches of arms in return for promises of personal support, and a few were suspected of rebel sympathies. Only a handful of leading figures in the state had avoided the squabbling and the conspiracies. Pérez Soto singled out for special praise those

> men of prestige and worth, but without pretension, such as Eduardo Colmenares in Duaca, Nerio Dunin in Quibor, [Florencio] Giménez Loyo and Miguel Oberto in Barquisimeto, etc., etc., who have not supported individual aspirants and have contracted and sustained their obligations directly with you, thereby avoiding the infighting and anarchy.[82]

Thus Colmenares cast his lot with the center. Perhaps he understood the growing momentum of political centralization, or perhaps he simply distrusted the scheming politicians in Barquisimeto, just as Gómez (who also spent years as a small hacendado before his rise in politics) never trusted the Caracas elite.

The same day that Pérez Soto informed Gómez of the intrigues in Lara, the atmosphere of national crisis intensified as Gómez announced an imminent rebel uprising. Given Pérez Soto's doubts concerning the loyalty of some of the army commanders in Lara, the defense of the regime in Lara would have to rely heavily on informal paramilitary forces. Argenis Azuaje, a leading Gomecista in Lara, was aware of this when in early August he advised Gómez of the regime's military position in the state. Rather than rely solely on the professional army, Azuaje had spoken with

> friends [who] have shown themselves willing to make common cause with me here in the state, such as Generals Eduardo Colmenares, Tomás Rojas [Vélis], Blas Romero, and Colonels Sotero Ortiz and Pablo Arrieche, so that I am sure to organize part of the army to sustain peace, given the qualities that such officers bring together. These individuals have offered to bring their followers [aportar su contingente].[83]

The "generals" and "colonels" named by Azuaje did not hold commissions in the regular army; they had won their titles in the civil wars at the turn of the century. Rojas Vélis and Arrieche were followers of Colmenares from the Libertadora; they clearly retained the ability to mobilize a clientele, just as they in turn were clients to Colmenares. Local networks of informal power endured beyond the eclipse of caudillismo that came with the defeat of the Libertadora and, at least in Duaca, were integrated into the central state under Gómez.

Just as leading politicians in Lara supported and protected Colmenares because of his numerous following, so his position as jefe civil enabled him to maintain his clientele. Colmenares remained the leader of the dominant political faction in Duaca for nearly two decades in part because he succeeded in distributing the spoils of office among his followers. Ramón Vásquez's temporary assumption of the office of jefe civil in 1907 can be viewed in this context. During his own tenure as jefe civil, Colmenares increased the number of jobs under his control, appointed his friends to fill them, and did what he could to raise their salaries.[84] Torres also allowed Colmenares and his allies to determine who sat on the district council.[85] And, just as Colmenares asked his patrons for money for himself, so he asked them to make "spontaneous and generous offerings" to his principal followers.[86]

Colmenares used his connections to the central regime to benefit his associates in other ways as well. In late 1906, for example, he asked Torres to secure the discharge of a friend's nephew who had been dragged into Castro's army during a campaign against Montilla.[87] Ten years later, while serving another stint as jefe civil, Colmenares wrote to Gómez to ask that Alfredo Jiménez Sorondo, the son of a prominent Duaca family, be released from prison after serving four years for involvement in a plot against the regime.[88] These were not isolated incidents. For decades into the future, Colmenares would be affectionately remembered by well-to-do Duaqueños for the protection he afforded against political persecution during the Gómez dictatorship.[89] The local strongman, who became a large landowner following the partition of the Indian community lands in 1916, used his influence to safeguard the local elite's economic interests as well, and in exchange many of the wealthiest men in the district gave Colmenares their active support.[90]

Although we lack a systematic study of the jefes civiles under Castro and Gómez, it seems clear that the rapport between Duaca's elite and Colmenares was not a common state of affairs in the nation as a whole. Few district elites, apparently, could count on having one of their own appointed to the office of district governor. Particularly during the Gómez era, influential clients of the regime often won appointment as jefe civil in a district outside their home base.[91] They commonly used their offices to advance their personal interests in ways that alienated the locally prominent. Thus even men like Eustoquio Gómez (the dictator's autocratic cousin and not usually one to fret about public opinion) worried that some jefes civiles would offend those with local influence.[92] District governors who came from outside the areas they governed were probably the most likely to abuse their office. By contrast, Colmenares, a Duaca native, was repeatedly appointed jefe civil of Duaca from 1906 through the first decade of the Gómez regime and consistently served the interests of the local elite. Only in the late 1910s, as he approached seventy years of age, did Colmenares leave office for good.

The position soon passed to another native son, Ramón Antonio Vásquez, who served as jefe civil through most of the 1920s. Having fought as Colmenares's second in command during the Libertadora, Vásquez was a logical choice to continue to guard the regime's military interests in the district. He was also well placed to serve Duaca's well-to-do. One of the wealthiest coffee growers and merchants in the district by the late 1910s, Vásquez proved especially vigorous in advancing the elite's economic interests against the peasantry.

The police under his command enforced debt peonage much more effectively than the officials of the nineteenth century, and in the mid-1920s Vásquez used his authority as jefe civil to approve new estate regulations that were harsher than any in Duaca's history (see chapter 7). Colmenares and Vásquez, having risen to prominence during the Libertadora, together governed Duaca as loyal clients of the central regime for most of the period between 1906 and the Great Depression. At the same time, they used their position to benefit the local class to which they both belonged.

To be sure, the phenomena emphasized in this chapter—factional politicking, the pursuit of patronage, and the advancement of class interests—did not constitute the whole business of government in Distrito Crespo. On occasion those in power pursued the ideal of government, the common good.[93] But the principal development in Duaca from the early 1900s onward was the elite's increasing power over local society, and elite control of the newly established district government was part of this process of growing domination. Thus the developments examined in this chapter—the winning of independent district status, the alliance with central state, and the local elite's control of district offices—take on historical significance primarily because they advanced the interests of the few at the expense of the many.

Conclusion

During the years that Cipriano Castro and Juan Vicente Gómez built an increasingly centralized state, Duaca's elite expanded their own political power. In contrast to a simplistic paradigm of centralization, which assumes that the national state triumphs through its ability to break the influence of local elites, the relationship between Duaca and the national state proved more nuanced. The Duaqueños managed to consolidate their own position through an accommodation with the center (like other local elites confronting centralization from a position of strength in other times and other places).[94] In the end, there proved to be no irreconcilable conflict between those interested in building central power and those interested in consolidating their control over local affairs. Like most historical processes, the working out of this accommodation was unplanned and encompassed contradictory tendencies.

Inspired by Duaca's growing prosperity following the completion of the railroad in 1891, the local elite began their struggle for political power by petitioning the state government to elevate the municipality of Duaca to a district and eventually achieved their goal through their support for Castro in his 1899 rebellion. But when Castro then denied them control of the newly created district, the Duaqueños joined in the rebellion against their former ally. Although the uprising failed to overthrow Castro, during its two and a half years the Duaqueños distinguished themselves as tenacious guerrilla fighters capable of controlling the strategically important railroad between Barquisimeto and Tucacas. Moreover, Eduardo Colmenares established his reputation as a military leader, and the influence he built during the war survived the rebellion's defeat.

It was only natural, then, that Castro and later Gómez, through their state presidents, sought an alliance with Colmenares and his faction. Through this accommodation with the locally powerful, the central regime gained authority and legitimacy in Duaca, as well as the assurance that if another war erupted Colmenares and his men would secure the railroad into Barquisimeto. As Santiago Briceño reminded Gómez in 1907, the government's interests in Distrito Crespo lay in keeping order during times of peace and controlling the railroad in times of war, and Colmenares was the best man to safeguard these interests. The same considerations allowed Ramón Antonio Vásquez, Colmenares's lieutenant and another representative of the district elite, to carry on as jefe civil through most of the 1920s.

In the end, both the national regime and the local elite emerged more powerful than before. Although those interested in building a strong central state and those interested in establishing their power locally at times perceived themselves to be locked in a win-or-lose struggle, and although they fought a costly war because of that perception, their interests proved compatible after all. Following two civil wars and a good deal of political maneuvering, prominent Duaqueños and the central state arrived at an arrangement that was beneficial to both. It often transpires, however, that when elites make peace among themselves, the cost is ultimately borne by society's subordinate groups. This would prove to be the case in Duaca, for the local elite that consolidated their political power in the early twentieth century held interests completely opposed to those of the peasant majority.

6 The Struggle for Land on Two Duaca Estates, 1909–1921

As the local elite strengthened their political position in the early 1900s, peasant access to the Indian lands and baldíos remained a fundamental feature of life in Duaca. This existence of large amounts of land outside the sphere of private ownership set limits on the elite's control over society. Most of the district's peasants did not live under a landlord, and those who did benefited from the system of low rents that resulted from the widespread availability of land outside the private estates. These conditions had shaped Duaca's agrarian structure at the onset of the coffee boom in the 1860s, and they remained in place a half century later.

During the 1910s and 1920s, however, prominent Duaqueños transformed local society. The resguardos and baldíos were brought under private ownership, the peasantry occupying these lands were reduced to estate tenants, and the old system of low rents was abandoned forever. The elite imposed these new relationships by applying their recently established political influence. Through their actions, they indicated that the pursuit of political power was not an end in itself but, rather, was part and parcel of the struggle to protect and advance economic interests.

The struggles between public land occupants and the owners of two estates between 1909 and 1921 illuminate one aspect of the elite's growing monopolization of land. In each case, estate owners succeeded in enclosing public land and reducing the peasant occupants to the status of estate tenants, and in each case the illicit appropriation of national lands was sanctioned by the state. These conflicts were adjudicated in Duaca's newly established district court, but at every turn litigants' political influence—rather than a strict application of the laws—guided the judicial process. These cases, then, illustrate how members of Duaca's elite translated political influence into expanded control over land, often in the face of popular resistance.

The Struggle for Los Chipas

The estate of Los Chipas and its environs had long been a scene of struggle between landowners and occupants of public land. The history of Los Chipas began in 1714 when the Spanish crown granted six fanegadas of land to Don Santiago Gaspar Ruíz de la Parra. This small tract of roughly forty-eight hectares lay well to the east of the Indian lands and was surrounded by public land on all sides. As frequently occurred in Venezuela and throughout Latin America, subsequent owners of the estate illegally expanded the boundaries to enclose more and more territory that legally formed part of the national domain until, by 1851, the estate of Los Chipas measured thousands of hectares, encompassing most of the land between the eastern border of Duaca's resguardos and the neighboring state of Yaracuy.[1] Subsequent owners sold land from the northern part of Los Chipas, creating the smaller estates of Licua, Batatal, and Limoncito.[2] The boundaries of Los Chipas and the smaller estates carved out of it remained relatively stable throughout the late nineteenth and early twentieth centuries (see figure 1).

The people of Duaca were fully aware that the owners of Los Chipas had expanded its boundaries to enclose public lands. During a survey of the estate in 1869, the inspector of public lands for the state of Lara observed that "for years we have heard it constantly said that most of Los Chipas is public land, because they say that its old area did not exceed eighteen [sic] fanegadas . . . and the enlargement of its boundaries has been noted."[3] Nevertheless, the owners of Los Chipas exercised authority over much of the estate, continually collecting rents in the southern and western portions of the estate. The hamlets of Agua-fría, Los Chipas, and Rincón-hondo, for example, were firmly under landlord control.[4] By contrast, the occupants of the northeastern

Figure 6.1 The Estates of Los Chipas, Licua, and Limoncito

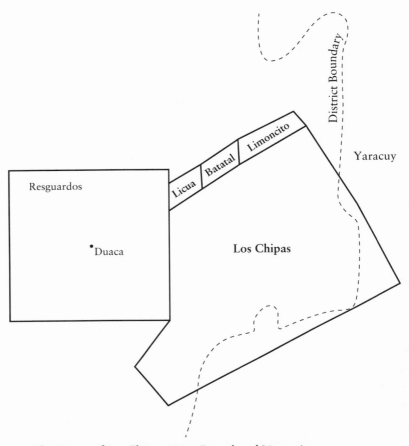

Figure 1. The Estates of Los Chipas, Licua, Batatal, and Limoncito

Source: RPEL, juicios civiles (1910), bulto 136, doc. 6.298, "Juicio Los Chipas, Giménez, Camejo, Rojas Vélis, 2a. pieza," folio 114.

section of the estate successfully resisted the owners' attempts to collect rent throughout the late nineteenth century. The occupants of this disputed zone—which included the hamlets of La Danta, Pajaritos, San Miguel, Quebrada de Oro, and Los Volcanes—lived free of landlord control. In 1885, José Antonio Torrealba, the owner of Los Chipas, sought to assert his authority over the disputed zone by petitioning the national government to confirm his ownership of all the land within the estate boundaries. His request, however, was rejected. Torrealba died soon after.[5] Subsequent sales of Los Chipas continued to declare the old boundaries enclosing the disputed zone, but in practice the owners controlled only the southern and western areas of the estate (see figure 2).

Figure 6.2 The Disputed Zone of Los Chipas

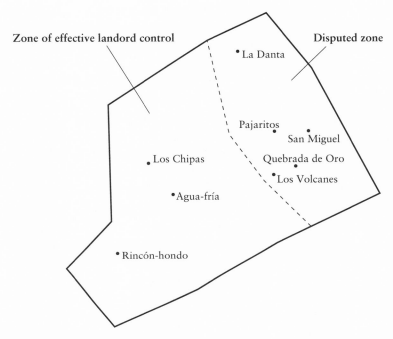

Zone of effective landord control

Disputed zone

• La Danta

Pajaritos
• San Miguel

• Los Chipas

Quebrada de Oro
• Los Volcanes

• Agua-fría

• Rincón-hondo

Figure 2. The Disputed Zone of Los Chipas

Sources: RPEL, juicios civiles (1910), bulto 136, doc. 6.298, "Juicio Los Chipas, Giménez, Rojas Vélis, 2a. pieza," folio 83; and map entitled "Barquisimeto," produced by Venezuela's Ministerio de Obras Públicas, Dirección de Cartografía, 1976.

The conflict in the northeastern part of Los Chipas came to a climax soon after Generals Avelino Giménez Méndez and Leopoldo Camejo purchased the estate in 1908. Camejo had no previous ties to the district. He had served in the Hernandista army in Lara in 1899, but after the war he had resided in the city of Valencia, in the central state of Carabobo, and then moved to Duaca only after purchasing his share of Los Chipas.[6] By contrast, Avelino Giménez Méndez had been an important local figure ever since he and his brother Aurelio arrived in Duaca from Quibor in the early 1890s. The Giménez Méndez brothers had acquired several coffee haciendas in the southern section of Los Chipas. Aurelio and Avelino also became the leaders of the Hernandista faction in Duaca and, following the reconciliation between Hernández and Castro, aided the government in subduing the Libertadora rebellion in Lara. Even after Castro made an alliance with the opposing Duaca faction led by Eduardo Colmenares, the Giménez Méndez brothers retained influence with the central regime. Colmenares and his ally Ramón Antonio Vásquez controlled the office of jefe civil during most of the period between 1906 and

1929, but Avelino managed to gain the position for several months in 1908.[7] It may have been Avelino's political stature that led him and Camejo to believe they could establish control over the disputed section of Los Chipas.

In 1909, Camejo and Giménez Méndez initiated a legal suit against five occupants of the disputed zone, claiming that the five occupied land within the estate of Los Chipas but refused to pay rent. The defendants named by Camejo and Giménez Méndez—General José Tomás Rojas Vélis (a close associate of Eduardo Colmenares), Saturnino Tovar, Homobono Rivero, Francisco Fonseca, and Saturnino Palacio—were clearly among the wealthier occupants of the disputed area. According to the suit filed by the landowners in Duaca's district court, the hacienda owned by Rojas Velis produced two hundred sacks of coffee annually, as well as a moderate amount of sugar, while the haciendas of Tovar, Rivero, and Fonseca produced one hundred sacks of coffee each, and the hacienda owned by Palacio, fifty sacks. Camejo and Giménez Méndez presented a copy of the estate's regulations, which called for rental payments of 6 percent of tenants' annual coffee production and demanded that the five pay accordingly.[8] Clearly, however, more was at stake than the fate of the five defendants, for if these submitted to the estate owners' demands, the poorer occupants of the disputed zone presumably would have little choice but to follow suit and recognize the landowners' dominion.

The five defendants chose to resist the estate owners and a five-year court battle ensued. Throughout the litigation, the alleged tenants insisted that the land they occupied was legally part of the national domain. Their lawyers introduced documentary evidence aimed at proving that virtually all of Los Chipas was public land, which previous owners of the estate had enclosed through illegal boundary changes.[9] Furthermore, they collected oral testimony to demonstrate that no previous owner of Los Chipas had collected rents in the disputed area.

The most important testimony came from Eloy Parra, who had administered Los Chipas on behalf of its owners in the late 1880s and 1890s. Parra began by candidly admitting he believed the estate lacked clear and definitive titles. He testified that he had attempted to collect rent throughout the estate, and tenants in some areas paid while those in other areas refused. According to Parra, the tenants who resisted rent collection "explained their refusal by saying that the land was public." When asked why he had never brought legal action against the recalcitrant tenants, Parra stated, "I never sued anyone for fear of involving myself in a case that might become interminable, or might turn out unfavorably for those I represented [the estate owners] . . . those whom I represented did not want me to attempt such a thing, and ordered me to continue collecting [rent] in the zones where it could easily be done."[10] By showing that previous owners had not exercised control over the disputed area, the defendants hoped to demonstrate that even the previous owners of Los Chipas doubted the legitimacy of the estate's boundaries.

Although the formal court proceedings revolved around legal claims to land, Duaca's factional politics had a profound impact on the course of the case. When Camejo and Giménez Méndez, two Hernandistas, faced the decision of which occupants of the disputed zone to name in their suit, it was hardly a coincidence they chose to name General José Tomás Rojas Vélis, who had fought against the Hernandistas in both the Restauradora and the Libertadora. Rojas Vélis was a close ally of Eduardo Colmenares, against whom Avelino and Aurelio Giménez Méndez had struggled for control of the district in the aftermath of the Libertadora. Colmenares and his faction won the struggle by forging an alliance with the central state; the decision by Avelino Giménez Méndez and Leopoldo Camejo to name Rojas Vélis in the legal suit signaled an eagerness to continue the conflict through other means.

As the two factions squared off in court, other members of the local elite sought to avoid involvement in the dispute. Soon after the proceedings began, the district judge excused himself from hearing the case on the grounds that he was related to Avelino Giménez Méndez. Duaca's district council then selected five members of the local elite as candidates to serve as judge in the case. In rapid succession, all five declared themselves relatives or intimate friends of at least one of the principals in the case and therefore ineligible under national law, until at last a sixth candidate agreed to hear the case.[11]

Now, judges drawn from the local elite did not hesitate to preside over cases that matched their intimate friends against the peasantry, as subsequent disputes made clear. When faced with the prospect of arbitrating an important suit between powerful rivals, however, men gladly submitted to the law and withdrew, in order to avoid offending either one side or the other. Similarly, some of the witnesses who were called to testify concerning the collection of rents in the disputed zone of Los Chipas disqualified themselves, explaining that they too were close friends of one or more of the principals in the case.[12] They, like most of the prospective judges, apparently concluded that the power wielded by both sides made involvement in the case too risky a proposition.

Most important, the political magnitude of the case resulted in the intervention of the Ministry of Development. Rojas Vélis and the other defendants, not content to remain on the defensive, declared in May 1910 that they were initiating a countersuit intended to prove that all of Los Chipas (with the exception of the land granted by the Spanish crown in 1714) was public land. Since the Ministry of Development had authority over national lands, Rojas Vélis and the other defendants petitioned the ministry to send a representative to Duaca so their countersuit could move forward.[13] The lawyers representing Camejo and Giménez Méndez opposed the petition, but on November 22, 1910, the minister of development ordered Antonio Alamo, the state prosecutor, to assume the post of public land inspector and to represent the national government in the conflict over Los Chipas.[14] The ministry's decision to intervene was an important setback for Camejo and Giménez Méndez and presumably resulted from Rojas Vélis's close ties to Eduardo Colmenares and the influence both men wielded within the Gomecista regime.

In April 1911, Alamo formally brought suit on behalf of the government against the owners of Los Chipas. He charged that all the territory within the estate was legally public land, with the exception of the small area alienated by the Spanish crown two hundred years before. Alamo's suit called on the owners of Los Chipas to surrender their claim to the estate and to recognize the state's right over virtually all the land within the boundaries of Los Chipas.[15] In essence, then, Alamo adopted the same position taken by Rojas Vélis and the other occupants of the disputed zone. If Alamo succeeded, Camejo and Giménez Méndez would lose their claim not only to the disputed zone, but also to the thousands of hectares where owners of Los Chipas had traditionally collected rents. In response to Alamo's demands, the lawyers for the estate owners raised a series of technical objections, which the judge approved, and the litigation became mired in procedural questions.[16]

In early 1912, as the dispute entered its fourth year, the government grew increasingly anxious to resolve the case and began to search for an expeditious settlement. On May 12, the minister of development, Pedro Emilio Coll, instructed Alamo to propose a compromise to the owners of Los Chipas. Coll wrote:

> In view of your messages and other documents received in this office concerning the controversy over the estate "Los Chipas," the National Government finds that it is necessary and urgent to put an end to this matter, for the tranquillity and prosperity of the agricultural region in question depend upon such a resolution, as you have said to this Ministry. To this purpose, the National Executive . . . authorizes you to propose the following transaction to the interested persons: the nation will recognize Generals Avelino Giménez

Méndez and Leopoldo R. Camejo as owners of the six fanegadas indicated in the old title, *as well as the lands that they cultivate,* leaving the rest [of the estate] as public land and its occupants therefore subject to the relevant laws concerning the acquisition [of the land they occupy], understanding that the nation recognizes the rights that they have acquired in virtue of article seven of the [public land] law. If the interested parties do not accept this transaction, the matter will continue its judicial course.[17] (Emphasis in original)

The government thus offered to grant the estate owners title to land where they owned haciendas, as well as to land that had been alienated by the crown in 1714, if they would renounce their claim to the rest of Los Chipas. Although it would deprive Camejo and Giménez Méndez of all land occupied by tenants, the offer represented a softening of the government's position. Rather than continue to press for the full application of the law, the government was entering into negotiations with Camejo and Giménez. The ministry had concluded, on the basis of information from Alamo and unnamed others, that the dispute was disrupting Duaca's economy, apparently because of the doubt it cast on land rights in an extensive area within the district. The desire for economic stability in Duaca led the ministry to seek an accommodation with the powerful men on each side of the conflict, rather than impose a settlement by fiat. The estate owners, however, rejected the government's offer and continued to defend their right to all of Los Chipas. In response, Coll ordered Alamo to "carry forward the pending litigation to its final resolution."[18]

Despite this ominous directive, the government eventually accepted a resolution that contained even greater concessions to Camejo and Giménez Méndez. In February 1914, the government and the original defendants in the dispute—Rojas Vélis, Palacio, Fonseca, Rivero, and Tovar—agreed to recognize Camejo and Giménez Méndez as rightful owners of the vast majority of Los Chipas, including all the areas where estate owners had traditionally collected rents. The new estate boundaries even enclosed part of the disputed zone where the owners had not previously exercised control. In exchange, Camejo and Giménez Méndez relinquished their claim to most of the disputed zone.[19] The court documents do not reveal how the parties in the dispute established the boundaries of the land that was declared public. In legal terms, Camejo and Giménez Méndez had as little claim to the land they retained as to the territory they surrendered. The final boundaries apparently resulted from negotiations between Alamo, the estate owners, and the defendants named in the original suit.

The resolution of the controversy was in many ways a victory for Camejo and Giménez Méndez. Because the national government formally recognized the new boundaries of Los Chipas, the estate owners' claim to their land was immune to future legal challenge. Now that the old doubts concerning the legitimacy of the estate's titles were settled, the market value of the estate increased dramatically.[20] Most important, perhaps, the owners now exercised control over more land than before the litigation, for the new boundaries of Los Chipas enclosed part of the disputed zone, where previous owners had proved unable to collect rents.

From this more advantageous position, Camejo and Giménez Méndez moved aggressively against tenants who still refused to recognize their dominion. In January 1916 they initiated a lawsuit against three such tenants, Manuel Rivero and his brothers Marcos and Crispín.[21] The Riveros' holdings were in Los Volcanes, a hamlet in the formerly disputed zone of Los Chipas, where occupants traditionally had not paid rent, but which fell within the new estate boundaries ratified by the national government. Significantly, the estate owners decided to prosecute the Riveros in a way that would intimidate other tenants who might resist the imposition of landlord control. Rather than demand only that the Riveros pay rent for the eight years since Camejo and Giménez Méndez had purchased Los Chipas, the estate owners also demanded that the Rivero brothers pay damages for the supposed deterioration of the land they cultivated. And, while peasant debtors such as the Riveros usually could cede part or all of their holdings to settle debts, Camejo and Giménez Méndez demanded that the three brothers destroy all their crops and buildings on the estate, which would force them to pay the back rents and damages with other resources, which they probably did not possess.[22] In short, the estate owners threatened the Riveros with complete impoverishment.

The Riveros promptly mortgaged their holdings in order to retain a lawyer, but since the new estate boundaries had been sanctioned by the national government, they could not deny that the land they occupied was part of Los Chipas. In March 1916, after less than two months of litigation, the estate owners halted their prosecution of the case, presumably because they had reached a settlement with the defendants, and in July the Riveros sold their holdings. The court records do not indicate the terms of the settlement, nor do they give any further indication of the fate of the Rivero brothers.[23]

Nevertheless, Camejo and Giménez Méndez had clearly succeeded in asserting their authority over the land formerly occupied by the Riveros. Within the larger context of Duaca's history, the case represents a telling episode in the erosion of peasant autonomy in the early twentieth century. The Riveros' origins were typical of Duaca's precipitate peasantry in at least two respects. First, like many of the district's inhabitants, they were not natives of the area but had migrated from a nearby jurisdiction (in this case the district of Yaritagua, in the neighboring state of Yaracuy). Second, the Rivero brothers had established their coffee groves on contiguous plots, thus conforming to the family-cluster pattern of settlement so typical of rural Duaca.[24] They presumably knew of the land dispute with the owners of Los Chipas when they settled in Los Volcanes sometime before 1908, but like other residents of the area they lived as de facto public land occupants until, in 1914, the national government agreed to the new boundaries of Los Chipas—boundaries that placed the Riveros and the other residents of Los Volcanes under the control of landlords for the first time. The Riveros, it seems, were unique only in their refusal to recognize the dominion of the owners of Los Chipas after the new estate boundaries were established, and their refusal cost them dearly. The economic demise of the Rivero brothers, then, was a direct result of the central state's willingness to negotiate the boundaries of Los Chipas rather than to reclaim all the public land that had been illegally enclosed.

During the 1910s, Camejo and Giménez Méndez also instituted changes in the administration of Los Chipas that were not directly related to the question of the estate's boundaries. Most important, they allowed elite tenants to purchase the land they occupied within the estate. José Tomás Rojas Vélis, the most prominent of the defendants in the legal battle of 1909–1914 and whose hacienda was within the boundaries agreed to by the national government, bought the ninety hectares of land under his hacienda in early 1915.[25] General José de la Paz Alvarado, who like Rojas Vélis was an ally of Eduardo Colmenares and therefore (presumably) a political adversary of Giménez Méndez and Camejo, similarly purchased the land he occupied in the southern part of Los Chipas.[26] During the 1910s, at least three other large tenants on the estate purchased plots ranging from 25 to 120 hectares.[27] The rationale behind these sales was apparently political. Despite the economic benefits that landowners derived from large tenants, the presence of members of the elite among the tenantry placed unwelcome limits on landlord authority, as Camejo and Giménez Méndez had learned when the Ministry of Development responded to Rojas Vélis's petition to intervene in the dispute over Los Chipas. Selling land to elite tenants, therefore, represented a strategy for the estate owners to tighten their authority over the peasant majority among the tenantry, who, without well-to-do allies, had little chance of resisting landowner demands.

To conclude, the relationship between landlords and tenants on Los Chipas changed dramatically during the decade after Camejo and Giménez Méndez purchased the estate in 1908. Previous owners, who often had lived outside the district and played a limited role in the administration of the property, had not attempted to enforce rent collection throughout the entire estate. Unable to establish a clear claim to their land, and confronted with an alliance of elite and peasant tenants in the northeastern section of Los Chipas who refused to submit to their dominion, the absentee owners had found themselves limited to controlling only part of the territory within the estate's boundaries. By contrast, Giménez Méndez and Camejo determined to establish absolute control over the entire estate. Both men lived in the district and Giménez Méndez, who was deeply enmeshed in district politics, must have been particularly anxious to brandish his power as a landowner. Although their assertion of authority involved Camejo and Giménez Méndez in an unforeseen and costly dispute with the national government, in the end they exercised effective control over more land than any of their predecessors. Furthermore, land sales to elite tenants drove a wedge between them and the poorer tenants, and occupants of the estate who still resisted landlord control could be easily subdued. While owners of Los Chipas before 1908 had tended to be distant and weak, Camejo and Giménez Méndez were true masters of their domain.

Conflict on the Estate of Limoncito, 1916–1920

Shortly after the conflict over Los Chipas, two more cases came before Duaca's district court involving the illicit enclosure of public lands, this time by the owners of Limoncito, one of the three smaller estates that had been carved out of Los Chipas during the mid-nineteenth century (see figure 1). The two cases that arose from the expansion of Limoncito's boundaries again demonstrate the state's willingness to sanction illegal appropriations of public land at the expense of the peasantry.

The conflict between the owners of Limoncito and the peasants who lived near the estate began in 1915, when the owner of Limoncito, Medardo Alvarado, carried out a "survey" of the estate's boundaries. The crucial portion of the survey involved the southern boundary of the estate, which bordered the area of the disputed zone of Los Chipas that had been reclaimed as national lands in the settlement of 1914. The settlement had merely stated that the reclaimed public lands bordered Alvarado's estate but did not define the actual boundary; this, ostensibly, was the purpose of Alvarado's survey.[28]

In early 1916, shortly after completing the survey, Alvarado initiated a lawsuit against Francisco, Andrés, Ramona, Epifania, and Juan Zenon Giménez, who allegedly occupied land on the southern part of Alvarado's estate but refused to pay rent. The five Giménez siblings were fairly prosperous peasants.[29] Aside from their coffee groves, conucos, pasture, and pottery shed located on land claimed by Alvarado, they had other holdings outside the estate. In responding to Alvarado's charges, the Giménez siblings argued that the land he claimed was really public. They explained that the farm Alvarado believed to be within the estate had been established by their father, Amalio Giménez, over forty years before. They had worked the holding continually since their father's death in 1904, but neither he nor they had ever been charged rent by owners of Limoncito—until now.[30]

Alvarado's lawyers never denied that the defendants and their father had occupied the land in question for decades without paying rent. Instead, they asked the judge to make a visual inspection of the Giménez holdings and to certify that they were within the estate's boundaries. The judge, Leoncio Guillén (an important merchant and hacendado in the district, and a close friend of Alvarado), made the inspection using as his guide Alvarado's 1915 survey of Limoncito and declared that the Giménez holdings were indeed on estate land.[31] Afterward, the defendants' lawyer objected that his clients had not been informed of the inspection and thus had not been able to participate. He also reiterated the charge that part of the land claimed by Alvarado was in fact public and had been illegally enclosed during the 1915 survey. The judge never responded to either point: he simply accepted the boundaries in the 1915 survey as legal and in June 1916 decided the case in Alvarado's favor. Guillén ruled that the Giménez family, aside from owing 600 bolívares in back rent, would also have to pay 867 bolívares in court costs. To guarantee payment, he placed an embargo on all the defendants' property.[32]

The Giménez family, however, proved determined to resist the judge's decision. When the court's representative attempted to take possession of the family's embargoed livestock, Juan Zenon Giménez refused to surrender a cow and her calf. Ten days later the court's representative returned to make preparations for the harvest of the embargoed coffee groves and conucos, only to find that the crops had already been harvested and removed. The Giménez family still refused to pay what they ostensibly owed for rents and court costs, and in 1917 their embargoed property was auctioned off to Pedro José Sandoval Vargas, who had recently purchased Limoncito from Medardo Alvarado. Before the auctioned property could be transferred, however, three of the livestock mysteriously died and one of the huts seized from the Giménez family was burned down. By April 1918, Juan Zenon and Francisco Giménez had reoccupied their farm within the estate and refused to allow Sandoval Vargas to take possession. In the last document in the case, the judge ordered the jefe civil to assist Sandoval Vargas in evicting the Giménez brothers.[33]

The tenacity with which the Giménez family resisted the court's decision reflected a conception of property rights that was deeply rooted in the history of Duaca's precipitate peasantry. Their harvesting of embargoed crops and their refusal to part with embargoed livestock was, on one level, simply part of their struggle for survival. But in their original reply to Alvarado's suit, the Giménez family—addressing the court directly rather than through a lawyer—clearly expressed why they resisted Alvarado's claim to the land they occupied. Their father had settled the land over forty years before, they had continued to work the holding he established, and neither they nor their father had ever been charged rent by the owners of the neighboring estate of Limoncito. Rather, they understood the land to be part of the public domain and thus open to free colonization. Under local custom and under the national public land law, they claimed usufruct rights to the land based on their continual occupation. Like all peasants who had settled on Duaca's public lands, the Giménez family depended on the integrity of the public domain to guarantee their access to land. The judge's sanction of the enclosure of the Giménez holding within Limoncito, however, made a mockery of usufruct rights to land, and the assessment of back rents and court costs must have appeared to the family to be a punishment for defending what was theirs by law as well as by custom.

The fate of the Giménez siblings, however, did not deter other peasants from resisting the enclosure of their lands by the owners of Limoncito. By early 1918, Pedro José Sandoval Vargas, the new owner of the estate, still faced opposition to rent collection on Limoncito from at least nine peasant cultivators. Like the Giménez family, the nine claimed that the land they occupied was part of the public domain and had been illegally enclosed within the estate boundaries during the 1915 survey. In February 1918, Sandoval Vargas initiated a lawsuit against the nine, demanding that they pay back rents and an indemnization, raze their crops and buildings, and vacate the estate.[34] Two of the defendants, rather than risk complete ruin, negotiated individual settlements with Sandoval Vargas, agreeing to pay two years' rent and a small indemnization in return for the opportunity to purchase the plots they occupied. The other seven resolved to continue their struggle and hired a lawyer—a very diligent lawyer, as it transpired—in the person of Afrodirio Vásquez, of Barquisimeto.[35]

Vásquez assembled extensive evidence to support the peasants' contention that the land they occupied was part of the national domain and had been illegally enclosed during the 1915 survey of Limoncito. He called as witnesses longtime residents of the disputed area who testified that the land in question had always been considered public and that no one had ever attempted to collect rent from the occupants.[36] Delving into the estate's previous deeds of sale, Vásquez presented evidence that the boundaries established in the 1915 survey were different from those in the estate's nineteenth-century titles. Therefore, when an acting judge, Félix García, made an inspection of the defendants' holdings and declared that they were within the estate boundaries, Vásquez dismissed the inspection as irrelevant because it had been based on the 1915 survey of the estate.[37] The real issue, he insisted, was whether the survey had changed the boundaries of Limoncito to enclose public land.

The crucial moment in the case came on September 17, 1918, when Vásquez led the district judge, Leoncio Guillén, on an inspection of the disputed area. In outlining the boundaries of Limoncito, Vásquez used a copy of the estate's title from 1868. He showed Guillén that the defendants' holdings were outside the boundaries established in the title. Since no owner of Limoncito had purchased land to add to Limoncito in the years since 1868, Vásquez reasoned, the defendants' holdings were not on estate land. If their holdings were inside the boundaries established in the 1915 survey, this merely proved that the survey had been used to expand Limoncito's boundaries. At the end of the inspection, Vásquez asked the judge to record the results of the inspection and to certify that the defendants were outside the boundaries of the 1868 title. Guillén, however, refused to make any declaration concerning what he had seen, arguing that this would constitute a premature ruling on the case as a whole.[38] The contrast with other judicial inspections could not have been more dramatic. On a visit to the disputed area a few months earlier, the acting judge had readily declared that the defendants were within the 1915 boundaries, and during a 1916 inspection Guillén himself had declared that the Giménez family occupied estate lands. Now, however, faced with evidence that the owners of Limoncito had usurped public lands occupied by peasant cultivators, Guillén refused to make any statement at all regarding what he had seen.

Later, in his closing argument, Vásquez presented a detailed review of the evidence he had assembled concerning the illegal expansion of Limoncito's boundaries. Significantly, though, he began his argument by drawing attention for the first time to what may have been the most important fact in the entire case: he charged that Guillén was an intimate friend of the Alvarado family and therefore should have declared himself ineligible to hear the dispute. Even though Medardo Alvarado was not directly involved in the litigation, the case—at least in Vásquez's view—hinged on whether he had used the 1915 survey to enlarge the boundaries of Limoncito before selling the estate to Sandoval Vargas. (Vásquez made no mention of the fact that Guillén had also presided over the suit brought by Alvarado against the Giménez siblings.) After quoting from a recent declaration by Juan Vicente Gómez on the need for judicial impartiality, Vásquez reviewed the documentary evidence in his clients' favor, reminded Guillén of their inspection of the boundaries of Limoncito as outlined in the 1868 title, and called on him to decide the case in favor of the defendants. Finally, Vásquez declared that he had petitioned the Ministry of Development to intervene in the dispute to defend his clients' access to the public lands enclosed by the 1915 survey.[39]

Guillén, however, decided the case in favor of Sandoval Vargas. Ignoring the question of whether Alvarado's survey had enlarged Limoncito's boundaries, and without making any reference to his inspection of the disputed area with Vásquez, he simply stated that the defendants occupied lands that Sandoval Vargas had legally acquired from Alvarado.[40] Guillén ordered the defendants to pay rent, court costs, and an indemnization for the use of estate land but refused to impose Sandoval's demand that they raze their crops and buildings and vacate the estate.

The lawyers for both sides appealed the decision to the state court in Barquisimeto. The state judge, in contrast to Guillén, proved willing to consider the legal history of Limoncito and ordered an on-site inspection to compare the boundaries established in the 1915 survey with those in the 1868 title. The inspector found important discrepancies between the two boundaries, and the judge ruled in favor of the peasants, overturning Guillén's decision on every point.[41]

Sandoval Vargas appealed once more, though, and in late 1921 the state supreme court reinstated Guillén's ruling. The court noted that the state inspector of public lands, as required by law, had participated in the 1915 survey and had approved the boundaries of Limoncito. In the high tribunal's opinion, civil courts were not the proper forum to challenge decisions made by public land inspectors.[42] Ultimate authority over public lands, of course, was vested in the Ministry of Development, which Vásquez had petitioned to intervene in the dispute, but the ministry never responded. The seven peasants—lacking the political connections that had prompted the ministry to intervene in the Los Chipas dispute on behalf of General Rojas Vélis—were forced to submit to their landlord.

Conclusion

Between 1909 and 1921, the owners of Los Chipas and Limoncito established authority over land that previously had been beyond their control, thus reducing public land occupants to the status of tenants. On both estates, the enclosure of public lands received the sanction of the state through a judicial process that was shaped more by political power than by regard for the law. In the case of Los Chipas, men on each side of the dispute enjoyed influence—largely as a result of their participation in the civil wars at the turn of the century—and pushed the legal proceedings to a compromise, a negotiated settlement in which the Ministry of Development, after initially attempting to recover usurped public lands, ultimately approved their enclosure. The conflicts on Limoncito matched members of the local elite who enjoyed connections to the district judge against peasants who—unlike the elite defendants on Los Chipas—could not persuade the Ministry of Development to intervene on their behalf. As a result, the struggle on Limoncito ended not in compromise or negotiation, but in victory for the estate owners and defeat and ruin for the peasants.

These conflicts also provide insight into the relationship between the local elite and the central state under the Gómez regime, for the events reviewed in this chapter indicate the regime's willingness to accommodate the local elite in questions regarding land. To be sure, the Ministry of Development originally intervened in the Los Chipas dispute with the aim of recovering all of the public lands that had been illegally enclosed. As it dragged on year after year, however, the case created uncertainty regarding land rights in a large section of the district, and the ensuing economic disruption persuaded the government to seek a negotiated settlement. The reclamation of national lands proved less pressing than the preservation of stability, which in turn required respect for the interests of those holding political and economic power within the district. The resulting settlement, however, sacrificed the interests of those who occupied most of the land enclosed in Los Chipas. In effect, the national state accepted a compromise between members of the local elite that had been achieved at the expense of the peasantry.

The dispute over Los Chipas, however, was far from typical. The national state generally refrained from intervening in local disputes over land and left the resolution of such conflicts to the district courts, which in turn were entrusted to local elites. From its creation in 1900 through at least the mid-1930s, Duaca's district court was presided over by a series of judges drawn from the local elite. Such a judicial policy was not universal in Latin America. In Brazil during the mid-nineteenth century, for example, the central state developed a corps of magistrates to administer justice—and, some hoped, to impose central authority—in local courts throughout the nation. Although they might in time develop ties to powerful local families, Brazilian judges came from outside the areas where they served and remained dependent on the national state for their salaries and promotions.[43]

By contrast, the Venezuelan state allowed members of local elites to serve as judges in the districts where they lived. Under such a system, locally prominent families could often count on the district judge as a friend, or even a relative. The results of Venezuelan judicial policy were evident in the disputes on Limoncito. The district judge who presided over both cases steadfastly refused to question the legitimacy of the survey carried out by his friend Medardo Alvarado, despite strong evidence that Alvarado had usurped public lands. In sum, the creation of a district court in Duaca, a result of the district status won through support for Castro in 1899, allowed the local elite to exercise considerable control over the resolution of local disputes, including land conflicts, and so added to their power over the peasantry.

7 The Transformation of Duaqueño Society

WHILE THE STRUGGLES for land on Los Chipas and Limoncito ran their course in Duaca's district court, the local elite imposed even more far-reaching changes on Duaca's peasantry. The 1910s and 1920s witnessed the privatization of the district's communal and national lands, the two bastions of free peasant settlement. In 1910, a group within the local elite initiated a movement to transfer the Indian community lands to private ownership, and the partition of Duaca's resguardos was complete by 1916. Shortly thereafter, large tracts of Duaca's national lands—close to thirty thousand hectares in all —were also privatized. In less than a decade, the elite had radically changed the structure of land tenure in the district.

The land privatization of the 1910s and 1920s represented a critical watershed in the history of Duaca's peasantry. Before 1916, many of the district's peasants—perhaps a majority—had occupied the resguardos or baldíos, living free of landlord control. But privatization allowed the elite to transform peasant occupants of the baldíos and resguardos into rent-paying tenants on new estates. Moreover, as the elite converted virtually the entire district into their private domain, they abandoned the old system of low rents that had prevailed on Duaca's estates since the beginning of coffee production and decreed new rental conditions that increased landowner profits at the expense of tenants. Land privatization also facilitated the imposition of a harsher system of debt peonage than had prevailed during the nineteenth century. In short, the elite's newly established control over land enabled it to subordinate Duaca's rural working population as never before.

The peasantry did not passively accept the new rural order of privatized land, high rents, and more coercive labor conditions. Peasant tenants frequently refused to pay rent and indebted peons attempted to flee their employers. These unorganized forms of individual resistance, however, were easily overcome by Duaca's judges and jefes civiles, who were themselves members of the district elite. By the same token, the power wielded by local authorities precluded more violent or sustained forms of mass resistance. As elsewhere in Venezuela, the authority of the Gómez regime allowed Duaca's elite to pursue their interests ruthlessly without fear of organized popular opposition.

Peasant Society, circa 1916

Before examining the privatization of Duaca's resguardos and baldíos, however, we must ask whether other, less dramatic changes had already begun to alter peasant society before the onset of wholesale land privatization in 1916. For, despite the crucial importance of land tenure systems in determining the structure of peasant society, we cannot ignore other factors such as demographic growth, which can alter rural society just as thoroughly as changes in the ownership of land. The peasant economy that emerged in Duaca during the nineteenth century depended on the availability of unoccupied land, and the amount of such land steadily decreased as the district's population grew. Peasant migrants had already reached the district's northern boundary during the 1890s, thus closing Duaca's frontier of vacant public lands. As the population continued to increase in the early twentieth century, easy access to unused land could no longer be taken for granted, even before the process of privatization that began in 1916.

Historians of agrarian society have demonstrated how growing population pressure on a limited land base has transformed the structure of society in such varied settings as preindustrial Europe, colonial Mexico, and late nineteenth-century Chile. A growing ratio of population to land generally works against the peasantry by lowering wages, raising rents, and forcing the division of peasant holdings into progressively smaller units. As Arnold Bauer argues in his synthesis of Spanish American rural history from 1870 to 1930, demographic pressures formed a crucial part of the context of agrarian change during this period, which witnessed a long-term deterioration in the condition of peasants and other rural workers.[1]

In Duaca, however, mounting demographic pressure wrought only limited changes in the structure of society before the onset of privatization in 1916. Population growth and (just as important) the ecological deterioration of parts of the district gradually turned the ratio of people to arable land against the peasantry after the turn of the century. As a result, access to land became more problematic than during the dynamic, expansive days of the nineteenth century. Nevertheless, population pressure did not affect rents, which remained stable until after privatization was complete in the mid-1920s, nor (apparently) did it depress real wages to a significant degree. In sum, while the availability of good land had become limited before the resguardos and baldíos were partitioned in 1916–1923, demographic and ecological factors had not yet pushed peasant society to a point of crisis.

An examination of the censuses of 1891 and 1920—unfortunately no census was undertaken between these two years—indicates significant population growth. The 1891 count found 12,868 inhabitants in the municipality of Duaca, and in 1920 the population of Distrito Crespo stood at 20,338.[2] The figures are somewhat misleading, however, since two large *caseríos* (hamlets) outside the municipality were added to Duaca's jurisdiction when it was made a district at the turn of the century. One hamlet, Tacarigüita (which included land in the Generals' Estate), had a population of 2,184 in 1891, while the other, Rincónhondo (which included land in the estate of Los Chipas), was apparently counted with the hamlet of Nonavana's population of 722. If we adjust Duaca's 1891 population to include these two hamlets, we find that the increase between 1891 and 1920 was from 15,774 to 20,338 (28.9 percent), a relatively modest rate of growth. Given the district's area of 81,500 hectares, there were slightly more than four hectares per inhabitant in 1920.[3]

The land in question, however, did not constitute a fixed, unchanging resource. Rather, Duaca's growing population took its toll on the area's ecology, and the deterioration of district lands reinforced the gradual increase in demographic pressure. As early as the turn of the century, deforestation had become a problem throughout eastern Lara and was blamed by the Barquisimeto press for erosion and periodic droughts.[4] In 1901 a Duaca newspaper called for the increased protection of woodlands, noting that "the forests of this district have recently suffered a great deal." The paper observed that the cutting of trees to fuel railroad engines had contributed to the problem but argued that the greatest danger was agriculturalists' clearing of land along streams, which led directly to their desiccation. "We have already felt the fatal consequences of that imprudence of cutting down trees at the headwaters and along the course of our streams," the newspaper asserted.[5] But the "imprudent" practice continued in the years that followed as peasants and hacendados searched for scarce virgin land to clear and cultivate. Duaca's district council received numerous denunciations against agriculturalists of all classes who had cleared land along streams, in violation of state and national law.[6] The authorities spent a good deal of time identifying and punishing the transgressors, but the constant flow of denunciations suggests that they were powerless to put an end to the practice.

In his classic study of Vassouras, a municipality in Brazil's Paraíba Valley, Stanley Stein emphasized the ecological degradation that resulted from intensive coffee production for the world market. Stein argued convincingly that the rapid expansion of coffee, along with a disregard for the long-term consequences of poor agricultural techniques, resulted in deforestation, erosion, changes in the cycle of rainfall, and the declining fertility of the soil.[7] Expansion of the coffee economy lay at the heart of ecological change in Duaca as well, but at least one observer, the Barquisimeto lawyer and politician Leopoldo Torres, stated emphatically that the techniques used to grow food crops did more damage to the land in eastern Lara than the spread of coffee groves. Although a peasant family might plant roughly equal areas in coffee and food crops, a coffee grove produced for over twenty years, whereas land under food crops wore out and had to be abandoned after only a few years.[8] Fundamentally, the ecological histories of Vassouras and Duaca were driven by the same forces: the intensification of land use by growing populations engaged in production for the world market, and a continued reliance on techniques that had been developed in a bygone era of seemingly limitless expanses of virgin forest.

Ecological change in Duaca was more apparent in the western part of the district than in the eastern because of long-standing environmental differences between the two areas. The Bobare mountains, which begin on the outskirts of the town of Duaca and stretch westward to the arid plains of Carora, had always been drier than the Aroa mountains, which dominate the eastern half of the district. Soil exhaustion occurred first and more dramatically in the fragile environment of the west. When, in 1911, shares were sold in the Generals' Estate, located to the west of the resguardos, the diminishing value of the land was explained by its increasing "sterility" in recent years.⁹ The deterioration of land in the west of the district has continued to the present, whereas the ecology of the eastern mountains has proven more resilient. Indeed, as one surveys the barren hills in the west of the district today, it is difficult to believe that coffee ever could have been grown there, and a query as to the location of the best lands in the district will invariably be answered with a litany of hamlets well to the east.

Caught between the opposing forces of population increase and ecological deterioration, peasants in the early twentieth century found that access to good land became more difficult as the years passed. Some peasants in search of land on which to establish their holdings were obliged to buy usufruct rights to uncultivated land from their neighbors. Under local custom, peasants on the resguardos and baldíos exercised control not only over the land they cultivated, but also over adjoining patches of forest bordering their crops, and over land they had cleared but not planted. Traditionally, these rights to uncultivated areas had been used to establish a small reserve for a new conuco or for the expansion of a coffee grove. But as land became scarce in the early twentieth century, rights to uncultivated areas acquired greater value and were occasionally sold to peasants in search of vacant land. Thus, upon mortgaging his coffee grove in 1911, Marcos Rodríguez Cortés declared, "I established [the grove] at my own expense in a cleared area and in forest [*en un rastrojo y derechos de montaña*] which I bought from Eustoquio Gutiérrez for 80 bolívares in the year 1905."¹⁰ Similarly, Demitrio Canelón paid Juan Manuel Campos and Raimundo Coronel for access to a cleared area to cultivate, and Francisca Rodríguez planted her coffee grove only after buying Manuel María Parra's rights to a patch of forest (*unos derechos de montaña sin cultivar*) and clearing it herself. For at least some members of the peasantry, access to land —even untitled land, outside the estates—now had to be purchased.¹¹

Land scarcity altered another aspect of the peasant economy that had developed in the nineteenth century. Before 1900, the widespread availability of unoccupied land had allowed peasant families to maintain a large degree of economic self-sufficiency from one generation to the next. Adult children had found it possible to leave home and establish their own holdings while their parents were still alive, thus avoiding the prospect of dividing the family holding into small, uneconomical units upon their parents' death. It had also been common for children to establish their holdings on plots contiguous to those of their parents or siblings, which facilitated labor sharing among kin. Such a pattern of expansion, which depended on continual access to unoccupied land, had been vital to the reproduction of Duaca's peasant society in the second half of the nineteenth century.

After the turn of the century, however, land scarcity altered the family settlement pattern. Notarial documents from the early 1900s contain scarcely any examples of peasants establishing groves next to their parents' holdings, and the family-based settlement pattern in general becomes less prevalent than during the nineteenth century. Adult children establishing their own households now had to search further for available land, thus disrupting labor-sharing arrangements with family members who stayed behind. In other cases, they remained at home and continued to work with their parents: there are numerous examples of parents and adult children mortgaging or selling farms that they worked together.[12] By the mid-1910s, if not before, demographic pressure had begun to restrict the ability of peasant households to reproduce themselves from one generation to the next through the traditional pattern of expansion.

Nevertheless, the extent of change should not be exaggerated. In several important ways, peasant life around 1916 continued much as during the nineteenth century. Although population growth and a diminished ecological base were gradually reshaping peasant society, these forces had not yet gathered sufficient strength to produce higher rents, lower wages, or other signs of intense demographic pressure. On Duaca's landed estates, the system of low rents from the nineteenth century—5 or 6 percent of the harvest for coffee groves and one fanega of corn for each hectare of food crops—remained the rule throughout the 1910s and into the early 1920s.[13] It was only around 1925, after the privatization of the resguardos and public lands, that the local elite imposed a new system of rents. Population pressure alone was not sufficient to bring about any radical change in conditions of tenancy.

Moreover, a true demographic crisis would have impelled dramatically greater numbers of peasants to join the wage labor force, thus depressing wages. Unfortunately, documentation concerning wages—and, just as important, prices, which must be taken into account in calculating real wages—is too sketchy to allow any firm conclusions on this point. I have found no documentation of wage rates in the 1910s, but in the early 1930s (that is, during the Depression), day laborers in rural Duaca received 1.5 bolívares a day, a 50 percent rise over the 2 reales (or 1 bolívar) paid in the second half of the nineteenth century.[14] If we use the price of corn as a rough measure of the cost of living, we again confront fragmentary data, but the best available information suggests that changes in the price of corn in Venezuela as a whole between the late nineteenth century and the year 1930 (despite wide fluctuations from year to year) were roughly equivalent to the 50 percent increase in Duaqueños' money wages during the same period.[15] It is thus plausible to suggest that Duaqueños' real wages were holding roughly steady during the period in question, despite growing population. More telling is that shortages of hacienda labor continued to be reported in the press through the 1910s—a surer indication that peasant access to land still restricted the supply of labor to the elite.[16]

Finally, it is worth emphasizing that the changes that occurred in peasant society before 1916 took shape gradually and resulted from what must have been perceived as "natural" forces. Ecological deterioration (in reality a man-made change) and demographic growth created new pressures on the land but did not appear to result from any conscious human design. Moreover, the pressures mounted slowly and produced little change from one year to the next. In several fundamental respects, the peasant world continued as it had during the nineteenth century. Many households still lived primarily from the production of their own farms, wage labor continued to be largely a seasonal activity, real wages remained relatively stable, and rents on private estates remained as low as ever. The privatization of Indian and national lands that began in 1916, therefore, constituted the first fundamental transformation of peasant society to occur in Duaca during the age of coffee. And, rather than resulting gradually from natural forces, the revolution in land tenure was imposed suddenly and by a specific class.

The Privatization of Duaca's Indian Lands

Duaca's resguardos remained under the control of the district's Indian community until 1916, well after Indian lands in most of Venezuela had passed to private ownership. The long delay in privatization resulted primarily from conflicts between Duaca's indigenous community and outsiders who owned extensive haciendas on the resguardos. In the early 1890s, the community had attempted to privatize the resguardos under a law that would have given its members preference in the distribution of land, but the community could not overcome the opposition of Cipriano Bracho, one of the largest non-Indian hacendados on the resguardos. In the ensuing struggle, Bracho and the community had fought to a stalemate, and there the matter remained for the rest of the century.

In 1904, the national government established a new law, which revised the process for privatizing Venezuela's remaining Indian lands. The new legislation abandoned the precedent of giving preference to members of indigenous communities in the distribution of resguardo lands. Under the 1904 statute, all de facto occupants of the resguardos, regardless of their ethnic origin, would receive title to the land they occupied. Thus the 1904 law, to a greater extent than previous statutes, simply legitimated the existing pattern of occupation on the resguardos and removed the objections of non-Indian hacendados such as Bracho. In drafting the legislation, lawmakers clearly intended to expedite the privatization of Venezuela's few remaining Indian lands.

In Duaca there was no move to begin division of the resguardos until 1910. The timing of privatization resulted as much from local factors as from the new national law. In 1908, a series of conflicts broke out concerning the boundaries between the resguardos and adjacent estates. In several instances, estate owners encroached on community land and attempted to expel the peasant occupants. In another dispute, Juan Bautista Pacheco Romano initiated a lawsuit against Aurelio Giménez Méndez (whose brother Avelino was co-owner of the Los Chipas estate), claiming that Giménez owned coffee groves on his estate but refused to pay rent. Giménez responded that his hacienda was within the resguardo boundaries, and in early 1910 the district judge ruled in his favor.[17] Pacheco Romano, however, appealed the case to the state court. With the appeal still pending, Giménez instigated a broadly based movement to privatize the resguardos, clearly hoping that in the process he would gain title to the disputed land under his hacienda.

Giménez, who was born and raised in the district of Quibor and arrived in Duaca around 1890, could not claim membership in Duaca's Indian community, but following the passage of the 1904 law non-Indians had no reason to oppose partition of the resguardos. Indeed, given the struggles against neighboring estate owners, all occupants of the resguardos may have seen privatization—with its promise of individual title to the land they occupied—as the best way to defend their holdings against future usurpation. In a series of meetings between April and December 1910, resguardo occupants gathered in the town of Duaca under Giménez's direction and organized a junta to protect the resguardo boundaries and to direct the process of privatization.[18] Giménez himself was named director general of the junta. Other officers included hacendados and merchants who claimed membership in the Indian community, such as Juan Antonio Mollejas (president), Martín Aguilar (vocal, or voting council member), and Juan Bautista Cambero (first vice president). In

August, Juan José Rivero, also a member of the community, reported to Leopoldo Torres that the junta enjoyed "the approval of many people within the [Indian] community."[19] Aside from including Indians and non-Indians, the junta also brought together members of the district's opposing political factions. Giménez was a prominent Hernandista, but Miguel José Tovar, one of the junta's vice presidents, was a leading member of the rival faction led by Eduardo Colmenares and Ramón Antonio Vásquez. Apparently, then, there was broad support for the junta's mission of protecting the resguardo boundaries and partitioning community lands.

The establishment of the junta assured that privatization would, at last, be accomplished. Only after Juan Antonio Mollejas, the junta president, introduced a judicial motion in 1912 to partition the resguardos did occupants come forward to register their farms in accordance with the 1904 law.[20] The junta also kept the process of privatization moving despite conflicts concerning the boundary between the resguardos and surrounding estates.[21] Disputes over the resguardos' true boundaries had paralyzed the attempt at partition in the 1890s, but the junta of the 1910s pushed the process to completion despite ongoing boundary disputes. The privatization of the resguardos was finalized in August 1916 when Duaca's district judge approved the division of land as recommended by the junta.[22]

Members of the junta, however, managed the privatization of community lands in accordance with their own class interests. Under their direction, most of the Duaca resguardos went to a few members of the elite. Table 4 clearly demonstrates the inequality of landownership resulting from the resguardo privatization. At one extreme, nineteen persons received lots ranging from 100 to almost 1,600 hectares, encompassing a total of 6,808.31 hectares. By contrast, the poorest seventy-six recipients, who gained title to plots of up to 20 hectares, received a total of only 644.75 hectares.

Some of the largest tracts received in the privatization derived from claims predating the partition. Juan Antonio Mollejas, the junta president, received title to most of his 1,092.11 hectares because he had purchased rights to community lands originally privatized in the 1850s.[23] Other large tracts were purchased from the junta well before the partition was completed in 1916. Beginning in 1913, the junta sold several large lots of community land to private owners, ostensibly to raise money to hire lawyers and surveyors. Thus Clemente Alvarado, the junta's treasurer, received title to 1,007.20 hectares, and Cipriano Bracho, who had obstructed partition in the 1890s, purchased 319.33 hectares from the junta at the unusually low price of one bolívar (the

Table 4. Land Distribution in the Partition of Duaca's Resguardos

Amount of Land Received (hectares)	No. of Recipients	Total Land (hectares)
1–5	27	74.20
5–20	49	570.55
20–50	34	1,092.83
50–100	12	807.92
100–200	8	1,198.37
200–500	8	2,345.73
over 500	3	3,264.21
Total	141	9,353.81

Source: RPEL, PDC, pro. 1, esc. 7, fols. 6–11, October 16, 1916.

Note: In addition, 394.74 hectares within the resguardos were set aside for towns and roads.

equivalent of two reales) per hectare. In the junta's other sales, Miguel Oberto, a prominent Barquisimeto merchant and politician, bought 180 hectares, and Isidro Ruíz, a local hacendado, purchased 162 hectares. In the partition itself, political influence apparently led to the alienation of other large tracts. Argenis Azuaje, a pillar of the Gomecista regime in Barquisimeto, received 588.16 hectares; Eduardo Colmenares, the political boss who served as jefe civil through much of the 1910s, received 228.75 hectares; and Aurelio Giménez, the junta's director, received 163.64 hectares. Clearly, most of Duaca's Indian lands were converted into large estates owned by members of the local and regional elite.[24]

Within these new estates were the holdings of many peasants who never received title to the land they occupied, despite the intent of the 1904 law under which the resguardos were privatized. Notary records contain numerous indications of resguardo occupants being converted into tenants during the partition. In late 1914, for example, Antonio Perdomo and his children mortgaged "a coffee grove in lands that used to belong to the Indigenous Community, and today are adjudicated to the attorney Domingo A. Yépez," who received forty-five hectares of resguardo land for legal assistance in the partition. Tomás Rojas suffered a similar fate. The founder of a small coffee grove in Agua Viva, Rojas registered a title for his holding in 1912 but never received title to the land he occupied. Instead, his plot was enclosed in the 320 hectares sold by the junta to Cipriano Bracho.[25] It is impossible to specify how many resguardo occupants were enclosed in the new estates created by the partition, but the available documentation suggests that hundreds of households were denied title to the land they occupied. In a number of cases, occupants' failure to contribute to the cost of surveying the resguardos provided a pretext for granting title to someone who could pay the appropriate fee.[26] Regardless of the particular means employed, and whatever the precise number of affected households, many occupants of the resguardos now found themselves living as tenants on private estates.

Although the partition of the resguardos was primarily the work of the junta led by Aurelio Giménez Méndez, Juan Antonio Mollejas, and others, final authority over the partition was held by the district judge, Leoncio Guillén. Himself a member of the local elite, Guillén acted to facilitate and support the junta's work rather than to enforce the laws that ostensibly regulated the partition. Guillén raised no objection when the junta's division of the resguardos left many occupants without title, thus violating the intent of the 1904 law. He also failed to enforce a 1912 statute establishing that all resguardos not privatized by July 4, 1914, would be reclassified as *ejidos* (lands controlled by the district council). Mollejas asked the court on July 20, 1914, to exempt the junta from the deadline because unusually heavy rains had delayed the surveying of the resguardos.[27] Guillén agreed, disingenuously ruling that an 1885 resguardo law could be used to justify the exemption.[28] Thus, despite national laws regulating the privatization of the resguardos, Duaca's local elite —acting through the junta, which in turn received unconditional support from Guillén—remained free to carry out the partition on its own terms.

The privatization of the resguardos did not provoke organized peasant resistance, but it did create lasting tensions between peasant occupants and their new landlords, as two conflicts from the 1920s illustrate.[29] The disputes involved former resguardo lands claimed by estate owners but occupied by peasants—Trina Méndez and Manuela Camero—who refused to recognize their landlords' dominion. In each case, the landowner presented his titles (originating in the 1916 partition) to the district judge and requested that the court uphold his authority over the occupants. In response, Méndez and Camero asserted their own rights to the land they occupied. The two peasant women based their claims on the tradition of usufruct rights that had prevailed before the 1916 partition. Méndez claimed a right to her plot on the basis of her continual occupation since 1902 and also referred to her membership in Duaca's indigenous community. Camero similarly attempted to defend access to her plot by claiming membership in the community and by arguing that her mother had occupied the land for more than forty years before passing it to her. Both occupants, then, continued to view land rights in terms of the traditions that had regulated access to the resguardos before privatization. These traditions, which centered on the principle of usufruct, had lost all legal force once the partition was carried out, but the cases demonstrate how doggedly peasants cleaved to the principle, even after privatization. The judge paid no heed to the arguments made by Méndez and Camero; he ruled that they were tenants on private estates and ordered them to come to terms with their landlords. Clearly, only private title could guarantee rights to land on what had been Duaca's resguardos.

The Privatization of Duaca's Public Lands

With the demise of the Indian community lands, only the baldíos—public lands controlled by the national government—remained open to free peasant occupation. Between 1919 and 1923, however, huge expanses of Duaca's baldíos were granted to private owners, thus continuing the assault against the district's peasantry that had begun with the partition of the resguardos. In 1919 alone, 14,425 hectares of national lands in Duaca were privatized. Between 1920 and 1923, a roughly equivalent area of Duaca's baldíos passed to private owners. Although these lands had been settled by peasant migrants, most of the privatized baldíos were acquired in large lots by members of the district elite. As in the partition of the resguardos, most of the peasants who occupied Duaca's national lands were forced to live as tenants on newly created private estates.

Given the widespread alienation of baldíos in Venezuela under the Gómez regime (1908–1935), the experience of Duaca's public land occupants was probably far from unique. Almost immediately after seizing power, Gómez sought to accelerate the alienation of public lands as a means of stimulating agricultural development. Legal reforms in 1909 and 1910 facilitated the sale of baldíos and increased from fifteen to two hundred hectares the area that individuals could receive in free grants. Moreover, the political stability imposed by Gómez, in contrast to the upheavals of the previous decades, proved conducive to the orderly processing of petitions for national land. The result was dramatic. The annual rate of privatization in Venezuela increased from 11,984.68 to 116,519.34 hectares between 1910 and 1914. Much of the public land alienated during this period was located in remote, sparsely populated states; the southern state of Bolívar alone accounted for over one-fourth of all lands privatized between 1910 and 1914. By contrast, the central coastal zone, long a center of settlement and economic activity, accounted for less than 1 percent of the public lands privatized during the same period, undoubtedly because most land there was already privately owned. Nevertheless, between 1910 and 1914 the government alienated almost one hundred thousand hectares in the western states of Zulia and Trujillo, which, like Lara, had experienced rapid growth in population and agricultural production since the end of the Federal War. In all regions, the privatized land passed to a few owners, creating new large estates. Although we lack figures for public land grants and sales during the entire period of the Gomecista dictatorship, the alienation of baldíos clearly continued at a significant (albeit decreasing) rate through the 1920s.[30]

In Duaca, where only a few hundred hectares of baldíos had been privatized since the 1870s, large expanses of land still formed part of the public domain when Gómez seized power in 1908. As table 5 demonstrates, the alienation of Duaca's public lands under Gómez began in 1913 and continued until 1929 but was most concentrated in the period between 1919 and 1923. It is impossible to specify how many hectares within the district were privatized during the dictatorship because two large grants in 1923, totaling 11,379.80 hectares, extended northward into Distrito Urdaneta, and documents relating to the two grants do not indicate how many hectares were located in each district. Nevertheless, an examination of the boundaries of the two tracts suggests that at least half of the area (5,689.9 hectares) was within Duaca's jurisdiction. If so, then at least 28,100.13 hectares of national lands were privatized in the district between 1913 and 1929. Almost all the land was classified as agricultural; only 711 hectares were classified as grazing land. Also, only 545 hectares of baldíos were privatized through sale in Duaca during the Gómez dictatorship (in 1929). The remainder passed to private owners through grants rather than sales, although grant recipients had to pay fees for surveys and titles.

Public land grants in Duaca illustrate, at the local level, two aspects of the Gómez dictatorship that have often been noted by scholars discussing the regime as a national political system. First, historians commonly emphasize the abuses and fraud that accompanied public land transactions under Gómez, and the experience of Duaca's peasantry supports their assertions.[31] Throughout the Gómez dictatorship, public land laws continued the nineteenth-century tradition of giving the current occupants preference in the acquisition of their plots, offering them free title to the land they cultivated plus an equivalent area of forest for future expansion. In practice, however, Duaca's public lands passed almost exclusively into the hands of the elite, and peasant occupants rarely received title to the areas they cultivated.

Table 5. Public Land Grants and Sales in Distrito Crespo Under Gómez, 1908–1935

Year of Grant or Sale	No. of Recipients	Area (hectares)
1913	1	48.00
1914	1	80.00
1917	1	195.90
1917	6	378.00
1919	1	82.62
1919	2	80.90
1919	1	165.60
1919	6	413.90
1919	5	615.60
1919	24	4,743.00
1919	44	8,324.00
1920	1	185.00
1920	25	4,583.83
1921	5	905.94
1921	3	711.00
1921	1	100.15
1923	1	92.75
1923	1	159.04
1923	40	6,629.20[a]
1923	28	4,750.60[a]
1929	3	545.00

Source: Registro Principal del Estado Lara, Protocolos del Distrito Crespo, 1908–1935.

a. Includes an unspecified area of land in Distrito Urdaneta.

Second, the privatization of Duaca's baldíos illustrates the patrimonial style of administration so often attributed to Gomecista functionaries. Members of the regime, historians maintain, treated the nation and its resources as means for their personal enrichment, using the increasingly centralized power of the state to exploit and appropriate the nation's wealth on an unprecedented scale.[32] Indeed, Gomecistas with influence at the state and district levels carried out the privatization of Duaca's national lands largely to advance their private economic interests. To be sure, many within Duaca's elite benefited from the privatization of baldíos, but those with close ties to the regime gained the most.

The five large collective grants between 1919 and 1923 that accounted for the great majority of land privatized in Duaca all followed a similar pattern. In each grant, over twenty recipients received title to more than four thousand hectares of baldíos. Each recipient gained ownership of a plot of land measuring between 150 and 200 hectares, the upper figure being the largest grant of free land allowed by law. The recipients ranged from prominent members of the local elite to illiterate peasants. In reality, though, most never exercised control over the lands to which they gained title. Within months of each grant, most or all of the recipients were obliged to cede their lands to one or two influential individuals, who thus acquired ownership of several thousand hectares. The new owners, who may be called brokers, then sold the land to its definitive owners, usually members of the local elite, who often acquired hundreds and even thousands of hectares. The final distribution of privatized land, then, was determined by the system of brokered sales and re-sales and bore no resemblance to the distribution outlined in the original grants from the national government.

The activities of three public land brokers—Miguel José Tovar, Domingo Antonio Yépez, and José Luis Pérez—will serve as focal points for a closer examination of the process through which Duaca's public lands were distributed. Their activities make clear that land privatization in Duaca was a profoundly political process. Public land brokers were important figures in state and local politics, and those to whom they sold land were also men of political influence. The privatization of Duaca's baldíos thus illustrates how a centralized, well-integrated state could control Venezuela's resources and distribute them among those loyal to the regime.

One of Duaca's most active land brokers was Miguel José Tovar, an aging general who had fought in the civil wars at the turn of the century under the command of Eduardo Colmenares. In his chronicle of life in Duaca in the early twentieth century, Rómulo Delgado Segura also identifies Tovar as a close friend of Ramón Antonio Vásquez, Duaca's jefe civil throughout most of the 1920s and another of Colmenares's generals.[33] Moreover, Tovar served on the junta that oversaw the partition of Duaca's resguardos and held a seat on Duaca's district council in the late 1910s. He undoubtedly exercised considerable influence in district politics.

In 1920–1921, Tovar acted as broker in the redistribution of a large collective grant in the eastern part of the district. The grant was issued by the national government on July 30, 1920, giving twenty-five individuals title to 4,583.83 hectares of public land along the Duaca-Aroa road. Four months later, all twenty-five "recipients" ceded their land to Tovar, who then divided the entire tract among six individuals.[34] Tovar sold the largest portion (thirteen hundred hectares) to David Gimón, a resident of the north-central state of Miranda, whose father, General David Gimón, was a close associate of Gómez and served as president of Lara between 1916 and 1920.[35]

State presidents were required to approve petitions for public land grants before they passed to the national government, and Gimón's tenure coincided with several large grants of baldíos in Duaca, including the one brokered by Tovar. The general's son, however, only retained his land in Duaca until 1925, when he sold it to Ramón Antonio Vásquez, Duaca's jefe civil and Tovar's friend. Vásquez had already purchased 100 hectares directly from Tovar, so in all he came to control 1,400 hectares, roughly 30 percent of the land in the original grant. Tovar sold another 1,000 hectares to Leoncio Guillén, the Duaca merchant who served as district judge during most of the 1910s. Carlos José Guillén, a Barquisimeto merchant, also purchased 1,000 hectares from Tovar. Hermelindo Oberto, a merchant and hacendado who, in the 1890s, had been one of the leaders of the movement to elevate Duaca to a district, and who had served on Duaca's district council in 1912–1913, purchased 800 hectares. Finally, Tovar sold the remaining 383.83 hectares to Domingo Antonio Yépez, another public land broker, who later divided the tract between Casimiro Casamayor and Pedro Javier, two Duaca entrepreneurs.[36]

Tovar did not appear to profit financially from his role as a land broker: he acquired the tract at ten bolívares per hectare and sold it at the same rate. Nevertheless, he clearly benefited from the public land bonanza in other ways. Aside from receiving his own grant of 185 hectares directly from the government, Tovar purchased a total of 2,253.65 hectares from other public land brokers between 1919 and 1924, of which he resold only 980 hectares.[37] Through the privatization of Duaca's baldíos, Tovar became one of the largest landowners in the district.

Another of Duaca's public land brokers was Domingo Antonio Yépez, who, like Tovar, had already played a role in directing the resguardo partition when he turned his attention to the district's baldíos. A lawyer by education, Yépez occupied a series of positions in state government during the Gómez dictatorship.[38] Yépez's successful political career attests to his connections to Lara's prominent Gomecistas, and because of these connections he was frequently employed by private citizens who sought concessions from the state government. Thus between 1912 and 1916, dozens of people (including Tovar) hired Yépez to help them secure title to public lands in Duaca and the neighboring municipality of Bobare.[39] That so many people seeking title to public land chose Yépez as their representative attests to his reputation as a facilitator within the state government.

Between 1919 and 1923, Yépez acted as a broker in three large collective grants in Duaca. He began by providing some financial backing for each of the grants; in at least two cases he hired the surveyor.[40] As a result, many of the land recipients owed money to Yépez when they received their titles, and transferred most or all of their land to him in payment.[41] Yépez thus gained title to at least 7,360 hectares from the three grants, which totaled 19,703.8 hectares. (Other brokers also acquired lands from these grants, two of which included land in Distrito Urdaneta.) When he resold the land, Yépez was often represented by José Luis Pérez, a resident of Barquisimeto who served as inspector of public lands for the state of Lara in 1918 and 1922.[42] In addition to periodically representing Yépez, Pérez acted as a land broker on his own account, acquiring over six thousand hectares. Yépez and Pérez sold most of the land they acquired to members of the Duaca and Barquisimeto elite in large tracts ranging from two hundred to almost fifteen hundred hectares.[43] Neither broker retained title to much, if any, land in Duaca. They simply acted as intermediaries in the transfer of national lands to members of the elite, allowing prominent individuals to acquire lands far in excess of the two-hundred-hectare limit established in the public land laws.

Peasant families occupied much of the land sold by Yépez, Pérez, Tovar, and other brokers. In a few rare instances, brokers allowed small and medium cultivators to purchase the plots they occupied. For example, four occupants in Caraquitas, the site of an 8,324-hectare grant in 1919, purchased plots of between 5 and 15 hectares each.[44] It was more common, however, that land occupied by peasants passed to the well-to-do. Members of the elite owning haciendas on the baldíos purchased not only the land under their own holdings, but also contiguous plots occupied by peasant families. In one instance, Yépez, upon selling 106.40 hectares to Francisco Rafael Fonseca, declared:

> Within this lot, aside from the crops belonging to the buyer, señor Fonseca, there are coffee groves and food crops belonging to Victor José Colmenares, Luciencia Márquez, Juan Santana López, Eufemia Agüero, José Luis Delgado, Daniel Antonio Lobos, and part of those belonging to Hermelindo González, which remain the property of their owners, since I sell to señor Fonseca only the land which they occupy.

When selling land to Ramón Antonio Vásquez, Yépez specified that part of the lot was occupied by "Juan Canelón, Lorenzo Peroza, Francisco Prado, Edmundo Valenzuela, Tomás Marchán, Manuel Tua, and others." In these and similar cases, the land sold by brokers became private estates, in which the landowner cultivated part of the estate directly and rented out other plots to peasant tenants.[45]

The network of political influence behind the privatization of Duaca's baldíos clearly extended to the state presidents, who had to approve all public land grants before they passed to the national government for final consideration. The largest grants in Duaca coincided with the administration of two state presidents closely associated with Gómez, General David Gimón (1916–1920) and General Rafael María Velasco (1921–1925). An important caudillo in his native state of Guárico, Gimón had rebelled against Castro during the Libertadora (1901–1903), but he supported Gómez when the latter seized power in 1908 and was rewarded with a series of important posts. Aside from his term as president of Lara, Gimón governed the states of Guárico and Bolívar and served as chief customs collector (a potentially lucrative position, given the opportunities for graft) in La Guaira and Maracaibo. Velasco's ties to Gómez were even older and stronger than those of Gimón. A native of Táchira and a distant relative of Gómez, Velasco served as an officer under Castro and Gómez during their successful revolution in 1899. After administering the customhouses in Ciudad Guyana, Puerto Cabello, and La Guaira, Velasco was named president of the state of Aragua in 1918. After leaving the presidency of Lara in 1925, he became governor of the Federal District.[46] As trusted servants of Gómez enjoying considerable influence within the regime, Gimón and Velasco could approve grants without fear that they would be blocked by the congress or the president himself.

Both Velasco and Gimón received compensation for their approval of public land grants in Duaca. While Gimón's son acquired 1,300 hectares from a broker, Gimón himself purchased 2,026.15 hectares from a different broker, and Velasco bought 1,000 hectares from a third intermediary. Clearly, the state presidents worked hand in glove with the brokers and extracted their share of the spoils. Nevertheless, Gimón, his son, and Velasco sold their lands in Duaca in 1925, and each accepted a price below what he had paid for the land.[47] Given the rapid development of Venezuela's petroleum industry after World War I, it seems plausible that they had acquired the land on a speculative basis, hoping to discover oil (and collecting rents from agriculturalists in the meantime) but losing interest when none was found.[48] Whatever their rationale, Gimón and Velasco both had personal stakes in the partition of Duaca's baldíos and both used their office to pursue entrepreneurial interests.

Other prominent Gomecistas in Lara also shared in the bounty of Duaca's national lands. General José Garbi, who served as jefe civil of Barquisimeto during much of the Gómez dictatorship and who owned several agricultural enterprises in Duaca and in the neighboring municipality of Bobare, is one example.[49] In transactions with Duaca's public land brokers, Garbi purchased 974 hectares near the western edge of the district, contiguous to his estate La Escalera.[50] Garbi acquired another 763 hectares of privatized land, also bordering La Escalera, from four individuals who received the land in a 1921 grant.[51] Similarly, General Argenis Azuaje, an occasional business partner of Gómez described in the Barquisimeto press as "a well-known figure in the politics of Lara and an irreproachable friend of [state] President David Gimón," acquired 158 hectares from a public land broker.[52] This tract was contiguous to the 588 hectares Azuaje had already received in the partition of Duaca's Indian lands. The privatization of Duaca's public lands thus allowed Garbi and Azuaje—two of the state's leading Gomecistas—to expand their estates.

Political influence also shaped the distribution of Duaca's baldíos among the elite residing within the district. None benefited more from the privatization of the baldíos than Ramón Antonio Vásquez, Duaca's jefe civil throughout most of the 1920s. In addition to the 1,400 hectares of land that he acquired in the grant brokered by Miguel José Tovar, Vásquez bought 758.49 hectares of prime coffee land in Camburito from another broker in 1920 and received his own grant of 136.60 hectares directly from the government.[53] Tovar (a close associate of Vásquez) and Leoncio Guillén (the district judge) also acquired large amounts of land through brokered sales. Many members of Duaca's elite acquired lots of a hundred hectares or more through public land grants and subsequent sales. When the rush to privatize the district's baldíos subsided in the mid-1920s, virtually every member of the local elite had become a landowner. But, as a rule, the largest tracts went to men closely linked to the dictatorship.

The privatization of Duaca's public lands demonstrated to the local elite the benefits of centralized political authority. Members of Duaca's elite had petitioned the state for sales of public land in the late nineteenth century, only to see a number of their requests languish in the hands of the authorities. The tumultuous politics of the decades before Gómez, characterized by frequent civil wars and by tensions between state and national authorities, made it difficult to push a request for land through the bureaucracy.

After the Libertadora Revolution (1901–1903), however, the increasingly powerful national army relegated caudillo warfare to the past, state presidents became loyal agents of central authority rather than guardians of regional interests, and an integrated system of national power was forged. Under Gómez, positions at all levels of government were reserved for so-called *amigos de la causa* (friends of the cause), men loyal to Gómez. By the mid-1910s (the period that witnessed the consolidation of the Gomecista state), this well-articulated political structure had fastened its hold on the nation and its resources to an extent beyond the means of the fractured, caudillo-ridden governments of the nineteenth century.[54] Gómez built the system first of all as an instrument of repression and political control, but the same system provided those loyal to the regime with connections to the center, which guaranteed that their petitions—including those for baldíos—would be heeded.

The Imposition of New Rental Conditions

With the privatization of Duaca's resguardos and baldíos, prominent Duaqueños, as a class, controlled access to land throughout virtually the entire district. As a result, the balance of power between landlord and peasant was altered forever. One manifestation of this shifting balance of power was the imposition of harsh conditions of tenancy by the landed class. Before the widespread privatization of land, rents on Duaca's estates had remained low in order to attract tenants. But by the mid-1920s, the great majority of peasants no longer had any alternative to settlement on private estates. Access to land now depended on coming to terms with a landlord, and the local elite soon took advantage of this new source of power.

In the mid-1920s, landowners ended the traditional system of rents-in-kind, which had prevailed on Duaca's estates since the nineteenth century, and established a new system of cash rents. Whereas the old system had favored tenants, the new cash rents clearly favored landowners. Under the old system, tenants had paid 5 or 6 percent of their harvest for land planted in coffee. Not only was the percentage low, the actual quantity of coffee paid in rent fluctuated with the quantity of the harvest, so that tenants owed less in years of low harvests. The cash value of rents rose and fell in a similar way with the changing value of coffee, which meant that tenants and landlords shared the consequences of falling prices. For land planted in food crops, tenants had paid one fanega of corn per hectare, an arrangement that granted tenants some protection against low prices, though none against poor harvests. On the whole, the old system had divided the risks inherent in agricultural production between landowner and tenant.

By contrast, the system of cash rents introduced around 1925 guaranteed landlords a safe profit while shifting risk entirely to tenants.[55] Estate owners now demanded between twenty-four and thirty-six bolívares per hectare for land planted in mature coffee bushes, regardless of the harvest or the market price of the crop. Coffee groves too young to produce a harvest, which had been rent-free under the old system, were now assessed at the rate of eighteen bolívares per hectare. Most tenants still paid in kind for land planted in food crops, but the rate rose from 184 to 276 kilograms of corn per hectare. Moreover, landowners now demanded that tenants pay rent at the beginning of the year rather than later, after the harvest. Since coffee farmers usually delivered their crop to merchants in February or March, rental payments in January would find tenants at the leanest part of the year. The imposition of the new schedule would also subject tenants to a one-time payment of two rental charges (that is, March and January) from the earnings of a single harvest.[56] Thus, landowners in Duaca pushed home the advantages created by a transformed agrarian structure, like the English landlords who doubled or tripled rents following the enclosure of common lands.[57]

Landowners established the new rental conditions simply by writing new *reglamentos* (regulations) for their estates and submitting them, as required by state law, to the jefe civil for approval. Once approved by the jefe civil, the new reglamentos governed relations between the landowner and all those occupying land within his estate. At least one elite observer, Leopoldo Torres, the former president of Lara who now practiced law in Barquisimeto, lamented the passing of the traditional system of rents (which he deemed "rational and equitable") and believed that jefes civiles should refuse to approve new regulations that imposed unfair burdens on tenants. But Duaca's jefe civil during the 1920s, Ramón Antonio Vásquez, who acquired several large estates during the privatization of the district's baldíos, readily endorsed the new regulations and soon imposed the new system on his own tenants as well.[58]

The combination of massive land privatization and new, more onerous rents changed peasant life throughout the district. Families who had occupied the resguardos or baldíos suffered the forced transition to estate tenancy, and peasants who had long resided on estates found themselves hard-pressed to meet the new rents. These changes, unlike those resulting from gradual population increase and ecological degradation, were relatively sudden, dramatic, and could be attributed directly to the local elite and their allies outside the district.

But even greater hardship was soon thrust upon the peasantry. The price of coffee declined sharply in 1929 and continued to tumble downward during the early and mid-1930s as the world sank into the Great Depression (see table 6). The 1935 export price of 33.08 bolívares per 60 kilograms represented a decrease of almost 75 percent in relation to the 1928 price of 129.98 bolívares. Finally, as though to make the calamity complete, a series of severe droughts struck Duaca in the early 1930s.[59] The full injustice of the new rents was thus revealed, as tenants were obliged to continue paying landlords the same rents from one year to the next, without any compensation for the double blow of poor harvests and plummeting coffee prices.

Landlord-Tenant Conflict

One can readily imagine peasants' outrage at the abuses that accompanied Duaca's agrarian transformation. Given the repressive strength of the Gómez regime, though, peasants realized that coordinated, large-scale resistance would be suicidal. Many Duaqueños nonetheless sought less dramatic ways of blunting or delaying the new hardships imposed upon them. Most important, dozens of peasant households resisted the new order of privatized land

Table 6. Prices for Venezuelan Coffee Exports, 1910–1935

	Price per 60-Kilogram Sack (bolívares)		*Price per 60-Kilogram Sack (bolívares)*
1910	69.60	1923	99.43
1911	85.04	1924	135.12
1912	85.64	1925	143.23
1913	71.34	1926	129.34
1914	60.76	1927	122.06
1915	61.43	1928	129.98
1916	61.96	1929	97.78
1917	51.32	1930	74.43
1918	83.82	1931	66.80
1919	137.60	1932	68.98
1920	72.86	1933	47.75
1921	75.68	1934	38.19
1922	87.25	1935	33.08

Source: Miguel Izard, *Series estadísticas para la historia de Venezuela* (Mérida: Universidad de los Andes, 1970), 164–65.

and harsher rents by refusing to make the payments demanded by their land-lords. In response, between 1923 and 1935, landowners in Duaca filed thirty-two legal actions against estate tenants who refused to pay rent. Twenty of these court cases (almost two-thirds) originated on estates composed of for-mer public lands that had been privatized under Gómez, compared to only four on estates composed of former resguardo land, and eight on the older es-tates of Los Chipas and the Generals' Estate. So, while peasants throughout the district resisted landlord authority, conflict was centered on the recently privatized public lands.

Landlords prevailed in all thirty-two cases, and most of the disputes fol-lowed a similar course. In many instances, a summons to appear before the judge proved sufficient to persuade the peasant tenants to pay rent. If not, the landowner had only to present the title to his land for the judge to rule in his favor. If the tenants still refused to comply, the judge ordered that their hold-ings be seized for sale at auction. Thus the district court played an important role in imposing the new order of privatized land and cash rents.

Tenants who offered some defense before the judge indicated, directly or indirectly, the importance of land privatization, new rents, and increasing poverty in creating the surge of landlord-tenant conflict. Remigio Lozada, a tenant on the estate of Los Chipas, explained that he refused to pay rent for his young coffee grove because it had not yet begun to produce a harvest. In-deed, under the pre-1925 system of rents, Lozada's young grove would have been rent-free until it entered production. But upon confronting Lozada in court, Leopoldo Camejo, the owner of Los Chipas, pointed out that his new regulations established a tariff of eighteen bolívares per hectare for young coffee groves. Lozada recognized that further resistance was fruitless and came to terms with Camejo.[60] In four other suits, the defendants claimed to lack sufficient resources to satisfy their landlords' demands.[61] Only one such de-fendant actually lost part of his holding for unpaid rents.[62] The others reached an accommodation with their landlords soon after their holdings had been embargoed for judicial auction; apparently these desperate tenants managed, at the last moment, to borrow enough money to pay what they owed in rents.

But most tenants who resisted rental payments did not plead poverty, nor did they protest against particular provisions in the reglamentos. Rather, they raised the more fundamental issue of whether their landlord was the legiti-mate owner of the land they occupied. Following privatization, some occu-pants of Duaca's Indian lands (as we have seen) challenged the authority of their new landlords by appealing to the tradition of usufruct rights that had long guaranteed the peasantry's access to community land. These appeals, however, carried no legal force once the resguardos had passed to private ownership, and resguardo occupants had little choice but to acknowledge the authority of their new landlords. Peasant resistance to rent collection on the privatized baldíos was also informed by the tradition of usufruct rights that had guaranteed peasant access to land during the long period before privatization.

Of particular interest are Juan Esteban Cordero and Nicomedes Castillo, two peasants who opposed landlords for years after the public land they occupied in Camburito was privatized. The area they cultivated passed to private ownership in 1919, and a broker later sold it to Ramón Antonio Vásquez. By early 1926, Vásquez had come into conflict with several occupants, including Cordero and Castillo, who refused to pay rent for the plots they occupied.[63] Despite Vásquez's position as jefe civil, which involved command of the police, the peasants would not accept his dominion without a struggle. They acceded to Vásquez's demands only after being brought before the district judge and threatened with the loss of their holdings. When the Great Depression struck, Cordero and Castillo again refused to pay rent and again were called before the judge.[64] Castillo quickly reached an agreement with Vásquez, but Cordero resisted longer, protesting that his holding was really on public land (even though all of Camburito and the surrounding area had been privatized in 1919). The judge ignored the statement and ordered Cordero to pay court costs as well as rents. Cordero was obliged to cede part of his farm to Vásquez in order to settle accounts.

Nevertheless, Castillo and Cordero soon saw a new opportunity to oppose landlord authority. In 1933, Vásquez sold his estate in Camburito to Jorge Zoghby, an Arab immigrant.[65] Four tenants on the estate, including Castillo and Cordero, refused to pay rent to Zoghby, perhaps believing that he would prove a less formidable opponent than Vásquez. Zoghby, however, quickly filed a legal action against them. When they appeared in court, the tenants refused to recognize Zoghby as the rightful owner of the land they occupied. They explained to the judge:

> In that region, we were virtually the first inhabitants, and we have always lived in the knowledge that the land we cultivate belongs to the Nation. It has never come to our knowledge that any person has acquired ownership of these lands and it would be wrong for us to recognize any dominion except for that of the Nation.[66]

The defendants, then, believed that their long occupation of the area entitled them to continue working the land free from landlord control. Whether they knew that national law gave public land occupants preference in the acquisition of their plots is unclear. But they certainly held to the conviction that no private individual had a moral claim to the land stronger than that of the original settlers.

Peasants in other parts of the district shared their outlook. In La Titiara, another area visited by privatization in 1919, a similar conflict occurred between Homobono Rivero, who purchased 145 hectares from a broker, and Modesto Rodríguez, a longtime occupant of the land. Rodríguez, whose eight-hectare farm included coffee groves, food crops, pasture, and two houses, had no intention of recognizing Rivero's claim to the land. Between 1925 and 1929, Rodríguez steadfastly ignored demands for rent, despite several encounters with persons sent by Rivero to persuade him to pay. Finally, in early 1930, as the depression deepened, Rivero initiated a lawsuit against Rodríguez, demanding that he pay 2,835 bolívares for five years' rent. Rodríguez refused, because

> in the twenty-two years that I have lived in the hamlet of Titiara, . . . where I have established my properties which are mentioned in this lawsuit, all of them with my own effort and personal labor, I have never been disturbed or troubled by anyone until now, when I have been disturbed and injured by the lawsuit attempted against me. Land surveys and topographical charts made by one man cannot take away what another has gained by his own work.[67]

Rodríguez went on to claim that the land he occupied was baldío but asserted that, even if the national government had alienated the land, his long occupation should guarantee his right to the area he cultivated. Thus Rodríguez, like the peasants in Camburito (and in other parts of the district where public lands were privatized)[68] asserted the primacy of usufruct rights long after privatization had deprived such rights of their legal force.

Quite clearly, Duaca's peasantry and elite, like opposed classes in other settings, adhered to different notions of property rights.[69] For the elite, landownership was conferred by a formal title granted by the previous owner and entered in the district registry. In the eyes of the peasantry, however, rights to land had more to do with its occupation and use. In effect, peasants viewed property rights primarily through the lens of custom. For generations, access to land on Duaca's public domain and resguardos had remained relatively unfettered, a matter of de facto occupation. Those who cleared and planted a given area enjoyed usufruct rights over the land until they sold their holding (that is, crops, buildings, and other improvements) or passed it on to their heirs. As long as the land remained public, this customary system of usufruct coincided with law and hence with the elite's view of property rights. But when privatization occurred, the two notions of property came into conflict. Members of the elite acquired legal title to the land but the peasantry, who rarely had an opportunity to acquire title during privatization, refused to believe that mere papers could negate their customary rights as occupants. When members of the elite demanded that they begin to pay rent for land they had long occupied, peasants on the former baldíos saw themselves as victims of a blatant fraud.

The privatization of the resguardos and baldíos, the enclosure of peasant farms by the owners of Los Chipas and Limoncito, and the imposition of new rents, transformed the agrarian structure of Duaca between the mid-1910s and the mid-1920s. Such sudden dislocation has sparked violent rebellion in other peasant societies. In Duaca, by contrast, popular reaction through 1935 did not go beyond the refusal to pay rent, the occasional tearing down of a landowner's fence,[70] or (in the case of the Giménez family on Limoncito, discussed in the previous chapter) a willingness to withhold or destroy embargoed property rather than surrender it to a landlord. Only in early 1936, shortly after the death of Juan Vicente Gómez, did peasant protest in Duaca feature coordinated action and widespread violence (see chapter 9). As long as the dictator lived, popular resentment in Duaca—and in most rural areas of Venezuela—stopped well short of open rebellion. The only organized movements against Gómez to arise from the countryside were elite-led caudillo rebellions like the one headed by José Rafael Gabaldón in 1929. By the 1920s, the Gomecista army easily crushed such anachronistic revolts.[71] Meanwhile, offenses less serious than armed rebellion could lead to imprisonment, induction into the army, or forced labor on highways under the blazing sun of the llanos. Not without reason, many Venezuelans lived in fear of the regime and its allies. The limited scope of peasant resistance in Duaca, then, was less remarkable than the courage of many Duaqueños who refused to accept landlord authority until the moment the district judge threatened to seize their farms.[72]

Factors other than the repressive apparatus of the state also worked to prevent the outbreak of open rebellion before 1936. Estate owners in Duaca used sales of land to medium and large tenants to drive a wedge between discontented peasants and their potential allies. In the conflict between the owners of Los Chipas and occupants of the estate's disputed zone, resistance to rent collection was led by members of the elite who, like their peasant neighbors, contended that the land they occupied was public rather than part of the estate. Once the conflict was settled, the estate owners allowed several large tenants to buy the land they occupied, apparently to prevent future confrontations. Similarly, during the years when Duaca's resguardos and baldíos were privatized and the new system of rents imposed, landowners throughout the district frequently allowed medium and large tenants to purchase the land they occupied. Sales of plots measuring twenty-five hectares or more by owners of larger estates were common.[73] More rarely, tenants on smaller plots also acquired title to the land they cultivated.[74] By selectively spreading the benefits of landownership, Duaca's estate owners defused the possibility of cross-class alliances. As a result, resistance to rent collection on Duaca's estates, though common, remained scattered and unorganized to the point that it could be easily contained by landowners and district authorities.

And yet it would be wrong to dismiss the resistance of these years as completely ineffectual. By demonstrating their willingness to confront landlords over issues of land rights and rents, peasants may have given pause to landlords who would have moved further and faster if they had met no resistance at all. As it was, landowners felt wary enough of the peasantry to settle dozens of disputes through the courts, drawing a veil of legality (however transparent) over their actions, rather than ride roughshod over popular sentiment at every turn. Landlords thinking of imposing still higher rents (akin to those in the central coastal zone) or a formal labor obligation on tenants would recall rents withheld, embargoed fields picked clean, embargoed livestock killed, fences destroyed—and they would think again. Even with the support of the Gomecista state, the elite were made to wonder if further impositions might carry a cost they would come to regret. Peasants who, in pursuit of frankly individual goals, resisted and lost may have won a small breathing space for their class.[75]

Changing Relations of Production

The conditions of wage labor on the elite's haciendas had long been shaped by the structure of land tenure in the district and they, too, were dramatically altered during the Gómez era. In the nineteenth century, widespread peasant access to land had limited the supply of wage workers and prevented the elite from establishing firm control over their labor force. But the loss of land and new cash rents made peasant households increasingly dependent on wage labor, diluting their bargaining power vis-à-vis employers. Also, between 1920 and 1926, the district's population rose sharply, from 20,338 to 28,719, an increase of 41 percent in only six years.[76] Such rapid growth must have driven more peasants to look for wage work. As households became ever more dependent on wages earned away from the family farm, and as state power was consolidated both locally and nationally, employers came to control hacienda labor more tightly than ever before.

Whereas hacendados in the nineteenth century relied primarily on *temporales* (temporary workers) drawn from peasant families residing outside the hacienda, by the 1920s *peones fijos* (permanent laborers) residing on the hacendado's land became more common. The origins of such workers can be readily deduced from the trends of the period. Given the growing scarcity of land for new farms, peasants who lost their holdings amid the dire conditions of the 1920s and early 1930s had little opportunity to establish new farms; accepting positions as permanent hacienda workers was one of the few options available to them. In addition to their wages, resident workers received access to small plots of land within the hacienda where they planted food crops, with one-third of the harvest claimed by the hacendado.[77] Totally dependent on the hacienda for their subsistence, permanent workers could be controlled more easily than laborers from outside the hacienda. Temporary workers, for example, often refused to accept work weeding coffee groves, which was backbreaking labor and poorly paid compared to harvest work.[78] Hacendados could now assign such unwelcome tasks to permanent, resident workers rather than bargain with reluctant day laborers.

Resident workers, like the seasonal laborers who continued to be drawn from outside the hacienda, were often in debt to the hacendado. And, by the 1920s, debt peonage had become a more effective system of labor coercion than it had been early in coffee boom. Whereas indebted hacienda workers in the nineteenth century had often escaped their debts, the police commanded by Duaca's jefe civil in the 1920s regularly apprehended indebted workers who attempted to evade their employers. Once captured, the peons were transported (often in fetters) back to their employer's hacienda to fulfill their labor obligations.[79] With labor now effectively immobilized, employers could enforce a harsher work regime. Indebted peons were often forced to work seven days a week, those who failed to complete the entire twelve-hour workday received no wages at all, and many laborers found it impossible to work off their debts. Moreover, some hacendados paid their workers in fichas, tokens that could be exchanged only for goods at the hacendado's store. Although Gómez issued an order in 1911 to end payments in fichas, police in Duaca and throughout much of Venezuela failed to implement the policy. Eulogio Segura Sánchez, a Duaca merchant and landowner who frequently served on the district council and who acquired hundreds of hectares of land in the 1910s and 1920s, paid coffee harvesters in fichas until the end of the dictatorship.[80] On at least some of Duaca's estates, then, a labor regime approaching classic debt peonage emerged during the last fifteen years or so of the Gómez era, with an indebted and immobilized workforce, effective police support, and workers obliged to spend their earnings at hacienda stores.

Duaca's rural working population, we may conclude, became increasingly stratified in terms of access to land and the conditions of labor during the 1920s. The most fortunate among the peasantry had acquired ownership of small or medium plots of land during the privatization of the resguardos and baldíos, but they constituted a small minority. Estate tenants, by contrast, maintained access to land only at an ever greater cost. New rents and, after 1928, low coffee prices and frequent droughts pushed tenant households toward a greater reliance on wages earned off the family farm, and day laborers from peasant households in the 1920s often became enmeshed in a coercive system of debt peonage. At the bottom of the rural hierarchy were the growing numbers of resident hacienda peons who had access only to a small plot of ground for food crops, produced no marketable surplus, and were subject to the labor demands of hacendados throughout the year.

The Progress of the Local Elite

The decade of the 1920s, then, stands out as a turning point in the history of Duaca's peasantry, in that it marked the beginning of a period of unprecedented hardship, which continued through the Great Depression. For the elite, though, the 1920s was a time of exuberant prosperity, a decade that marked the apogee of their economic fortunes. Rómulo Delgado Segura and Angel María Núñez, two members of the local elite who published chronicles of Duaca in 1971, both evoked the 1920s as a kind of golden age in the history of the district.[81] Within the limited perspective of their own class, their view was well founded. Favorable coffee prices during most of the 1920s, together with the extraction of greater surplus from tenants and workers, created a particularly favorable conjuncture for Duaqueño entrepreneurs. Before examining the changes in Duaca's economic structure brought by the depression (see chapter 8), let us briefly examine the progress of Duaca's well-to-do during the decade preceding the crisis.

The prosperity of the local elite during the 1920s is particularly significant because it contradicts those historians who have argued that the rapid development of the nation's oil industry after World War I resulted in the decline of Venezuelan agriculture.[82] Although this process may have taken hold in some regions, Duaca's coffee economy remained strong until the Great Depression, at least in terms of its ability to generate profits for the elite. Annual coffee production within the district remained between fifty and sixty thousand sacks of forty-six kilograms each, approximately the level reached toward the end of the nineteenth century.[83] Loans continued to flow from Duaca merchants to rural producers in return for coffee to be sent on the railroad to the coast. Indeed, Duaca's importance as a regional commercial center increased as transportation to neighboring jurisdictions was improved and producers from outside the district sent their crops to Duaca for shipment to the coast. According to Núñez:

> From the pueblos of Urachiche and Yaritagua in the state of Yaracuy, and from Aguada Grande, Parúpano and Siquisique in Urdaneta District of the state of Lara, long mule trains arrived daily [in Duaca], carrying sacks of coffee to be deposited in the warehouses at the railroad station, and returned with merchandise shipped from Barquisimeto and Puerto Cabello for the aforementioned pueblos.[84]

As in the nineteenth century, members of the local elite invested in all aspects of the coffee economy. Most combined the role of merchant and hacendado, and by the mid-1920s many owned land occupied by peasant tenants as well. Those with sufficient capital also invested in mechanized coffee-processing centers. During the first three decades of the twentieth century, several members of Duaca's elite built extensive enterprises that combined the production, processing, and marketing of coffee. Three such men whose large diversified investments placed them at the pinnacle of Duaqueño society in the 1920s deserve special attention.

Pedro Javier, an Arab immigrant who never learned to read or write Spanish but adopted a Hispanic name, settled in Duaca just after the turn of the century. He began his career as a merchant, extending credit to coffee producers in Duaca and in the neighboring municipality of Bobare. Like most

Duaca merchants, Javier soon expanded his investments to include the ownership of coffee groves.[85] And, like most members of the local elite, Javier became a landowner in the late 1910s and early 1920s. He received a grant of public land in Camburito in 1917, and in the years that followed he purchased thousands of hectares of land scattered throughout Duaca and Bobare.[86] In 1924, Javier became a co-owner of Duaca's principal coffee-processing plant. Later that same year, he and the other owners (Eulogio Segura Sánchez and José Luis Delgado) replaced the plant's nineteenth-century machinery with new equipment imported from Scotland.[87] Javier's investment of over thirty thousand bolívares in the plant reflected his faith in the future of Duaca's coffee economy while the high prices of the 1920s prevailed.

Eulogio Segura Sánchez, one of Javier's partners in the processing plant, followed a somewhat different path to the top of Duaca's coffee economy. Born into a prominent Duaca family, Segura emerged as an important entrepreneur in the 1890s, when, still a young man, he acquired two important sugar and coffee haciendas as well as a merchant enterprise.[88] Segura headed Duaca's municipal government in the mid-1890s and also served as editor on *El Eco del Norte,* one of Duaca's earliest newspapers; he used both positions to promote the idea of elevating Duaca to a district, and he held a seat on Duaca's district council on numerous occasions between 1905 and 1936.[89]

Segura received title to over 400 hectares of prime agricultural land in the partition of Duaca's resguardos in 1916, then acquired 198 hectares through a public land grant in 1919, and bought hundreds of hectares more in the years that followed.[90] To complement his growing productive and commercial enterprises, Segura purchased a share of Duaca's main coffee-processing plant in 1919. Three years later, he established the firm of Segura e Hijos (Segura and Sons), financed with a loan of fifty thousand bolívares from the Banco de Venezuela. As one of Duaca's wealthiest merchants during the 1920s, Segura could afford to make large loans to other members of the local elite. He loaned forty thousand bolívares to Leopoldo Camejo, the owner of the estate of Los Chipas, and twenty-six thousand bolívares to Juan de Dios Valero Yépez, also a large landowner. Segura's diversified investments formed the foundation of a family enterprise that would continue to control much of Duaca's agrarian economy into the 1990s.[91]

Whereas Segura was primarily an entrepreneur who at times participated in local politics, Ramón Antonio Vásquez rose to prominence first through warfare and politics and later used political influence to advance his economic enterprises. Vásquez was at best a small-scale merchant when he followed

Eduardo Colmenares into the Libertadora Revolution in 1901. But, as Colmenares established his political dominance in the district, Vásquez, as his ally, shared in his influence and eventually rose to the position of jefe civil. By the 1910s, Vásquez's merchant enterprise was prospering and he began to invest in the production of livestock and coffee. Vásquez was also among the Gomecistas who profited most from the privatization of Duaca's public lands, and by the early 1920s he had become one of the largest landowners in the district. In 1923, as coffee prices climbed upward, Vásquez further diversified his investments by establishing an electrically powered processing plant in Licua.[92]

He also continued to invest in cattle, an enterprise that attracted a number of Gomecista officials—and Gómez himself—because of their ability to control the local supply and price of beef.[93] No record remains of a formal monopoly to supply Duaca with beef, but Vásquez butchered more cattle for local sale than any other Duaqueño entrepreneur during the 1920s. In at least one year, 1920, he owned more than half of the cattle brought to Duaca's slaughterhouse.[94] Just as Vásquez's political influence facilitated his acquisition of land, so it may have aided him in controlling the local beef market.

In reporting the achievements of Vásquez and others, the press often lauded them as *progresistas,* that is, people who worked for the material progress of the region. Such a characterization was in keeping with the Gómez regime's embrace of positivism, a philosophy that justified dictatorship as being necessary in order for "backward" nations to achieve modernity. To be sure, some of the elite's activities before the depression did serve to modernize certain aspects of Duaca's economy. Javier, Vásquez, and Segura imported new coffee-processing equipment, and some of the district's sugar hacendados upgraded their machinery as well. The privatization of Indian and national lands and the shift to cash rents were also consistent with notions of capitalist development. Moreover, Duaca's elite financed the expansion and upgrading of the district's road system. Pedro José Ramones, for example, built a highway (suitable for his new automobile) from the town of Duaca to his estate in Tucuragua. Similarly, Ramón Antonio Vásquez constructed a highway between Duaca and his property in Agua Colorada.[95] And, in 1927, Vásquez, Segura, and Dr. C. F. Figueredo agreed to provide 8,550 bolívares for the construction of a highway between Duaca and Yaritagua; they sealed their pact by opening a bottle of champagne and drinking the health of Juan Vicente Gómez.[96]

And yet, it would be a mistake to portray Duaca's elite simply as "modernizers" or proponents of capitalism, just as there is little to gain by following historians who, by emphasizing the Venezuelan elite's attachment to latifundia and debt peonage, conclude that landowners practiced "feudalism." In reality, neither theoretical model explains all important aspects of the transformation of Duaqueño society that culminated in the 1920s. The most salient aspect of this period was that the local elite—aided by their connections to the Gómez dictatorship, high coffee prices during most of the 1920s, and a surge in population growth between 1920 and 1926—pursued their interests more ruthlessly and with greater success than during any previous period in Duaca's history. These interests centered upon the extraction of greater profits from the production, processing, and marketing of coffee. Thus the elite engaged in some modernizing activities, such as road construction, importing new equipment, and shifting to a more "capitalistic" system of cash rents. At the same time, however, they imposed an increasingly noncapitalistic, unfree system of labor on Duaqueño workers, because this, too, advanced their interests. The result was not full-blown agrarian capitalism, understood as free wage labor, but rather a more effective system of exploitation in which established features of the system of production (indebted labor and landlord-tenant relationships) became more pervasive, more easily enforced, and more profitable.

Conclusion

Agrarian change in Duaca during the first three decades of the twentieth century occurred in two distinct phases. During the first phase, which extended to 1916, demographic and ecological factors produced relatively modest alterations in the structure of peasant society. Following the arrival of settlers at the furthest reaches of Duaca's public land frontier in the 1890s, the slow yet steady population growth of the early twentieth century brought mounting demographic pressure on the district's land base. Moreover, population growth hastened the deterioration of Duaca's ecology, which further reduced the supply of good land. The changes brought by demographic and ecological factors, however, proved modest. Peasants seeking a plot on which to establish their holdings found access to new land increasingly problematic, but most aspects of the peasant economy remained unchanged. Many of Duaca's peasants—probably a majority—continued to live beyond landlord control on the resguardos or public lands; peasant households continued to depend primarily on the production of their own holdings, despite seasonal wage labor on the elite's haciendas; real wages apparently held steady; and, on Duaca's handful of private estates, rents remained low and flexible throughout the 1910s. In short, although demographic pressure had become a tangible force by 1915, it produced only limited change.

By contrast, the years from 1916 to the late 1920s witnessed the transformation of Duaqueño society. The elite appropriated most of Duaca's resguardos and baldíos, changing forever the structure of land tenure in the district. Although laws governing the alienation of community and national lands gave de facto occupants preference in the acquisition of the land they cultivated, only a handful of peasant occupants gained title to their plots. Most were converted into rent-paying tenants on new private estates, or they became dependent hacienda laborers. The transformation of Duaca's agrarian structure culminated around 1925, when the elite discarded the traditional system of low rents and imposed a harsher system of fixed cash rents.

The local elite's political power was instrumental in this process of social and economic change. Politically influential men within the local elite controlled the privatization of Indian and public lands, in the first case through the junta that oversaw the partition of the resguardos, and in the second case through the system of brokered redistribution of public lands. Political connections to the Gómez regime proved particularly important in the appropriation of public lands, which depended upon cooperation between the Duaca elite, state presidents, and the central regime. Moreover, the power of the state, which in Duaca was in the hands of the local elite, was crucial in enforcing the new agrarian structure based on privatized land, cash rents, and debt peonage. The district court consistently supported landlord authority against peasants who resisted the appropriation of their lands and the collection of rent. The jefe civil and district police assisted the elite in asserting tighter control over hacienda workers. Between 1916 and the late 1920s, Duaca's elite used the power of the Gomecista state, both within and beyond the district, to establish firm control over local society.

8 Economic and Political Change in Duaca During the Depression

THE GLOBAL DEPRESSION THAT began in 1929 brought important changes to Duaca. As in many Venezuelan districts, these years witnessed the end of the dominance of coffee in the local economy. Many Duaqueños—again, like Venezuelans elsewhere—found that the production of food crops for growing urban markets was a more viable strategy than the continued production of coffee. Others in the district decided to abandon agriculture altogether in favor of jobs in Barquisimeto. As migration out of the district mounted, Duaca's population began to decline for the first time in over a century. The export cycle that had begun after independence, fueled by in-migration and the spatial expansion of coffee, drew to a close as declining coffee production and out-migration signaled the end of an era.

These years also marked a turning point in the relationship between the local elite and the Gomecista state. A failed uprising against Gómez in the neighboring state of Portuguesa, in 1929, resulted in the imposition of a more repressive state government in Lara and ended the political privileges formerly enjoyed by Duaca's elite. Members of the local elite were thereafter excluded from the office of jefe civil, and some prominent Duaqueños faced active persecution by the Gómez regime. Neither the economic nor the political crises of the depression, however, brought any fundamental change to the structure of class relationships within the district. The systems of land and labor established during the 1910s and 1920s remained intact and became the focal point of the peasant protests of 1936.

The Changing Agrarian Economy

The declining importance of coffee in Duaca is best understood within the context of changes in the Venezuelan coffee economy as a whole. The depression (which brought a 75 percent decline in coffee prices between 1928 and 1935) did not have a uniform effect throughout the nation.[1] In the Andes, producers responded to the crisis by expanding their fields to grow the additional coffee needed to settle accounts with creditors. Venezuelan producers outside the Andes, by contrast, tended to abandon the crop as its price plunged. Thus coffee, which had been widely cultivated in Venezuela before 1930, became progressively concentrated in the Andean states of Táchira, Trujillo, and Mérida. The new lands planted in coffee in the Andes after 1930, however, were increasingly ill-suited to the crop, leading to a decline in Andean productivity as the area under cultivation grew.[2]

These trends led to a modest contraction in the volume of Venezuelan coffee exports during the 1930s (see table 7). At the same time, however, other coffee-producing nations increased exports, despite the depression. Whereas Venezuela had supplied 3.7 percent of global exports in 1925, it accounted for only 1.4 percent in 1933. During this eight-year period, Venezuela went from being the world's fourth-largest coffee exporter to the eighth.[3]

Historians have long sought the underlying causes of Venezuela's marginalization in the world coffee economy. If other countries could expand exports despite the depression, why did Venezuela fail to do so? Some scholars point to the allegedly pernicious effects of Venezuela's petroleum economy. Edwin Lieuwen and Luis Cipriano Rodríguez, for example, argue that the oil industry drew agricultural workers from the countryside to the oil camps, converted cropland into drilling sites, and diverted capital from agriculture to speculative ventures linked to the emerging petroleum economy.[4] Although all these processes certainly occurred, it is not clear that they achieved a magnitude sufficient to undermine the coffee economy. Moreover, there was a time lag between the onset of the oil boom and the decline of coffee, which makes any direct correlation problematic. Venezuela's oil industry began to

Table 7. Venezuelan Coffee Exports, 1920–1935

	Amount (tons)	Value (thousands of bolívares)
1920–1921	37,348	45,357
1921–1922	62,157	78,411
1922–1923	45,655	66,394
1923–1924	56,509	93,655
1924–1925	52,260	117,689
1925–1926	48,224	115,120
1926–1927	43,044	92,791
1927–1928	43,698	88,900
1928–1929	60,406	130,861
1929–1930	48,548	79,118
1930–1931	57,612	71,474
1931–1932	47,622	53,021
1932–1933	39,306	45,190
1933–1934	38,081	30,308
1934–1935	46,760	29,769
1935–1936	58,180	32,077

Source: Miguel Izard, Series estadísticas para la historia de Venezuela (Mérida: Universidad de los Andes, 1970), 193.

grow rapidly after World War I, but it did not immediately affect agriculture. Coffee exports, as Roseberry observes, held steady through 1928. Furthermore, he notes, "it is clear that, although coffee was dramatically displaced from its position of prominence in the Venezuelan economy in the third decade of this century, the coffee sector itself had not shown any signs of dissolution during the twenties."[5] In sum, there was no contradiction between the rapid development of the oil industry and the continuation of the coffee economy, at least in the short term.

The fundamental cause of Venezuela's declining share of the world coffee market seems to have been the chronically low productivity of Venezuelan groves in comparison to those in other nations. The average yield of Venezuelan coffee bushes had long been inferior to that obtained in most other Latin American coffee economies. As early as 1888, David Burke, the U.S. consul in Puerto Cabello, commented on the fact. Burke noted that in Lara and Carabobo, the largest states in his jurisdiction, coffee bushes usually produced only one and one-quarter pounds each, whereas in Costa Rica and other (unspecified) parts of Central America the yield was two pounds per bush.[6] He reported that some observers attributed the low yields to Venezuela's inferior soil and climate, while others believed that Venezuelan producers failed to care for their groves as scrupulously as growers elsewhere. Burke preferred the latter explanation and indicated several common shortcomings in Venezuelan coffee cultivation, such as failure to prune the bushes regularly, prepare the soil for planting, and irrigate fields.

A number of historians have made a similar case. Consuelo Ascanio notes Venezuela's failure to keep pace with Colombian or Brazilian production and asserts that the low technical level of Venezuelan agriculture was largely to blame for its low yields. She emphasizes poor harvesting techniques that damaged trees, failure to carry out regular weedings, and a widespread tendency to use seedlings that took root spontaneously in productive groves rather than to produce young bushes selectively in separate seedbeds. To these factors, Alicia Ardao adds a failure to replace old, unproductive bushes and an occasional absence of one of coffee's most basic requirements: shade trees. Finally, Gastón Carvallo and Josefina Ríos de Hernández emphasize the lack of anti-erosion techniques, such as terraces, and note that Costa Rican and Colombian growers were much more conscientious than their Venezuelan counterparts in keeping bushes properly pruned, a practice that boosts yields. The low technical level of Venezuelan coffee cultivation, these scholars conclude, rendered many growers unable to maintain production under the disastrous market conditions of the depression.[7]

But while there is a broad consensus concerning Venezuela's poor productivity and the low technical level of its coffee production, the existing literature does not satisfactorily explain why Venezuelan growers never adopted the practices that prevailed elsewhere. Some scholars suggest that Venezuelan hacendados lacked the capital to hire enough workers to care properly for their coffee groves.[8] It is not clear, however, that labor or capital were more plentiful in other coffee economies, nor does the argument apply to peasant groves worked with family labor.

Along with poor technical practices, whatever their ultimate cause, ecological factors also contributed to the low productivity of Venezuelan coffee, particularly in the twentieth century. The nation's frontier of new coffee lands, which had been extensive in the middle of the nineteenth century, had been settled by the early twentieth century, and in some areas soil exhaustion became a problem. This surely contributed to the declining yield of coffee per hectare from the nineteenth century to the twentieth.[9] Moreover, Venezuelans frequently planted coffee in areas where the climate and soil had always been less than ideal. One early twentieth-century agronomist noted the prevalence of low yields across the nation and suggested that up to one-half of Venezuela's groves were located on land more suited to other crops.[10] Thus it seems likely that low productivity, rooted in a combination of ecological and technical factors, rendered the coffee sector particularly vulnerable to the depression, forcing many growers to cease production of the crop. The government's decision to support and even revalue the Venezuelan currency in the mid-1930s, undertaken largely to satisfy oil companies needing to import supplies and machinery, further undermined the competitive position of Venezuela in the global coffee market.[11] Only a handful of districts—located almost entirely in the Andes, where the nation's best coffee lands were concentrated—could still hope to produce large quantities at a profit by the end of the 1930s.

Duaca was among those districts where the crisis of the 1930s marked the close of the coffee cycle. Having produced between 2.5 and 3 million kilograms annually from the 1890s through the 1920s, Duaqueños saw their coffee harvests fall to less than 1 million kilograms by the mid-1930s, and to less than 0.5 million by 1950.[12] In Duaca, as elsewhere outside the Andes, the land was simply not productive enough to sustain the coffee economy once the market collapsed. The Aroa mountains, which dominate the eastern portion of Duaca and extend into the neighboring state of Yaracuy, were heavily planted in coffee before the depression, but a recent study of soils there found only 2.54 percent of the area to be appropriate for coffee cultivation.[13] Duaqueños also grew coffee extensively in the Bobare mountains of the western part of the district, where the soil and climate were even less suited to the crop than in the Sierra de Aroa. Although land in Duaca deteriorated under the pressure of intensified cultivation during the late nineteenth and early twentieth centuries, it seems likely that a good deal of the district's coffee had always been planted on land only marginally suited to the crop. Thus whereas Duaca's coffee economy could prosper during periods of high prices (such as occurred during the 1870s, part of the 1890s, and most of the 1920s), many producers quickly went bust when the depression struck.

Duaqueños who abandoned coffee often turned to the production of food crops. Indeed, the transition would probably have come about eventually even without the impetus of a crisis in the coffee sector. Barquisimeto's steady rise in population from 23,109 to 36,429 inhabitants between 1926 and 1936 created a growing demand for staples, and Duaca, only some forty kilometers away and linked by the railroad, was ideally situated to supply the city. In the northern part of the district, growers began to plant new commercial crops such as potatoes, tomatoes, and onions. Around the town of Duaca, the shift toward food crops meant an expansion of corn and black beans at the expense of coffee. Further south, in the flatlands near El Eneal, some landowners began to cultivate sisal, a fibrous plant used to make cordage and burlap bags. To be sure, coffee was not completely abandoned. As late as 1941 an observer could refer to Duaca's remaining coffee haciendas as being among the richest in the state.[14] But the transition from the dominance of coffee to that of food crops and sisal was clear.

The crisis of the 1930s brought hardship to all sectors of Duaqueño society, but the peasantry, still reeling from the effects of land privatization and the imposition of fixed cash rents, bore the brunt of the crisis. Many small cultivators lost their holdings in the early and mid-1930s because of unpaid debts, and many coffee farms were abandoned. Rather than look for new ways to make a living in the district, many left Duaca for good. The district's population declined from 28,719 to 22,864 inhabitants between 1926 and 1936 and continued to decline through 1950, when census takers found only 21,904 inhabitants.[15] Some migrants may have gone to rural areas in neighboring jurisdictions. Many others, however, headed for Barquisimeto to seek jobs on public works projects, which the government continued to finance from rising oil revenues.[16] During the 1930s, then, a large number of peasants from Duaca became urban wage workers after losing their farms. The combined effects of the agrarian changes of the 1920s and the depression of the 1930s transformed numerous Duaqueños from peasants into proletarians, but many of those who suffered this transformation emerged as an urban rather than a rural proletariat.

Venezuela's first census of coffee farms, completed in 1939 and published the following year, reveals the structure of production, by farm size, after the effects of the depression and out-migration had been absorbed (see table 8). At the time of the census, the district's coffee production was only a third of what it had been at the height of the boom. The census allows one to distinguish between the small peasant farms with fewer than five thousand trees, which generally could be worked with family labor alone, and the medium-to-large peasant farms with up to twenty thousand trees, which, depending on family size and composition, generally would require labor from outside the household at harvest time.[17] In aggregate, Duaca's peasant sector as a whole—that is, all farms up to twenty thousand trees—accounted for 93.36 percent of all coffee farms (943 out of 1,010) but owned only 42.69 percent of

Table 8. Structure of Coffee Production in Distrito Crespo (Duaca), 1939

Coffee Trees per Farm	No. of Farms	Total Trees	Total Production (kilograms)
Fewer than 5000	673	1,555,000	178,940
5,000–20,000	270	2,343,908	253,414
20,000–50,000	32	1,073,700	122,682
50,000–100,000	21	1,537,400	132,710
Over 100,000	14	2,622,950	271,722
Total	1,010	9,132,958	959,468

Source: Instituto Nacional del Café, *Censo cafetero,* 125–26.

trees in the district (3,898,908 out of 9,132,958) and produced 45.06 percent of the district's coffee (432,354 kilograms out of a total of 959,468). Meanwhile, the largest farms in the district—those with over a hundred thousand trees— accounted for only 1.39 percent of all farms but owned 28.72 percent of all trees and produced 28.32 percent of the district's coffee.

The lack of any comparable quantitative data for earlier periods makes it difficult to fit the census figures into the long-term pattern of agrarian change. And yet some attempt must be made to place the "snapshot" provided by the census into the overall pattern of Duaca's historical development. This can be done only by juxtaposing the 1939 statistics to the much more impressionistic data drawn from a century of notarial and judicial records. Although a juxtaposition of these distinct types of information— each gathered through different means for different reasons—is fraught with methodological hazards,[18] and although even the apparently objective census data must be treated with caution,[19] such a comparison does present a reasonable picture of the changing structure of local coffee production.

The qualitative data gleaned from notarial records make it entirely plausible that in earlier decades—into the 1910s, perhaps—the peasantry accounted for a considerably greater share of coffee production than the 45 percent recorded in the census.[20] When considered together, then, data gleaned from notarial records and the census suggest that by the late 1930s Duaca's peasants had seen their share of coffee production eroded by the cumulative weight of the changes of the previous three decades—the growing scarcity of vacant land for new peasant holdings (which meant that transfers of peasant farms to members of the elite steadily shrank the peasant sector), the revolution in land tenure and rents, the onset of the Great Depression, and the apparent tendency of poorer Duaqueños to abandon their farms in search of jobs in

Barquisimeto and other urban centers. One important question that cannot be addressed through any available data is whether peasants, during the depression, abandoned coffee in favor of other crops as rapidly as the larger producers did, a factor that could color our reading of the 1939 statistics. Still, with due caution, it is plausible to suggest that the census presents a picture not only of a local coffee economy in rapid decline (which is beyond dispute), but also of a peasant sector providing a diminishing share of local production relative to the period before Duaca's agrarian transformation.

While the peasantry confronted the depression already weakened by recent developments, Duaca's elite entered the crisis after enjoying the prosperity of the 1920s. The crisis clearly caught local entrepreneurs by surprise. Many, having taken out loans to expand operations while the high coffee prices of the 1920s prevailed, could not meet their creditors' demands once the crisis hit. Some of the well-to-do obtained assistance from the Banco Agrario y Pecuario (BAP), a government institution founded in 1928 to provide long-term, low-interest loans to the rural sector. During the late 1920s and early 1930s, dozens of Duaca's entrepreneurs received BAP loans ranging from seven to a hundred thousand bolívares. The terms of these loans—5 percent interest and a twenty-year repayment schedule—were much more favorable than those offered by the major Barquisimeto and Puerto Cabello merchant firms, which generally charged 9 or 12 percent and demanded repayment in one to five years. In Duaca, as seems to have been the case elsewhere in Venezuela, the BAP's loans went exclusively to members of the landed elite.

The state's financial assistance, though, did not spare the district elite from the worst effects of the crisis. Duaca's jefe civil, Ramón Antonio Vásquez, received a loan of a hundred thousand bolívares from the BAP during its first year of operation, before the depression struck in full force. Nevertheless, Vásquez had to use eighty thousand bolívares of this credit to pay existing debts to large merchant firms and soon needed new loans from private sources. In 1931, a year of drought in Duaca, Vásquez informed one of his creditors, R & O Kolster of Puerto Cabello, that his haciendas had produced only one-half their normal harvest. Vásquez also explained to Kolster that because he had to make immediate payments to the BAP, Blöhm and Company, and several Duaca merchants, he would not be able to deliver any coffee to the firm until the following year. Kolster responded with a lawsuit against Vásquez, and in 1932 Vásquez sold several of his smaller haciendas to pay debts to Kolster and to the Barquisimeto firm of Calderón e Hijos. One year later, Vásquez had to sell his main coffee estates in Camburito and San Mateo, which were heavily mortgaged to the BAP and to two Duaca merchants. In short, the state's credit program did little to shield Vásquez from the effects of the depression.[21]

Nor was the experience of Vásquez unique. Other members of the local elite also lost their properties for debt, even though they had received loans from the BAP. Luis Bracho—whose father, Cipriano Bracho, had been one of Duaca's largest coffee growers in the late nineteenth century—mortgaged his family's principal estate to the BAP for sixty thousand bolívares in 1930 but soon proved unable to meet payments on the loan. In 1935, the BAP was obliged to acquire the estate at judicial auction for one-half its declared value.[22] Similarly, Pedro Javier, one of Duaca's most prominent entrepreneurs, received a loan of one hundred thousand bolívares from the BAP in 1930. He used the entire credit to pay existing debts but only went deeper into debt as the depression continued. Several years later, Javier had to cede several mortgaged properties to a Barquisimeto merchant firm to settle a debt of 266,240 bolívares.[23]

Indeed, few members of the local elite who mortgaged properties to the BAP during the crisis ever redeemed them.[24] Rather than bailing out Duaca's entrepreneurs, then, government loans only delayed the day of reckoning by allowing them to retain their properties for a few more years before ceding them to the BAP or private creditors. Some elite observers even complained that the BAP actually had a negative impact on the district economy.[25]

On balance, the BAP probably benefited merchants more than landowners. Many of those receiving credit from the BAP used some or all of the credit to pay existing debts to private creditors, usually merchants in Puerto Cabello, Barquisimeto, or Duaca. (The BAP often stipulated, in the mortgage contract itself, that certain amounts of a loan would be used to pay certain creditors.) Had government credit not been available, these private lenders would have been obliged to foreclose on rural properties whose values were steadily declining. Instead, they received cash. Whether money from BAP loans allowed large import-export firms to survive the depression is a question beyond the scope of the present study, but at least two major firms involved in the coffee economy—Blöhm and Boulton—did survive the depression despite the huge drop in coffee prices.[26]

In the case of one Duaca merchant, Eulogio Segura, the benefits derived by the commercial sector from the BAP's loans are more clear. During the early decades of the twentieth century, Segura built one of Duaca's largest agricultural and commercial enterprises, combining coffee and sugar production with extensive credit operations, including large loans to other members of the local elite. Several of Segura's debtors received loans from the BAP, and their mortgages to the BAP specify that at least 85,300 bolívares in government credit passed directly to Segura.[27] This flow of cash may explain why Segura managed to ride out the depression with his properties intact, while other prominent Duaqueños such as Ramón Antonio Vásquez, Pedro Javier, and Leopoldo Camejo all suffered large-scale losses. The Segura family, having weathered the crisis, went on to expand their operations still further in the decades that followed, and they remain one of the most prosperous families in Duaca today.

The Political Crisis of the Local Elite

The depression brought political as well as economic challenges to the local elite. Since the last years of the Castro regime, Duaca's elite had enjoyed a position of influence within the increasingly centralized Venezuelan state. Whereas many districts in the nation were placed under jefes civiles who came from outside the jurisdiction, in Duaca the office of jefe civil went to local men of standing who respected and served the interests of the local elite. General Eduardo Colmenares, who held the office during most of the period between 1906 and 1919, repeatedly used his influence to prevent the political persecution of Duaqueños during the Gómez regime.[28] Colmenares's friend and successor, Ramón Antonio Vásquez, demonstrated his commitment to the interests of the local elite by opening new roads, enforcing the contracts between indebted workers and their employers, and approving the new estate regulations of the mid-1920s. While some districts suffered abuses at the hands of jefes civiles sent from other jurisdictions, the Duaca elite clearly benefited from the repeated appointment of native sons to govern the district.

But by the late 1920s, changes in Venezuela's political structure rendered the relationship between the local elite and the central state increasingly anachronistic. Colmenares and Vásquez had risen to political prominence during the Revolución Libertadora at the turn of the century when they proved their skill at controlling the railroad passing through Duaca to Barquisimeto. Their appointments reflected an implicit bargain, in which Castro and Gómez allowed Duaca's elite to control local government in exchange for guaranteeing the regime's security interests in the district. By the late 1920s, however, local uprisings had ceased to pose a serious threat to Gómez. The security of the regime had come to rest squarely on the national army, a force capable of subduing any civilian uprising. Simply put, the central state no longer needed the local elite to safeguard their military interests in Duaca.

Nevertheless, it took a revolt against Gómez in 1929, centered in the neighboring state of Portuguesa, to set in motion the events that were to redefine the relationship between Duaca's well-to-do and the national regime. The revolt in question—one of the most important to disturb the relative calm of the Gómez years—was led by José Rafael Gabaldón.[29] Like so many political figures of the era, Gabaldón first rose to prominence during the civil wars at the turn of the century. Having stood by Castro during the Libertadora, he went on to serve as jefe civil in Puerto Cabello and in Boconó, in the Andean state of Trujillo. Gómez named Gabaldón president of Portuguesa state in 1909, but Gabaldón then broke with the government in 1913 over Gómez's decision to cancel elections and remain in power. Forced to spend more than two years in hiding, Gabaldón received a government amnesty in 1916.

Over the next thirteen years, Gabaldón maintained an ambivalent relationship with Gómez, one that alternated between cordial respect and thinly veiled opposition. Gabaldón retired to his cattle, sugar, and coffee haciendas in Biscucuy, a district in the northwestern corner of Portuguesa, near the border with Trujillo and Lara (some 120 kilometers southwest of Duaca). But if the persecution of previous years had been intended to cow him into cooperation with the regime, it failed. Instead, he gained a reputation for protecting peasants against the abuses of Gomecista officials in the area. He refused to cooperate with the forced military recruitment drives so common in rural Venezuela and also gave refuge to people on the run from local authorities. At the same time, he remained on good personal terms with Gómez. He occasionally visited the dictator and sometimes wrote to him to complain of excesses committed by local officials.[30]

Relations between Gabaldón and Gómez reached a turning point following the antigovernment student protests of early 1928 in Caracas. The student demonstrators—including Gabaldón's son, Joaquín—were easily arrested, but they awakened widespread sympathy among the Venezuelan populace, sparking more demonstrations and, in April, an unsuccessful revolt within the armed forces. The regime, which had gone without serious challenge since the purge of 1913–1914, suddenly faced a growing and increasingly open opposition. Seizing the moment, Gabaldón visited Gómez one last time and advocated a political opening, but Gómez made no response. In September

Gabaldón took the decisive step of writing a public letter to Gómez urging him to surrender power and hold free elections.[31] He boldly warned Gómez not to follow the example of Porfirio Díaz of Mexico, who suppressed opposition until a popular revolution engulfed the nation. It would be far better for Venezuela, and for Gómez's reputation in history, if the old Andino ended his political career by overseeing a transition to democracy. Copies of Gabaldón's letter circulated widely in western Venezuela and among students in Caracas. Now the regime would have to respond.[32]

Gómez had no intention of surrendering power and ordered that Gabaldón be arrested if he left his hacienda, Santo Cristo, in Biscucuy. Meanwhile, Gabaldón attempted to organize a revolt against the dictatorship. Believing that he would be supported by several simultaneous uprisings in other regions (including one to be led by General Eleazar López Contreras, a top general in the national army),[33] Gabaldón led a band of armed followers from his hacienda to the city of Guanare, which he captured on April 28, 1929.

He soon realized, though, that no large supporting revolts had materialized. Feeling betrayed and doomed, Gabaldón headed toward Lara, picking up more recruits along the way and bringing his force to several hundred men. After learning that the Gomecista army was waging a campaign of terror against his sympathizers (both real and imagined), Gabaldón hurried to surrender in late June.[34] It was a fittingly chivalrous end to one of Venezuela's most quixotic revolts. Perhaps to his surprise, Gabaldón was imprisoned rather than executed and was released five years later.

While sparing Gabaldón, Gómez took decisive action to prevent any further unrest in the region. Among other measures, he dispatched his cousin, Eustoquio Gómez, to assume the presidency of Lara and to oversee military operations in several western states. It was an ominous decision. Eustoquio Gómez had become one of the most feared and despised figures in the regime when, as president of Táchira (1914–1925), he carried out a particularly brutal program of repression.[35] His appointment as president of Lara signaled the dictator's determination to deal harshly with those who had sympathized with Gabaldón. No one seemed to doubt that many people in Lara were disloyal to the regime; indeed, some of Gabaldón's supporters criticized him for not striking at Barquisimeto after his initial capture of Guanare, so certain were they that he would have raised a large following around Lara's capital.[36] Now it was Eustoquio Gómez's job to ferret out potential rebels throughout the state.

As president of Lara, Gómez preferred to name jefes civiles from outside the state, probably because he believed that men without ties to the areas they governed would be more reliable in carrying out orders violating the interests and the personal safety of the local elites.[37] It was around this time that the office of jefe civil of Duaca passed from Ramón Antonio Vásquez, the Duaqueño who had held the post for most of the 1920s, to General Pedro Molina, who had no discernible ties to the district. Moreover, Duaca's district council lost much of its power and was reduced to granting automatic approval to decisions made by appointed officials.[38] As the Gómez regime entered its third decade, Duaca's elite experienced the imposition of central authority as never before.

On December 4, 1930, Eustoquio Gómez received two coded telegrams ordering the arrest of ten men who had been implicated in conspiracies against the regime. Some of those named—including General Bártolo Yépez of Duaca —stood accused of conspiring in Gabaldón's revolt.[39] Whether an actual conspirator or not, Yépez had been on uneasy terms with the regime for years. After establishing his reputation in the civil wars at the turn of the century, Yépez had served as jefe civil of Carúpano, in the eastern state of Sucre, early in the Gómez regime, but, like Gabaldón, he soon retired from public life because of political differences with the dictator. Gomecistas identified Yépez as an ally of Gabaldón as early as 1913 and forced him to abandon his home in El Tocuyo, Lara, presumably because of its proximity to Gabaldón's base in Biscucuy.[40] Yépez resettled in Duaca, where he purchased an estate for the handsome sum of forty thousand bolívares in 1916. Over the years, Yépez (again, like Gabaldón) gained a reputation for granting protection to men fleeing the authorities. People in Duaca and neighboring districts knew that Yépez regularly granted refuge to fugitives, provided they agreed to work on his hacienda.[41]

Upon decoding his instructions of December 4, Eustoquio Gómez ordered Duaca's jefe civil, General Molina, to arrest Yépez.[42] Warned of Molina's approach, Yépez fled his estate. But rather than go into hiding, Yépez traveled directly to Maracay, the city west of Caracas where Juan Vicente Gómez lived during most of his years in power, and he presented himself before the general. Yépez protested that he had not participated in Gabaldón's plot, a claim he would repeat years later after Gómez had died.[43] Gómez apparently believed him, for instead of imprisoning Yépez he merely confined him to the city of Maracay. Few Venezuelans accused of conspiring with rebels escaped so lightly, but Yépez's confinement contributed to the ruin of his properties in Duaca over the next five years.

Nor was Yépez the only member of Duaca's elite to suffer persecution during Eustoquio Gómez's tenure as state president. In 1931, General Pablo María Arrieche, a Duaca merchant and hacendado, also found himself obliged to flee the authorities. Like Yépez and Gabaldón, Arrieche had been in the good graces of the Gómez regime during its early years. In 1913, Argenis Azuaje—a leading Gomecista in Barquisimeto—identified Arrieche as one of the local strongmen who could be counted on to defend the regime in the event of renewed civil war.[44] In 1916, Azuaje and Arrieche jointly sponsored a cockfight in Duaca, and later, with Eduardo Colmenares and Ramón Antonio Vásquez, they could be seen inspecting a new bridge on the Duaca-Barquisimeto highway.[45] It is not clear when or why Arrieche began to distance himself from the regime, although his declining economic fortunes in the early 1920s may have contributed to his political disaffection.[46] Whatever the reason, Gomecista officials were hot in pursuit of Arrieche when, in late 1931, he and his son took refuge in the house of Juancho Gudiño Bracho, another prominent Duaqueño. The authorities soon discovered Gudiño's role in Arrieche's escape, and in December 1931, Gudiño was murdered in cold blood by men under the orders of Eustoquio Gómez.[47] The incident shocked Duaqueños, in part because Gudiño, a grandson of coffee planter Cipriano Bracho, belonged to one of the district's most respected families. Perhaps Duaqueños reflected that such a brutal act would have been unthinkable during the years before the arrival of Eustoquio Gómez, when natives like Vásquez and Colmenares were jefe civil and could still act as a shield between the central regime and the locally prominent.

Nevertheless, the harsh political rule imposed on Duaca's elite beginning in 1929 did not directly add to their economic problems. There is no indication, for example, that General Molina, Duaca's jefe civil during this period, muscled his way into the local elite's economic enterprises or even became very involved in the local economy. Nor did the elite's political problems undermine their economic hold on the peasantry. Molina's mission of safeguarding the security of the regime did not imply a reordering of Duaca's class relationships. Moreover, a member of the local elite continued to preside over the district court, and through 1935 the court continued to enforce landlord demands against recalcitrant tenants. The systems of land tenure and labor imposed during the 1910s and 1920s remained unchallenged until late 1935. In December of that year, news reached Duaca that Juan Vicente Gómez had died following an extended illness. Within weeks it became clear that the local elite's control over land and the peasantry was no longer secure.

Conclusion

The depression that began in 1929 marked the end of an era in Duaca. As in other areas of Venezuela outside the Andes, the depression forced many coffee growers in Duaca to shift their production to food crops that could be marketed in the nation's growing cities. Despite the rising demand for food-stuffs in Barquisimeto, however, the depression brought hardship to all sectors of Duaqueño society. For the peasantry, the depression added another weight to the burden created by the recent revolution in agrarian structures. Thousands responded by migrating out of the district, many to seek wage work in Barquisimeto.

For Duaca's elite, the depression spelled the end of the abundance of the 1920s. When the crisis struck, a number of prominent Duaqueños drew loans from the government's Agricultural and Livestock Bank in an attempt to preserve their commercial and agricultural enterprises, but many failed. In addition, Duaca's elite suffered the imposition of a new state government in 1929, which curtailed their control over district government. Even in the midst of these political and economic changes, however, the class relationships imposed during the Gómez dictatorship remained in place and assured a basic continuity in Duaca's social structure through late 1935.

9 The Peasant Protests of 1936

THE DEATH OF Gómez in December 1935 triggered an explosion of violent unrest in several of Venezuela's major cities as well as in the oil camps of the western state of Zulia. Driven by a combination of resentment against the dictatorship, desire for revenge against local Gomecistas, and, on occasion, a simple quest for easy loot amid the disintegration of public order, ordinary citizens attacked the symbols of the old regime. The popular outbursts were soon suppressed, but they initiated the period of greatest political ferment in Venezuela since the nation won independence from Spain in the early nineteenth century. It soon became apparent that long-term political stability depended on the new government's willingness to broaden political participation and to address (however nominally) the social and economic problems plaguing the nation. The process of deciding the limits of reform, however, proved to be laden with conflict between the conservative government of President Eleazar López Contreras (1935–1941) and his fragmented opposition.

Although the actions of urban groups and oil workers usually dominate analysis of Venezuelan politics in the years immediately following the death of Gómez, rural areas also experienced agitation for change. After all, agrarian grievances were widespread in Venezuela in the mid-1930s. The concentration of landownership and the imposition of increasingly onerous work conditions had characterized the Gómez era throughout much of the nation, and the Great Depression had only added to the hardships suffered by Venezuela's rural population. As John Duncan Powell observes, the "skirmishes" between peasants and landowners that occurred throughout rural Venezuela in the months and years following the death of Gómez were a reaction against the agrarian structure imposed during the dictatorship.[1] Peasants seeking revenge for the abuses of recent years destroyed landowners' property and invaded usurped lands, even while they petitioned the new government for lawful reform.

One such skirmish between landlords and peasants occurred in Duaca, where violent protests erupted following Gómez's demise. Into April 1936, peasants in the district attacked their landlords' property, destroyed fences, and set fire to buildings and fields. Virtually no estate in Duaca escaped the popular wrath, and for months local authorities seemed powerless to control the unrest. As peasants settled on Duaca's estates without landowners' consent and as rent collection came to a virtual halt, some concluded that the estate system created over the past two decades was on the verge of disintegration. Events in Duaca lend clear support to Powell's thesis that the rural skirmishes beginning in 1936 were the direct result of changes imposed during the dictatorship. For, in the case of Duaca, there is no doubt as to the cause of the violence: peasants were protesting the appropriation of land and the imposition of oppressive rents, processes that had characterized the Gómez era in the district.

A Framework for Analysis: Moral Economy and Frontier Peasantries

To place Duaca's 1936 protests in proper context, we must leave aside the narrative of historical events, at least for a moment, to consider a theoretical framework for the study of peasant rebellion. Of particular relevance is the body of literature built around the concept of moral economy. This theory, which emphasizes the defensive, even conservative, nature of popular protest, has been widely applied to peasant resistance to economic change in Latin America. Recently, however, scholars have raised the question of whether this framework can be applied to precipitate peasantries, and if so, what modifications in the theory might be necessary to accommodate the specific history of peasants whose class origins are found in conditions of export expansion.

Exploring these questions in relation to the 1936 rebellion in Duaca sheds light both on the theoretical debate and on the character of the rebellion itself.

Some of the controversy over the theory's applicability to particular social groups results from a long-term dilution of the concept's initial clarity. Ever since British historian E. P. Thompson introduced the theory of moral economy into modern scholarship in his 1971 study of food riots in eighteenth-century England, the concept has been applied to an ever increasing range of topics and social groups, a development that, as Thompson himself observed, led to a corresponding decline in the precision of the theory and that today renders any definition problematic.[2] It seems clear, however, that the fundamental insight of moral economy analysis is the assertion that protests against economic modernization or growing intrusion by the state are, in many instances, informed by popular ideologies wedded to established traditions. Resistance to change, the theory insists, is rooted in people's belief that a preexisting social and economic order (one in which the principles of the market are not yet all-powerful) is better suited to the common good than the new order that elites wish to impose (one in which capitalist ideals or state power will redefine the marketing of grain, the organization of labor, or some other fundamental aspect of local life). Popular movements against such changes, then, are based on a desire to preserve or re-create a way of life that, by virtue of experience, has become ingrained in the popular consciousness as a just and legitimate social order. In applying the theory to "traditional" rural societies undergoing rapid change, a number of scholars have argued that the "moral economy" defended by peasant rebels is governed by principles of paternalist relations (between an hacendado and his workers, or between a village headman and his villagers) and reciprocal exchanges (that is, exchanges outside the market) among peasants themselves.[3]

As William Roseberry observes, scholars who use the moral economy framework are sometimes too eager to lump together all preindustrial societies as "traditional" or "precapitalist"; this failure to acknowledge the distinctive histories of particular social groups, he believes, is one of the sources of imprecision in the literature.[4] He goes on to question the applicability of moral economy analysis to precipitate peasantries, particularly the peasant society of the Venezuelan Andes. Roseberry argues that, because frontier peasantries have their origins in the expansion of the global market for tropical products in the nineteenth and twentieth centuries, their history and their political consciousness are quite different from those of the peasants who normally appear in the moral economy literature—that is, indigenous villages whose origins stretch back into time immemorial, before the modern commercial world had come into being. He argues that precipitate peasantries, having been shaped at their origin by commercial capitalism, lack an alternative (noncapitalist) vision of society around which they can rally when their livelihood is threatened, because they have no precapitalist institutions in living memory on which to base their notions of social justice. Thus, Roseberry suggests, the central element in the moral economy dynamic is absent, giving the theory only limited value in the study of frontier peasantries.

Jeffrey Gould, in a finely detailed study of the political ideologies of a frontier peasantry in Chinandega, Nicaragua, has acknowledged the importance of the questions raised by Roseberry but provides a more nuanced response. Gould finds that, although Chinandega's peasantry was formed in a period of export expansion, peasant protest did draw—selectively—on certain aspects of the local, collective past, including the "sacred right" of access to land. At several junctures, his analysis suggests that moral economy theory is not irrelevant to precipitate peasantries, but rather that scholars must give due attention to the specificities of local history in applying the insights of the theory to any particular setting.[5] Even precipitate peasantries, it seems, cannot all be lumped together.

In its general outlines, the analytical framework developed in the moral economy literature is clearly relevant to the protests that swept across Duaca following the death of Gómez. Like other groups to whom the theory has been applied, rebels in Duaca sought to overturn the dramatic restructuring of social relationships that had been thrust upon them, in the hopes of returning to a previous way of life, which, in their experience, had proven to be more just, legitimate, and equitable. Here, as in the rebellions considered by the moral economy theorists, Duaca's peasants used their own history to construct a standard by which to gauge the injustices of the present.[6] In particular, they harked back to the formative years of their class, when widespread access to land, low rents, a weak state, and a labor market that granted workers some leverage with employers had created conditions favorable to the expansion and reproduction of the peasant household. To be sure, the moral economy embedded in Duaqueños' experience lacked some of the "classic" features identified by Thompson and others (such as a strong ideology of paternalism serving to restrain exploitation). But such particulars should not obscure the larger outlines of the political dynamic that took hold. The popular memory of the peasantry's formative period provided a standard—a "moral heritage," in James Scott's phrase, or a "retrospective norm" in Alan Knight's —powerful enough to form a shared basis for collective political action.[7]

Of equal significance, Duaqueños' attachment to their own past was not constrained by its inextricable ties to the unfolding of commercial capitalism. One suspects that they had not forgotten the abuses and the risks that had always accompanied the coffee economy, but they also recalled that commercial production had created a livelihood for many households—as long as the elite had been held at bay. The key to re-creating the relative prosperity of this bygone era was to break the elite's hold on land, not to reverse the advance of commercial capitalism. Because Duaqueños found little in their own history to turn them against the market per se, it was entirely logical for their protest to share the nostalgic nature of those featured in the moral economy literature; but given their particular, local experience, Duaqueños' nostalgia for the favorable conditions of the past did not involve a rejection of commercial capitalism.[8]

One could also object that the "traditions" that claimed Duaqueños' loyalty were of such recent creation they cannot be compared to those of village peasantries or the preindustrial workers of Europe, whose customs stretch back much further in time. Nevertheless, by the mid-1910s, when the agrarian revolution began, Duaqueños could look back on two or three generations of involvement in the commercial economy under the generally favorable conditions that had prevailed since the end of the Federal War. Peasants and workers in other settings have attached the weight of "custom" to conditions with even shorter histories than this.[9]

In the minds of those who lived through Duaca's agrarian revolution, it ended the local "tradition" of relatively free access to land and thus overturned an established way of life. As the revolution was carried out beginning in the mid-1910s, peasants limited their protest to individualized, everyday forms of resistance, realizing that more coordinated or aggressive action would have been suicidal under the Gomecista regime. But when Gómez died, they seized the moment and undertook more concerted action to overturn the agrarian structure that had been imposed during the dictatorship. Through violence and through petitioning the new government for legal reform, Duaca's peasants sought to break estate owners' control over access to land and to reassert the primacy of usufruct rights.

The Protests of 1936

Whereas agrarian change provided the fundamental rationale for the turmoil in Duaca, political changes at the national and state levels were equally important in determining the timing of the protests. As in many cases of rural rebellion, the imposition of an onerous system of land and labor is not in itself a completely satisfying explanation for the onset of mass resistance.[10] Peasants often wait to act upon their grievances until they perceive a weakening of state control, a division within the elite, or the possibility of forming an alliance with another social class.[11] These political factors all played a role in the outbreak of peasant protest in Duaca. Perhaps most important, Venezuela experienced a marked relaxation of political repression in the months following the death of Gómez. It was within this climate of political opening that Duaca's peasants chose to launch their protest.

Gómez's successor was General Eleazar López Contreras, who had served as minister of war during the last four years of the dictatorship and who had been known as a moderate within the regime. During his first months as president, López haltingly steered Venezuela toward a more open political system. Political parties, proscribed under Gómez, were allowed to organize in early 1936 and included the Progressive Republican Party (PRP), an heir of the clandestine Venezuelan Communist Party of the early 1930s, and the Venezuelan Organization (Orve), a reformist party that included some leaders of the anti-Gómez student movement of 1928. In response to increasingly vociferous calls for change, López also announced his so-called February Program, the first comprehensive policy by a Venezuelan president aimed at broad social and economic reform. Although many Gomecistas remained in high government positions, López made clear his intent to lead the nation beyond the stifling confines of the old regime.[12]

Late 1935 and early 1936 also brought political crises and a relaxation of repression within the state of Lara. Since 1929, Lara had been governed by Eustoquio Gómez, the dictator's cousin, sent to Barquisimeto following the Gabaldón revolt. Don Eustoquio, already "one of the most hated men in Venezuela [because of] his cruelty and high-handedness," had governed Lara with an iron fist for the last six years of the dictatorship.[13] Determined to perpetuate his family's hold on Venezuela after Juan Vicente's death, Eustoquio Gómez contested López's control of the national government and was shot dead while leading an assault on the presidential palace in late December 1935. López then named Vincencio Pérez Soto, a native of Lara, as state president.

But as one of Venezuela's most prominent Gomecistas, Pérez Soto could do nothing to ameliorate popular resentment against the old regime. On January 18 and 19, 1936, popular outbursts erupted in Barquisimeto as crowds attacked individuals and property linked to the Gomecista dictatorship. The most dramatic incident occurred on January 19, when a crowd attacked a house in the city belonging to the family of General Pedro Molina, who had served as jefe civil of Duaca under Don Eustoquio and who was believed to be hiding inside. By the time troops arrived to quell the riot, one of Molina's sons had shot a protestor and the crowd had retaliated by setting fire to the house. Amid the confusion, a rock hurled at one of the Molinas hit the troops' commander, and the soldiers opened fire into the crowd, killing nine and wounding fourteen, hitting most in the back as they attempted to flee.[14]

In the resulting furor, it became apparent that Pérez Soto could not impose stability in the state. On February 14, the same day that police in Caracas opened fire on a mass demonstration and threw the regime into crisis, López, in an extensive reorganization of his government, replaced Pérez Soto with none other than José Rafael Gabaldón, who had led the 1929 revolt against Gómez. Gabaldón, in keeping with the spirit of López's recent pronouncements, moved to liberalize the political climate in the state, which earned him the implacable enmity of Lara's economic elite.[15]

While raising legalistic objections to the organization of new conservative parties, Gabaldón placed no restrictions on the activities of new reformist and left-wing parties, including Orve and the PRP, each of which established local branches in March. These two parties drew their membership primarily from the middle class, but each clearly hoped to establish a base among peasants and urban workers, and the PRP strongly advocated land reform. Throughout the spring, the two parties held a series of rallies in Barquisimeto, with Gabaldón's apparent blessing.[16] Between late 1935 and early 1936, then, the political atmosphere in Lara had changed dramatically. It was within this context of crisis and political change that Duaca's peasants initiated their protest against the district's estate owners.

Attacks on landowners' property, which became the most common form of protest in Duaca, began sporadically in late 1935 and the early weeks of 1936. Casimiro Casamayor's estate of Tucuragua (formerly part of the Generals' Estate) became an early focal point of these attacks. On December 24, 1935, a group of men tore down the estate's main gate, and during the following two months, tenants repeatedly burned Casamayor's equipment and cut his fences. By early March, they were setting fire to pastures and to buildings used to store harvested crops. Similar attacks occurred at El Toro, which belonged to Domingo Javier, the son of Duaca entrepreneur Pedro Javier, where tenants destroyed the fences separating livestock from cultivated fields. In declarations before the district judge, Casamayor and Javier accused thirty-six men of taking part in the attacks.[17]

Even as Duaqueños launched attacks against landowners' property, they petitioned the state for legal redress of their grievances. In a letter to López Contreras dated March 3, 1936, a group of Duaca's peasants called the president's attention to the conditions of landlessness and high rents that had come to define life in the district over the previous two decades. As they described abuses in the district, the Duaqueños made clear the connection between their grievances and the Gómez dictatorship:

> General: We, members of the proletariat of this locality, direct ourselves to you in the firm belief that we shall be heard. We desperately wish to work to bring bread to our humble homes, thus fulfilling a sacred mission, but in reality all our efforts are in vain and every hope is frustrated because we do not have a piece of earth to cultivate, and wherever we try to raise a dwelling and plant crops, powerful hands forbid us such work, as though we were loathsome people, without any right to life. . . . These privations are carried out brazenly and at times with unspeakable abuses by those who call themselves owners of estates [dueños de posesiones], charging us ever higher rents, in unfair proportion to the fruit of our labor. . . . Such proceedings in this jurisdiction date from when General David Gimón exercised the Presidency of the State of Lara. It was he who permitted and with few or no scruples carried out the distribution of land, giving to his favorites as much as he pleased and leaving the destitute without aid. At that time, we can say, we began the most infamous martyrdom, for we are condemned not to possess a piece of land to cultivate from which to give food to our children.[18]

Duaca's peasants, then, clearly perceived a watershed in their history—the administration of state president David Gimón (1916–1920)—that marked the beginning of their "martyrdom." To be sure, in the months following Gómez's death it was safe (and even fashionable) to blame the fallen dictatorship for many national problems. In Lara, however, such accusations usually focused on Eustoquio Gómez, the last Gomecista president of the state and the dictator's cousin, rather than on Gimón. The Duaqueños, then, were not simply couching their protest in the political rhetoric of the moment. Rather, they pointed to the period in their history when landlessness and high rents became inescapable realities in the district. Gimón's tenure as state president coincided with the alienation of some twenty thousand hectares of public land in Duaca, much of which became the property of men connected to the regime, men whom the peasants saw as Gimón's favorites. True, the first record of fixed cash rents comes from 1925, five years after Gimón's departure from Lara. The peasantry nevertheless collapsed the beginning of landlessness and the imposition of high rents into a single historical moment, perhaps because they believed (correctly, as I argue) that the two developments were inextricably linked. The petition may be read as a plea for López Contreras to help the peasants return to conditions that prevailed before the onset of privatization.

The letter brought no immediate response from López, and in the weeks that followed peasant attacks against the estates intensified. By mid-March the press could report that "almost all the estates of this jurisdiction" had suffered attacks, indicating that the protests had spread to all corners of the district. Not a day went by without landowners seeing their fences cut, their buildings destroyed, their pastures and cultivated fields burned. At the urging of Duaca's jefe civil, President Gabaldón sent detachments of the civil guard to patrol the countryside, but the attacks continued. Landowners began to wonder if the unrest would soon move beyond attacks on property. On March 18, a newspaper correspondent in Duaca reported that the very lives of estate owners were in grave danger.[19]

Meanwhile, the estate owners attempted to organize in their own defense. They tried to hold a meeting one evening at Duaca's Club Bolívar, a social center of the well-to-do, but the gathering was prevented by a group of peasants armed with machetes. In the aftermath of the incident, Leopoldo Camejo, owner of the estate Los Chipas, emerged as the spokesman for Duaca's large landowners. In a statement to the Barquisimeto press, Camejo roundly criticized Duaca's newly appointed jefe civil, Rómulo Delgado Segura, for not acting decisively to end peasant attacks against the estates.[20]

Camejo accused Delgado of leniency toward the peasantry and even of freeing some peasants that had been apprehended in the act of destroying property.[21] Rather than enforcing the law, Delgado was allegedly encouraging "the intensification of peasant vandalism that is sowing ruin in the countryside." Moreover, according to Camejo, the *jefes de caseríos* (minor officials in the outlying hamlets appointed by the jefe civil) had led "the peasant hordes" in attacking the estates and in breaking up the landowners' meeting at the Club Bolívar. Indeed, two of the jefes de caseríos singled out by Camejo— Francisco R. Villegas and Juan Antonio Oviedo—had signed the letter of protest to President López Contreras. Camejo called on President Gabaldón to dismiss Delgado—and, by extension, his jefes de caseríos—"for being the cause of all the peasant outrages." According to the landed elite, the true cause of the protests was purely a matter of deficient civil authority; it had nothing to do with usurped lands and exploitative rents.

Camejo's assertion that Delgado sympathized with the peasantry was not without foundation. In an interview published in the Caracas daily *El Universal,* which reported regularly on the protests in Duaca, the jefe civil made it clear that, in his opinion, the protests resulted from Duaca's inequitable agrarian structure. Although he never argued that the land privatization of the Gómez era had been illegal (a clear implication in the peasants' letter to López Contreras), Delgado maintained that the highly concentrated ownership of land, coupled with exorbitant rents, had produced the polarization of Duaqueño society. "In honor to the truth," he told the interviewer, "what we have in Duaca is an agrarian problem."[22]

For Duaca's jefe civil to speak of an "agrarian problem" in the district was as unprecedented as the protests themselves. Clearly, Delgado, who had been appointed jefe civil by reformist state president Gabaldón, was not an instrument of Duaca's large landowners. True, he was a nephew of Eulogio Segura, probably Duaca's wealthiest entrepreneur, and he owned a few small landholdings in the district. But Delgado had never joined the privileged group of large estate owners who controlled access to land in Duaca. As an adolescent he had worked in his uncle Segura's commercial house in Duaca, and he had later been employed as a traveling agent for several Barquisimeto merchant firms with interests in the district.[23] Delgado had also acquired (and often resold) agricultural properties in Duaca, and he occasionally operated as a merchant on his own account. Nevertheless, his enterprises always remained small-scale, probably because he had begun his investments just before the onset of the depression and was thus prevented from expanding his operations. In two articles written in early 1935 for Duaca's newspaper, *La Senda,* Delgado complained bitterly of the situation facing the district's struggling entrepreneurs.[24] It seems likely that the essays flowed largely from Delgado's own unfulfilled ambitions. If he had hoped to follow in the footsteps of his uncle Segura, he was sadly disappointed. Despite his family connections, Delgado remained well outside the top echelon of Duaqueño society.

Delgado's class position is important, for he was part of a growing group that found itself between the peasantry and the wealthiest in local society. This emerging middle sector was composed largely of elite families who had suffered downward mobility in recent years. They were removed from the

peasantry by birth, education, and the accumulation of small amounts of entrepreneurial capital, but they were no longer among the elite who dominated the local economy. Duaca's elite had always been a varied group in
terms of wealth and power, but the Great Depression increased the distance
between its upper and lower levels. Some upper-class families lost most of
their property during the crisis of the early 1930s, often through foreclosures
by the BAP. At the same time, young members of prominent families such as
Delgado found it all but impossible to carve out new fortunes for themselves.
Some probably joined the ranks of Duaca's salaried workers—teachers, jour-
nalists, lawyers, and managers—even as they maintained small agricultural
and commercial enterprises. Delgado found himself within this emerging
middle sector.

A large segment of Duaca's middle sector gave public support to the peasantry in its struggle against the district's large estate owners. Only days after
the landowners issued their first statement criticizing Delgado's handling of
the crisis, a group of forty-four Duaqueños sent a letter to the Barquisimeto
press in which they defended the peasantry and Delgado while denouncing
the abuses of the estate owners.[25] The group, which identified itself as representing commerce, agriculture, and "the arts" (the liberal professions), included members of several well-known Duaca families. Like Delgado, they
came from prominent clans enjoying a status well above that of the peasantry,
but they were not among the large estate owners who had profited most during the Gómez era. Some, such as Donato Bracho and César Couput, belonged to old Duaca families who had seen their fortunes disappear during
the depression, whereas others, such as Oblen Ablan and Pascual Candia, had
come from immigrant families who had entered commerce and agriculture
but never amassed large enterprises.

In their letter, the forty-four boldly protested estate owners' oppression of
the peasantry. They dismissed the estate owners' assertion that the peasantry's
attacks resulted from a lack of civil authority or from the work of "agitators."
They claimed instead that the unrest was born of "an agrarian problem in
which a few individuals monopolized the lands of the District, many of them
using subterfuges which shall be juridically proven, and who established
a harsh feudalism on their large estates; justice now calls them to stand face
to face with the innocent and defenseless whom they have abused." While
indicting the estate owners, these members of Duaca's middle sector also dis-
tanced themselves from the peasants' assault on property. They condescend-
ingly noted that "rustic men" were bound to respond violently in the face of

oppression, but they refused to condone the peasant attacks. The best solution to Duaca's problems, the correspondents suggested, would be for the peasants to allow their social betters to guide them in a peaceful, legal search for justice. Thus the letter reflects a reformist position of the type often associated with Latin American middle sectors: on the one hand they sought retribution for the abuses of the Gómez era, while on the other hand they insisted that reform be carried out through legal channels.[26]

The 1936 protests, then, provide a window for viewing a growing political and economic rift within the upper levels of Duaqueño society. On one side, those who owned the largest estates in the district found themselves targets of the protests and stood firmly together in opposing any concessions to the peasantry; indeed, they refused to recognize the legitimacy of any peasant grievances. Meanwhile, those among the elite who had suffered downward economic mobility during the depression and who had not shared in the land bonanza of the Gómez era were not directly threatened by the protests. Instead, they sensed an opportunity to denounce the district's oppressive (in their word, "feudal") agrarian structure and thus allied themselves with the peasants' cause. As already mentioned, the timing and ultimate outcome of peasant protest are often influenced by the emergence of divisions within the elite and by the peasantry's ability to establish cross-class alliances. In the case of Duaca, the split between the large landowners and the emerging middle sector, as well as the alliance between the latter and the peasantry, may help to explain why the protests in Duaca continued unchecked during the early months of 1936.

Moreover, some Duaqueños who supported the peasantry were affiliated with the newly formed PRP, led by members of the proscribed Communist Party.[27] On Sunday, March 22, several representatives of the party arrived in Duaca from Barquisimeto to hold a public meeting. Many of the peasants who gathered in Duaca's plaza that day came to town under the guidance of the jefes de caseríos—the same minor officials blamed by the estate owners for leading attacks in the countryside.[28] The speakers from the PRP imparted a double-edged message to the peasants who attended the meeting. While assuring them that their grievances had reached the proper officials and that justice would be done, the PRP representatives also urged the peasants to continue their struggle. Perhaps most important, they affirmed the peasants' belief that Duaca's land was rightfully theirs. The speakers thus declared their solidarity with the peasants while avoiding an outright approval of attacks against private property. The ambiguity was undoubtedly intentional, a studied attempt by the newly legalized party to avoid an endorsement of illegal acts, while doing what it could to make connections with its potential supporters among the peasantry.

The attacks continued through late March, despite earlier reports that virtually all estates in the district had already suffered damages. To the north of the town of Duaca, a coffee grove was burned on Eulogio Segura's hacienda La Quinta. To the west, peasants cut fences on Manuel Anzola Tamayo's estate El Otro Lado. To the east, in Tumaque Arriba, a group cut fences separating Felix Elyuris's cattle from his cane fields, while in Agua-fría peasants set fire to Nefatalí Sanchez's coffee groves and destroyed fences on an hacienda belonging to Sabás Rodríguez.[29] In early April, peasants on three estates near El Eneal cut fences, stole barbed wire, burned fence posts, and freed cattle to wander into cultivated fields. It was around this time that peasants invaded lands on El Pegón and La Tigrera, estates belonging to the widow of Argenis Azuaje, the well-known Gomecista. Occupying the land as though it were their own, the peasants cleared small plots and planted food crops as they wished. Other estates suffered similar invasions.[30]

As their assaults on landowners' property continued, Duaca's peasants received growing support—at least at the rhetorical level. On April 6, one of Barquisimeto's two leading newspapers, *El Heraldo,* published an editorial entitled "The Problem of the Large Estates," which denounced the appropriation of land by powerful individuals during the Gómez dictatorship.[31] Although the editorial did not refer to Duaca explicitly, its description of agrarian problems reads like a blow-by-blow account of Duaca's history during the preceding decades. The editors denounced the loopholes in public land legislation such as the lack of a ban on the immediate resale of privatized land, which had allowed a few individuals to amass large estates, sometimes using surrogates (*testaferros o prestanombres*) who acquired title on their behalf. In some instances, the editorial asserted, a member of the elite would facilitate a land grant in favor of peasant settlers but then overcharge them for his services (such as land surveys, legal services, and title registrations), thus forcing the recipients to sign over their newly acquired land. Once the estates were formed, landowners imposed conditions "under which tenants were obliged to pay high rents, and on no few occasions had to cede their crops to the master in order to settle debts arising from rents and interest that could not be satisfied on schedule." The worst abuses, the editors charged, were sometimes committed by the jefes civiles. Such conditions, of course, had characterized Duaca's agrarian transformation from the mid-1910s onward. By publishing the editorial at the height of the protests in Duaca, the editors of *El Heraldo* gave thinly veiled support to the peasants' cause.

The following day, however, an event occurred that would quickly bring about the suppression of the protests and a muffling of public support for the peasantry. Late on the afternoon of April 7, the horribly mutilated corpse of Casimiro Casamayor, one of Duaca's largest landowners, was found in the road between the town of El Eneal and his estate in Tucuragua. Casamayor had been killed with a machete, but many of the blows had been struck to disfigure the body after death had already occurred. The fatal blow, perhaps struck while he was still mounted on his horse, had been to Casamayor's side, producing a wound deep enough that the lungs protruded. But the killers had also decapitated the corpse, severed the ears, hands, feet, and genitals, and stuffed the latter in the corpse's mouth. The ghastly scene in the road spoke vividly of the hatred that Casamayor's assailants felt for their victim. They had not even bothered to take his money or other valuables; clearly this was not a case of robbery. No one doubted that Casamayor's murder was linked to his being an estate owner, or that the killing signaled an escalation of the peasant protests.[32]

Local reaction to the murder was colored by the fact that Casamayor was one of the most hated landlords in the district. Over the past twenty years, his propensity for initiating lawsuits against his fellow Duaqueños had earned him a reputation as a *picapleito*—someone overly fond of litigation.[33] Not only had Casamayor repeatedly sued tenants who failed to pay rent, he had taken legal action to settle boundary disputes with neighboring landowners as well.[34] Although some Duaqueños were repulsed by the brutality of the murder, few showed any surprise that Casamayor had come to a violent end. Some local residents saw no reason to pity the man. Upon hearing of the murder, Rómulo Delgado, the jefe civil, was heard to exclaim, "What an agreeable victim!"[35]

The district judge opened an investigation into the murder, focusing immediately on the protests that had plagued Casamayor's estates since late December. The victim's widow, his administrator on the estate of Tucuragua, and a neighboring landowner all told the judge that the murder was connected to the conflict between Casamayor and his tenants.[36] Beginning in December, the estate's fences had been destroyed in several places, tenants had set fire to fields, buildings, and equipment. Men repeatedly gathered at

Casamayor's house at night and called him out, though he refused to leave the security of his home.[37] By late March, Casamayor believed that he could identify thirty of the men who had participated in the attacks on his estate. On March 28, he formally asked the district judge to initiate criminal proceedings against them.[38] He had gone to town on April 7 to take care of some matters related to the case; it was on his way home that he was killed.

Casamayor's widow, Esther Parra de Casamayor, provided a particularly compelling picture of the tensions between Casamayor and his tenants.[39] Most of the attacks against the estate had been carried out under the cover of darkness, but tenants had lost all fear of Casamayor in their face-to-face dealings with him as well. Parra declared that tenants refused to pay rents according to the estate regulations. Some paid only as much as they wished rather than the established tariff, others paid nothing, and many refused to recognize any form of landlord authority at all. Indeed, Parra emphasized that the tenants believed Duaca's landed estates had ceased to exist. "The word among all those who live in Tucuragua," she told the judge, "is that the estates have fallen and that they can do whatever they want." Just two days before his death, Casamayor had confronted a peasant erecting a house on the estate without permission. The peasant told Casamayor that he needed no permission "because the estates have fallen," and when Casamayor lectured him on the estate's regulations, he simply smiled and began to whistle a tune. Finally, Parra testified that she had overhead one of the thirty men accused by Casamayor say that the fences destroyed on the estate "were worth nothing because the estates had already fallen." Casamayor's tenants, and presumably those on other estates as well, had apparently concluded that Duaca's private estates had passed away with Gómez.

Given the conditions that prevailed in Duaca in March and early April, it must have seemed obvious to the peasantry that the district's system of landed property was indeed crumbling. The entire course of events in the district since the death of Gómez pointed to the decline of landlord authority. Only a few individuals had been arrested for the destruction of property, with most attacks against the estates going unpunished. As the jefe civil and local elite argued openly in the press, and as Barquisimeto politicians and editors voiced support for peasant grievances, a concerted campaign to suppress the peasantry did not seem an immediate possibility. While the peasantry's actions had clearly played a major role in undermining landlord power, the shifts in regional politics following the death of Gómez had also worked in the peasants' favor. Just as the Gómez dictatorship had been a crucial factor in the elite's growing control over land and over the peasantry, so the dictator's demise seemed to signal a shift back toward greater peasant autonomy.

There is no explicit indication of what land tenure system the peasantry believed should prevail in Duaca following the demise of the private estates. No specific proposals for agrarian reform emerged from the unrest of early 1936. But we can surmise that the peasantry may well have sought a return to an agrarian system based primarily on usufruct rights, a system such as the one that had prevailed on Duaca's public domain and resguardos prior to privatization. Several facts lend support to this conclusion: the peasants' letter to López Contreras, in which they identified the privatization of land under state president Gimón as the beginning of their "martyrdom," peasants' unauthorized settlement on estate lands during the protests, and the popular belief that the end of the private estates had freed the peasantry to live and work the land as they chose. Moreover, landowner-peasant conflicts from the 1910s through the early 1930s provide strong evidence of peasant attachment to the principle of usufruct rights, as peasants repeatedly appealed to the principle in their attempt to defend themselves against the claims of landowners. Historical experience had taught the peasantry that use rights provided the most just method of regulating access to land. For, just as an agrarian system built around usufruct rights was associated with the most expansive, dynamic phase of the peasantry's past in Duaca, so the world of private estates was undeniably linked to peasant oppression. The protests of 1936 represented the peasantry's attempt to return to the system of land use that in their experience had served them best.

The attempt proved to be in vain. Following the murder of Casimiro Casamayor, the state government moved decisively to restore order in Duaca. President Gabaldón dispatched additional units of the state guard to Duaca to protect lives and property, and the protests were quickly repressed. Some of those who had participated in the peasant movement fled the district, fearing for their lives.[40] Despite his willingness to use force to end the protests, however, Gabaldón remained faithful to his reformist mission. He raised the issue of Duaca's agrarian problem with President López Contreras during a meeting in Caracas. López referred the matter to his minister of agriculture, Alberto Adriani, who in turn dispatched a team of lawyers to Duaca to scrutinize the acquisition of public lands during the dictatorship.[41] The investigation may have resulted from a sincere desire to correct past abuses, or it may have been a calculated attempt to ease popular discontent. In any event, it did not lead to the widespread reclamation of public lands but only began the slow process of measuring and privatizing most of Duaca's remaining baldíos.[42]

The political opening that had created the context for the protests of 1936 soon came to an end. Gabaldón remained in office only a few months and was replaced by Honorio Sigala, a staunch defender of landowner interests and allegedly one of the more brutal and corrupt state presidents to serve under López Contreras.[43] In a surprising development, Rómulo Delgado Segura became Sigala's ally. Turning his back on what he had declared to be Duaca's agrarian problem, Delgado would later support the rightist Pérez Jiménez dictatorship before retiring from politics to spend his final years reading theosophy and attempting to develop a herbal cure for baldness.[44] López Contreras, in late 1936 and early 1937, turned decidedly to the right, repressing opposition parties, sending his most militant opponents into exile, and dashing hopes for a sustained political opening. His only nod in the direction of agrarian reform was to confiscate the vast rural properties that had belonged to Gómez, but he never intended to distribute the land to peasants.[45] Moreover, Gómez owned no property in Duaca or elsewhere in Lara, so estates there were not affected.[46] Contrary to peasant hopes, Duaca's large estates did not fade away: they remained intact.[47]

Epilogue

The years following the 1936 protests witnessed a perpetuation of the agrarian structure that took shape in Duaca during the Gómez period. Although the data gleaned from agricultural censuses must be treated with caution, such figures nonetheless confirm that most peasants in Duaca continued to live and work on land they did not own. Venezuela's first agricultural census, that of 1937, found that less than one-third of Duaca's farms—539 out of 1,695 (31.8 percent)—were located on land belonging to the farm owner. By contrast, a clear majority—990 out of 1,695 (58.4 percent)—were tenant farms. The smallest group—comprising only 166 farms (9.8 percent)—occupied public land.[48] Because the census counted farms (*fundos*) rather than farm owners, and because some individuals owned multiple farms, these figures cannot be taken as an exact reflection of Duaca's social structure. In all probability, most landowning farmers were members of the elite who owned a number of the fundos counted in the census, whereas most tenants and public land occupants owned only one fundo apiece. Thus landowning farmers were almost certainly less than 31.8 percent of all farm owners, while tenants and public land occupants probably accounted for much more than two-thirds of farm owners.

The situation deteriorated even further in the years that followed. The 1950 census found that the control of land in Duaca had become increasingly concentrated since 1937. While the number of farms increased to 2,470, the number of farms belonging to landowning farmers actually decreased, to 326 (a mere 13.2 percent).[49] This was the lowest figure for the entire state of Lara.[50] At the other extreme, 67.8 percent of farms in Distrito Morán and 73 percent of those in Distrito Torres were located on land to which the farmer had title in 1950, and many of these were small peasant farms. Meanwhile, small cultivators in Duaca remained without title to the land they occupied.

This basic continuity of agrarian structure, however, does not mean that the old struggles over land have receded completely into the past. Land conflicts remain a common feature of district life. The most important land dispute since the 1936 protests occurred in the late 1980s. Beginning in May 1987, Duaca's district government attempted to establish public control over the ten thousand hectares that had formerly comprised Duaca's Indian community lands. Proceeding on the basis of a report authored in part by historian Reinaldo Rojas, the district council asserted that the 1916 privatization of the resguardos had not been carried out in accordance with the land law of 1912 and was therefore null and void. Observing that the same law stated that any resguardo lands not duly privatized would become ejidos, municipal lands administered by the district government, the council announced that it would assume control over the entire ten thousand hectares.

In the uproar that followed, several local entrepreneurial organizations took the lead in opposing the council.[51] These organizations included members of families who had formed part of Duaca's elite as far back as the late nineteenth century. In declarations to the press, they pointed to the large agricultural production that would be jeopardized if the council seized the land. They vigorously defended the legality of the 1916 privatization but, at the same time, emphasized that even if some provisions of the law had not been fulfilled, the current owners of the land had acquired their properties in good faith. In a pivotal development, the Federation of Chambers of Commerce and Production (Fedecámaras), Venezuela's most powerful business organization, entered the dispute on behalf of Duaca's embattled landowners. By late

1988, the tide of events had turned against the council, and it was forced to suspend the reclamation. Once again, an attempt to reform Duaca's agrarian structure had been rebuffed.

Conclusion

The protests of 1936 represented a dramatic challenge to landlord power in Duaca. As in other areas of Venezuela, peasants in Duaca saw the political opening of that year as an opportunity to overturn the agrarian structure imposed during the dictatorship. Duaqueño peasants destroyed landlord property sporadically from late December 1935 through February 1936; their attacks intensified dramatically during March and early April. As the attacks went unpunished, and as land invasions occurred and rent collection came to a virtual halt, the underpinnings of landlord authority appeared to disintegrate, leading peasants to conclude that the district's large estates had ceased to exist. If only briefly, land in Duaca seemed to be under the control of those who worked it. This illusion of a return to the dominance of usufruct rights ended abruptly in mid-April, when armed forces sent from outside the district quelled the protests and restored landlord power.

That matters went as far as they did in Duaca was due largely to a growing rift within the elite. Members of an emerging middle sector, many of whom came from elite families hard hit by the depression, sided with the peasantry against the large estate owners. Duaca's jefe civil, himself a struggling member of an elite family, openly sympathized with the peasants and was reluctant to use his authority to repress them. The jefes de caseríos, appointed by the jefe civil as his representatives in the outlying hamlets, also supported the peasants. Finally, the Barquisimeto press and the PRP sided with the peasantry and called for the reform of Duaca's "feudal" agrarian structure. Middle-class sympathy for the peasantry, however, did not lead to any formal multiclass alliance in 1936, largely because of disagreements over political tactics. While the peasantry continued to engage in direct action against the system of landed estates, the middle sectors were only willing to endorse a more gradual strategy of legal reform.

The 1936 protests in Duaca and other parts of rural Venezuela mark a moment of transition. Even as the peasantry looked backward, hoping to restore the agrarian order that had preceded the changes brought under Gómez, a new era was beginning in Venezuela. A political alliance between reformist middle sectors and the Venezuelan peasantry eventually became one of the defining characteristics of this new era. It provided the basis for the multiclass political parties that increasingly dominated national politics. The priorities of the parties have rarely been those of the peasantry, however, and agrarian reform in Venezuela has been halting, driven by political considerations, and largely ineffective. Any land redistribution that has occurred has been most extensive in the central coastal zone; in peripheral areas such as Duaca, land reform has by and large been limited to the distribution of small plots of marginal lands.[52] In Duaca, the agrarian structure imposed by the Gomecista state and its local allies has remained largely in place during the intervening decades.

10 Coffee and Social Transformation
    in Latin America

THE EXPERIENCE OF Duaca's peasantry between independence and the 1930s had much in common with that of other rural Latin Americans. Throughout the region, the expansion of agricultural export economies was accompanied by the thorough transformation of society. Although the pattern of change varied widely from one locale to the next, its most salient characteristic was the growing subordination of labor to owners of land and capital. Whereas rural cultivators in the early nineteenth century often enjoyed some degree of autonomy and subsistence security, by the early or mid-twentieth century the rural working class had generally been reduced to a condition of dependence and deepening poverty. In some cases the subordination of workers occurred primarily through the spread of free wage labor and the emergence of a fully developed capitalist mode of production, in others through credit relationships that increasingly favored creditors over direct producers, and in others through landlords' imposition of increasingly harsh conditions of tenancy. In many instances combinations of these modalities (and others) took hold.[1]

The coffee economies of Central and South America and the Caribbean vividly demonstrate the range of socioeconomic processes associated with the expansion of export agriculture. During the century that ended with the Great Depression, the proliferation of coffee radically changed the face of society in nations such as Brazil, Guatemala, El Salvador, Colombia, Costa Rica, Puerto Rico, and Venezuela. Coffee in each nation enriched a small minority of the population while in the long run impoverishing those who toiled to produce the valued bean. And yet this common outcome was in no way predetermined. It resulted instead from the varied social and political settings into which coffee was introduced, from choices made by historical actors and, above all, from struggles among the social groups whose fate was somehow linked to coffee. Thus the pattern of change in each nation—and often within various regions of the same nation—was unique, despite the production of the same crop for an increasingly integrated world market.

To conclude this study of Duaca, I shall review the patterns of agrarian change in Latin America's major coffee economies, focusing on questions of land tenure, relations of production, and where possible, the role of the state in directing or conditioning agrarian change. At the least, such a review will help to place Duaca in its proper historical context by suggesting how Duaqueños' experiences resembled or differed from those of other Latin Americans engaged in coffee production. In addition, a review of developments in the region's coffee economies will serve to suggest comparative questions concerning the transformation of rural Latin America during the nineteenth and early twentieth centuries. Most important, the comparative history of coffee points to the primacy of political factors in conditioning the evolution of social structures.

To begin, it is crucial to differentiate between those areas where coffee developed from the beginning as a plantation crop and those where it was largely a peasant crop. In the former group, Brazil, Guatemala, and El Salvador are particularly important examples. Each of these nations witnessed the development of coffee plantations worked by dependent labor in the nineteenth century. Although agrarian change in each country had its unique characteristics, in all three nations the political influence wielded by coffee planters was fundamental in integrating land and labor into the plantation economy.

Brazil, Latin America's largest coffee producer, provides one of the clearest examples of a planter class using state power to protect and expand a plantation system of concentrated land holdings and dependent workers. Planters' success in turning government policy to their own advantage reflected their prominent role in the consolidation of a national state. As the coffee boom began in the 1830s, Brazilian elites—still searching for new political institutions following independence from Portugal in 1822—had experimented with a series of reforms aimed at decentralizing political power. By the late 1830s, the propertied class in general, and the increasingly prosperous yet anxious coffee growers in particular, had come to view these reforms as the cause of a rising tide of social and political unrest, and they clamored for a powerful central state capable of restoring order. In the years that followed, Brazilian landowners led the move toward a more centralized political structure but, in doing so, ensured that the central state remained responsive to the interests of men of property.[2]

Coffee planters were particularly influential among the landowners who controlled the levers of central power, whether by occupying important posts themselves or by putting in place functionaries beholden to them. Indeed, coffee planters from Rio de Janeiro province (the richest coffee region of the early and mid-nineteenth century) may well have formed the most powerful local elite under the constitutional monarchy that held sway until 1889, and coffee planters from São Paulo (whose production exceeded that of Rio by the late nineteenth century) held a disproportionate share of national power under the Old Republic of 1889–1930.[3]

Planters consistently used their political pull to establish and maintain a pattern of concentrated landownership in the most productive coffee zones. As coffee took hold in Rio de Janeiro's Paraíba Valley in the 1820s and 1830s, control over land was often contested, due to the vague boundaries of colonial-era land grants and the legal recognition of squatters' rights. In the struggles that ensued, local potentates effectively used the courts (and, on occasion, armed thugs) to dislodge smaller cultivators, who were either marginalized within the valley's plantation economy or driven westward to the frontier.[4]

In 1850, as coffee continued to expand westward into the province of São Paulo, the imperial government attempted to regularize landholdings and to assert greater control over public lands on the frontier. But planter interests shaped both the new land law and its subsequent application.[5] While the 1850 statute curtailed squatters' rights and prevented the growth of a landowning peasantry on the frontier, large planters continued to integrate public lands into their plantations through a variety of means, including purchase from the government, the legitimation of fictitious claims allegedly established before 1850, and the intimidation of anyone who dared challenge their pretensions. When disputes arose on the São Paulo frontier, "courts invariably awarded land title to the strongest among the pretenders," as occurred earlier in the Paraíba Valley.[6]

Planters also used their political influence to guarantee themselves a dependent labor force amid the erosion of slavery. Indeed, as Emília Viotti da Costa argues, the ending of squatters' rights in the 1850 land law responded to planters' anxieties concerning the continued viability of the plantation system at a time when Brazil's Atlantic slave trade was coming to an end.[7] Planters hoped to replace their slaves gradually with European immigrants, who first came to Brazil in significant numbers in the late 1840s; the ban on unauthorized settlement of public lands was intended to ensure that immigrant farmers became tenants on plantations. As it happened, only a limited number of immigrants were interested in coming to Brazil under the conditions offered by planters in the 1840s and 1850s, and slaves continued to work most coffee plantations until abolition in 1888. By that time, Paulista planters had instituted a new program of government subsidized immigration, which, when combined with more lenient tenancy contracts on the plantations, provided a steady flow of European workers until World War I. Some immigrant tenants, known as *colonos,* eventually fulfilled their dream of becoming independent farm owners, but usually in areas where coffee-based prosperity had already come and gone.[8] The most fertile lands, those on the steadily moving western frontier, continued to be dominated by large estates worked by tenants. In sum, planters' influence over immigration policy, like their control over land policy and the courts, proved crucial to the reproduction of the plantation system as coffee cultivation extended westward.

In Guatemala, the growth of coffee plantations in the late nineteenth century reflected the program of the Liberal Party, most notably during the rule of President Justo Rufino Barrios (1873–1885).[9] Aggressively promoting the spread of coffee, Liberals sold large tracts of public lands at low prices and facilitated the privatization of Indian community lands, especially in the prime coffee-growing areas of the western piedmont. To be sure, small cultivators produced substantial amounts of coffee in some areas of Guatemala's highlands, but by 1890 the country's large planters controlled a larger share of national production than any of their Central American counterparts.[10]

The Liberal state also aided planters by supplying them with Indian workers through two forms of coerced labor, the village-based labor drafts known as *mandamientos* and a codified system of debt peonage. Both systems were far from ideal in the planters' view, as they tied up large sums of capital in wage advances while usually failing to provide a reliable supply of workers. Planters, though, could not obtain adequate numbers of seasonal workers through any other method as long as communities retained substantial amounts of land, which many did. In short, government policy played an indispensable role in establishing and maintaining coffee plantations in Guatemala.

But the government's ability to impose the new agrarian order depended on the creation of a more powerful, centralized state system; Guatemalan Liberals realized that the transformation of the state itself had to be part and parcel of the coffee revolution. Without a more developed apparatus of coercion and control, popular resistance might have derailed the Liberal program. Consequently, as David McCreery has observed, the Guatemalan Liberals professionalized the national army, made the militia a more credible force, and utilized technological advances such as the telegraph, the railroad, and the repeating rifle "to build a state of unprecedented power."[11] Indigenous opposition could still push the regime to compromise as it sought to enforce the labor laws, and Liberal leaders thought it wise to proceed cautiously and selectively in the breakup of Indian lands, but the new state proved strong enough to push through the wide-ranging changes needed for planters to prosper.[12]

Elites in El Salvador employed the power of the state to engineer one of the most drastic transformations of land and labor in nineteenth-century Latin America. As early as the 1840s, the Salvadoran government had sought to encourage the cultivation of coffee through a series of tax exemptions, but it became clear that a more fundamental reordering of society would be required to boost production. A large portion of the nation's land was not privately titled, having been granted during the colonial era to Spanish towns as ejidos or to Indian villages as *tierras comunales* (common lands). As late as the 1870s, Indian lands comprised fully one-quarter of the country, and in the central highlands (the region most suited to coffee) Indian lands and ejidos together accounted for the greater part of all land. Widespread peasant access to ejidos and Indian lands slowed the growth of a wage labor force and hindered the progress of plantation agriculture, despite the small nation's high population density.[13]

In the late nineteenth century, Liberal governments initiated more aggressive policies designed to transform El Salvador in the interests of the planter class. Between 1879 and 1881, the national government mandated the privatization of all ejidos and Indian lands. It seems that El Salvador's national state had not yet achieved the degree of centralized power wielded by the Guatemalan government at the time of that nation's assault on communal lands, but Salvadoran planters had fastened their hold on municipal governments, which took the lead in implementing the new laws, often in the face of peasant resistance. The general effect of privatization was for the elite to expand dramatically their control over the best coffee lands, even though in certain areas many small and medium cultivators did receive title to their plots. As most peasants lost their land, they had little choice but to seek work on expanding coffee plantations. Meanwhile, the judiciary, the army, and a rural police force introduced after a peasant rebellion in 1889, aided planters in controlling workers. By the end of the century, the national state was increasingly stable, centralized, and under the control of coffee planters, whose interests it steadfastly defended.[14]

In all three nations, then, the state played a crucial role in the development and maintenance of a plantation economy. Significantly, in all three cases, the formative decades of the coffee economy coincided with advances in the consolidation of state power, and planters gained dominant positions within the emerging governmental structures. Indeed, it is difficult to imagine the emergence and continuation of large coffee plantations in these three nations without the active support of the state apparatus. But in other areas of Latin America, particularly on sparsely populated frontiers where land was plentiful, labor was free and mobile, and policies restricting peasant access to land were either not enacted or not enforced, coffee became a peasant crop.

Precipitate Peasantries in Latin American Coffee Zones: Shared Origins and Divergent Paths

The development of coffee-based peasant societies in Costa Rica, Puerto Rico, and parts of Venezuela and Colombia all followed a broadly similar outline. The dominant pattern consists of two distinct phases: an initial phase in which an emergent precipitate peasantry enjoyed relative prosperity and autonomy, and a second phase in which the peasantry, for a variety of reasons, experienced growing poverty and subjugation to elites.

The first period in the history of frontier peasantries was that of their formation and expansion. In Costa Rica, Puerto Rico, the Venezuelan Andes, and parts of Colombia, the growth of the coffee economy during the nineteenth century drew waves of settlers to sparsely populated frontier areas. The resulting societies fit Roseberry's description of precipitate peasantries, that is, groups of small cultivators created in frontier areas during the height of the agro-export boom. These peasantries shared similar characteristics at their origins and for some years thereafter. In the four cases under review, as in

Duaca, early settlers in the coffee zones enjoyed considerable autonomy compared to laborers in the plantation economies of Brazil, Guatemala, and El Salvador. To be sure, they experienced a degree of internal differentiation, with some households hiring labor in while others hired out. In addition, virtually all peasant households engaged in coffee production received loans from merchants. This link to commercial capital brought with it certain risks, but the risks were partially mitigated by the generally favorable coffee prices of the latter part of the nineteenth century.

Most important, precipitate peasants in their formative phase benefited from the frontier's high ratio of land to population. As long as land was abundant, rising generations and families who lost their farms for debt could migrate to the frontier and establish new farms instead of becoming dependent laborers. Moreover, widespread peasant access to land limited the supply of wage workers and thus gave laborers more bargaining power with employers. In general, then, the first peasant settlers succeeded in maintaining themselves and their children as peasants. During this initial phase, precipitate peasantries were, on the whole, geographically expansive and economically resilient.

But as time passed, conditions invariably began to deteriorate, initiating the second phase in the history of precipitate peasantries, that of impoverishment and subjugation. The decline of precipitate peasantries occurred through two distinct scenarios, one driven primarily by demographic factors and another driven by elites' use of political influence to seize control of land and labor. Even though the two scenarios could operate simultaneously, it is useful for purposes of analysis to consider each one separately.

Demographic forces most commonly became the principal factor in the decline of precipitate peasantries. After several decades of prosperity, and sometimes sooner, peasantries began to suffer the effects of growing population pressure as the frontier became completely settled, vacant land became scarce and expensive, and family holdings with each passing generation were subdivided into progressively smaller farms. Under these conditions, peasants who lost their farms to creditors or who inherited uneconomically small farms could only turn toward wage labor. Meanwhile, the expanding labor pool might exert a downward pressure on wages. The markets for land and labor—which did not undermine peasant prosperity as long as land remained abundant—began to erode peasants' livelihood as the ratio of population to land increased. Thus demographic change (rather than the existence of markets per se) stood as a formidable threat to frontier peasants' long-term pros-

perity. The case of Costa Rica provides the clearest evidence of the role of demographic forces in threatening household self-sufficiency.

But in some cases precipitate peasantries suffered impoverishment and
subjugation at the hands of local elites even before demographic forces had
undermined the viability of the peasant economy. On the Colombian frontier, as in Duaca, this process of domination involved the appropriation of
public lands occupied by small cultivators who were converted into estate tenants. In both cases, political factors played a fundamental role in shaping society as members of the elite used their connections to the state to seize control
of land already settled and occupied by peasants. In terms of their long-term
fate, then, precipitate peasantries can be divided between those pauperized
largely through demographic forces (as occurred in Costa Rica), and those
who suffered impoverishment due primarily to the political machinations of
land-hungry elites (as occurred in Colombia).

My aim is now to trace the origins, development, and ultimate impoverishment of peasantries in Costa Rica, Puerto Rico, Colombia, and the
Venezuelan Andes. This discussion is intended to demonstrate general patterns in the formation, expansion, and eventual decline of frontier peasantries
engaged in coffee production from the mid-nineteenth century to roughly the
1930s. It will then serve as a comparative framework for a review of the history of Duaca.

Lowell Gudmundson's fine analysis of Costa Rica demonstrates how the
transition to a coffee economy created a new class of independent small cultivators. Prior to the introduction of coffee, the vast majority of Costa Ricans
lived in towns and villages and either cultivated nearby subsistence farms,
often located on municipal land, or worked on local haciendas. This pattern
of nucleated settlement, when combined with Costa Rica's small population,
left large amounts of land unoccupied at independence. The introduction of
coffee in the early and mid-nineteenth century, however, brought about a
rapid dispersal of Costa Rica's population, as peasant families migrated to
new lands to engage in production for export. Gudmundson believes that this
ruralization of the population resulted in a more egalitarian system of land
tenure than had prevailed during the colonial era. In his words, "coffee's initial task was to transform the inegalitarian colonial order, one based on both
landed inequality and occupational diversity, toward an order that featured a
more dispersed and privatized agrarian capitalism in which outlander small-
holding became predominant for the first time." Gudmundson makes clear
that many peasants who grew coffee on their own farms also worked as hired

hands on larger farms, but he argues that their wages "did not necessarily account for the greater share of the total family income." After the turn of the century, however, many rural Costa Ricans became increasingly dependent on wage labor, and by the 1930s a process of proletarianization was well advanced in some areas.[15]

Mario Samper provides a detailed analysis of the gradual transformation of rural society in one locale on the Costa Rican frontier. His nuanced analysis of migration, changing land use, and peasant inheritance practices reinforces many of Gudmundson's arguments and highlights again the importance of demographic factors in bringing about the gradual impoverishment of the Costa Rican peasantry. Focusing on the northwestern section of the Central Valley, Samper finds that landownership became widespread during the initial phase of settlement in the early and mid-nineteenth century. The size of landholdings varied among settlers from the beginning, but variations in wealth were less extreme on the frontier than in areas settled during the colonial era. By the late nineteenth century, however, population growth, land scarcity, and the subdivision of farms through inheritance began to undermine the autonomy of many peasant families, pushing them toward wage labor. Inhabitants of the region were obliged to migrate in ever greater numbers to search for increasingly scarce lands still open to colonization. Whereas migration into the northwest had remained high through the early 1890s, by 1900 out-migration had become the dominant pattern, in spite of the bleak prospects for success elsewhere. Among those who remained in the northwest, variations in wealth became increasingly dramatic from the late nineteenth century onward. During the early and mid-twentieth century, when "land scarcity became acute in the northwest," the size of most family holdings continued to decline, leading to an ever greater dependence on wage labor among the majority of the population.[16]

The role of the state in directing agrarian change, which was crucial in the plantation economies of El Salvador, Guatemala, and Brazil, was less pronounced in Costa Rica's principal coffee zones, despite the political influence of the nation's coffee bourgeoisie from the mid-nineteenth century until the 1948 Revolution.[17] Some entrepreneurs used their political influence to obtain large tracts of public land on the Costa Rican frontier, but most divided their holdings into smaller plots for sale to settlers.[18] These sales played a fundamental role in the rise of a landowning peasantry in the nineteenth century. The Costa Rican elite never mounted a concerted attempt to establish a system of large estates worked by dependent laborers, although they did occasionally develop haciendas worked by seasonal labor drawn from peasant households.[19] With such a high ratio of land to population during the formative years of the coffee economy, binding large numbers of workers to the land as tenants or peons would have required a highly coercive system of labor control, and there is no indication that the state had achieved sufficient power to impose such a system. Instead, entrepreneurs concentrated their investment in merchant enterprises, establishing control over the financing, processing, and marketing of coffee produced by their peasant clients. By the early twentieth century, a limited number of processor-creditor firms had consolidated their market position and imposed increasingly unfavorable terms on direct producers. Thus in Costa Rica—in contrast to most of rural Latin America, where conflicts tended to pit landowners against small cultivators or dependent workers—political tensions revolved around divisions between direct producers and merchant-processors.[20]

Agrarian change in the Venezuelan Andes followed a pattern similar to that observed in Costa Rica, with demographic factors playing a decisive role. Here, the development of the coffee economy involved two patterns of migration in the decades following the Federal War (1859–1863). Coffee zones most commonly received migrants who moved from the higher elevations (*tierra fría*) of the wheat-growing regions of the Andes to lower elevations (*tierra templada*) where conditions were suitable for coffee.[21] In the state of Táchira, situated on Venezuela's western border, many migrants into the coffee zones came from Colombia. Although politicians and entrepreneurs dreamed of attracting white European immigrants to make the nation prosperous, Venezuelan and Colombian settlers laid the foundation of the coffee boom in the Andes. Here, as on other coffee frontiers, the peasantry's economic fortunes depended largely on the availability of land and on cooperative exchanges (especially labor exchanges) among peasant households.[22]

In his study of the Andean district of Boconó, Roseberry emphasizes the exploitative features of the Boconó coffee economy from the time of its formation in the mid-nineteenth century, pointing especially to peasants' dependence on commercial capital. He also describes the internal differentiation of the peasantry and the need of poorer families to earn wages through seasonal employment. Nevertheless, household production predominated in nineteenth-century Boconó, and Roseberry concludes that "The formation of a coffee economy implied the creation of a peasantry."[23] Into the late nineteenth century, peasants in Boconó enjoyed widespread access to land. Indian community lands and private estates were divided and sold, enabling many settlers to gain title to the plots they cultivated, while other peasants settled on public land.

As in Costa Rica, the expansive phase of the peasant economy could only continue as long as new lands remained available. A few coffee districts in the Andes still had vacant lands to attract settlers as late as 1920, but in Boconó the supply of land for new settlement was exhausted two decades earlier. There, Roseberry observes, "the coffee economy had lost its 'progressive' aspect" by the turn of the century. The reproduction of peasant households could no longer be achieved through mere spatial expansion. The twentieth century, therefore, witnessed processes similar to those in Costa Rica as small and medium farms "experienced fragmentation and decreasing returns" and farm owners "experienced a type of proletarianization" without completely losing access to land. By the 1970s, "coffee farmers . . . [were] no longer working off the farm to supplement farm income. Rather, the farm, reduced to a garden, [was] supplementing wages." During the twentieth century, then, capitalist relations of production gradually superseded those of the peasant household, but without creating an absolutely landless proletariat.[24]

In the coffee zones of Puerto Rico, the creation and impoverishment of a precipitate peasantry took place within a shorter time span than in Costa Rica or Venezuela. Works by Laird Bergad, who has focused on the municipality of Lares, and by Fernando Picó, who has studied the municipality of Utuado, suggest that demographic factors were crucial in bringing about the decline of Puerto Rico's peasantry, but they also indicate that political factors played an important secondary role.[25] Both municipalities, like most of the island's interior highlands, were sparsely settled frontier areas when the coffee economy began to develop in the early nineteenth century. As in Costa Rica and the Venezuelan Andes, the rise of coffee in Puerto Rico drew migrants to vacant land. Many settlers gained title to public land, sometimes with the assistance of local officials eager to spread the burden of land taxes imposed on the municipalities. In Utuado and Lares, however, the supply of public land was already exhausted by 1870, and rising generations had to choose between dividing the family farm into ever smaller units or moving to haciendas as dependent laborers. A small class of independent smallholders survived, but a large segment of the rural population was pushed toward proletarianization during the final three decades of the nineteenth century.

Puerto Rico's relatively swift movement toward wage labor stands in contrast to the more gradual changes observed in Costa Rica and the Venezuelan

Andes. Picó and Bergad both suggest that the unusually high ratio of population to land on the island may explain its sudden shift toward proletarianization. Bergad notes that, whereas the frontier of unsettled land in Puerto Rico "was closed by the 1870s and land scarcity resulted," unsettled land still remained abundant in other Latin American agrarian economies. "Puerto Rico's high population density," he observes, "contrasted with the demographic situation in Costa Rica, Colombia, Brazil, and even Cuba."[26] The equation of land and population, then, was critical in undermining the peasant economy that flourished briefly in the Puerto Rican interior.

Nevertheless, the colonial state also played a role in converting Puerto Rican peasants into dependent hacienda laborers. In 1849, Puerto Rico's governor general issued a vagrancy law requiring all persons who did not own land or practice a skilled trade to sign labor contracts with landowners and to carry a *libreta* (notebook) recording their obligations, debts, and work performance. Unlike many similar laws in nineteenth-century Latin America, the Puerto Rican statute succeeded in binding the rural population to landowners and in undercutting workers' bargaining power with employers.[27] The documented instances of hacendados invoking the law, the numbers of people registered as workers under the law, and the surviving libretas, all leave no doubt that the law was enforced and that it increased the pool of labor available to hacendados. But the impact of the law (which was abolished in 1873) probably resulted as much from demographic and ecological factors as from the power of the Spanish colonial state. The limited extent of Puerto Rico's frontier and the high concentration of population kept most of the rural poor within reach of the law. Moreover, the need for wages probably pushed more peasants to sell their labor than were pressured to do so by the state.

On the Colombian frontier, however, elites often used their connections to the state to subjugate the peasantry before demographic pressures reached a critical stage. As Catherine LeGrand has demonstrated, the development of Colombia's frontier economy repeatedly brought peasant settlers into conflict with entrepreneurs attempting to appropriate land occupied by small cultivators. Settlers migrated to public lands throughout the nineteenth century, many of them planting coffee or other export crops. But after they made the land productive, Colombian peasants were confronted by members of the elite who asserted control over the land either by securing a grant from the government or by using judicial "surveys" of local estates to enclose settlers' farms. Elites who acquired title to public lands forced the occupants to sign tenancy contracts or face eviction from their farms. Peasants often struggled to defend their right to the land they cultivated, but they rarely won. According to LeGrand, the period of free peasant access to land was usually brief. "In most parts of the country," she writes, "peasant settlers could hope to remain undisturbed on their claims for at most ten to thirty years; at this point large land entrepreneurs invariably appeared on the scene."[28]

The formation of coffee estates in Colombia, then, often involved the expropriation of peasants who had already cleared the land and planted their own coffee groves.[29] In contrast to the dominant trends observed in Brazil, Guatemala, and El Salvador, entrepreneurs in Colombia established large estates by using the state (and sometimes private thugs) to dispossess settlers already engaged in coffee production. The expropriation of Colombian settlers, however, proved to be only the first act in a long struggle. In the 1920s and 1930s, estate tenants organized to reclaim their lands, and due to a combination of economic and political pressures, some estates were divided among occupants who received title to the land they worked. Struggles over coffee lands continued through the mid-twentieth century, played an important role in the upheavals known as the Violence (1946–1958), and did not completely subside thereafter.[30] LeGrand concludes, "Colombian frontier expansion gave rise to an ideology of peasant protest centered on the reclamation of public lands that remains a vital tradition in the rural areas today."[31] The history of Colombia's precipitate peasantry, then, presents a vivid contrast to its Costa Rican counterpart, for in Colombia peasant access to land has often depended on political struggle rather than demographic or economic factors.

Agrarian Change in Duaca

In Duaca, as on the Colombian frontier, the fundamental impetus behind agrarian change was the elite's use of political influence to appropriate land occupied by peasant settlers. The transformation of rural Duaca depended upon the local elite's alliance with Cipriano Castro and Juan Vicente Gómez, the two national leaders who consolidated the power of the national state between 1899 and 1935. Duaca's elite, which had exercised only limited control over land and over the peasantry in the nineteenth century, used the power of the state to impose a radically new agrarian order during the first three decades of the twentieth century.

Like most areas of Latin America that came to be populated by precipitate peasantries, Duaca had occupied a marginal place in the economy of the colonial era and thus remained an isolated frontier region into the early nineteenth century. Only during the decades following independence, as Duaqueños began to cultivate coffee, did the region's large expanse of vacant land attract a steady stream of migrants. As population increased, peasants and elite hacendados pushed coffee cultivation beyond Duaca's Indian community lands—long the center of agricultural production—to public lands and private estates. Into the 1860s, however, the growth of Duaca's coffee economy was limited by poor transportation and by the area's weak integration into the network of credit that served the central coastal zone to the east. These same factors restrained the spatial expansion of production, leaving a large portion of Duaca's territory still unoccupied.

As the local export boom began in earnest in the mid-1860s, Duaca experienced many of the same developments that occurred on other coffee frontiers characterized by widespread peasant settlement. Ever larger numbers of migrants came to work the land, especially as new transportation systems and merchant networks facilitated ties to the global market. Cooperative arrangements among households, particularly those linked by kinship, gave peasant society much of its vigor and resiliency. Migrants often settled in family clusters, an arrangement that facilitated the exchange of labor among households, and loans of cash and goods among peasants made it possible to meet many of the exigencies of the commercial economy. Although peasants often sought work on haciendas to supplement household income, and although many borrowed in advance of wages, a system of tightly controlled peonage did not emerge in Duaca during the nineteenth century, largely because widespread access to land restrained the supply of labor, increased workers' bargaining power with employers, and thus bolstered peasant autonomy. Clearly these patterns of household economy were not unique to Duaca; they paralleled developments during the formative period of the coffee economy in other regions where frontier peasantries took hold.

A critical development that set Duaca apart from most other coffee frontiers was the long delay in the privatization of public and communal lands. In many settings, coffee producers or elite interlopers secured private title to land within the first two decades or so following the beginning of commercial production. By contrast, most of Duaca's Indian and national lands remained untitled until at least the mid-1910s, a half century after the onset of the export boom. To be sure, some of Duaca's Indian lands were privatized in the early 1850s, but most continued under community ownership until 1916. Several tracts of national land passed to private ownership soon after the Federal War, but a large expanse of Duaca's territory—at least forty thousand hectares, or half the district's terrain—remained as public lands through the first decade of the twentieth century. Attempts to establish private ownership over additional areas of the resguardos and public lands in the nineteenth century often failed as the decentralized structure of political power in Venezuela, the repeated outbreak of civil war, and local rivalries frustrated elite ambitions. With so much land untitled and open to settlement, estate owners offered unusually favorable conditions to tenants well into the twentieth century, recognizing that only low rents could attract cultivators who enjoyed the alternative of occupying community or public land.

In Venezuela, the consolidation of the central state occurred not during the formative decades of the coffee economy (as in Brazil and Guatemala) but many years after coffee was established as the leading export. In theory a more powerful national state might constitute a threat to local elites, but as prominent Duaqueños became integrated into the new political order they enhanced their control over local society. Having won district status through their support of Castro's 1899 revolt, Duaca's elite later won control over the office of jefe civil (a position given to nonlocal appointees in many parts of Venezuela) in exchange for safeguarding the regime's security interests in the district. The pivotal figures in this alliance were Eduardo Colmenares, who led the Duaqueños in the Revolución Libertadora (1901–1903) and commanded the largest following in the district, and his ally Ramón Antonio Vásquez. Their ability to control the railroad into Barquisimeto during political upheavals provided them with leverage that few local elites could match as they bargained with the new national leaders. As a result, either Colmenares or Vásquez held the office of jefe civil during most of the period between 1906 and 1929. And, as in virtually all Venezuelan districts, members of the local elite also controlled Duaca's district court and district council. In less than a decade, then, Duaca's local elite won district status, assumed control of the new district government, and cemented their ties to the central state.

Having originated during the previous era of political fragmentation, peasant society in Duaca was radically transformed once political consolidation occurred. Most important, the local elite used their newly established power to seize lands occupied by peasant settlers. Beginning in the mid-1910s, prominent Duaqueños appropriated Indian community lands, won title to public lands through a system of grants and brokered redistribution, and used the courts to legitimize the illegal expansion of estate boundaries. In every instance, occupants of public or community lands came under the control of newly established landlords. By the mid-1920s, the elite exercised almost complete control over access to land in the district, the great majority of Duaca's peasants had become estate tenants, and the landlord class had imposed a new, more onerous system of rents. Few coffee frontiers have undergone such a radical revolution in land tenure in such a compressed period of time.

Through the end of the Gómez dictatorship, the power of the state proved critical to the enforcement of the new agrarian order. Between the early 1920s and 1935, the district court supported landlords' claims against their tenants in dozens of cases. Defendants in these cases repeatedly claimed that because they were longtime occupants of public or community land, their rights to the areas they cultivated superseded those of their landlords. The court, however, refused to question the legality of the land privatization of the 1910s and 1920s. Meanwhile, as the conditions of the 1920s and 1930s drove more peasants to search for wage work, the jefe civil and the police assisted employers in imposing the most tightly controlled system of peonage in Duaca's history. Despite mounting popular grievances, the repressive apparatus of the Gomecista state discouraged collective protest in Duaca and throughout Venezuela.

In the conflict that erupted after Gómez's demise, peasants demonstrated both their abhorrence of the changes imposed during the past twenty years and their continued attachment to the system of land tenure that had marked the early expansion of the coffee economy. As in peasant rebellions elsewhere, Duaqueños' goals were shaped by memories of an earlier period of prosperity and relative autonomy. Sensing a political opening at the national and state levels, and receiving support from an emerging middle sector of local society, the peasantry made a last-ditch effort to recover the past. They petitioned the new national president to reverse the injustices of the Gómez era, destroyed landlord property, invaded estate lands, refused to pay rent, and brutally murdered one of the district's most prominent landowners. At the height of the protests, some peasants concluded that they were winning their struggle, that Duaca's system of private estates was about to disappear, and that the land would soon be reclaimed by those who worked it. But soon thereafter the state government moved decisively to repress the peasantry, the movement disintegrated, and the estate system survived.

The agrarian history of Duaca, then, points to the connection between politics and agrarian change. Changes in the prevailing system of land and labor did not simply represent the cumulative effects of market or demographic forces; rather, the transformation of Duaqueño society grew out of political changes at the local and national levels. The estate system that by the 1920s had come to define Duaca's agrarian structure was not simply the result of a century of production of coffee for the world market. It was also—and, in the eyes of peasants, it was primarily—the local face of Gomecismo.

As the evidence from other Latin American coffee zones demonstrates, political factors often played a critical role in shaping agrarian structures. Political factors loom particularly large in the history of coffee zones because—in a number of countries, including Brazil, Costa Rica, Colombia, and Venezuela—coffee spread to public lands under the control of the national state. The agrarian structures that took shape on the coffee frontiers of each of these nations reflected, to a greater or lesser degree, the action of the state in the allocation of land. Our understanding of the different patterns of agrarian change on Latin America's coffee frontiers, therefore, will depend upon future research into the structure and dynamics of the states that controlled land in those regions.

Given the progress of current research, it is possible to trace with some specificity the patterns of agrarian change that occurred in many of Latin America's frontier regions. But developing a typology of such patterns does not explain why a particular area developed as it did. Why plantations on the São Paulo frontier and precipitate peasantries elsewhere? Or, why a demographic decline of Costa Rica's peasantry but outright expropriation in Colombia? Perhaps in each setting the elite exercised the control they desired. It is possible, for example, that the Costa Rican elite chose to impose a different structure of production than the Brazilian elite. It seems more likely, though, that differing degrees of elite control over land resulted from the relative strength or weakness of ruling classes in particular places at particular moments. If so, the comparative history of coffee-based societies should begin with comparative studies of national states and of local elites' triumphs and failures in using state power to assert control over land and people on the coffee frontiers of Latin America.

Notes

Where several archival documents cited in a note have the same protocolo number, the number is included only in the citation of the first document in the series. All translations are by the author, unless otherwise indicated.

Abbreviations Used in the Notes

AANH	Archivo de la Academia Nacional de la Historia
ACMB	Archivo del Concejo Municipal de Barquisimeto
ACMDC	Archivo del Consejo Municipal del Distrito Crespo
ANH	Academia Nacional de la Historia
BAHM	*Boletín del Archivo Histórico de Miraflores*
CAP	Colección Ambrosio Perera
CJMH	Colección José Manuel Hernández
doc.	document
esc.	escritura
fol.	folio
j.civ.	juicios civiles
j.pen.	juicios penales
leg.	legajo
no fol.	unnumbered folios

PDB	Protocolos del Distrito Barquisimeto
PDC	Protocolos del Distrito Crespo
pr.	protocolo
RPEL	Registro Principal del Estado Lara

Chapter 1. Introduction

1. Roseberry, *Coffee and Capitalism in the Venezuelan Andes,* esp. 206–08, and chaps. 3, 4. Compare Eric R. Wolf's discussion of "open" peasant communities in "Types of Latin American Peasantry," 452–71. For a debate concerning Roseberry's conceptualization of peasants, see C. Smith, "Anthropology and History," and Roseberry, "Something About Peasants."

2. Roseberry, *Coffee and Capitalism,* esp. 109.

3. For Costa Rica, see Samper, *Generations of Settlers.* For the Colombian frontier, see Catherine LeGrand, *Frontier Expansion.* For Puerto Rico, see Bergad, *Coffee,* and Picó, *Amargo café.* See also chapter 10.

4. See Aston and Philpin, *The Brenner Debate.*

5. Acosta Saignes, *Latifundio,* and "Los orígenes históricos del problema agrario" (1959), in *Estudios,* 151–61; Brito Figueroa, *Historia económica y social.*

6. Carvallo and Ríos de Hernández, *Temas;* Ríos de Hernández, *La hacienda venezolana;* Ardao, *El café;* Muñoz, *El Táchira fronterizo;* Price, "Hands for the Coffee: Migration"; and Roseberry, *Coffee and Capitalism.*

7. Samper makes a similar point regarding Roseberry's work in *Generations of Settlers,* 251.

8. This is a recurring theme in Price, "Hands for the Coffee: Migration"; see also the discussion of migration in Gudmundson, *Costa Rica Before Coffee,* 130–36.

9. Roseberry, "Images of the Peasant in the Consciousness of the Venezuelan Proletariat," in *Anthropologies and Histories,* esp. 63–64.

10. For example, Graham, *Patronage and Politics,* 7, 271. Useful discussions of clientelism are also found in Bailey, *Stratagems and Spoils;* Vincent, "Political Anthropology"; and Kettering, "Political Clientelism."

11. These alternative approaches to the Venezuelan state have been pursued successfully by Kornblith, "Estado y políticas"; Germán Carrera Damas, "Simón Bolívar, el culto heróico y la nación," in *Venezuela: Proyecto nacional y poder social* (Barcelona, Spain: Editorial Crítica, 1986), 178–223; and Segnini, *La consolidación.*

12. Velásquez, *La caída del liberalismo amarillo;* Quintero, *El ocaso de una estirpe;* Pino Iturrieta, "Estudio preliminar." For a thoughtful discussion of Gómez, see Caballero, *Gómez.* Velásquez has been especially influential through his direction of the *Boletín del Archivo Histórico de Miraflores (BAHM),* which publishes documents relating to the Castro and Gómez eras, and Pino has led the important Castro-Gómez research project at the Universidad Central de Venezuela.

Chapter 2. The Early History of Duaca

1. "Memoria del P. Miguel de Madrid," in Carrocera, *Misión de los capuchinos*, 374–75.

2. Perera, *Historia político-territorial*, 10–12; Lombardi, *Venezuela*, 66–68.

3. Little is known concerning preconquest society in this region of Venezuela. See Molina, "Proposiciones"; also Vila, *Notas*, 40–49.

4. Arcila Farías, *El régimen de la encomienda*, 118–19, 194–95, 202–03, 218–21, 279–81.

5. Rojas, "Aproximaciones," 364, 366. Except where otherwise indicated, my discussion of Duaca during the colonial period relies on this work, 340–407.

6. Ibid., 340–43.

7. Ibid., 349; and Arcila Farías, *El régimen de la encomienda*, 189–90.

8. Rojas, "Aproximaciones," 344–47.

9. For the history of the mines, see Verna, *Las minas del Libertador*.

10. Ibid., 82–83. See also, "Descripción geográfica y relación individual del Valle de Nuestra Señora del Carmen de Aroa" (1745), in Altolaguirre y Duvale, *Relaciones geográficas*, 138–39.

11. Rojas, "Aproximaciones," 355–56; Arcila Farías, *El régimen de la encomienda*, 69.

12. The malleability of such categories in Mexico is demonstrated in John K. Chance, *Race and Class in Colonial Oaxaca* (Stanford: Stanford University Press, 1978).

13. If the term *mulatto* were used in this broad sense, it would be synonymous with the more widely used term *pardo*. John V. Lombardi writes of this group: "The pardos formed by far the largest ethnic group [in colonial Venezuela]. Their distinguishing and identifying characteristics were mostly negative: being neither white nor Indian, neither black nor slave, they were called and called themselves pardos." Lombardi, *Venezuela*, 48.

14. Martí, *Documentos*, vol. 6 (Compendio), 376.

15. Arcila Farías, *El régimen de la encomienda*, 292–94, 297–302.

16. "Ynstruzión y notizia de la Ciudad de Barquisimeto y su Jurisdición" (1745), in Arellano Moreno, *Relaciones geográficas de Venezuela*, 374.

17. The landscape of what is now Distrito Crespo is described in Perales Frigols, *Geografía económica*, 17–21. I have also relied on the topographical maps produced by the cartography division of the Ministerio de Obras Públicas.

18. Some officials believed the proper allotment was one league surrounding each indigenous village, while others believed that villages should receive one league in each of the four cardinal directions, for a total of four square leagues. Many Venezuelan villages, including Duaca, had their resguardos measured according to both systems, creating disputes into the national period. For Duaca, see Martí, *Documentos*, 2:62–63; for the Andes, Lucas Guillermo Castillo Lara, *Raices pobladores del Táchira: Táriba, Guásimos (Palmira), Capacho* (Caracas: ANH, 1986), 341–42, 523–26. For comments from a post-independence land surveyor, see "El agrimensor José Tomás Tyler representa ante el Gobernador de la Provincia de Barcelona acerca de la situación de la propiedad territorial en la región" (1834), in Gómez Rodríguez and Camacho Zavala, *Materiales*, 105–08.

19. Arcila Farías, *El régimen de la encomienda*, 294–99.

20. Rojas, "Aproximaciones," 376–77.

21. RPEL.PDC, pr. 1, esc. 11, fols. 9–17, October 10, 1912. This document is a copy of Zidardia's 1778 *censo* (mortgage).

22. Rojas, "Aproximaciones," 376.

23. The colonial cacao economy is discussed in detail in Ferry, *Colonial Elite of Early Caracas*, pp. 45–71, 105–38.

24. Martí, *Documentos*, 2:66; Rojas, "Aproximaciones," 370–73.

25. Cunill Grau, *Geografía del poblamiento*, 1:281–82.

26. Verna, *Las minas del Libertador*, 111–13. Humboldt judged that Aroa's copper "is of an excellent quality," superior to that found in Sweden and Chile. Humboldt, *Personal Narrative*, 4:251. Cunill Grau, *Geografía del poblamiento*, 1:305–06, 312.

27. Hawkshaw, *Reminiscences*, 182, 177–79.

28. Cunill Grau, *Geografía del poblamiento*, 1:312.

29. Izard, "La agricultura venezolana," esp. 122–45; Lombardi and Hanson, "First Venezuelan Coffee Cycle."

30. Carvallo and Ríos de Hernández, *Temas*, 11–28.

31. RPEL.PDB, pr. 8, fols. 3–4, July 26, 1856, and pr. 7, fols. 2–3, August 12, 1857.

32. RPEL.PDB, pr. 7, fol. 5, June 27, 1840, and no fol., May 30, 1857.

33. Cunill Grau, *Geografía del poblamiento*, 2:998, 1376–77; Lombardi, *Venezuela*, 325.

34. "Ley de 2 de abril de 1836," in Armellada, *Fuero indígena venezolano*, 2:39.

35. "Ley de 7 de abril de 1838," in ibid., 2:41–42.

36. Martínez Guarda, "Las tierras de resguardos indígenas," 108–09.

37. "Resolución ejecutiva de 21 de enero de 1852," in Gómez Rodríguez and Camacho Zavala, *Materiales*, 461–62.

38. See the resolution of the dispute between hacendados and the Indian communities of Píritu and San Miguel. "Decreto del Gobernador de la Provincia de Barcelona," in Gómez Rodríguez and Camacho Zavala, *Materiales*, 473–74.

39. Scholars disagree over how much resguardo land was lost through illegal enclosure, and how quickly the process occurred. Eduardo Arcila Farías, who emphasizes Spain's protection of the Indians during the colonial era, argues that after independence Venezuelan elites quickly seized control of most Indian lands. By contrast, Manuel Pérez Vila emphasizes the slow rate of privatization over the course of the nineteenth century. Arcila Farías, "Régimen de la tenencia de la tierra," in *Diccionario histórico de Venezuela*, 3:325–26; Pérez Vila, "Resguardos indígenas," in ibid., 3:374–77.

40. Both the 1828 and the 1840 episodes are documented in RPEL.j.civ. (1840) bulto 74, leg. 1.562, "El Doctor Ignacio Oropeza apoderado de los indígenas de la parroquia de Duaca, pidiendo se ampare a éstos en la legua de tierra que les pertenece." The offenders are not named.

41. RPEL.PDB, 1850, pr. 8, fols. 6–9, September 27, 1850, and fols. 1–4, November 4, 1850.

42. For a more detailed discussion of the sale of community lands, see Yarrington, "Duaca in the Age of Coffee," 34–35.

43. See the *poder* (power of attorney) dated August 14, 1865, in RPEL.j.civ. (1869) leg. 2.690, "Contiene el deslinde pedido por los ciudadanos Anselmo y Salustiano Alcalá," fols. 18–19. It is unclear whether Colonel Félix Aguilar is identical to the Félix Aguilar

Oviedo who purchased 70 fanegadas (48.9 hectares) from Gumercindo Giménez, in RPEL.PDB, pr. 8, fol. 4, December 27, 1851.

44. Telasco A. MacPherson, *Diccionario del Estado Lara,* 3rd ed. (Caracas: Ediciones de la Presidencia de la República, 1981), 286–89.

45. The history of some of these privately owned plots can be traced in sales and mortgage documents. See, for example, RPEL.PDC, pr. 1, esc. 71, fols. 56–57, May 14, 1917, in which Juan Antonio Mollejas traces the history of his estate in Perarapa to the sale of resguardo lands in 1850.

46. RPEL.PDB, pr. 8, fol. 4, September 17, 1850, and fol. 1, January 2, 1852.

47. RPEL.PDB, 1850, pr. 8, fol. 2, September 12, 1850, and fol. 4, July 29, 1864.

48. RPEL.j.civ. (1900) bulto 120, suit between the heirs of Gumercindo Giménez and the Ferrocarril Suroeste de Venezuela, documents without title or number, fol. 12. Giménez's heirs successfully defended their title to the land, as documented in ibid. (1906) bulto 128, "Escrito del Dr. Juan G. Colmenárez, demandando la Compañía de Ferrocarril Suroeste de Venezuela por una faja de terreno que pertenece a la sucesión del General Gumercindo Giménez."

49. Public land policy and administration are reviewed by Gómez R., "Política de enajenación," vii–lxxii.

50. Ibid., xviii, xxvi.

51. "Ley de 10 de abril de 1848 sobre . . . tierras baldías," in Gómez Rodríguez and Camacho Zavala, *Materiales,* 377–80.

52. Gómez R., "Política de enajenación," xxxiii, lii, liii.

53. "Informe de la Junta Económica de la Provincia de Barquisimeto," in ibid., 322.

54. "Ley sobre enagenación de tierras baldías y creación de oficinas de agrimensura" (1821), in *Materiales . . . , 1800–1830,* 312–14; and "Ley de 10 de abril de 1848 sobre . . . tierras baldías," in Gómez Rodríguez and Camacho Zavala, *Materiales,* 377–80.

55. Gómez R., "Política de enajenación," xx, xxxvii.

56. The movement of peasant settlers to public lands throughout the nineteenth century is a prominent and well-documented theme throughout Cunill Grau, *Geografía del poblamiento.*

57. "El Gobernador de la provincia de Barquisimeto," in Gómez Rodríguez and Camacho Zavala, *Materiales,* 192–97.

58. RPEL.PDB, pr. 8, fol. 6, August 19, 1864.

59. The early history of Los Chipas can be traced through the documents collected for an early twentieth-century lawsuit concerning the estate in RPEL.j.civ. (1913) bulto 142, leg. 6.866, "Documentos presentados por los doctores Escovar Albizu y J. R. Giménez en el acto de la contestación de la demanda 'Los Chipas,' 7a pieza" (see chapter 6 for a detailed discussion of this case).

60. RPEL.j.civ. (1869) leg. 2.690, "Contiene el deslinde pedido por los ciudadanos Anselmo y Salustiano Alcalá de la posesión 'Los Chipas,'" fols. 14–15.

61. The earliest mention of tenants on Los Chipas paying rent in kind dates from 1843. See RPEL.j.civ. (1910) bulto 136, leg. 6.298, "Juicio Los Chipas, Giménez, Camejo, Rojas Velis, 2a pieza," fol. 95.

62. RPEL.PDB, pr. 8, fol. 1, February 18, 1862.

63. RPEL.PDB, pr. 4, fols. 3–5, May 16, 1838.

64. The debts of workers on one Venezuelan hacienda, in the province of Carabobo, reportedly ranged from 5 to 109 pesos in 1858, when the annual wage amounted to only 24 pesos. Brito Figueroa, *Historia económica y social*, 4:1584–85.

65. Ibid., 4:1579–86.

66. Lombardi, *Venezuela*, 177. For a similar view, see Camacho, "Aportes," xlv, lvi.

67. Matthews, "Rural Violence and Social Unrest," 71–86. A published version of Matthews's work is also available: *Violencia rural en Venezuela, 1840–1858* (Caracas: Monte Avila, 1977).

68. My discussion of police codes in the province of Barquisimeto is based on "Reglamento general de policía de la provincia de Barquisimeto" (1835), in *Materiales . . . , 1810–1865*, 150–51; Barquisimeto, *Ordenanzas, resoluciones, decretos*, 33–36; Barquisimeto, *Ordenanzas y resoluciones*, 28–32.

69. *Gaceta de Venezuela*, November 16, 1845, 294, and January 10, 1847, 601.

70. Cunill Grau, *Geografía del poblamiento*, 2:978.

71. Matthews, "Rural Violence and Social Unrest"; Brito Figueroa, *Tiempo de Ezequiel Zamora* (Caracas: Universidad Central de Venezuela, 1981); Camacho, "Aportes"; Gómez R., "Política de enajenación."

72. Perera, *Historia político-territorial*, 131, 198. The standard narrative of the war is Alvarado, *Historia de la Revolución Federal*. See also Lombardi, *Venezuela*, 187–90.

73. RPEL.PDB, pr. 8, fol. 1, February 18, 1862.

Chapter 3. The Coffee Boom and Peasant Society, 1863–1899

1. Izard, "El café."

2. Roseberry, *Coffee and Capitalism*, 207.

3. Roseberry indicates his awareness of the problem of reducing the peasantry to an object of larger historical forces (*Coffee and Capitalism*, 207), but his argument throughout the book nonetheless tilts strongly in that direction.

4. In the early 1870s, the municipalities of Duaca and Bobare together produced 1,386,272 kilograms of coffee annually. Venezuela, *Apuntes estadísticos*, 295. My review of the protocolos from Bobare and Duaca leads me to believe that between two-thirds and three-fourths of this production came from Duaca. The figure for the early 1890s represents the low end of the Duaca government's estimate of the municipality's coffee production in 1893. Perera, *Historia político-territorial*, 311.

5. For population figures, see Cunill Grau, *Geografía del poblamiento*, 2:998, 1377. Núñez, *Bosquejo histórico*, 94. For in-migration to Duaca, see RPEL.PDB, pr. 1, esc. 65, no fol., May 9, 1876; pr. 4, esc. 6, fols. 1–4, July 2, 1877; and pr. 4, esc. 8, fols. 2–3, November 30, 1883. For out-migration from Quibor, see Cunill Grau, *Geografía del poblamiento*, 2:1394.

6. This view of the changing geography of settlement is based on my review of the protocolos.

7. For examples of large Barquisimeto merchants making loans directly to Duaqueño peasants, see RPEL.PDB, pr. 7, fol. 4, July 13, 1865; pr. 2, esc. 8, no fol., April 25, 1871; pr. 2, esc. 24, no fol., May 25, 1874; and pr. 2, esc. 26, no fol., May 31, 1875.

8. Gormsen, *Barquisimeto,* 50–51. For information on the railroad, see Verna, *Las minas del Libertador,* 211–15.

9. Throughout this study, I use the term *peasant* in a broad sense, applying it to all agriculturalists of low status who enjoy a large degree of control over the disposition of their labor, and who live primarily from the fruits of household-based production. This definition embraces persons with access to land through a variety of systems of tenure—including renters on private estates, public land occupants, small cultivators with title to their plots, and members of landowning communities—but does not include landless workers. This broad definition is appropriate for a study of Duaca because of the similar organization of household production among rural producers there, regardless of the system whereby they gained access to land. For discussion of the issues involved in defining peasants, see Henry A. Landsberger, "The Role of Peasant Movements and Revolts in Development," in Landsberger, ed., *Latin American Peasant Movements* (Ithaca: Cornell University Press, 1969), 1–5; Mintz, "A Note on the Definition of Peasantries"; G. Smith, *Livelihood and Resistance,* 18–28; C. Smith, "Anthropology and History"; and Roseberry, "Something About Peasants," 69–76.

10. In defining the term *hacienda* in this way, I am departing from the usual understanding found in Latin American historiography, which assumes the hacendado owns the land where his or her enterprise is located. Duaqueños themselves regularly used the term in the sense that I am using it: Large farms on untitled or community-owned land, as well as large tenant farms on landed estates, are regularly referred to as haciendas in notarial and judicial documents. When referring to a tract of privately owned land, Duaqueños tended to speak of *una posesión de tierras;* if the landowner also owned improvements, these would constitute his or her hacienda within the estate.

11. Many public lands in the Venezuelan Andes remained untitled as long as those in Duaca, whereas indigenous lands tended to be privatized earlier than Duaca's (see later this chapter and chapter 7).

12. Williams, *States and Social Evolution,* 94–95. Williams attributes the endurance of untitled land largely to the weakness of the national state (p. 98), the same factor that I highlight in the case of Duaca.

13. Throughout this study, the term *Duaca* refers to the area that became Distrito Crespo (with its administrative center in the town of Duaca) in 1899, including some hamlets such as Agua-fría, Rincón-hondo, and Tacarigüita that were not part of the municipality of Duaca before 1899. Thus some of the discussion in this chapter and the next relies on documents from areas that belonged to the municipalities of Catedral and Concepción before being transferred to the jurisdiction of Duaca in 1899.

14. Montiel Acosta, "El conuco."

15. RPEL.PDB, pr. 8, fols. 4–5, April 22, 1867; pr. 1, esc. 56, no fol., April 23, 1876; pr. 2, esc. 16, no fol., April 22, 1876; pr. 2, esc. 18, fols. 7–8, April 10, 1877; and pr. 2, esc. 77, fols. 8–9, October 31, 1883. See also the cases cited below of sons establishing coffee groves next to those of their living parents.

16. RPEL.PDB, pr. 1, esc. 36, no fol., March 11, 1874; pr. 1, esc. 84, fols. 134–35, June 1, 1881; pr. 2, esc. 4, fol. 6, February 14, 1881; and pr. 1, esc. 61, fols. 69–72, March 10, 1898.

17. RPEL.PDC, pr. 1, esc. 19, fols. 23–24, June 8, 1901.

18. This was a common practice among peasants in Venezuela and elsewhere in Latin America. Carvallo and Ríos de Hernández, *Temas,* 139.

19. For examples of sons establishing coffee groves next to those of their living parents, see RPEL.PDB, pr. 1, esc. 73, fols. 106–07, March 27, 1878; pr. 1, esc. 115, fol. 2, October 15, 1883; pr. 2, esc. 46, no fol., September 7, 1874; pr. 2, esc. 17, no fol., April 21, 1874; pr. 1, esc. 16, no fol., March 16, 1873; and pr. 1, esc. 175, fols. 55–56, December 21, 1877. It should be assumed that some sons established groves on nearby plots that did not border those of their parents, but such cases cannot be documented using the protocolos, which only specify the holdings that directly bordered the property being mortgaged or sold.

20. Gudmundson, "Peasant, Farmer, Proletarian," esp. 237–38, 243–44, 252–57. For similar trends in a different region, see Johnson, "Impact of Market Agriculture," esp. 633–34, 640–48.

21. Price, "Hands for the Coffee: Migration," 305–06.

22. Examples include RPEL.PDB, pr. 2, esc. 46, no fol., September 7, 1874; esc. 24, no fol., May 25, 1874 (see the note in the document's margin); and esc. 29, fols. 21–23, April 27, 1877.

23. Price, "Hands for the Coffee: Migration," 309–10.

24. RPEL.PDB, pr. 1, esc. 166, no fol., December 22, 1876; esc. 126, no fol., October 1, 1874; esc. 29, fols. 41–42, March 25, 1882; esc. 150, fols. 12–13 (protocolo supletorio), September 4, 1884; and esc. 143, fols. 157–58, June 5, 1895.

25. Examples include RPEL.PDB, pr. 1, esc. 126, no fol., October 1, 1874; esc. 166, no fol., December 22, 1876; and esc. 143, fols. 157–58, June 5, 1895.

26. For a different view, in which mortgages to merchants are seen as more detrimental to the household economy, see Roseberry, *Coffee and Capitalism,* esp. chap. 4.

27. For examples of Duaqueño peasants who lost their holdings to creditors, see RPEL.PDB, pr. 1, est. 113, fols. 180–82, August 17, 1879; esc. 106, fols. 173–75, July 20, 1880; esc. 37, fols. 54–55, April 1, 1880; esc. 84, fols. 134–35, June 1, 1881; and esc. 29, fols. 41–42, March 25, 1882. For examples of small producers who abandoned their coffee groves, see ibid., pr. 1, esc. 132, fols. 31–33, August 14, 1884, and pr. 2, esc. 36, fols. 10–11, May 2, 1885.

28. Compare Arcondo, "La crisis de la agricultura," 392.

29. Miguel Otero Silva, *Casas muertas* (Buenos Aires: Editorial Losada, 1955), 145. For Felipe Días and his wife, see RPEL.PDB, pr. 1, esc. 20, fols. 32–34, February 28, 1880. For Antonio Camacho, see RPEL.PDB, pr. 1, esc. 143, fols. 157–58, June 5, 1895. It is worth noting that in both cases tenants turned to nearby hacendados within the estate rather than to the landlord.

30. For Jesús Méndez, see RPEL.j.civ. (1878) leg. 2.950, "Sobre la demanda que ha intentado Ramón Machado, contra Jesús Méndez por cobro de venezolanos," esp. fols. 4, 6. For an account of the unhealthy conditions prevailing in rural Venezuela in the 1930s, see Acosta Saignes, *Latifundio,* 85–103.

31. These arrangements were notarized as rental agreements, with the rental "payments" being used to cancel the peasant's debt. For examples, see RPEL.PDB, pr. 1, esc. 126, no fol., October 1, 1874; pr. 2, esc. 28, fols. 14–15, June 3, 1887; pr. 1, esc. 64, no

fol., May 12, 1874; pr. 2, esc. 18, no fol., March 1, 1878; pr. 2, esc. 25, fols. 3–4, August 4, 1886; and pr. 1, esc. 14, fols. 15–16, July 18, 1888.

32. For Juan Eusebio Colmenares, see RPEL.PDB, pr. 2, esc. 33, no fol., June 19, 1875, and esc. 36, no fol., July 9, 1876. For Miguel and Manuel Rodríguez, see RPEL.PDB, pr. 2, esc. 17, no fol., April 21, 1874. For other examples of peasants helping their kin to fend off creditors, see RPEL.PDB, pr. 2, esc. 56, fols. 10–11, July 12, 1877, and fols. 1–2, May 4, 1865. The latter document, presented by Juan Bautista Agüero, is erroneously bound with pr. 12 (*poderes*) but does not appear at the beginning of the bundle, despite its folio numbers.

33. For José del Carmen's description of a loan to his son-in-law Apolinario Mendoza, see RPEL.PDB, pr. 4, esc. 6, fols. 1–4, July 2, 1877. For small loans in other peasant wills, see RPEL.PDB, pr. 4, esc. 5, no fol., April 7, 1875, and fols. 12–13, May 11, 1881.

34. RPEL.PDB, pr. 2, esc. 18, fols. 7–8, April 10, 1877, and pr. 1, esc. 24, fols. 42–44, April 7, 1879.

35. RPEL.PDB, pr. 2, esc. 35, no fol., June 26, 1874; pr. 1, esc. 54, no fol., April 21, 1876; pr. 1, esc. 27, fols. 37–38, March 21, 1877; and pr. 1, esc. 25, fols. 29–31, April 13, 1893.

36. RPEL.PDB, pr. 1, esc. 20, fols. 22–25, October 26, 1897, and pr. 4, esc. 6, fols. 1–4, July 2, 1877.

37. For an example of a well-to-do peasant, Venancio Soto, employing peon labor, see RPEL.j.civ. (1888) leg. 3.583, "Venancio Soto contra Luis González," fols. 7–8. On the use of kinship ties to recruit labor, see Gudmundson, "Peasant, Farmer, Proletarian," 231.

38. For peasants who made loans, see RPEL.PDB, pr. 2, esc. 18, fols. 7–8, April 10, 1877, and pr. 1, esc. 21, fols. 22–24, April 13, 1891. For Lorenzo Sánchez, see RPEL.PDB, pr. 1, esc. 113, fols. 168–70, June 3, 1878.

39. For complaints of labor shortages in Duaca, see RPEL.PDB, pr. 2, esc. 12, fols. 16–18, March 4, 1879. Bauer, "Rural Society," 127.

40. Bauer forcefully argues that advances to workers were very often incentives rather than part of an effective system of coerced labor. Bauer, "Rural Workers," 34–63.

41. For the Virgües family, see RPEL.PDB, pr. 11, fols. 1–3, June 9, 1866. For Avelino and Aurelio Giménez Méndez, see ibid., pr. 1, esc. 52, fols. 51–58, February 16, 1897. Intermediate amounts of peon debts are documented in ibid., pr. 1, esc. 22, fols. 30–32, October 18, 1890, and pr. 4, esc. 4, fols. 8–12, April 28, 1880; also RPEL.j.civ. (1888) leg. 3.668, "Diligencias relativas sobre inventario, valuo y partición de los bienes dejados por el finado Francisco Peralta," fols. 4–5.

42. RPEL.PDB, pr. 1, esc. 52, fols. 98–101, August 13, 1893.

43. This was the common wage for rural workers throughout Spanish America during the last third of the nineteenth century, according to Bauer, "Rural Society," 126. Although no wage data is available for Duaca in this period, two reales is identified as the customary wage in the neighboring municipio of Bobare. RPEL.j.civ. (1878) leg. 2.951, "Contiene la demanda que ha intentado Pilar Hernández contra Isidro Rojas por cantidad de venezolanos."

44. Particularly large advances to selected workers appear in hacienda accounts

from other parts of Latin America. Herbert Nickel has referred to the practice as "an indirect wage increase." Quoted in Bauer, "Rural Workers," 47.

45. For Altagracia López, see RPEL.PDB, pr. 6, esc. 47, no fol., December 23, 1871. For Cecilio Carrera, see ibid., esc. 42, fol. 8, September 21, 1883.

46. For the children of Juan Manuel Palencia, see RPEL.PDB, pr. 1, esc. 131, no fol., November 1, 1873. For Justiniano Herrera, see ibid., pr. 2, esc. 98, fols. 164–67, November 26, 1880. For Carlos Carmona, see ibid., pr. 2, esc. 26, fols. 39–41, May 21, 1881.

47. For examples of indebted workers who owned conucos and coffee groves independently of their employers, see RPEL.j.civ. (1878) leg. 2.951, "Contiene la demanda que ha intentado Pilar Hernández, contra Isidro Rojas por cantidad de venezolanos"; and RPEL.PDC, pr. 1, esc. 19, fols. 16–17, February 4, 1915.

48. The only documented case of an hacienda with a resident workforce in this period is the sugar hacienda El Buco on the outskirts of the town of Duaca, where workers had huts and subsistence plots within the hacienda. RPEL.PDB, pr. 1, esc. 18, fols. 23–26, August 7, 1892.

49. This was true of indigenous villages throughout the northern regions of Venezuela. Sanoja and Vargas, *Antiguas formaciones,* 247.

50. Cunill Grau, *Geografía del poblamiento,* 2:1005, 1045–49; Roseberry, *Coffee and Capitalism,* 85–87. For the case of Sanare, in the state of Lara, see RPEL.j.civ. (1887) legs. 3.788, 4.019; for Guarico (Distrito Morán), see ibid. (1885) leg. 3.423, and (1887) leg. 3.569; for other resguardos in Distrito Morán, ibid. (1888), (1890) bulto 110, (1891) bulto 111, and (1893) bulto 113.

51. Rents on communal land elsewhere in Lara appear to have been relatively low. In Santa Rosa, agricultural plots on the *ejidos* (common land) in 1830 rented for one or two pesos per almud, depending on whether the plot was irrigated. RPEL.j.civ. (1830) leg. 693, "Expediente de Recaudación de terreno y demás concerniente a los propios de la Parroquia de Santa Rosa." For the widow in Tarana, see RPEL.PDB, pr. 1, esc. 160, no fol., December 17, 1875. For contracts mentioning rental payments, see RPEL.PDB, pr. 1, esc. 116, no fol., August 29, 1874; esc. 147, no fol., November 17, 1875; esc. 36, fols. 47–49, April 3, 1882; also esc. 141, fols. 155–56, June 4, 1895.

52. The original reads: "Conviene advertir, que el comprador debe entenderse con el representante de los indígenas, con relación al pago de la pensión de arrendamiento del terreno que va a ocupar, pues si yo nada pagaba, era porque, como indígena también tenía derecho en aquel." RPEL.PDB, pr. 1, esc. 23, no fol., February 17, 1874.

53. RPEL.PDB, pr. 1, esc. 156, fols. 23–26, July 28, 1885, and esc. 76, fols. 90–91, November 29, 1895.

54. Because the community's original title to the resguardos had been lost around 1850, Torres and the community representatives had to gather testimony concerning the boundaries and legal history of the resguardos, which they used to secure a new title. The relevant documents were registered together in RPEL.PDB, pr. 1, esc. 161, fols. 10–14, June 26, 1890.

55. For General Juan de la Rosa Vásquez, see RPEL.PDB, pr. 8, fols. 3–4, January 22, 1866, and fols. 4–5, April 22, 1867. For the sale to Cipriano Bracho, see ibid., pr. 1, esc. 137, fols. 214–18, July 17, 1878. Bracho received 319 hectares in Tinajitas in the privatiza-

tion of the resguardos in 1916. RPEL.PDC, pr. 1, esc. 7, fols. 6–11, October 10, 1916. For testimony of coercive tactics used to enlarge haciendas in other parts of Venezuela, see Ríos de Hernández, *La hacienda venezolana,* 24–25, 165–66.

56. "Ley de 25 de mayo de 1885," in Armellada, *Fuero indígena venezolano,* 2:211–15.

57. For Pantaleón Heredia and Leopoldo Torres, RPEL.PDB, pr. 1, esc. 35, fols. 46–49, February 9, 1892. For evidence of Heredia's membership in Duaca's Indian community, ibid., esc. 38, fols. 41–42, November 7, 1896. Indian communities in other parts of Lara faced similar attempts to appropriate their land, as indicated in RPEL.PDB, pr. 6, esc. 23, fol. 9, May 7, 1885. For Justiniano Herrera, RPEL.PDB, pr. 3, esc. 19, fols. 16–18, May 26, 1893.

58. This explanation for the delay in the privatization of Duaca's resguardos was first suggested to me by Professor Reinaldo Rojas.

59. AANH.CAP, tomo 44, sección 13, Juan B. Cambero to Leopoldo Torres, February 1, 1909.

60. AANH.CAP, tomo 10, sección 28, J. J. Rivero M. to Leopoldo Torres, August 11, 1910.

61. For a similar view of Colombian public land settlers, see LeGrand, *Frontier Expansion,* 24–26, 32. For interpretations of migration onto public lands in Costa Rica, see Gudmundson, *Costa Rica Before Coffee,* 130–36.

62. For evidence of this northward movement, see RPEL.PDB, pr. 2, esc. 56, fols. 10–11, July 12, 1877; pr. 1, esc. 142, fols. 235–37, October 15, 1880; pr. 1, esc. 79, fol. 97, June 10, 1882; pr. 1, esc. 132, fols. 31–33, August 14, 1884; pr. 1, esc. 41, fols. 47–48, August 9, 1888; pr. 1, esc. 27, fols. 30–31, July 21, 1890; and pr. 1, esc. 36, fols. 39–40, November 5, 1896.

63. The process of public land settlement by peasants and subsequent appropriation of the land by elites is a central theme in LeGrand, *Frontier Expansion.*

64. The sale of land to Herrera is documented in RPEL.PDB, pr. 2, esc. 27, no fol., September 19, 1869. For the sale to Aguilar and Escalona, ibid., pr. 1, esc. 29, no fol., May 29, 1871. Aguilar and Escalona failed to exercise ownership over their land and it soon reverted to the public domain. The history of this land, known as El Huso, was reviewed by the state inspector of public lands, José Luis Pérez, in 1917. Pérez found that part of El Huso was later included in three sales of public lands made in 1890–1891, and that these later sales proceeded without opposition. José Luis Pérez (Barquisimeto) to Ministerio de Fomento, November 17, 1917, in Archivo General de la Nación (Caracas), Ministerio de Agricultura y Cría, in packet titled "Ministerio de Fomento, Dirección de tierras baldías, industrias y comercio; ramo: tierras baldías 1917 y 1918. Interesados: Juan Mollejo [*sic*] y Felix García. Asunto: Tierras en El Huso." The folder containing these and other packets is marked "32," but in practice it seems that no filing system is used for these documents at the Archivo.

65. RPEL.PDB, pr. 11, fols. 1–2, June 29, 1868. For similar cases elsewhere in Venezuela, see Linder, "Agriculture and Rural Society," 154–55; and Price, "Hands for the Coffee: Migration," 227.

66. RPEL.PDB, pr. 7, fols. 1–2, June 27, 1868; pr. 1, esc. 10, no fol., December 21, 1868; and pr. 1, esc. 37, no fol., March 12, 1874.

67. For the case of Buenavista, see RPEL.PDB, pr. 4, esc. 2, fols. 2–6, June 10, 1893. For Bobare, see ibid., pr. 2, esc. 7, fols. 5–6, March 2, 1878; pr. 1, esc. 46, no fol., March 2, 1878; and the agreement among María del Carmen Agüero, Pedro de la Asunción Agüero, Francisco Rodríguez, Fabian Mendoza, and Mateo Alvarado, protocolos de 1869 (unnumbered), esc. 57, August 12, 1869.

68. Dionisio Castillo mortgaged two mature coffee groves on public lands in Cambural and El Aserrado in 1865. When he sold one of the groves in 1870, he declared he was up to date on rent payments to General Santos Herrera, who bought the land from the national government in 1867. RPEL.PDB, pr. 7, fols. 4–5, March 28, 1865, and pr. 1, esc. 17, no fol., November 10, 1870. For the Generals' Estate, see RPEL.PDB, pr. 7, fols. 1–2, June 27, 1868; pr. 1, esc. 10, no fol., December 21, 1868; and pr. 1, esc. 37, no fol., March 12, 1874.

69. RPEL.PDB, pr. 1, esc. 70, fols. 80–81, August 20, 1890; esc. 106, fols. 131–32, August 28, 1891; esc. 53, fols. 67–68, November 10, 1891; and esc. 52, fols. 66–67, November 10, 1891.

70. RPEL.PDB, pr. 1, esc. 8, fols. 8–10, July 9, 1896; esc. 78, fols. 118–19, December 31, 1893; and esc. 75, fols. 114–15, December 31, 1893.

71. The references to public land petitions are found in RPEL.PDB, pr. 1, esc. 15, fols. 22–23, January 22, 1878; pr. 1, esc. 38, fols. 58–60, November 8, 1893; pr. 3, esc. 19, fols. 16–18, May 26, 1893; and RPEL.PDC, pr. 1, esc. 4, fols. 4–6, July 6, 1901, and esc. 29, fols. 30–33, November 25, 1908. Petitions to buy public land did not have to be registered in the protocolos; it would be remarkable if these were the only unsuccessful petitions from this period.

72. References to petitions from Granado and Parra are found in RPEL.PDC, pr. 1, esc. 4, fols. 4–6, July 6, 1901, and esc. 29, fols. 30–33, November 25, 1908. Peña's attempt to gain title to the land is referred to in RPEL.PDB, pr. 1, esc. 15, fols. 22–23, January 22, 1878. Peña's participation in the revolt is mentioned in Vásquez, *Apuntaciones*, 38. Juan de la Rosa Vásquez, who owned a large coffee hacienda on Duaca's resguardos, is also identified as a participant in the revolt.

73. RPEL.PDB, pr. 1, esc. 136, fols. 174–77, June 14, 1893.

74. General works on nineteenth-century Venezuelan politics include Velásquez, *La caída;* Gilmore, *Caudillism and Militarism;* and Urbaneja, "Caudillismo y pluralismo."

75. Floyd, *Guzmán Blanco,* 146–47. For further information on late nineteenth-century politics in Lara, see Perera, *Historia político-territorial,* 217–26, 228–46, 287–93, 303–06.

76. José Ramón Brito, *Gobernantes del Estado Lara, 1552–1977* (Barquisimeto: Gobernación del Estado Lara, 1978), 136–38.

77. For a list of uprisings in this period, see Francisco González Guinán, *Historia contemporánea de Venezuela,* 2nd ed. (Caracas: Ediciones de la Presidencia de la República, 1954), 15:836–49.

78. Price, "Hands for the Coffee: Migrants," 75.

79. Acosta Saignes, "Los orígenes históricos del problema agrario," in *Estudios,* 151–61, and *Latifundio;* also Brito Figueroa, *Historia económica y social.*

80. This discussion of landlord-tenant relations is based on "Reglamento de la Posesión 'Los Chipas'" (1908) in RPEL.j.civ. (1910) bulto 136, leg. 6.298, "Juicio Los Chipas, Giménez, Camejo, Rojas Velis, 2a pieza," fol. 102; and on rental conditions in the neighboring *municipio* of Bobare, as described in AANH.CAP, tomo 50, sección 33, "Condiciones . . . ," and tomo 3, sección 25, "Estudio del reglamento . . . ," which includes a discussion of rental conditions in eastern Lara as a whole.

81. Rents are outlined in the documents cited in the previous note. For supporting evidence see RPEL.PDB, pr. 2, esc. 31, no fol., June 3, 1874, and pr. 1, esc. 43, fols. 56–57, March 10, 1887.

82. The advantages and disadvantages for landlords and tenants of various rental systems are discussed in Scott, *Moral Economy of the Peasant*, 44–52, 65–90.

83. Brito Figueroa, *Historia económica y social*, 1:290, and 2:392–93, 414–16; Salvador de la Plaza, "La reforma agraria en Venezuela," *Revista del Colegio de Abogados del Distrito Federal* (January–March 1960), 41; and Carvallo and Ríos de Hernández, *Temas*, 21, 24–27.

84. Price, "Hands for the Coffee: Migration," 86–87, 241, 375.

85. For São Paulo, see Stolke, *Coffee Planters, Workers, and Wives*, and Dean, *Rio Claro*. For Cundinamarca, see Palacios, *Coffee in Colombia*, chap. 4, and Jiménez, "Traveling Far in Grandfather's Car."

86. However, oral history interviews have confirmed that some tenants in Lara and Yaracuy in the early twentieth century were free from any coercion to work in the landlord's fields. Ríos de Hernández, *La hacienda venezolana*, 31.

87. RPEL.j.civ. (1896) leg. 4.621, "Expediente que contiene el inventario . . . de bienes quedados al fallecimiento intestado de Apeles Pereira."

88. For details on the methodology that led to these conclusions, see Yarrington, "Duaca in the Age of Coffee," 101–03.

89. In this analysis of mortgages, I have included not only those transactions formally recorded as *hipotecas* (mortgages) but also the transactions recorded as *ventas con pacto de retracto* (sales with retraction agreement). Under the conditions of these "sales," the purchaser left the property in the hands of the seller for a specified period of time (usually one or two years), during which time he or she could buy back the property by refunding the purchase price. In many cases, the original owner was also required to make monthly "rental" payments equal to 1 or 2 percent of the purchase price, during the time that he reserved the option to repurchase the property. If the original owner failed to buy back the property or did not make the "rental" payments, then the new owner took possession. Clearly, these "sales" were really dressed-up mortgages, complete with monthly interest payments disguised as rental payments. The difference was that these transactions were drawn up to make it easier for creditors to take control of debtors' property.

90. RPEL.PDB, pr. 2, esc. 55, fol. 94, July 9, 1880.

91. For large tenants extending credit to their workers, see RPEL.PDB, pr. 4, esc. 4, fols. 8–12, April 28, 1880; pr. 1, esc. 22, fols. 30–32, October 18, 1890; and pr. 1, esc. 52, fols. 51–58, February 16, 1897. For housing and pulperías, see ibid., pr. 1, esc. 17, fols. 19–20, April 13, 1894, and esc. 17, fols. 17–19, April 8, 1897.

92. For Castillo, see RPEL.PDB, pr. 1, esc. 71, fols. 9–10, November 25, 1891, and esc. 7, fols. 11–12, October 9, 1890. For Giménez, see ibid., esc. 34, fols. 3–4, April 5, 1877; Perera, *Historia político-territorial,* 219.

93. For Los Chipas in the 1860s, see RPEL.j.civ. (1869) leg. 2.683, no title page, dispute between Eulogio Pérez, representing Anselmo Alcalá, and Bernardo Méndez. For José Regino Cadevilla, see RPEL.PDB, pr. 1, esc. 40, fols. 58–60, February 12, 1892; for Cadevilla's holdings, ibid., esc. 113, fols. 139–41, September 3, 1891.

94. Unless otherwise noted, this discussion of the conflict on Los Chipas relies on the testimony of Eloy Parra in RPEL.j.civ. (1911) bulto 137, leg. 6.480, "Juicio Los Chipas, Giménez, Camejo, Rojas Velis. 3a pieza," fols. 122–30.

95. For evidence of elite hacendados among the "tenants" in the disputed area, see RPEL.PDB, pr. 1, esc. 72, fols. 91–93, May 6, 1893; esc. 176, fols. 199–200, September 25, 1895; and esc. 1, fols. 1–2, January 3, 1897.

96. RPEL.j.civ. (1869) leg. 2.673, "El Cdno. Manuel Antonio Ramírez demanda a José de la Paz Parra por cantidad de pesos que le adeuda"; ibid. (1883) bulto 104, leg. 3.307, "Ramón Briceño, con poder del Grl. Reyes Quiñones demanda a Eusebio Escobar por pago de pisos"; and RPEL.PDB, pr. 1, esc. 43, fols. 56–57, March 10, 1887.

97. *Gaceta Oficial* (Caracas), July 28, 1885, 1.095.

98. For an excellent discussion of the complex relationship between structure and agency, see Ortner, "Theory in Anthropology," 126–66.

99. Marie Price emphasizes the strong element of agency in peasant migration in the Venezuelan Andes in "Hands for the Coffee: Migration," esp. iv, 6–7, 261, 354–56.

Chapter 4. Commerce and the Local Elite, 1863–1899

1. Costa, *The Brazilian Empire,* chap. 4; Dean, *Rio Claro,* chaps. 4, 6; and Stolke, *Coffee Planters, Workers, and Wives,* chaps. 1–2.

2. On access to land, see Gudmundson, *Costa Rica Before Coffee;* on credit, processing, and marketing, see Cardoso, "Formation of the Coffee Estate."

3. References to the destruction of property during the Federal War appear in RPEL.PDB, pr. 11, fols. 1–2, July 27, 1865; pr. 4, esc. 6, no fol., September 6, 1871; and pr. 2, esc. 1, fols. 1–3, January 22, 1884.

4. For Juan Aguilar's will, see RPEL.PDB, pr. 4, esc. 2, no fol., August 1, 1870. For the document in which Aguilar and over a hundred other members of Duaca's indigenous community appoint Francisco Palma as their representative, see ibid., pr. 6, esc. 8, no fol., February 4, 1871. Aguilar lost one of his coffee haciendas for unpaid debts in 1871, and his heirs lost the second in 1876. Ibid., pr. 1, esc. 15, no fol., March 31, 1871, and esc. 7, no fol., January 27, 1876.

5. RPEL.PDB, pr. 1, esc. 29, no fol., May 29, 1871, and esc. 76, no fol., October 24, 1872.

6. RPEL.PDB, pr. 2, esc. 76, fols. 120–22, May 17, 1878. For evidence of Heredia's membership in the indigenous community, see ibid., pr. 6, esc. 8, no fol., February 4, 1871. Heredia was the community's representative during the critical period of the

early 1890s, when the resguardos were in danger of being reclassified as baldíos. See ibid., pr. 1, esc. 161, fols. 10–14, June 26, 1890, and esc. 35, fols. 46–49, February 9, 1892.

7. For the Andrade family, see RPEL.PDB, pr. 8, fol. 4, January 28, 1868, and pr. 1, esc. 178, fols. 59–61, December 25, 1877. For the Ledesmas, see ibid., pr. 1, esc. 14, no fol., March 28, 1871, and pr. 2, esc. 21, no fol., May 24, 1874.

8. RPEL.PDB, pr. 7, fol. 1, July 4, 1865, and pr. 11, fols. 1–3, June 9, 1866.

9. A detailed inventory of Vásquez's property is contained in his will, RPEL.PDB, pr. 4, esc. 2, no fol., February 6, 1871.

10. For Cecilio Carrera, RPEL.PDB, pr. 2, esc. 43, no fol., July 30, 1874, and pr. 2, esc. 100, fols. 29–31, July 31, 1877. For José Maximiniano Soteldo, ibid., pr. 2, esc. 41, no fol., July 10, 1875, and pr. 2, esc. 21, no fol., May 10, 1876.

11. In 1878, Nicolás Alvarado owned three haciendas in addition to his commercial establishment in the town of Duaca. RPEL.PDB, pr. 2, esc. 105, fols. 169–72, August 6, 1878. For Segura's mercantile and agricultural operations, see ibid., pr. 2, esc. 23, no fol., May 10, 1875, and pr. 1, esc. 196, fols. 330–31, October 29, 1878.

12. For the case of Nicolás Alvarado, see RPEL.PDB, pr. 2, esc. 10, no fol., March 18, 1876, and pr. 1, esc. 130, fols. 4–7, October 13, 1877.

13. Examples include RPEL.PDB, pr. 2, esc. 29, no fol., June 3, 1874; pr. 2, esc. 96, fols. 154–55, July 11, 1878; and pr. 1, esc. 36, fols. 41–43, April 20, 1891.

14. Coffee-processing methods used in Lara, Carabobo, and Yaracuy are discussed in David N. Burke (Puerto Cabello) to U.S. Dept. of State, January 18, 1888, U.S. Consular Reports (microfilm), T-229, roll 10. For processing methods in Venezuela, see Ríos de Hernández, *La hacienda venezolana*, 67–72, 235–37, and Price, "Hands for the Coffee: Migration," 75–80.

15. For example, one hacendado-turned-merchant received coffee in the husk from a debtor at the price of 4.80 venezolanos (6 pesos) per 46 kilograms and sold it (presumably dehusked) for 6.40 venezolanos (8 pesos) per 46 kilograms. RPEL.PDB, pr. 2, esc. 29, no fol., June 3, 1874, and esc. 30, no fol., June 4, 1874.

16. RPEL.PDB, pr. 2, esc. 16, no fol., September 16, 1873; and Perera, *Historia político-territorial*, 219. Giménez's status as a recent arrival in Duaca may have been one reason for his appointment, for it was made directly by President Antonio Guzmán Blanco in the aftermath of General León Colina's revolt, which received support from members of the Duaqueño elite.

17. RPEL.PDB, pr. 2, esc. 28, no fol., June 3, 1874; esc. 29, no fol., June 3, 1874; esc. 21, no fol., April 28, 1875; esc. 34, no fol., June 23, 1875; and esc. 61, no fol., October 19, 1875. Giménez is identified as a Quiboreño in pr. 1, esc. 65, no fol., May 9, 1876.

18. Regarding Peralta's early commercial dealings in Duaca, see RPEL.PDB, pr. 2, esc. 5, no fol., February 15, 1874; esc. 31, no fol., June 3, 1874; and esc. 62, no fol., November 26, 1875. For Peralta's will, see RPEL.PDC, pr. 4, esc. 1, fols. 1–3, December 11, 1912.

19. When I refer to mortgages, I include the documents drawn up as *ventas con pacto de retracto,* which served as mortgages.

20. *El Eco Industrial* (Barquisimeto), May 26, 1905, 1.

21. Roseberry, *Coffee and Capitalism,* 92.

22. Ibid., 82–98.

23. RPEL.PDB, pr. 2, esc. 41, no fol., July 10, 1875; pr. 1, esc. 61, no fol., May 5, 1876; pr. 1, esc. 62, fols. 39–40, May 16, 1877; pr. 2, esc. 105, fols. 169–72, August 6, 1878; pr. 1, esc. 55, fols. 95–96, May 21, 1879; and pr. 1, esc. 220, fols. 36–37, November 23, 1886.

24. RPEL.PDB, pr. 2, esc. 5, no fol., February 15, 1874; esc. 31, no fol., June 3, 1874; and esc. 62, no fol., November 26, 1875.

25. RPEL.PDB, pr. 1, esc. 73, no fol., July 4, 1875; esc. 48, fols. 19–20, April 24, 1877; and esc. 39, fol. 54, February 21, 1878.

26. RPEL.PDB, pr. 1, esc. 205, fol. 343, November 1878 (final page missing).

27. RPEL.PDB, pr. 2, esc. 76, fols. 120–22, May 17, 1878; esc. 61, fols. 186–88, July 29, 1879; esc. 68, fols. 107–10, September 28, 1881; and esc. 64, fol. 54, October 11, 1882.

28. For Peralta's dealings with his brothers, see RPEL.PDB, pr. 2, esc. 30, fols. 7–9, September 2, 1886; pr. 1, esc. 178, fols. 47–48, September 5, 1886; pr. 1, esc. 30, fols. 47–52, November 7, 1888; and pr. 1, esc. 63, fols. 83–84, February 26, 1891. For his continuing acquisition of haciendas, see pr. 1, esc. 200, fols. 13–14, October 14, 1886; esc. 82, fols. 108–09, December 22, 1887; and esc. 87, fols. 110–11, March 9, 1891.

29. Venezuela, *Tercer censo*, 2:489.

30. RPEL.PDB, pr. 1, esc. 179, fols. 61–66, December 31, 1877; esc. 122, fols. 3–6, June 10, 1886; and esc. 18, fols. 15–16, April 14, 1899.

31. RPEL.PDB, pr. 11, fols. 1–2, June 29, 1868.

32. Pérez's purchase of Los Chipas in 1869, his loss of most of the land for debt in 1877, and his retention of the 139 hectares in Tumaque are documented in RPEL.PDB, pr. 1, esc. 179, fols. 61–66, December 31, 1877.

33. RPEL.PDB, pr. 2, esc. 55, fol. 94, July 9, 1880.

34. Though written and dated in 1881, Pérez's will was registered only in 1885. RPEL.PDB, pr. 4, esc. 2, fols. 2–5, March 1, 1885.

35. RPEL.PDB, pr. 1, esc. 51, no fol., March 31, 1877.

36. RPEL.PDB, pr. 1, esc. 54, no fol., April 21, 1876; esc. 170, fols. 49–50, December 17, 1877; and esc. 172, fols. 167–68, June 3, 1878.

37. RPEL.PDB, pr. 1, esc. 137, fols. 214–18, July 17, 1878.

38. RPEL.PDB, pr. 2, esc. 101, fols. 161–64, July 18, 1878.

39. RPEL.PDB, pr. 1, esc. 95, fols. 118–20, August 23, 1891. Other loans, though made in the 1890s, were registered only in 1900. See RPEL.PDC, pr. 1, esc. 12, fols. 15–16, August 18, 1900, and esc. 13, fols. 16–18, August 18, 1900.

40. For an inventory of Bracho's property, see RPEL.j.civ. (1917) bulto 150, doc. 7.496, "Partición de los bienes de la sucesión Bracho Díaz." For some of Bracho's first investments in properties in the town of Duaca, see RPEL.PDB, pr. 1, esc. 31, fols. 48–49, February 8, 1891, and esc. 89, fols. 113–14, March 11, 1891.

41. Two of these landholdings—the estates of Batatal and Licua—were separated from Los Chipas before the Federal War. See RPEL.PDB, pr. 8, fol. 4, January 28, 1868, and pr. 1, esc. 14, no fol., March 28, 1871. In the other four cases, members of the local elite owning haciendas as tenants bought the land they occupied, see ibid., pr. 1, esc. 42, fols. 57–60, February 23, 1878; esc. 208, fol. 352, November 21, 1878; esc. 209, fols. 353–54, November 23, 1878; and esc. 205, fol. 343, November 1878 (final page missing).

42. The sale to Herrera is referred to in RPEL.PDB, pr. 2, esc. 27, no fol., September 19, 1869. The sizes of most small estates are not given in the protocolos during this period.

43. This is my impression from the protocolos, which contain many sales and mortgages of farms belonging to tenants on Los Chipas and the Generals' Estate, but very few referring to tenants on the smaller estates.

44. Floyd, *Guzmán Blanco,* esp. 133–56; and Quintero, "La muerte del caudillismo," 43–49.

45. See the documents gathered in AANH.CAP, tomo 12, sección 5; *El Occidental* (Barquisimeto), July 8, 1879, "Plausible noticias," and December 16, 1879, "La voz del pueblo"; and George Edmund Carl, *First Among Equals: Great Britain and Venezuela, 1810–1910* (Syracuse: Dellplain Latin American Studies no. 5, 1980), 59.

46. The importance of the railroad and highway are discussed in Gormsen, *Barquisimeto,* esp. 50–51 (the remarks of the nineteenth-century geographer, Wilhelm Sievers, are on page 51).

47. Plans for the dedication of the church appeared in "El 8 de Diciembre en Duaca," *El Occidental* (Barquisimeto), October 21, 1879.

48. *El Occidental* (Barquisimeto), December 9, 1879.

49. For a discussion of the Venezuelan economy in this period, see Arcondo, "La crisis de la agricultura."

50. For some of García's early loans, see RPEL.PDB, pr. 7, fols. 2–3, July 7, 1865; pr. 7, fols. 2–3, March 8, 1865; and pr. 7, fols. 2–4, August 16, 1866.

51. See the government decree in AANH.CAP, tomo 12, sección 5.

52. RPEL.PDB, pr. 2, esc. 118, fols. 52–53, September 12, 1877, and esc. 53, fols. 81–83, April 16, 1878.

53. RPEL.PDB, pr. 2, esc. 31, fols. 49–53, May 21, 1880; esc. 32, fols. 53–59, May 21, 1880; and esc. 76, fol. 132, September 3, 1880.

54. RPEL.PDB, pr. 1, esc. 156, fol. 38, October 6, 1881; esc. 157, fol. 45, October 8, 1881; and esc. 158, no fol., October 8, 1881.

55. RPEL.PDB, pr. 1, esc. 37, fols. 49–51, April 6, 1882, and esc. 135, fols. 16–17, June 9, 1887.

56. RPEL.PDB, pr. 1, esc. 44, fols. 57–59, April 16, 1882; pr. 2, esc. 36, fols. 24–26, June 22, 1887; pr. 1, esc. 14, fols. 19–21, July 8, 1893; and pr. 1, esc. 56, fols. 58–60, November 23, 1896.

57. RPEL.PDB, pr. 1, esc. 7, fols. 6–7, October 12, 1889; esc. 35, fols. 38–41, December 24, 1892; and esc. 38, fols. 58–60, November 8, 1893.

58. RPEL.PDB, pr. 1, esc. 25, fols. 30–31, November 7, 1889, and esc. 105, fols. 11–13, November 27, 1894.

59. Venezuela, *Memoria* (1888), 181–82.

60. Venezuela, *Memoria* (1890), 195. In violation of the monopoly, another processing plant began commercial operation at around the same time. The owners of the "legitimate," officially sanctioned plant retained Barquisimeto lawyer Leopoldo Torres to defend their rights. Torres's papers from the case are preserved in AANH.CAP, tomo 3, sección 16.

61. David N. Burke (Puerto Cabello) to U.S. Dept. of State, January 18, 1888, U.S. Consular Reports (microfilm), T-229, roll 10.

62. The plant was owned briefly by Jefferson Davis Bell, an American who also had dealings with the rival processing plant mentioned above. RPEL.PDB, pr. 1, esc. 94, fols. 118–20, December 24, 1890, and esc. 68, fols. 94–97, April 29, 1892.

63. Cardoso, "Formation of the Coffee Estate"; and Bergad, *Coffee,* esp. 152, 159.

64. *La Integridad* (Duaca), December 2, 1897, 4–6, 8–10.

65. RPEL.PDC, pr. 1, esc. 40, fols. 38–39, September 28, 1908.

66. Nelson Paredes Huggins reviews the history of railroad in the Andean coffee region in *Vialidad y comercio,* 64–77.

67. *El Monitor* (Barquisimeto), January 30, 1892, 2.

68. For Lapp's local operations, see RPEL.PDB, pr. 1, esc. 13, fols. 15–17, October 5, 1894; esc. 221, fols. 245–47, September 23, 1896; esc. 229, fols. 253–54, September 30, 1896; and esc. 192, fols. 206–10, June 9, 1896. For his connection to Beselin and Company, see ibid., pr. 1, esc. 35, fols. 38–40, November 8, 1897.

69. Price, "Hands for the Coffee: Migrants," 65–66.

70. "La sangre italiana en Duaca," *Ecos de Guape* (Duaca), June 24, 1971.

71. RPEL.PDB, pr. 1, esc. 72, fols. 91–93, May 6, 1893; esc. 63, fols. 70–71, October 30, 1894; esc. 25, fols. 27–28, July 9, 1896; and esc. 68, fols. 79–80, March 23, 1898.

72. RPEL.PDB, pr. 1, esc. 159, fols. 20–23, September 6, 1884; esc. 60, fols. 82–85, May 27, 1888; and esc. 178, fols. 47–48, September 5, 1886.

73. For Peralta and Rojas Vélis, see RPEL.PDB, pr. 1, esc. 62, fols. 98–101, August 13, 1893. For Andrade and Guillén, ibid., esc. 134, fols. 166–68, June 5, 1891; esc. 80, fols. 19–21, November 26, 1891; and their advertisement, along with those of other Duaca merchants, in *El Eco del Norte* (Duaca), February 26, 1892, 4.

74. I examined the protocolos for all years within the period of this study, but limited time prevented the recording of all transactions for every year after 1880. Again, my count of mortgages includes not only documents written as mortgages (*hipotecas*) but also those written as sales with provisions for the original owner to repurchase his or her property (*ventas con pacto de retracto*).

75. *La Integridad* (Duaca), December 2, 1897, 4–6.

76. See Izard, "El café," 215.

Chapter 5. Rebellion and Accommodation

1. The classic statement of this view is Velásquez, *La caída;* see also Quintero, *El ocaso de una estirpe.*

2. For a concise overview, see Segnini, *La consolidación.* On the armed forces, see Ziems, *El gomecismo.*

3. Kornblith, "Estado y políticas," 93–101. See also Segnini, *La consolidación,* 51–60.

4. *El Eco del Norte* (Duaca), February 6, 1892, 4.

5. Ibid., 2.

6. Ibid., February 26, 1892, 1–2.

7. The petition is reprinted in Perera, *Historia político-territorial,* 310–12. For the state president's deliberations, see 307–10, 312–14.

8. ACMB, Libro de actas de sesiones del concejo municipal de Barquisimeto, 1896, fol. 3, January 13, 1896; and Actas de sesiones, 1899, fol. 39, June 13, 1899.

9. The concejo municipal's 1899 edict, which refers to an earlier 1892 ruling, is copied in RPEL.PDC, pr. 1, esc. 12, fols. 17–19, October 10, 1912. See also ACMB, Actas de sesiones, 1899, fol. 18, February 27, 1899, and fol. 23, March 13, 1899.

10. *El Heraldo* (Barquisimeto), August 13, 1897, "Circular."

11. AANH.CJMH, tomo 25, M. Bracho Orozco to José Manuel Hernández, May 13, 1897.

12. Manzanarez, *La Revolución.* Unless otherwise cited, my discussion of the Restauradora in Duaca is based on this source.

13. Ibid., 6.

14. Jacinto Lara to Cipriano Castro, November 3, 1899, in *Boletín del Archivo Histórico de Miraflores (BAHM)* 70 (January 1972), 16–17.

15. Manzanarez, *La Revolución, 6,* 3.

16. Ibid., 10.

17. Norberto's military activities are mentioned in Alvarado, *Historia de la Revolución Federal,* 121, 268, 542. On Aurelio, see Pepper, *A través de Lara,* 264.

18. Armas Chitty, "Trayectoria del caudillo," in Armas Chitty, *El Mocho Hernández,* 11–13.

19. Manzanarez, *La Revolución,* 11–16.

20. Ibid., 16–20.

21. AANH.CJMH, tomo 29, telegrams headed "Duaca octubre 6 de 1899 . . . para Gral. E. Garmendia" and E. Garmendia to Luis Loreto Lima, October 7, 1899.

22. Manzanarez, *La Revolución,* 30–33; and AANH.CJMH, tomo 29, E. Garmendia to Luis Loreto Lima, October 27, 1899.

23. Jacinto Lara to Carlos Liscano, November 4, 1899, and Liscano to Lara, November 6, 1899, in *BAHM* 22–24 (January 1963): 228–31.

24. Velásquez, *La caída,* 365–66.

25. Manzanarez, *La Revolución,* 37–52.

26. Jacinto Lara to Ramón Ayala, November 19, 1899, in *BAHM* 70 (January 1972): 96–97; and Lara to Diego Colina, November 18, 1899, in ibid. 22–24 (January 1963): 237–38.

27. Manzanarez, *La Revolución,* 57–61, 70–74.

28. Jacinto Lara to Ramón Ayala, November 19, 1899, in *BAHM* 70 (January 1972): 96–97.

29. Jacinto Lara to Diego Colina, November 18, 1899, in *BAHM* 22–24 (January 1963): 237–38.

30. See Domingo Irwin G., "Notas," 15–20.

31. Manzanarez, *La Revolución,* 65–70, 74–76; and Jacinto Lara to Cipriano Castro, February 9, 1900, in *BAHM* 72 (May 1972): 29–30.

32. Perera, *Historia político-territorial,* 332–36, 340.

33. Ibid., 334.

34. Quintero, *El ocaso de una estirpe,* 51–70.

35. Ibid., 39–50.

36. *Veinte de febrero* (Duaca), October 22, 1900, 2.

37. Ismael Manzanarez to Cipriano Castro, April 2 and 19, 1900, in *BAHM* 74 (September 1972): 7, 125, and February 28, 1901, in ibid. 91 (May 1976): 128. For Duaqueño commanders, *El Heraldo* (Duaca), June 23, 1900, 2.

38. Silva Uzcátegui, *Enciclopedia larense,* 365.

39. Nuñez, *Bosquejo histórico,* 107–08.

40. Silva Uzcátegui, *Enciclopedia larense,* 365–66.

41. Luther T. Ellsworth to Ambassador Herbert W. Bowen, May 15, 1902, in Consular Post Records (U.S. National Archives, Washington, D.C.), Puerto Cabello, C8.2, 2:301–02.

42. Silva Uzcátegui, *Enciclopedia larense,* 368.

43. Ibid., 369–75.

44. Velásquez, *La caída,* 402–03.

45. AANH.CAP, tomo 20, sección 60, Leopoldo Torres to Torres Cárdenas, February 3, 1907; see also Vásquez, *Apuntaciones,* 85–86.

46. Velásquez, *La caída,* 403–07.

47. Ibid., 409–42.

48. Vásquez, *Apuntaciones,* 86.

49. AANH.CAP, tomo 20, sección 60, Leopoldo Torres to Torres Cárdenas, February 3, 1907.

50. Silva Uzcátegui, *Enciclopedia larense,* 377–78.

51. Briceño Ayestarán, *Memorias,* 257–58, 270, 867–69.

52. Silva Uzcátegui, *Enciclopedia larense,* 383–85.

53. Ibid., 386–89; Velásquez, *La caída,* 446–50.

54. Quintero, *El ocaso de una estirpe,* 102–03.

55. Quoted in ibid., 103.

56. Silva Uzcátegui, *Enciclopedia larense,* 389–90.

57. AANH.CAP, tomo 27, sección 31, E. Colmenares, R. A. Vásquez, and Paulo E. Piña to Leopoldo Torres, September 22, 1905.

58. Torres refers to these conversations with González Pacheco in a letter to Torres Cárdenas, February 3, 1907, in AANH.CAP, tomo 20, sección 60.

59. AANH.CAP., tomo 36, fols. 87–90, Leopoldo Torres to Cipriano Castro, July 15, 1906.

60. Many of the documents concerning Gómez's interim presidency and the Acclamation have been published in *BAHM* 15 (1961); the introduction, 161–62, offers a useful summary. Additional commentary is found in Carlos Siso, *Castro y Gómez: Importancia de la hegemonía andina* (Caracas: Editorial Arte, 1985), 197–206; and Caballero, *Gómez,* 85–91.

61. José Garbi to Juan Vicente Gómez, May 5, 1906, in *BAHM* 15 (1961): 180; also José Garbi to Juan Vicente Gómez, April 25, 1906, in ibid., 173–74.

62. AANH.CAP, tomo 40, sección 1, F. A. Colmenares to Leopoldo Torres, May 29,

1906, and Eduardo Colmenares, R. A. Vásquez, Cipriano Bracho, et al. to Leopoldo Torres, May 29, 1906.

63. AANH.CAP, tomo 36, fols. 87–90, Leopoldo Torres to Cipriano Castro, July 15, 1906.

64. Ibid. Torres reviews the affair in his letter of February 3, 1907, to Torres Cárdenas, in AANH.CAP, tomo 20, sección 60.

65. AANH.CAP, tomo 40, Paulo E. Piña to Leopoldo Torres, August 31, 1906; E. Colmenares to Leopoldo Torres, September 5, 1906; R. A. Vásquez to Leopoldo Torres, September 1, 1906

66. AANH.CAP, tomo 40, R. Paiva to Leopoldo Torres, November 21, 1906.

67. AANH.CAP, tomo 40, E. Colmenares to Leopoldo Torres, October 8, 1906.

68. Ibid., December 28, 1906.

69. AANH.CAP, tomo 36, fol. 144, Leopoldo Torres to Cipriano Castro, September 23, 1906.

70. Santiago Briceño A. to José Garbi, June 5, 1907, in Briceño Ayestarán, *Memorias,* 769.

71. ACMDC, Copiador de correspondencia de 1907–1908, fol. 39, July 8, 1907, entry no. 158, and fol. 48, September 22, 1907, entry no. 207.

72. AANH.CAP, tomo 20, sección 60, Torres Cárdenas to Leopoldo Torres, February 1, 1907.

73. AANH.CAP, tomo 20, sección 60, Leopoldo Torres to Torres Cárdenas, February 1, 1907.

74. AANH.CAP, tomo 20, sección 60, Leopoldo Torres to Torres Cárdenas, February 3, 1907.

75. J. V. Gómez to Santiago Briceño, June 14, 1907, in Briceño Ayestarán, *Memorias,* 905.

76. Santiago Briceño A. to J. V. Gómez, July 6, 1907, in ibid., 785.

77. Richard Graham makes this point regarding Brazilian patrons in *Patronage and Politics,* 249–51. Useful discussions of clientelism are also found in Bailey, *Stratagems and Spoils,* and in Vincent, "Political Anthropology," 175–94.

78. Malcolm Deas, "Colombia, Ecuador, and Venezuela, c. 1880–1930," in Leslie Bethell, ed., *The Cambridge History of Latin America* (Cambridge, England: Cambridge University Press, 1986), 5:678; and Velásquez, *La caída,* 37.

79. Ziems, *El gomecismo,* 166.

80. A useful discussion of the 1913 crisis is found in Caballero, *Gómez,* 151–60.

81. Vincencio Pérez Soto to Juan Vicente Gómez, July 29, 1913, in *BAHM* 31 (July–August 1964): 114.

82. Ibid., 115.

83. Argenis Azuaje to Juan Vicente Gómez, August 3, 1913, in *BAHM* 17–18 (March 1962): 175.

84. AANH.CAP, tomo 40, R. Paiva to Leopoldo Torres, September 8, 1906; ACMDC, Copiador de correspondencia de 1907–1908, fol. 6, January 10, 1907, and fol. 11, February 1, 1907; Copiador de correspondencia de 1905–1906, fol. 39, September 14, 1906.

85. AANH.CAP, tomo 40, R. A. Vásquez to Leopoldo Torres, November 21, 1906; E. Colmenares to Leopoldo Torres, January 2, 1907.

86. E. Colmenares to Briceño Ayestarán, March 8, 1908, in Briceño Ayestarán, *Memorias,* 916–17. Briceño was no longer state president at this time.

87. AANH.CAP, tomo 40, E. Colmenares to Leopoldo Torres, December 12, 1906.

88. E. Colmenares to Juan Vicente Gómez, August 29, 1916, in *BAHM* 49–51 (July 1967): 119. The text of the letter makes it clear that this was not the first time Colmenares had sought a personal favor from Gómez, whom he addressed as "my dear friend and chief."

89. Nuñez, *Bosquejo histórico,* 107–08. Núñez, Duaca's chief chronicler in this century, relied heavily on oral tradition.

90. *Ecos de Duaca* (Duaca), October 23, 1911, 1–2.

91. Examples of members of Lara's elite being appointed jefe civil outside their home districts appear in *Notas* (Barquisimeto), June 23, 1918, 4, and August 1, 1918, 2; and *El Loro* (Duaca), March 27, 1924, 2. See also Velásquez, *La caída,* 38. For a rare example of a state president who systematically appointed members of local elites to serve as jefes civiles in their home districts, see Pedro M. Guerra to Juan Vicente Gómez, March 8, 1915, in Segnini et al., *Los hombres del Benemérito,* 1:523.

92. This emerges in a number of the letters collected in Segnini et al., *Los hombres del Benemérito,* vol. 1. Examples include Eustoquio Gómez to Juan Vicente Gómez, September 5, 1913, 429; December 21, 1918, 439; June 20, 1930, 443; and Eduardo J. Dagnino to Juan Vicente Gómez, September 16, 1911, 190.

93. The district council and jefe civil, for example, continually tried to protect the district's streams, which were threatened when the forests along their banks were cut down. ACMDC, Copiador de correspondencia de 1907–1908, fol. 48, September 22, 1907; Copiador de correspondencia de 1911–1914, October 20, 1913, fol. 47, and September 15, 1914, fol. 87. The council also imposed a new water-use agreement with the owner of the sugar hacienda El Buco to assure townspeople and small cultivators access to water. Copiador de correspondencia de 1911–1914, April 27, 1911, fol. 15, and February 15, 1912, fols. 26–27.

94. See Richard Graham's comments concerning political centralization in Brazil in *Patronage and Politics,* esp. chap. 2; and William Beik, *Absolutism and Society in Seventeenth-Century France: State Power and Provincial Aristocracy in Languedoc* (Cambridge, England: Cambridge University Press, 1985), esp. 31–32, 198–99, 237, 245–46, 277–81, 333–35.

Chapter 6. The Struggle for Land on Two Duaca Estates

1. A copy of the 1851 *deslinde* (survey) of the boundaries of Los Chipas is in RPEL.PDB, pr. 8, esc. 16, no fol., May 14, 1869.

2. RPEL.PDB, pr. 8, fol. 4, January 28, 1868; pr. 1, esc. 14, no fol., March 28, 1871; and pr. 1, esc. 111, fols. 51–52, May 24, 1886.

3. The 1869 document, in which the inspector also states that the true boundaries

and area of the estate cannot be verified, is reproduced in RPEL.j.civ. (1908) bulto 131, doc. 5.935, "1ª pieza Los Chipas," fol. 38.

4. In the early 1890s, a tenant in Agua-fría attempted to have his land declared baldío. In rejecting the tenant's petition, the state government cited the continual collection of rents in the zone. The estate owners later registered the government's decision. See RPEL.PDB, pr. 1, esc. 40, fols. 58–60, February 12, 1892. Sales and mortgages of tenant holdings in the hamlets of Agua-fría, Rincón-hondo, and Los Chipas usually specified that the land was part of the estate of Los Chipas.

5. The government's rejection of Torrealba's petition appears in *Gaceta Oficial* (Caracas), July 28, 1885, 1095. Torrealba's heirs also refer to his failed efforts to obtain clear title to all of Los Chipas in RPEL.PDB, pr. 1, esc. 122, fols. 3–6, June 10, 1886.

6. For Camejo's service with the Hernandistas, see Manzanarez, *La Revolución,* 74. Camejo is referred to as a resident of Valencia in the purchase of Los Chipas, as recorded in RPEL.PDC, pr. 1, esc. 6, fol. 8, July 8, 1908.

7. Núñez, *Bosquejo histórico,* 54. Avelino aided Castro and Gómez in subduing the Libertadora Revolution following the government's defeat of the rebels at La Victoria. See *El Larense* (Barquisimeto), January 21, 1908, 3.

8. The landowners' original *demanda* (in which they established the rationale for the suit, named the defendants, and specified their objective in the proceedings) is dated September 28, 1909, and is found in RPEL.j.civ. (1908) bulto 131, doc. 5.935, "1ª pieza Los Chipas," fols. 4–5. The estate's *reglamento,* which contains rental conditions, is entered in ibid. (1910) bulto 136, doc. 6.298, "Juicio Los Chipas, Giménez, Camejo, Rojas Velis, 2a pieza," fol. 102.

9. RPEL.j.civ. (1908) bulto 131, doc. 5.935, "1ª pieza Los Chipas," fols. 32–57, 60–66.

10. RPEL.j.civ. (1911) bulto 137, doc. 6.480, "Juicio Los Chipas, Giménez, Camejo, Rojas Velis, 3a pieza," fols. 128–29.

11. RPEL.j.civ. (1908) bulto 131, doc. 5.935, "1ª pieza Los Chipas," fols. 6–11.

12. RPEL.j.civ. (1911) bulto 137, doc. 6.480, "Juicio Los Chipas, Giménez, Camejo, Rojas Velis, 3a pieza," fols. 139, 142.

13. RPEL.j.civ. (1908) bulto 131, doc. 5.935, "1ª pieza Los Chipas," fol. 57. The petition was repeated in August. See ibid. (1910) bulto 136, doc. 6.298, "Juicio Los Chipas, Giménez, Camejo, Rojas Velis, 2a pieza," fols. 84–85.

14. The estate owners' opposition is recorded in RPEL.j.civ. (1908) bulto 131, doc. 5.935, "1ª pieza Los Chipas," fol. 69; order from the minister of Fomento, in ibid. (1911) bulto 138, doc. 6.333, "Demanda, que sobre la posesión Los Chipas, intenta el Procurador General del Estado Lara contra varios por ocupar terrenos patrimonio de la Nación," fol. 1.

15. RPEL.j.civ. (1911) bulto 138, doc. 6.333, "Demanda, que sobre la posesión Los Chipas, intenta el Procurador General del Estado Lara," fols. 15–16; see also fols. 47–49.

16. Ibid., fols. 29–39, 44–46.

17. Ibid., fols. 51–53.

18. Ibid., fol. 55.

19. The final agreement was published in *Gaceta Oficial* (Caracas), February 9, 1914, and a copy was entered in the court documents. RPEL.j.civ. (1913) bulto 141, doc. 6.789,

"Pruebas introducidas por las partes demandadas en el Juicio Los Chipas, 6a pieza," fol. 181.

20. Between 1908 and 1920, the value of the estate increased from 13,400 to 140,000 bolívares. The 1908 value is the price paid by Camejo and Giménez Méndez when they purchased the estate, as recorded in RPEL.PDC, pr. 1, esc. 6, fol. 8, July 8, 1908, and esc. 11, fols. 12–13, July 11, 1908. When Giménez Méndez died in 1920, his half of the land in the estate of Los Chipas (excluding all buildings, crops, and other improvements) was valued at 70,000 bolívares. RPEL.j.civ. (1920) bulto 155, "Inventario de los bienes del Grl. Avelino Giménez Méndez," fol. 20.

21. RPEL.j.civ. (1916) bulto 147, doc. 7.399, "Demanda intentada por el Dr. R. Escovar Albizu, como apoderado de Avelino Jiménez Méndez y Leopoldo R. Camejo, contra Manuel, Marcos y Crispín Rivero, por desocupación de terrenos de la posesión Los Chipas."

22. The estate owners' demands are recorded in ibid., fol. 1.

23. The mortgage of the Riveros' holdings is recorded in RPEL.PDC, pr. 1, esc. 30, fols. 26–27, February 8, 1916; the sale is in ibid., esc. 15, fol. 15, July 12, 1916.

24. For the Riveros' origins and a description of their holdings, which together occupied only eight hectares, see ibid., esc. 30, fols. 26–27, February 8, 1916.

25. Ibid., esc. 44, fol. 38, February 23, 1915.

26. Ibid., esc. 26, fols. 22–23, July 15, 1918. See also RPEL.j.civ. (1910) bulto 136, doc. 6.298, "Juicio Los Chipas, Giménez, Camejo, Rojas Velis, 2a pieza," fol. 97.

27. RPEL.PDC, pr. 1, esc. 18, fols. 16–17, January 25, 1916; esc. 64, fols. 68–70, May 11, 1916; and esc. 114, fols. 101–02, September 23, 1916.

28. For a copy of the survey, see RPEL.j.civ. (1915) doc. 7.310 (cover sheet missing), lawsuit brought by Medardo Alvarado against Francisco, Andrés, Ramona, Epifania, and Juan Zenon Giménez, fol. 4.

29. Ibid., fol. 5.

30. Ibid., fols. 43–44.

31. Ibid., fols. 45, 48.

32. Ibid., fols. 56–61.

33. Ibid., fols. 62–77.

34. RPEL.j.civ. (1918) bulto 152, lawsuit brought by Pedro J. Sandoval Vargas (represented by Ramón Escovar Albizu) against Antonio Colmenares, Juan Anselmo Abarca, Juan Giménez, Juan Bautista Oviedo, Domingo Mejías, Juan Esteban Oviedo, Evaristo Mendoza, Felipe Eulogio Rodríguez, and Tomás Sánchez, fol. 2.

35. Ibid., fols. 4–9.

36. Ibid., fols. 30–32.

37. Ibid., fols. 30, 41.

38. Ibid., fols. 34–35.

39. Ibid., fols. 40–43.

40. Ibid., fols. 57–62.

41. Ibid., fols. 74, 79–85.

42. Ibid., fols. 95–99.

43. Scholars have disagreed over the extent to which judges acted as agents of cen-

tral authority or became integrated into the local elites in the areas where they served. The position that judges remained loyal to the center is argued in Pang and Seckinger, "Mandarins of Imperial Brazil," 215–44. Thomas Flory, by contrast, argues that judges became brokers between the imperial state and local elites, thus avoiding complete identification with either the center or the notables within their jurisdictions. See Flory, *Judge and Jury*, esp. chap. 10. For a discussion of this and related topics, see Graham's review essay, "State and Society," 223–36.

Chapter 7. The Transformation of Duaqueño Society

1. Bauer, "Rural Society," esp. 123, 126–27, 147. For an influential debate over the relative importance of demographic trends and class struggle in shaping European social structure before 1800, see essays by Robert Brenner and others in Aston and Philpin, *The Brenner Debate*. The significance of population growth in the transformation of the Mexican Bajío after 1750 is reviewed in Tutino, *From Insurrection to Revolution*, 41–61. On Chile, see Bauer, *Chilean Rural Society*, chaps. 5–6.

2. Venezuela, *Tercer censo*, 2:314; and Perales Frígols, "Geografía económica," 63.

3. For the inclusion of the two caseríos, see Perera, *Historia político-territorial*, 340. For populations, see Venezuela, *Tercer censo*, 2:319. For district's area, see Vila, *Aspectos geográficos*, 18.

4. *El Eco Industrial* (Barquisimeto), May 17, 1905, 1. Historians of Venezuela are only beginning to integrate ecological change into their economic and social analyses. See Cunill Grau, "Historia ambiental y regionalización," 139–53.

5. *La Voz del Norte* (Duaca), September 15, 1901, 3.

6. Examples include ACMDC, Copiador de correspondencia de 1907–1908, fol. 48, September 22, 1907, entry no. 206, and no fol., January 25, 1908, entry no. 26; Copiador de correspondencia de 1911–1914, fol. 12, March 17, (1911?), entry no. 267; fol. 25, January 24, 1912, entry no. 6; fol. 47, October 20, 1913, entry no. 112; and fol. 87, September 15, 1914, entry no. 214.

7. Stein, *Vassouras*, 214–22. For an excellent analysis of the changing ecology of a very different region, see William Cronan, *Changes in the Land: Indians, Colonists, and the Ecology of New England* (New York: Hill and Wang, 1983).

8. AANH.CAP, tomo 3, sección 25, "Estudio del reglamento de la posesión Santa Inés."

9. RPEL.PDC, pr. 1, esc. 34, fols. 26–27, August 7, 1911.

10. RPEL.PDC, pr. 1, esc. 63, fol. 52, May 12, 1911. Sales of rights to uncultivated areas include ibid., esc. 56, fols. 44–45, February 15, 1912; esc. 140, fols. 110–11, March 15, 1920 (the sale in this document was actually made in 1916); and esc. 12, fol. 12, March 12, 1904.

11. For Demitrio Canelón, RPEL.PDC, pr. 1, esc. 99, fols. 98–99, December 18, 1919. This document records Canelón's sale of the grove; the date he purchased the rights to the cleared land is not specified. For Francisca Rodríguez, ibid., esc. 64, fol. 53, May 13, 1911.

12. Examples include RPEL.PDC, pr. 1, esc. 35, fol. 26, April 27, 1910; esc. 40, fol. 32, February 6, 1912; and esc. 36, fols. 30–31, February 3, 1912.

13. "Reglamento de la posesión 'Santa Ana'" (1922), in RPEL.j.civ. (1928) bulto 173, "Demanda de Manuel Vicente Giménez Vásquez, apoderado de P. Vásquez de Giménez Perdomo contra Florencio Majano, Augustín Majano, Julia Majano, Salomé Durán y Ramón García"; and "Reglamento de la posesión 'San Rafael'" (1919), in RPEL.j.civ. (1927) bulto 171, "Demanda de Blas Delascio contra Trina Méndez." Even in early 1925, as the new rents began in Duaca, Leopoldo Torres wrote of the customary prevailing rent as being 5 percent of the coffee harvest. AANH.CAP, tomo 3, sección 25, "Estudio del reglamento de la posesión Santa Inés."

14. For wage rates in the nineteenth century, see chapter 3. Wages in the early 1930s are recorded in court documents concerning judicially embargoed haciendas. RPEL.j.civ. (1930) bulto 178, "Ejecución de hipoteca de Pedro Javier contra Regino Vásquez," fol. 14; and ibid. (1934) bulto 187, "José Garbi demanda á Melania Martínez de Tovar," fols. 23, 25–26.

15. Corn prices (per fanega) for Venezuelan regions in 1894 are found in Izard, *Series estadísticas,* 157; corn prices for Venezuela as a whole (per 100 kilograms) beginning in 1913 are found in ibid., 160. In order to calculate a representative price from 1894 to compare to the "national" prices from the twentieth century, I took the median 1894 price from among the nine regional prices, using the fanega equivalents, which varied by region, as listed in Lisandro Alvarado, "Pesos y medidas usados en Venezuela" (1923), in *Obras completas* (Caracas: Ministerio de Educación, 1958), 8:257. As it happens, the median 1894 price of 17.98 bolívares per 100 kilograms of corn comes from Lara. Between 1930 and 1934, the two years for which wages in Duaca can be documented, the price of corn fluctuated between 19.25 and 33.33 bolívares per 100 kilograms. A 50 percent increase in the price of corn relative to 1894 (an increase that matches that of wages for the same period) would yield a price of 26.97 bolívares, which falls near the middle of the 1930–1934 range.

16. *El eco industrial* (Barquisimeto), May 26, 1905, 1; *Notas* (Barquisimeto), October 21, 1917, 3, and July 3, 1919, 3.

17. For estate owners encroaching on peasant land, AANH.CAP, tomo 44, sección 13, Juan B. Cambero to Leopoldo Torres, February 1, 1909, and tomo 10, sección 28, J. J. Rivero to Leopoldo Torres, August 11, 1910. For Juan Bautista Pacheco Romano against Aurelio Giménez Méndez, see RPEL.j.civ. (1909) bulto 133, document 6.013, "Demanda intentada por el Dr Juan Jacobo Guédez contra Rudecindo Peralta y Aurelio Giménez Méndez," and ibid., bulto 134, doc. 6.026, "Juicio civil Giménez Méndez contra Pacheco Romano, 2a pieza," fol. 126.

18. These meetings are recorded in "Mensura y posesión de los Resguardos de Indígenas en la parroquia Duaca," broadsheet dated April 18, 1910, in RPEL.j.civ. (1908) bulto 131, doc. 5.935, "1ª pieza Los Chipas," fol. 58. RPEL.PDC, pr. 3, esc. 3, fols. 2–4, November 25, 1910.

19. AANH.CAP, tomo 10, sección 28, J. J. Rivero to Leopoldo Torres, August 11, 1910.

20. Many of these documents are gathered in RPEL.j.civ. (1912) bulto 140, "Dili-

gencias promovidas por Juan Antonio Mollejas, partición de terrenos indígenas, 2a pieza," and "Partición de terrenos indígenas, 3a pieza." The protocolos of Distrito Crespo from June 1912 through 1914 also contain many cases of resguardo occupants registering titles to their holdings.

21. In October 1912, Raimundo Sangronis attempted to halt the partition, charging that the resguardo boundaries were not well defined. RPEL.j.civ. (1912) bulto 139, doc. 59, "Diligencias promovidas port Juan Antonio Mollejas, 1a pieza," fol. 18.

22. RPEL.PDC, pr. 1, esc. 7, fols. 6–11, October 16, 1916. Although this document gave final legal approval to the partition, recipients of land began to sell plots "received" in the partition as early as late 1914.

23. See the declarations by Mollejas in RPEL.PDC, pr. 1, esc. 71, fols. 56–57, May 14, 1917, and esc. 4, fols. 3–4, April 9, 1917.

24. For Clemente Alvarado, RPEL.PDC, pr. 1, esc. 74, fols. 71–72, December 23, 1913; for Cipriano Bracho, ibid., esc. 5, fols. 4–5, January 18, 1915. Oberto bought his land in two transactions, see ibid., esc. 19, fols. 20–22, July 11, 1914, and esc. 66, fols. 62–63, August 8, 1914. For the sale to Ruíz, see ibid., esc. 12, fols. 10–11, January 19, 1914. For Argenis Azuaje, Eduardo Colmenares, and Aurelio Giménez, see the document finalizing the resguardo partition, ibid., esc. 7, fols. 6–11, October 16, 1916.

25. For Antonio Perdomo and his children, RPEL.PDC, pr. 1, esc. 35, fols. 31–32, November 3, 1914. The title registered by Rojas is found in RPEL.j.civ. (1912) bulto 140, "Diligencias promovidas por Juan Antonio Mollejas, partición de terrenos indígenas, 2a pieza," fols. 40–42. When Rojas mortgaged the grove two years later, he declared it was in land belonging to Bracho's heirs. RPEL.PDC, pr. 1, esc. 30, fols. 27–28, July 20, 1916.

26. A 1910 document composed by the junta lists 1,170 adult men and women as *comuneros* (joint holders) of the resguardos. See the printed broadsheet in RPEL.j.civ. (1908) bulto 131, doc. 5.935, "1ª pieza Los Chipas," fol. 58. By contrast, only 141 individuals received title to land in the partition. For examples of occupants losing land because they could not pay the required fee, see RPEL.PDC, pr. 1, esc. 91, fols. 90–91, May 17, 1915; esc. 52, fol. 52, September 6, 1915; and esc. 66, fols. 55–56, May 23, 1918.

27. RPEL.j.civ. (1912) bulto 139, "Partición de terrenos indígenas, 5ª pieza," fols. 235–36. Mollejas provided testimony from other witnesses including the surveyor aiding in the partition, Antonio S. Briceño, as to the delays caused by heavy rain. See fols. 237–38.

28. Guillén's ruling is emphasized at the conclusion of the document finalizing the partition. RPEL.PDC, pr. 1, esc. 7, fols. 6–11, October 16, 1916. A movement arose in the late 1980s (see chapter 9) to reclaim Duaca's former resguardo lands as ejidos, basing its case on the illegality of Guillén's ruling. Even some who opposed the reclamation agreed that Guillén had side-stepped the law. *El Informador* (Barquisimeto), June 16, 1987, B6.

29. RPEL.j.civ. (1927) bulto 171, "Demanda de Blas Delascio contra Trina Méndez"; ibid. (1923) bulto 161, "Manuela Camero contra Eulogio Segura," and bulto 163, "Demanda de Manuela Camero contra Eulogio Segura."

30. Paredes Huggins, "La incorporación de tierras baldías," 18–25, 29, 47, 48. Also

Brito Figueroa, *Historia económica y social,* 2:384, 386. According to Luis Cipriano Rodríguez, the regime alienated 187,091 hectares of baldíos between 1922 and 1929. See Rodríguez, "Gómez y el agro," in Pino Iturrieta, *Juan Vicente Gómez,* 93.

31. Examples of abuse and fraud include Paredes Huggins, "La incorporación de tierras baldías," 38–40, 48; and Brito Figueroa, *Historia económica y social,* 2:382, 385.

32. Diego Bautista Urbaneja, "El sistema político gomecista," in Pino Iturrieta, *Juan Vicente Gómez,* 56, 66 n. 12; and Pino Iturrieta, "Estudio preliminar," 1:21–25.

33. Delgado Segura, *Miscelaneas duaqueñas,* 21.

34. The grant was later registered in Duaca, in RPEL.PDC, pr. 1, esc. 14, fols. 11–13, October 9, 1920. The transfer was entered in the district registry the following month, in ibid., esc. 81, fols. 77–79, December 28, 1920.

35. RPEL.PDC, pr. 1, esc. 16, fols. 14–15, January 29, 1921.

36. For Ramón Antonio Vásquez, see RPEL.PDC, pr. 1, esc. 52, fols. 55–56, November 12, 1925. For Tovar's sales to Vásquez and Leoncio Guillén, see ibid., esc. 33, fols. 29–30, February 16, 1921. For Carlos José Guillén, see ibid., esc. 17, fol. 15, January 29, 1921; for Hermelindo Oberto, esc. 18, fol. 16, January 29, 1921. For Domingo Antonio Yépez, see esc. 33, fols. 29–30, February 16, 1921; esc. 129, fols. 139–40, June 10, 1925; and esc. 74, fols. 103–09, March 21, 1927.

37. The grant to Tovar is recorded in RPEL.PDC, pr. 1, esc. 90, fols. 83–84, May 6, 1920. For Tovar's purchases from other brokers, see ibid., esc. 19, fol. 21, October 7, 1919; esc. 92, fols. 69–71, February 20, 1920; esc. 94, fols. 71–72, February 20, 1920; and esc. 111, fols. 93–94, September 17, 1924. For his sales of parts of these lands, see ibid., esc. 142, fols. 144–45, June 2, 1921; and esc. 179, fols. 168–69, June 10, 1920.

38. *Gaceta Oficial del Estado Lara,* November 4, 1909, 1, and March 11, 1915, 2; and *Notas* (Barquisimeto), February 24, 1916, 2.

39. RPEL.PDC, pr. 3, esc. 2, fols. 1–2, October 17, 1912; pr. 3, esc. 2, fol. 5, November 28, 1912; pr. 3, esc. 1, fol. 1, January 5, 1914; pr. 3, esc. 2, fol. 1–2, April 6, 1915; and pr. 3, esc. 1, fol. 1, October 6, 1916; *Gaceta Oficial del Estado Lara,* August 13, 1913, 2, February 12, 1914, 2, and March 19, 1915, 4.

40. The three grants are recorded in RPEL.PDC, pr. 1, esc. 110, fols. 88–91, September 23, 1919; esc. 38, fols. 35–37, July 30, 1923; and esc. 39, fols. 37–38, July 31, 1923. Yépez's debt to the surveyor, Antonio Sebastian Briceño, for measurement of public land grants in Las Casitas and Las Carpas is indicated in ibid., esc. 26, fols. 24–26, October 25, 1924. Yépez provided financing for the 1919 grant in Caraquitas through Félix Antonio Urdaneta, as indicated in esc. 36, fols. 36–38, October 17, 1919.

41. For transfers to Yépez from the 1919 grant in Caraquitas, see RPEL.PDC, pr. 1, esc. 8, fols. 7–8, October 3, 1919; esc. 14, fols. 12–13, October 4, 1919; esc. 16, fols. 14–15, October 4, 1919; esc. 36, fols. 36–38, October 17, 1919. Six public land recipients transferred lots to Yépez from the 1923 grant in Las Casitas, as indicated in ibid., esc. 136, fols. 118–19, June 3, 1924. Twenty-three recipients from the 1923 grant in Las Carpas ceded their land to Yépez in ibid., esc. 135, fols. 116–18, June 2, 1924.

42. Some of Pérez's official correspondence can be found in the Archivo General de la Nación, Ministerio de Agricultura y Cría, folder titled "Ministerio de Fomento, Dirección de Tierras Baldías, Industrias y Comercio, Correspondencia 1918, Inten-

dente de Tierras Baldías del Estado Lara." Pérez's appointment in October 1922 is recorded in Venezuela, "Dirección de Tierras Baldías, Industrias y Comercio," in *Memoria* (Caracas: Tipografía Cosmos, 1923), 6–7. For cases of Pérez representing Yépez in the sale of recently privatized public lands, see RPEL.PDC, pr. 1, esc. 15, fols. 14–16, July 15, 1924; esc. 16, fols. 16–17, July 16, 1924; and esc. 26, fols. 24–26, October 25, 1924.

43. Thirty-two recipients of public lands in Las Casitas ceded their land to Pérez in RPEL.PDC, pr. 1, esc. 4, fols. 3–5, July 7, 1924, and esc. 25, fols. 27–29, January 28, 1925. Four recipients of public lands in Las Carpas ceded their property to Pérez in ibid., esc. 7, fols. 7–8, July 10, 1924. For Yépez and Pérez sales to local elite, ibid., esc. 5, fols. 11–13, July 7, 1920; esc. 79, fols. 68–71, May 1, 1920; esc. 67, fols. 57–58, August 15, 1924; esc. 28, fols. 28–30, April 15, 1925; esc. 16, fols. 16–17, July 16, 1924; esc. 111, fols. 93–94, September 17, 1924; esc. 39, fols. 42–44, February 6, 1925; and esc. 40, fols. 44–45, February 7, 1925.

44. RPEL.PDC, pr. 1, esc. 101, fols. 92–93, May 10, 1920; esc. 103, fols. 94–95, May 10, 1920; esc. 127, fols. 119–20, May 17, 1920; and esc. 133, fol. 126, May 18, 1920.

45. Yépez to Francisco Rafael Fonseca, RPEL.PDC, pr. 1, esc. 124, fols. 116–17, May 17, 1920. Yépez to Ramón Antonio Vásquez, ibid., esc. 126, fols. 118–19, May 17, 1920. In addition to these, see ibid., esc. 157, fols. 150–51, May 29, 1920; esc. 185, fols. 174–75, June 14, 1920; esc. 5, fols. 11–13, July 7, 1920; esc. 45, fols. 42–43, March 1, 1921; and esc. 88, fol. 113, May 21, 1927.

46. For Gimón, see *Diccionario histórico de Venezuela*, 2:299. For Velasco, ibid., 3:850–51. A sample of Velasco's correspondence with Gómez is collected in Segnini et al., *Los hombres del Benemérito*, 2:459–65.

47. For Gimón's purchase see RPEL.PDC, pr. 1, esc. 97, fols. 74–76, February 24, 1920. For Velasco, see ibid., esc. 15, fols. 14–16, July 15, 1924. The sales by Gimón, his son, and Velasco are recorded in ibid., esc. 98, fol. 100–01, September 9, 1925; esc. 52, fols. 55–56, November 12, 1925; and esc. 10, fols. 9–10, January 12, 1925.

48. Gimón participated in other speculative ventures linked to oil, as recorded in B. S. McBeth, *Juan Vicente Gómez and the Oil Companies in Venezuela, 1908–1935* (Cambridge: Cambridge University Press, 1983), 87, 89.

49. For Garbi's largest properties, see RPEL.PDC, pr. 1, esc. 4, fols. 4–5, January 22, 1909, and esc. 49, fols. 47–48, September 4, 1915.

50. RPEL.PDC, pr. 1, esc. 44, fols. 35–36, January 27, 1920, and esc. 70, fol. 54, February 7, 1920. La Escalera was located in the municipio of Bobare, but a small portion extended into Distrito Crespo. The privatized land was in Distrito Crespo.

51. RPEL.PDC, pr. 1, esc. 61, fols. 57–58, March 11, 1921, and esc. 68, fols. 67–68, May 2, 1921.

52. The quote is from *Notas* (Barquisimeto), June 23, 1918. For Azuaje's land acquisition, see RPEL.PDC, pr. 1, esc. 2, fol. 2, January 5, 1920. Azuaje and Gómez jointly purchased 125 hectares of grazing and agricultural land in Distrito Crespo in 1911; Gómez sold his shares in the land (and in two other properties in Lara) to Azuaje in 1914. See RPEL.PDC, pr. 1, esc. 85, fols. 67–69, May 29, 1911; esc. 61, fols. 57–59, August 7, 1914; and esc. 41, fols. 37–38, February 16, 1924.

53. RPEL.PDC, pr. 1, esc. 102, fols. 79–80, February 27, 1920, and esc. 132, fols. 103–04, March 11, 1920.

54. Segnini, *La consolidación*, 91–92; Ziems, *El gomecismo*, 160–68.

55. My description of the new rental system is based on "Reglamento de la Posesión Piedras Lisas" (1925), in RPEL.j.civ. (1928) bulto 174, "Demanda de Francisco Giménez Sorondo, apoderado de Belicio Díaz contra Benigno Pérez"; "Reglamento de las Posesiones Volcanes, Chigüiral, Chipas y La Reforma" (1928), in RPEL.j.civ. (1932) bulto 181, "Demanda de Leopoldo R. Camejo contra Juan Alvarado"; and RPEL.j.civ. (1932) bulto 181, "Demanda de Ramón Antonio Vásquez contra Nicolás Zavarce Riera, por cobro de cantidad de bolívares provtientes de pisos," fol. 1.

56. James Scott makes this point regarding a similar transition in rental arrangements in Malaysia, in *Weapons of the Weak*, 73.

57. Neeson, "Opponents of Enclosure," 139.

58. For Leopoldo Torres, AANH.CAP, tomo 3, sección 25, "Estudio del reglamento de la Posesión Santa Inés del señor Luis Díaz Quintero" (1925). Reglamentos approved by Vásquez include those from the estates of Los Chipas (1928) and Piedras Lisas (1925), cited above. For Vásquez imposing fixed cash rents on his own tenants, see RPEL.j.civ. (1926) bulto 170, "Demanda intentada por Ramón Antonio Vásquez contra José Colmenares," fol. 1, and (1932) bulto 181, "Demanda de Ramón Antonio Vásquez contra Nicolás Zavarce Riera, por cobro de cantidad de bolívares provientes de pisos," fol. 1.

59. References to droughts in Duaca are found in RPEL.j.civ. (1931) bulto 180, "Demanda de Rómulo Delgado Segura contra Sacramento Aguilar," fol. 5; Rodríguez Marrufo, "Aportes," 113; "Sobre el mismo tema," *La Senda* (Duaca), March 10, 1935; and "La agricultura y el reajuste de sus cuentas," *El Impulso* (Barquisimeto), April 16, 1937.

60. RPEL.j.civ. (1935) bulto 191, "Demanda intentada por Leopoldo Ramón Camejo contra Remigio Lozada por cobro de pisos."

61. RPEL.j.civ. (1927) bulto 171, untitled documents pertaining to the suit brought by Casimiro Casamayor against Magdaleno Heredia, Antonio Alejos, Isaías Rivero, and Basilio Alejos; ibid. (1928) bulto 174, "Demanda de Juan Rafael Sequera Sangronis contra Trinidad Martínez, por cobro de cantidad de bolívares"; ibid. (1935) bulto 190, "Demanda de Rafael Molina Herrera . . . contra Virgilio Riera por pensiones de arrendamiento como pisatario de la posesión Caraquitas"; and ibid. (1928) bulto 173, "Demanda de Juan Rafael Sequera Sangronis contra Cruz Alvarez por cobro de bolívares."

62. Cruz Alvarez ceded part of his holding to his landlord, Juan Rafael Sequera Sangronis, to settle a debt for unpaid rents. RPEL.PDC, pr. 1, esc. 83, fol. 102, May 3, 1929.

63. RPEL.j.civ. (1926) bulto 168, "Demanda intentada por el Doctor F. Seijas y J. M. Ponte [Vásquez's representatives] contra Juan Esteban Cordero, por cobro de bolívares"; ibid., bulto 170, "Demanda intentada por el Doctor Francisco Seijas y J. M. Ponte, apoderados de R. A. Vásquez, contra Nicomedes Castillo, por cobro de cantidades de bolívares"; and ibid., bulto 170, "Demanda intentada por Ramón Antonio Vásquez contra José Colmenares."

64. RPEL.j.civ. (1931) bulto 179, "Demanda de Ramón A. Vásquez contra Juan Este-

ban Cordero," and ibid. (1932) bulto 182, "Demanda de Ramón Antonio Vásquez contra Nicomedes Castillo."

65. RPEL.PDC, pr. 1, esc. 11, fols. 13–15, October 30, 1933.

66. RPEL.j.civ. (1934) bulto 189, "Demanda intentado por Jorge Zoghby contra Anastacio Véliz, Nicomedes Castillo, Juan Esteban Cordero, y Juan Pantaleón Leal, por cobro de cantidad de bolívares," fol. 6.

67. RPEL.j.civ. (1930) bulto 178, "Demanda intentada por Juan B. Luna, apoderado de Homobono Rivero, contra Modesto Rodríguez," fol. 9.

68. Juan Salcedo, a tenant on Eulogio Segura Sánchez's estate in Caraquitas, also claimed that the land he occupied, which had been privatized in 1919, was public land. RPEL.j.civ. (1930) bulto 177, "Demanda intentada por Eulogio Segura Sánchez contra Luis Morillo, Juan Salcedo y Felipe Castillo, por cobro de bolívares," fol. 5.

69. See, for example, Thompson, "Custom, Law, and Common Right," in *Customs in Common,* 97–184.

70. Several tenants on the estate of Perarapa joined in this act of resistance during a dispute over unpaid rents and (according to the landowner) unauthorized occupation of estate lands. RPEL.j.civ. (1928) bulto 174, "Demanda intentada por Francisco Giménez Sorondo, apoderado de Francisco Vivas contra Tomás Abarca, por cobro de bolívares," fol. 25; see also fol. 10.

71. Roseberry, *Coffee and Capitalism,* 183–86.

72. For discussions of political repression and labor control in Venezuela under Gómez, see Powell, *Political Mobilization,* 48–49; Otilia Rosas González and Juan José Salazar, *Orígen del latifundio caroreño* (Barquisimeto: Fondo Editorial Buría, 1988), 96–98; Segnini, *La consolidación,* 101–04; Zeims, *El gomecismo,* 166–68; and Linder, "Agriculture and Rural Society," chaps. 5–6.

73. Examples include RPEL.PDC, pr. 1, esc. 99, fols. 81–82, June 21, 1918; esc. 23, fols. 19–20, April 20, 1918; esc. 9, fols. 7–8, January 18, 1919; esc. 10, fol. 8, January 18, 1919; esc. 142, fols. 144–45, June 2, 1921; esc. 49, fols. 48–49, August 9, 1922; esc. 93, fols. 125–27, September 11, 1926; esc. 162, fols. 209–10, June 16, 1927; and esc. 163, fols. 210–12, June 17, 1927.

74. Examples include RPEL.PDC, pr. 1, esc. 45, fol. 38, May 4, 1918; esc. 66, fols. 55–56, May 23, 1918; esc. 20, fol. 20, July 18, 1924; esc. 71, fols. 61–62, August 18, 1924; esc. 32, fols. 61–62, February 11, 1926; esc. 34, fols. 65–66, February 12, 1926; esc. 164, fols. 212–13, June 17, 1927; and esc. 165, fols. 213–14, June 17, 1927.

75. For an elegant presentation of the thesis that "everyday" forms of peasant resistance undermine the willingness of elites to push exploitation to the maximum level possible, see Scott, *Weapons of the Weak.*

76. Perales Frigols, *Geografía económica,* 63.

77. Pepino Valenzuela, interview by author, Duaca, April 15, 1990; and RPEL.PDC, pr. 1, esc. 15, fols. 14–17, October 16, 1923, and also esc. 1, fols. 1–4, July 2, 1920.

78. In the neighboring municipio of Bobare, Antonio Pereira worked as a day laborer harvesting coffee on haciendas belonging to the Briceño family but refused nonharvest jobs such as weeding, for the reasons indicated. Antonio Pereira, interview by author, Barquisimeto, February 21, 1990.

79. Pepino Valenzuela, a resident of Duaca during the 1920s and 1930s, interview by author, Duaca, April 15, 1990. Worker debts were also strictly enforced at this time in the neighboring municipio of Bobare. Antonio Pereira, interview by author, Barquisimeto, February 21, 1990.

80. Rodríguez Marrufo, "Aportes," 122–26; Garriga, *Fichas, señas, y ñapas,* 16–17, 29; Pepino Valenzuela, interview by author, Duaca, April 15, 1990.

81. Delgado Segura, *Miscelaneas duaqueñas,* and Núñez, *Bosquejo histórico.*

82. Arguments concerning the oil industry's allegedly detrimental influence on agriculture are summarized in Lieuwen, *Petroleum in Venezuela,* 53, and Rodríguez, *Gómez,* 131–33.

83. "Sobre el mismo tema," *La Senda* (Duaca), March 10, 1935; and *El Impulso* (Barquisimeto), April 16, 1937, 1, 2.

84. Núñez, *Bosquejo histórico,* 64.

85. For Pedro Javier as a merchant, see RPEL.PDB, pr. 1, esc. 20, fols. 27–28, July 22, 1903; esc. 33, fols. 35–36, August 9, 1906; and esc. 34, fols. 36–37, August 10, 1906. Also RPEL.PDC, pr. 1, esc. 34, fols. 30–31, March 10, 1909, and esc. 89, fols. 84–85, May 13, 1914. For expanding his investments, RPEL.PDC, pr. 1, esc. 23, fol. 24, November 5, 1915. Also RPEL.PDB, pr. 1, esc. 4, fol. 5, January 4, 1911; esc. 116, fols. 158–60, March 3, 1914; and esc. 84, fols. 92–95, February 13, 1917.

86. The public land grant is recorded in RPEL.PDC, pr. 1, esc. 39, fols. 32–33, July 25, 1917. For Javier's subsequent purchases of land, see ibid., esc. 9, fols. 9–11, October 10, 1918; esc. 86, fols. 70–71, September 8, 1919; esc. 87, fol. 71, September 8, 1919; esc. 55, fols. 55–56, November 5, 1919; esc. 145, fols. 114–15, March 16, 1920; esc. 89, fols. 111–14, August 27, 1920; esc. 70, fols. 70–71, May 3, 1921; esc. 49, fols. 48–49, August 9, 1922; esc. 30, fols. 28–29, July 25, 1923; esc. 25, fols. 35–37, July 20, 1926; and RPEL.PDB, pr. 1, esc. 151, fols. 149–51, May 29, 1923.

87. RPEL.PDC, pr. 1, esc. 137, fols. 119–20, June 3, 1924, and esc. 164, fol. 145, June 16, 1924.

88. RPEL.PDB, pr. 1, esc. 1, fols. 1–8, October 3, 1893, and esc. 48, fols. 50–51, November 15, 1896.

89. I am grateful to Profesora Luisa Rodríguez for allowing me to borrow her list of men serving on Duaca's district council between 1905 and 1936, which she had compiled from council records. For Segura's efforts to have Duaca made a district, see Perera, *Historia político-territorial,* 310–12, and *El Eco del Norte* (Duaca), February 6, 1892, 4.

90. RPEL.PDC, pr. 1, esc. 7, fols. 6–11, October 16, 1916; esc. 110, fols. 88–91, September 23, 1919; esc. 115, fols. 94–95, September 25, 1919; esc. 53, fols. 57–59, November 28, 1924; esc. 2, fols. 2–3, October 1, 1926; and esc. 3, fols. 4–6, October 4, 1926.

91. For coffee-processing plant, see RPEL.PDC, pr. 1, esc. 45, fols. 46–48, October 27, 1919; for Segura e Hijos, ibid., esc. 88, fols. 84–85, September 8, 1922; for loans, esc. 1, fols. 1–3, April 4, 1922, and esc. 62, fols. 58–59, March 6, 1923.

92. RPEL.PDC, pr. 1, esc. 196, fols. 185–87, June 7, 1913; esc. 24, fol. 30, April 14, 1916; esc. 15, fols. 13–14, April 5, 1914; and esc. 4, fols. 3–4, January 7, 1916. For processing plant in Licua, *El Loro* (Duaca), November 24, 1923, 3.

93. Evidence surfaces repeatedly in the correspondence collected in Segnini et al., *Los hombres del Benemérito.* For examples in volume 1, see Félix Galavís to Juan Vicente Gómez, October 10, 1923, 331, September 24, 1925, 333–34, and September 23, 1926, 335–36. In volume 2, see Amador Uzcátegui to Juan Vicente Gómez, September 28, 1925, 448–49.

94. Cardozo, "Duaca a princípios del siglo," 50.

95. *Notas* (Barquisimeto), March 16, 1916, 4, and May 21, 1916, 3.

96. *El Heraldo* (Barquisimeto), February 7, 1927, 1.

Chapter 8. Change in Duaca During the Depression

1. Izard, *Series estadísticas,* 165.

2. Roseberry, *Coffee and Capitalism,* 134, 136, 142, 144.

3. Izard, "El café," 262.

4. Examples include Lieuwen, *Petroleum in Venezuela,* 53, and Rodríguez, *Gómez,* 131–33.

5. Roseberry, *Coffee and Capitalism,* 128.

6. David N. Burke (Puerto Cabello) to U.S. Dept. of State, January 18, 1888, U.S. Consular Reports (microfilm), T-229, roll 10.

7. Ascanio R., "Consideraciones," 613–28; Ardao, *El café,* 65–69; Carvallo and Ríos de Hernández, *Temas,* 86–87.

8. Carvallo and Ríos de Hernández, *Temas,* 86–87, and Izard, "El café," 230.

9. The decline is noted in Izard, "El café," 229. Roseberry suggests the Boconó coffee economy may have been reaching its spatial limits by the early twentieth century and notes that Rangel argues this was the case throughout the Andes. *Coffee and Capitalism,* 97.

10. Martínez Mendoza, *Manual del agricultor venezolano,* 221, 224.

11. See Roseberry, *Coffee and Capitalism,* 128, 132, and the sources cited therein.

12. "Sobre el mismo tema," *La Senda* (Duaca), March 10, 1935; *El Impulso* (Barquisimeto), April 16, 1937, 1, 2; Instituto Nacional del Café, *Censo cafetero,* 125–26; and Venezuela, *Segundo censo agropecuario* (1950), 2:589.

13. "No son aptos para el cultivo de café suelos de la Sierra de Aroa," *El Impulso* (Barquisimeto), August 27, 1989, C3.

14. For commercial crops, see Pepper, *A través de Lara,* 284–86; for corn and black beans, Gormsen, *Barquisimeto,* 135; for sisal, Pepper, *A través de Lara,* 167–68; for coffee haciendas, Silva Uzcátegui, *Enciclopedia larense,* 1:220.

15. Perales Frigols, *Geografía económica,* 63.

16. "Boletín oficial," *La Senda* (Duaca), January 5, 1936. See also V. Torrealba Silva, "Crónica sobre la fundación y desarrollo de Duaca," in *Guía económica y social del Estado Lara* (Barquisimeto: Editorial Continente, 1952), 213.

17. These correlations of farm size and labor needs are borrowed from Williams, *States and Social Evolution,* 86, 309 n. 112; and Bergquist, *Labor in Latin America,* 302–03.

18. On the methodological problems associated with the use of notary records or

censuses (not to mention the perils of the type of comparison that I attempt here), see Edelman and Seligson, "Land Inequality," 445–91.

19. The census's count of farms over a hundred thousand trees is especially suspect. My review of sales and mortgage records would suggest that fewer farms of this size existed in the district. It is possible, for example, that some estates with tenants were counted as single farms, masking the existence of tenant farms within the estate.

20. Unfortunately, the vast majority of notarial records for the period of this study do not indicate farm size, in either hectares or coffee trees. Nevertheless, the following observations, based on my reading of these records over a period of eighteen months, lead me to believe in the predominance of peasant production into the early twentieth century: the large number of transactions by individuals selling or mortgaging coffee groves for relatively modest sums and who declare that they established their farms with their own labor and that of their family; the number of such transactions involving illiterate or semiliterate farm owners who (on the basis of the total evidence gathered on Duaca) do not appear in any source as members of the local elite; and the number of similar individuals listed as owners of adjoining farms when establishing the boundaries of the farm being sold or mortgaged. In addition, one must remember how common it was for small cultivators to be found on the public and communal lands enclosed by the elite in the 1910s and 1920s.

21. For the BAP loan, RPEL.PDC, pr. 1, esc. 57, fol. 83, November 21, 1928. Vásquez's letter is included in the civil suit brought by Kolster against him, in RPEL.j.civ. (1931) bulto 180, "Mercantil: R & O Kolster demanda a Ramón Vásquez por pago de bolívares," fol. 1. For Vásquez's sale of smaller haciendas, RPEL.PDC, pr. 1, esc. 39, fols. 59–62, December 2, 1932; for sale of main coffee estates, esc. 11, fols. 13–15, October 30, 1933.

22. For the BAP loan, RPEL.PDC, pr. 1, esc. 87, fol. 120, June 14, 1930; for judicial auction, esc. 5, fols. 7–9, January 17, 1935.

23. For the BAP loan, RPEL.PDC, pr. 1, esc. 55, fols. 65–68, May 2, 1930; for his ceding mortgaged properties, esc. 35, fols. 49–51, December 4, 1934.

24. In many cases, the notaries added marginal notes to the original BAP loans indicating that the mortgaged property had been alienated before the terms of the loan were fulfilled. Examples include RPEL.PDC, pr. 1, esc. 66, fols. 101–04, December 4, 1928; esc. 76, fols. 111–16, September 6, 1928; esc. 11, fols. 11–15, April 4, 1930; esc. 30, fols. 47–50, November 7, 1929; esc. 30, fols. 48–51, October 29, 1930; esc. 57, fols. 71–74, May 3, 1930; and esc. 76, fols. 103–06, March 9, 1931.

25. "La agricultura y el reajuste de sus cuentas," El Impulso (Barquisimeto), April 16, 1937, 1, 2; Núñez, Bosquejo histórico, 81–82.

26. For a history of Blöhm, see Dupouy, "Las Casas Blöhm de Venezuela," 113–31. For comments on the Boulton family enterprise during and after the depression, see Ewell, Venezuela, 72.

27. RPEL.PDC, pr. 1. esc. 37, fols. 64–67, November 6, 1930; esc. 48, fols. 81–85, November 11, 1930; esc. 11, fols. 11–15, April 4, 1930; esc. 69, fol. 103, December 23, 1929; esc. 30, fols. 47–50, November 7, 1929; and esc. 79, fols. 108–12, March 11, 1931.

28. Núñez, Bosquejo histórico, 107–08.

29. Unless otherwise indicated, my discussion of Gabaldón and his revolt is drawn from Heredia A., *El año 29*, 41–123. See also Roseberry, *Coffee and Capitalism*, 183–86; and *Diccionario histórico de Venezuela*, 2:227–28.

30. José R. Gabaldón to Juan V. Gómez, November 7, 1917, and October 18, 1924, in Segnini et al., *Los hombres del Benemérito*, 1:302–03, 313–16.

31. José R. Gabaldón to J. V. Gómez, September 7, 1928, in ibid., 1:316–22.

32. Heredia, *El año 29*, 80.

33. Ibid.,87.

34. Caballero, *Gómez*, 314.

35. Ramón J. Velásquez, "Aspectos de la evolución política de Venezuela en el último medio siglo," in Velásquez, ed., *Venezuela moderna: Medio siglo de historia* (Caracas: Editorial Ariel, 1979), 19–20.

36. Heredia, *El año 29*, 112.

37. This preference was bitterly noted in the press soon after the dictatorship ended. See "La realidad larense," *El Impulso* (Barquisimeto), February 19, 1936, 1.

38. "Los concejos municipales," *La Senda* (Duaca), January 5, 1936.

39. González Bracho, *Verdad histórica*, 69–70. The telegrams are referred to in E. Gómez to General J. V. Gómez, December 10, 1930, in Segnini et al., *Los hombres del Benemérito*, 1:444–45.

40. See the biographical sketch of Yépez in Pepper, *A través de Lara*, 187; and Vincenzo Pérez Soto to Juan Vicente Gómez, July 29, 1913, in *BAHM* 31 (July 1964): 116.

41. Antonio Pereira, interview by author, Barquisimeto, February 21, 1990. The purchase is recorded in RPEL.PDC, pr. 1, esc. 10, fols. 16–19, April 10, 1916.

42. E. Gómez to General J. V. Gómez, December 10, 1930, in Segnini et al., *Los hombres del Benemérito*, 1:444–45.

43. González Bracho, *Verdad histórica*, 69–70.

44. Argenis Azuaje to Juan Vicente Gómez, August 3, 1913, in *BAHM* 17–18 (1962): 175.

45. *Notas* (Barquisimeto), February 20, 1916, 3.

46. In 1922, Arrieche had to cede fourteen haciendas, twenty houses, and other goods to his creditors, Blöhm and Company of Barquisimeto, to settle a debt of 46,642.09 bolívares. RPEL.PDC, pr. 1, esc. 25, fols. 24–29, October 25, 1922.

47. Núñez, *Bosquejo histórico*, 58.

Chapter 9. The Peasant Protests of 1936

1. Powell, *Political Mobilization*, 44–56.

2. For the original study, see Thompson, "Moral Economy," 76–136. Thompson comments on these later developments in "The Moral Economy Reviewed," in his *Customs in Common*, esp. 336–51.

3. Examples of moral economy analysis applied to rural settings include Scott, *Moral Economy;* Mallon, *Defense of Community;* Langer, "Labor Strikes and Reciprocity"; Tutino, *From Insurrection to Revolution*, 13–37; and Knight, *The Mexican Revolution*, 1:150–70.

4. Roseberry, "Images of the Peasant in the Consciousness of the Venezuelan Proletariat," in *Anthropologies and Histories*, 56–57.

5. Gould, *To Lead as Equals*, esp. 8, 134–35, 139, 297–302.

6. See Scott, *Moral Economy*, chap. 6.

7. Ibid., 167; Knight, *The Mexican Revolution*, 1:162.

8. Of course, both village and precipitate peasantries have rebelled against the prospect of becoming proletarians. This was the fate awaiting many Duaqueños in the 1930s, whether it was in the form of degrading, irregular wage labor in commercial agriculture or the more unpredictable prospect of migration to the city in search of employment. Thus the Duaqueños could qualify as "anticapitalist" rebels if one considers capitalism to be fundamentally a mode of production rather than a system of global commerce.

9. Hobsbawm, "Inventing Traditions," in Hobsbawm and Ranger, *The Invention of Tradition*, 2–3; Thompson, "Introduction: Custom and Culture," in *Customs in Common*, 1.

10. For a statement of this position, see Skocpol, *States and Social Revolutions*.

11. See, for example, Tutino, *From Insurrection to Revolution*.

12. Ewell, *Venezuela*, 74–75.

13. Ibid., 73.

14. Lameda Acosta, *Desde Gómez*, folleto 1, 55–59.

15. Ibid., folleto 2, 14–15; Rodríguez Marrufo, "Aportes," 77–79.

16. John D. Martz, *Acción Democrática: Evolution of a Modern Political Party in Venezuela* (Princeton: Princeton University Press, 1966), 28–31; Lameda Acosta, *Desde Gómez*, folleto 2, 23, 26–27.

17. RPEL.j.pen. (1936) bulto 164, "Denuncia criminal presentada por Casimiro Casamayor contra Juan Isabel Giménez y otros por ataque a la propiedad particular," and "Denuncia presentada por los ciudadanos Domingo Javier & Martín Orozco."

18. The letter appeared in the press under the heading "La crítica situación de los agricultores del Distrito Crespo: David Gimón repartió las tierras a sus favoritos," *El Impulso* (Barquisimeto), March 9, 1936, 4.

19. The quotation is cited in Rodríguez Marrufo, "Aportes," 135; for destruction of property, *El Heraldo* (Barquisimeto), March 18, 1936, 1, and March 20, 1936, 1; on detachments of the civil guard, Rodríguez Marrufo, "Aportes," 146–48. *El Heraldo* (Barquisimeto), March 18, 1936, 1.

20. Rodríguez Marrufo, "Aportes," 140, 141–42.

21. All quotations in this paragraph are cited in ibid., 141–42.

22. *El Universal* (Caracas), April 13, 1936, 9.

23. A short biographical sketch of Delgado appeared shortly after his death in K. Delgado, "La mujer de un viajante," F10.

24. Rómulo Delgado S., all in *La Senda* (Duaca), "La danza del café," January 20, 1935; "Sobre el mismo tema," March 10, 1935; and "En defensa de la agricultura," April 7, 1935.

25. *El Heraldo* (Barquisimeto), March 18, 1936, 1, 3.

26. Compare to the case of the *tinterillos* (rural lawyers) and other middle-sector allies of Colombian peasants in LeGrand, *Frontier Expansion*, 69–77; and Michael F.

Jiménez, "At the Banquet of Civilization: The Limits of Planter Hegemony in Early Twentieth-Century Colombia," in Roseberry et al., *Coffee, Society, and Power*, 279–81.

27. The short-lived PRP united radical members of the generation of 1928 with older communist activists. Gabaldón Márquez, *Archivos*, 306.

28. Rodríguez Marrufo, "Aportes," 145–46.

29. *El Heraldo* (Barquisimeto), March 25, 1936, 1, 4, and March 30, 1936, 1.

30. For El Eneal, RPEL.j.pen. (1936) bulto 163, "Denuncia intentada por Juan Rafael Sequera Sangronis." For El Pegón and La Tigrera, RPEL.j.civ. (1936) bulto 192, doc. 889, "Interdicto de restitución promovido por la Señora Genoveva Tamayo de Asuaje contra José de la O. Silva y Jesús Blanco." For similar invasions, RPEL.j.civ. (1937) bulto 197, "Demanda de Anelo Gargano contra Ignacio Arenas, José Arquimides Múgica y Bonifacio Gudiño."

31. "Editorial: El problema de los latifundios," *El Heraldo* (Barquisimeto), April 6, 1936, 1.

32. *El Heraldo* (Barquisimeto), April 8, 1936, 1; Octavio Rodríguez Armella, interview by author, Barquisimeto, March 30, 1990.

33. Pepino Valenzuela, interview by author, Duaca, April 15, 1990.

34. RPEL.j.civ. (1927) bulto 171, "Demanda de Casimiro Casamayor contra Magdaleno Heredia, Antonio Alejos, Isaías Rivero, y Basilio Alejos"; ibid. (1933) bulto 185, "Demanda de Casimiro Casamayor contra Manuel Julian Meléndez"; and RPEL.PDC, pr. 1, esc. 13, fols. 20–22, February 5, 1935.

35. The quote appears, with slight differences in wording, in K. Delgado, "La mujer de un viajante," and in RPEL.j.pen. (1936) bulto 164, "Causa penal que obra contra Eusebio Castillo y correos por delito de homocidio," fols. 29–30.

36. RPEL.j.pen. (1936) bulto 164, "Causa penal que obra contra Eusebio Castillo y correos por delito de homocidio," fols. 18, 19, 29–30.

37. Ibid., fols. 3–4.

38. RPEL.j.pen. (1936) bulto 164, "Denuncia criminal presentada por Casimiro Casamayor contra Juan Isabel Giménez y otros por ataque a la propiedad particular."

39. All the material from Parra's testimony referred to in this paragraph is found in RPEL.j.pen. (1936) bulto 164, "Causa penal que obra contra Eusebio Castillo y correos por delito de homocidio," fols. 3–4.

40. Rodríguez Marrufo, "Aportes," 153.

41. *El Heraldo* (Barquisimeto), April 11, 1936, 1, 4.

42. The process can be followed in Venezuela, Ministerio de Agricultura y Cría, *Memoria* (Caracas: Artes Gráficas, 1938), vol. 1, pt. 1, 152–53; *Memoria* (Caracas: Editorial Atlantida, 1939), vol. 1 (Dirección de Tierras), 52; and *Memoria* (Caracas: Tipografía Garrido, 1942), 357.

43. Gabaldón Márquez, *Archivos*, 267.

44. K. Delgado, "La mujer de un viajante."

45. Ewell, *Venezuela*, 76.

46. Lara was one of only eight states where Gómez owned no property at the time of his death. His property was concentrated in the central coastal zone and his home state of Táchira. Caballero, *Gómez*, 183.

47. The future of the peasant struggle in Duaca was undermined because the

parties of the left and center that remained committed to agrarian issues in Lara turned their attention to areas such as El Tocuyo, where modern sugar enterprises employed large concentrations of workers. See Rodríguez Marrufo, "Controversia entre AD y el PCV," 279–87.

48. Venezuela, *Censos agrícola y pecuario, 1937, Estado Lara*, x, 3. These figures must be treated with caution, because there are some glaring internal contradictions in the census. For example, another table in the same census (page 31) gives the number of farms on public land in the district as 314, in direct contradiction to the table on page 3, according to the categories explained on page x.

49. Venezuela, *Segundo censo agropecuario*, 2:76.

50. Perales Frigols, "Geografía económica del Estado Lara," *Revista de Fomento* (Ministerio de Fomento, Caracas), nos. 79–82 (1953): 64–65.

51. The dispute over Duaca's ejidos received extensive coverage in two Barquisimeto newspapers, *El Impulso* and *El Informador*. Particularly informative articles include "Resguardos de la comunidad indígena de Duaca," *El Informador*, June 16, 1987, B6; "Comunidad de Duaca se propone la recuperación de sus ejidos," *El Impulso*, June 26, 1987, sección C; "Más de 100 productores están afectados por ordenanza sobre ejidos del Concejo Municipal de Crespo," *El Impulso*, July 18, 1987, B1; "El Distrito Crespo apunta hacia el futuro," *El Informador*, January 28, 1988, C6; "Es un acto demagógico declarar la III independencia de Crespo (según presidente de APROPECO)," *El Impulso*, March 22, 1988; and "A la opinión pública: Los ejidos de Duaca," *El Informador*, May 26, 1988, C6.

52. The weaknesses of agrarian reform are explored in Powell, *Political Mobilization*. See also FUDECO, *Contribución al conocimiento del Distrito Crespo*, 43.

Chapter 10. Coffee and Social Transformation

1. The best introduction to agrarian change in this period is still Duncan and Rutledge, *Land and Labour in Latin America*. Theoretical aspects are more fully discussed in Goodman and Redclift, *From Peasant to Proletarian*.

2. Graham, *Patronage and Politics*, esp. chap. 2.

3. On the role of coffee planters under the constitutional monarchy, see Leslie Bethell and José Murilo de Carvalho, "1822–1850," in Leslie Bethell, ed., *Brazil, Empire, and Republic, 1822–1930* (Cambridge, England: Cambridge University Press, 1989), 78–79, 84; and Graham, *Patronage and Politics*, 12–14, 29–30, 51, 67–68, 176–77, 271. On São Paulo, see Joseph Love, *São Paulo in the Brazilian Federation, 1889–1937* (Stanford: Stanford University Press, 1980), esp. chaps. 4–6.

4. Stein, *Vassouras*, 10–17.

5. Dean, "Latifundia and Land Policy," 606–25.

6. Dean, "Ecological and Economic Relationships in Frontier History," 76.

7. Costa, *Brazilian Empire*, chap. 4.

8. Dean, *Rio Claro*, 190–92, and Stolke, *Coffee Planters, Workers, and Wives*, chap. 2. For more optimistic views of colonos' economic mobility, see Mauricio A. Font, "Labor System and Collective Action in a Coffee Export Sector: São Paulo," in Rose-

berry et al., *Coffee, Society, and Power*, 181–205, and Thomas Holloway, *Immigrants on the Land: Coffee and Society in São Paulo, 1886–1934* (Chapel Hill: University of North Carolina Press, 1980).

9. McCreery, *Rural Guatemala*, and Cardoso, "Historia económica del café," 21–22, 27–28.

10. Williams, *States and Social Evolution*, 64–66.

11. McCreery, *Rural Guatemala*, 174; see also 179–81.

12. Ibid., chaps. 8–9.

13. Browning, *El Salvador*, 155–221; and Cardoso, "Historia económica del café," 14–15, 22–23, 29–30.

14. Williams, *States and Social Evolution*, 75–77, 207, 211, 219.

15. The quotations are from Gudmundson, *Costa Rica Before Coffee*, 151–52, 48. For the 1930s, see Gudmundson's detailed study of a single district, "Peasant, Farmer, Proletarian," 221–57.

16. Samper, *Generations of Settlers*, 167.

17. For coffee entrepreneurs' political role, see Anthony Winson, *Coffee and Democracy in Modern Costa Rica* (New York: St. Martin's, 1989), esp. 23–27.

18. Cardoso, "Formation of the Coffee Estate," 171; and Samper, *Generations of Settlers*, 75–76.

19. For a detailed study of one coffee enterprise, which emphasizes the difficulty in establishing a large landed estate, see Gertrud Peters Solórzano, "La formación territorial de las fincas grandes de café en la Meseta Central: Estudio de la firma Tournón (1877–1955)," *Revista de Historia* 9–10 (1980): 81–167. Peters finds that this foreign-controlled firm could only accumulate scattered small and medium-sized farms, rather than a large unified enterprise.

20. Gudmundson, "Peasant, Farmer, Proletarian."

21. Price, "Hands for the Coffee: Migrants," 62–80. Price effectively refutes the long-held notion that migrants from the Venezuelan *llanos* (plains) pioneered the Andean coffee economy.

22. Ibid. On labor exchanges, see Carvallo and Ríos de Hernández, *Temas*, 138–39; Wolf, "San José," 104–07; and Samper, *Generations of Settlers*, 214, 244, 250.

23. Roseberry, *Coffee and Capitalism*, esp. chap. 4 (quotation, 99).

24. Quotations in this paragraph are from ibid., 97, 173, 180.

25. Picó, *Libertad y servidumbre* and *Amargo café*; Bergad, *Coffee*.

26. Bergad, *Coffee*, 219, 222.

27. Picó, *Libertad y servidumbre*, 63–66, 81, 109–11, 164; Bergad, *Coffee*, 92, 94, 116–34. See also Sidney Mintz, "The Role of Forced Labor in Nineteenth-Century Puerto Rico," *Caribbean Historical Review* 2 (1951): 134–41.

28. LeGrand, *Frontier Expansion*, chaps. 2–3. Quotation from LeGrand, "Labor Acquisition and Social Conflict," 48.

29. This pattern, however, was not universal in Colombia. See Keith Christie, "Antioqueño Colonization in Western Colombia: A Reappraisal," *Hispanic American Historical Review* 58 (1978), esp. 262–68.

30. These struggles are discussed in Bergquist, *Labor in Latin America*, 330–75.

31. LeGrand, *Frontier Expansion*, 170.

Selected Bibliography

Archival Sources

This work is based largely on unpublished materials from Venezuelan archives in Caracas, Barquisimeto, and Duaca. The archives are described here in order of their importance to the study, beginning with the most important.

1. Registro Principal del Estado Lara, Barquisimeto

Records used from this archive fall into two categories. First are the notarial records known as *protocolos,* which include sales, mortgages, documents granting power of attorney, and wills. These constituted my major source for reconstructing Duaca's economy, particularly regarding credit and land tenure. The protocolos are organized by district and by year. Through 1899, documents regarding the municipality of Duaca are with the district of Barquisimeto (now Distrito Iribarren). Beginning in 1900, documents for Duaca (Distrito Crespo) are separate. As is common in property registries throughout Venezuela, the protocolos from the decades between independence and the mid-1870s are in poor condition and many can no longer be read. But protocolos from that period forward are in very good condition, bound by trimester, with a name index in most volumes.

The second group of *registro* documents used for this study are the judicial documents. These are divided between civil and criminal cases. The civil documents are in fine condition but are organized only by year, not by district, and thus are very time-consuming. Nevertheless, the civil suits from Duaca provided crucial information on relationships between landlords and tenants, particularly for the twentieth century. The documents from criminal cases are stored in a separate room with no permanent personnel, which makes access more difficult. Again, they are organized by year but not by district.

2. Archivo de la Academia Nacional de la Historia, Caracas

This newly renovated archive includes a number of separate collections, most of which are dedicated to the colonial and independence eras. Of particular use for this study was the Colección Ambrosio Perera. A historian of Lara, Perera collected a wide assortment of documents, the most useful being the papers of Leopoldo Torres, a lawyer and politician whose career spanned the years from around 1880 through the mid-1920s. Torres's papers deal with all regions of Lara and include correspondence from his term as state president under Cipriano Castro, as well as papers originating from his work as a lawyer.

The archive also contains the Colección José Manuel Hernández, composed of papers relating to the career of the Venezuelan caudillo popularly known as El Mocho. This collection includes documents produced by Hernandistas in all regions of Venezuela—including a good run of correspondence from Lara—but the collection sheds little light on Duaca, undoubtedly because Hernández had so few supporters there.

3. Archivo del Consejo Municipal de Duaca

This archive holds a small assortment of documents from the district council between 1905 and the mid-1930s. The most useful were the records of the council meetings and the copy book of the council's correspondence, but each set was missing a number of years. Unfortunately, some council documents—such as maps showing the boundaries of the Indian lands—have been lost.

4. Archivo del Consejo Municipal de Barquisimeto

This archive holds documents of the same type found in Duaca but has very little from the period before 1900, when Duaca was under the jurisdiction of the Barquisimeto council. Nevertheless, the records from several years in the 1890s provided some material concerning tensions between Duaca and Barquisimeto.

5. Archivo General de la Nación, Caracas

Potentially very useful because of its manuscript records from the government agencies charged with administering public lands, this archive seems to give highest priority to collections relating to the colonial and independence eras. Special permission is required to use documents from the Ministry of Development or the Ministry of Agriculture and Livestock. Even though the archive's published guide indicates substantial holdings relating to public lands in Lara, little was found. Still, the papers here included some potentially useful documents for other geographic areas, such as letters between public land inspectors and the Ministry of Development and petitions from public land occupants claiming that the areas they cultivated were being usurped.

Published Sources

Acosta Saignes, Miguel. *Estudios en antropología, sociología, historia, y folclor*. Caracas: ANH, 1980.

———. *Latifundio*. Mexico City: Editorial Popular, 1938.

Altolaguirre y Duvale, Angel de, ed. *Relaciones geográficas de la gobernación de Venezuela, 1767–1768*. Caracas: Ediciones de la Presidencia de la República, 1954.

Alvarado, Lisandro. *Historia de la Revolución Federal en Venezuela*. Caracas: Ministerio de Educación, 1956. [Orig., 1909].

Arcila Farías, Eduardo. *El régimen de la encomienda en Venezuela*. 3rd ed. Caracas: Universidad Central de Venezuela, 1979.

Arcondo, Aníbal. "La crisis de la agricultura venezolana durante el período 1873–1889." *Tierra Firme* 20 (1987): 381–95.

Ardao, Alicia. *El café y las ciudades en los Andes venezolanos, 1870–1930*. Caracas: ANH, 1984.

Arellano Moreno, Antonio, ed. *Relaciones geográficas de Venezuela*. Caracas: ANH, 1964.

Armas Chitty, J. A., ed. *El Mocho Hernández (papeles de su archivo)*. Caracas: Universidad Central de Venezuela, 1978.

Armellada, Fray Cesáreo, ed. *Fuero indígena venezolana*. 2 vols. Caracas: Venezuela, Ministerio de Justicia, 1954.

Ascanio R., Consuelo. "Consideraciones sobre la situación del café venezolano entre 1908 y 1935." *Tierra Firme* 12 (1985): 613–28.

Aston, T. H., and C. H. E. Philpin, eds. *The Brenner Debate: Agrarian Class Structure and Economic Development in Pre-Industrial Europe*. Cambridge: Cambridge University Press, 1985.

Bailey, F. G. *Stratagems and Spoils: A Social Anthropology of Politics*. Oxford, England: Basil Blackwell, 1969.

Barquisimeto (Provincia). *Ordenanzas, resoluciones, decretos y acuerdos de la Diputación Provincial de Barquisimeto*. Barquisimeto: Oficina de Joaquín Pérez, 1853.

———. *Ordenanzas y resoluciones expedidas por la Diputación Provincial de Barquisimeto en 1856*. Barquisimeto: Oficina de Joaquín Pérez, 1857.

Bauer, Arnold. *Chilean Rural Society from the Spanish Conquest to 1930*. Cambridge: Cambridge University Press, 1975.

———. "Rural Society." In *Latin America: Economy and Society, 1870–1930*, ed. Leslie Bethell. Cambridge: Cambridge University Press, 1989.

———. "Rural Workers in Spanish America: Problems of Peonage and Oppression." *Hispanic American Historical Review* 59 (1979): 34–63.

Bergad, Laird W. *Coffee and the Growth of Agrarian Capitalism in Nineteenth-Century Puerto Rico*. Princeton: Princeton University Press, 1983.

Bergquist, Charles. *Labor in Latin America: Comparative Essays on Chile, Argentina, Venezuela, and Colombia*. Stanford: Stanford University Press, 1986.

Briceño Ayestarán, Santiago. *Memorias de su vida militar y política*. Caracas: Tipografía Americana, 1948.

Brito Figueroa, Federico. *Historia económica y social de Venezuela*. 4 vols. Caracas: Universidad Central de Venezuela, 1979–1987.

Browning, David. *El Salvador: Landscape and Society*. Oxford, England: Clarendon Press, 1971.

Caballero, Manuel. *Gómez, el tirano liberal*. 3rd ed. Caracas: Monte Avila, 1994.

Camacho, Antonieta. "Aportes para el estudio de la formación de la mano de obra en Venezuela: Esclavos y libres, 1810–1865." In *Materiales para el estudio de la cuestión agraria en Venezuela, 1810–1865: Mano de obra, legislación, y administración*. Caracas: Universidad Central de Venezuela, 1979.

Cardoso, Ciro F. S. "The Formation of the Coffee Estate in Nineteenth-Century Costa Rica." In *Land and Labour in Latin America*, ed. Duncan and Rutledge. Cambridge: Cambridge University Press, 1977.

————. "Historia económica del café en centroamérica (siglo xix): Estudio comparativo." *Estudios Sociales Centroamericanos* (San José), no. 10 (1975): 9–55.

Cardozo, Orlando. "Duaca a princípios del siglo." In *San Juan Bautista de Duaca*. Barquisimeto: Fondo Editorial Buría, 1988.

Carrocera, P. Buenaventura de, ed. *Misión de los capuchinos en los llanos de Caracas*. Vol. 1. Caracas: ANH, 1972.

Carvallo, Gastón, and Josefina Ríos de Hernández. *Temas de la Venezuela agroexportadora*. Caracas: Tropykos, 1984.

Costa, Emília Viotti da. *The Brazilian Empire: Myths and Histories*. Chicago: University of Chicago Press, 1985.

Cronon, William. *Changes in the Land: Indians, Colonists, and the Ecology of New England*. New York: Hill and Wang, 1983.

Cunill Grau, Pedro. *Geografía del poblamiento venezolano en el siglo xix*. 3 vols. Caracas: Ediciones de la Presidencia de la República, 1987.

————. "Historia ambiental y regionalización en Venezuela durante el siglo xix." *Tierra Firme* 30 (1990): 139–53.

Dean, Warren. "Ecological and Economic Relationships in Frontier History: São Paulo, Brazil." In *Essays on Frontiers in World History*, ed. George Wolfskill and Stanley Palmer. Austin: University of Texas Press, 1981.

————. "Latifundia and Land Policy in Nineteenth-Century Brazil." *Hispanic American Historical Review* 51 (1971): 606–25.

————. *Rio Claro: A Brazilian Plantation System, 1820–1920*. Stanford: Stanford University Press, 1976.

Delgado, Kotepa. "La mujer de un viajante." *El Nacional* (Caracas), August 25, 1985, F10.

Delgado Segura, Rómulo. *Miscelaneas duaqueñas*. Barquisimeto: Tipografia Nieves, 1971.

Diccionario histórico de Venezuela. 3 vols. Caracas: Fundación Polar, 1988.

Duncan, Kenneth, and Ian Rutledge, eds. *Land and Labour in Latin America: Essays on the Development of Agrarian Capitalism in the Nineteenth and Twentieth Centuries*. Cambridge: Cambridge University Press, 1977.

Dupouy, Walter. "Las Casas Blöhm de Venezuela." *Boletín de la Asociación Cultural Humboldt*, nos. 11–12 (1976): 113–31.

Edelman, Marc, and Mitchell A. Seligson. "Land Inequality: A Comparison of Census Data and Property Records in Twentieth-Century Southern Costa Rica." *Hispanic American Historical Review* 74.3 (1994): 445–91.

Ellner, Steve. "Venezuelan Revisionist Political History, 1908–1958: New Motives and Criteria for Analyzing the Past." *Latin American Research Review* 30.2 (1995): 91–121.

Ewell, Judith. *Venezuela: A Century of Change*. Stanford: Stanford University Press, 1984.

Ferry, Robert J. *The Colonial Elite of Early Caracas: Formation and Crisis, 1567–1767*. Berkeley and Los Angeles: University of California Press, 1989.

Flory, Thomas. *Judge and Jury in Imperial Brazil: Social Control and Political Stability in the New State*. Austin: University of Texas Press, 1981.

Floyd, Mary B. *Guzmán Blanco: La dinámica de la política del septenio*. Caracas: FUNRES, 1988.

FUDECO (Fundación para el Desarrollo de la Región Centro Occidental de Venezuela). *Contribución al conocimiento del Distrito Crespo*. Barquisimeto: FUDECO, 1971.

Gabaldón Márquez, Joaquín. *Archivos de una inquietud venezolana*. Caracas and Madrid: Ediciones Edime, 1955.

Garriga, Gorgias R. *Fichas, señas, y ñapas de Venezuela*. Caracas: Lagoven, 1979.

Gilmore, Robert. *Caudillism and Militarism in Venezuela, 1810–1910*. Athens: University of Ohio Press, 1964.

Gómez R., Carmen. "Política de enajenación y arrendamiento de tierras baldías." In *Materiales para el estudio de la cuestión agraria en Venezuela, 1829–1860: Enajenación y arrendamiento de tierras baldías*. Caracas: Universidad Central de Venezuela, 1971.

Gómez Rodríguez, Carmen, and Antonieta Camacho Zavala, eds. *Materiales para el estudio de la cuestión agraria en Venezuela, 1829–1860: Enajenación y arrendamiento de tierras baldías*. Caracas: Universidad Central de Venezuela, 1971.

González Bracho, Matías. *Verdad histórica de la revolución acaudillada por el Gral. J. R. Gabaldón en Santo Cristo, año 1929*. Caracas: N.p., 1958.

Goodman, David, and Michael Redclift. *From Peasant to Proletarian: Capitalist Development and Agrarian Transitions*. New York: St. Martin's, 1982.

Gormsen, Erdmann. *Barquisimeto: Una ciudad mercantil en Venezuela*. Caracas: Editorial Arte, 1966.

Gould, Jeffrey L. *To Lead as Equals: Rural Protest and Political Consciousness in Chinandega, Nicaragua, 1912–1979*. Chapel Hill: University of North Carolina Press, 1990.

Graham, Richard. *Patronage and Politics in Nineteenth-Century Brazil*. Stanford: Stanford University Press, 1990.

———. "State and Society in Brazil, 1822–1930." *Latin American Research Review* 22 (1987): 223–36.

Gudmundson, Lowell. *Costa Rica Before Coffee: Society and Economy on the Eve of the Export Boom*. Baton Rouge: Louisiana State University Press, 1986.

———. "Peasant, Farmer, Proletarian: Class Formation in a Smallholder Coffee Economy, 1850–1950." *Hispanic American Historical Review* 69 (1989): 221–57.

Hawkshaw, John. *Reminiscences of South America from Two and One Half Years' Residence in Venezuela*. London: Jackson and Walford, 1838.

Heredia A., Cipriano. *El año 29: Recuento de la lucha armada*. Caracas: Avilarte, 1974.

Humboldt, F. H. Alexander von. *Personal Narrative of Travels to the Equinoctial Regions of America During the Years 1799–1803*. 7 vols. Translated by Helen Maria Williams. London: Longman, Hurst, Rees, Orme and Brown, 1819.

Instituto Nacional del Café. *Censo cafetero.* Caracas: Instituto Nacional del Café, 1940.

Irwin G., Domingo. "Notas sobre los empresarios políticos de la violencia en la Venezuela de la segunda mitad del siglo xix." *Tierra Firme* 29 (1990): 15–20.

Izard, Miguel. "La agricultura venezolana en una época de transición, 1777–1830." *Boletín Histórico* 10 (1972): 81–145.

———. "El café en la economía venezolana del siglo xix (estado de la cuestión)." *Estudis* (Valencia, Spain), 1 (1973): 205–73.

———. *Series estadísticas para la historia de Venezuela.* Mérida: Universidad de los Andes, 1970.

Jiménez, Michael F. "Traveling Far in Grandfather's Car: The Life Cycle of Central Colombian Coffee Estates. The Case of Viotá, Cundinamarca, 1900–1930." *Hispanic American Historical Review* 69 (1989): 185–219.

Johnson, Ann Hagerman. "The Impact of Market Agriculture on Family and Household Structure in Nineteenth-Century Chile." *Hispanic American Historical Review* 58 (1978): 633–48.

Kettering, Sharon. "The Historical Development of Political Clientelism." *Journal of Interdisciplinary History* 18 (1988): 419–47.

Knight, Alan. *The Mexican Revolution.* 2 vols. Cambridge and New York: Cambridge University Press, 1986.

Kornblith, Miriam. "Estado y políticas de gasto público." In *Apreciación del proceso histórico venezolano,* by Ramón J. Velásquez, Arturo Uslar Pietri et al., 93–101. Caracas: Fundación Universidad Metropolitana and Fondo Editorial Interfundaciones, 1988.

Lameda Acosta, I. E. *Desde Gómez hasta la Revolución de Octubre: Historia de una década de sucesos políticos en Lara, de 1935 á 1945.* Barquisimeto: Tipografía Vásquez, 1953.

Langer, Erick D. "Labor Strikes and Reciprocity on Chuquisaca Haciendas." *Hispanic American Historical Review* 65 (1985): 255–77.

LeGrand, Catherine. *Frontier Expansion and Peasant Protest in Colombia, 1830–1936.* Albuquerque: University of New Mexico Press, 1986.

———. "Labor Acquisition and Social Conflict on the Colombian Frontier, 1850–1936." *Journal of Latin American Studies* 16 (1984): 27–49.

Lieuwen, Edwin. *Petroleum in Venezuela: A History.* New York: Russell and Russell, 1954.

Linder, Peter S. "Agriculture and Rural Society in Pre-Petroleum Venezuela: The Sur del Lago Zuliano, 1880–1920." Ph.D. diss., University of Texas, Austin, 1992.

———. "Coerced Labor in Venezuela, 1880–1936." *The Historian* 57 (1994): 43–58.

———. "Relaciones de producción en las haciendas del Sur del Lago Zuliano, 1880–1936: Algunas conclusiones preliminares." *Tierra Firme* 19 (1987): 283–93.

Lombardi, John V. *Venezuela: The Search for Order, the Dream of Progress.* Oxford and New York: Oxford University Press, 1982.

Lombardi, John V., and James A. Hanson. "The First Venezuelan Coffee Cycle, 1830–1855." *Agricultural History* 44 (1970): 355–69.

Mallon, Florencia. *The Defense of Community in Peru's Central Highlands: Peasant Struggle and Capitalist Transition, 1860–1940.* Princeton: Princeton University Press, 1983.

Manzanarez, Ismael. *La Revolución Liberal Restauradora en el norte del Estado Lara.* Barquisimeto: El Pueblo, 1900.

Martí, Mariano. *Documentos relativos a su visita pastoral de la diócesis de Caracas, 1771–1784,* ed. Lino Gómez Canedo. 7 vols. Caracas: ANH, 1969.

Martínez Guarda, María Antonieta. "Las tierras de resguardos indígenas: Un aspecto de la formación de la propiedad territorial en el siglo xix." *Revista Universitaria de Historia* 1 (1982).

Martínez Mendoza, Rafael. *Manual del agricultor venezolano, o compendio de todos los cultivos tropicales.* 2nd ed. Caracas: Tipografía Central, 1930.

Materiales para el estudio de la cuestión agraria en Venezuela, 1800–1830. Caracas: Universidad Central de Venezuela, 1964.

Materiales para el estudio de la cuestión agraria en Venezuela, 1810–1865: Mano de obra, legislación, y administración. Caracas: Universidad Central de Venezuela, 1979.

Matthews, Robert. "Rural Violence and Social Unrest in Venezuela, 1840–1858: Origins of the Federalist War." Ph.D. diss., New York University, 1974.

McCreery, David. *Rural Guatemala, 1760–1940.* Stanford: Stanford University Press, 1994.

Mintz, Sidney W. "A Note on the Definition of Peasantries." *Journal of Peasant Studies* 1 (1973): 91–106.

Molina, Luis E. "Proposiciones para una interpretación del pasado prehispánico del Estado Lara, Venezuela." *Revista de Ciencias Sociales de la Región Centro Occidental* 3 (1986): 65–90.

Montiel Acosta, Nelson. "El conuco como sistema productivo en las formaciones económico-sociales venezolanas." *Tierra Firme* 18 (1987): 177–81.

Muñoz, Arturo. *El Táchira fronterizo: El aislamiento regional y la integración nacional en el caso de los Andes, 1881–1899.* Caracas: Biblioteca de Autores y Temas Tachirenses, 1985.

Neeson, J. M. "The Opponents of Enclosure in Eighteenth-Century Northamptonshire." *Past and Present* 105 (1985): 114–39.

Núñez, Angel María. *Bosquejo histórico de la población de Duaca.* Barquisimeto: Editorial Cuyuní, 1971.

Ortner, Sherry B. "Theory in Anthropology Since the Sixties." *Comparative Studies in Society and History* 26.1 (1984): 126–66.

Palacios, Marco. *Coffee in Colombia, 1850–1970.* Cambridge: Cambridge University Press, 1980.

Pang, Eul-Soo, and Ron Seckinger. "The Mandarins of Imperial Brazil." *Comparative Studies in Society and History* 14 (1972): 215–44.

Paredes Huggins, Nelson. "La incorporación de tierras baldías al dominio privado en el quinquenio 1910–1914." *Revista Universitaria de Historia* 8 (1984): 15–50.

———. *Vialidad y comercio en el occidente venezolano (principios del siglo xx).* Caracas: Tropykos, 1984.

Pepper, José Vicente. *A través de Lara.* N.p., 1941.

Perales Frigols, Pedro. *Geografía económica del Estado Lara.* Caracas: Ministerio de Fomento, 1954.

Perera, Ambrosio. *Historia político-territorial de los Estados Lara y Yaracuy.* Caracas: Artes Gráficas, 1946.

Picó, Fernando. *Amargo café (los pequeños caficultores de Utuado en la segunda mitad del siglo xix).* Río Piedras, P.R.: Ediciones Huracán, 1981.

———. *Libertad y servidumbre en el Puerto Rico del siglo xix (los jornaleros utuadeños en vísperas del auge del café)*. Río Piedras, P.R.: Ediciones Huracán, 1979.

Pino Iturrieta, Elías. "Estudio preliminar." In *Los hombres del Benemérito,* ed. Yolanda Segnini et al. Vol. 1. Caracas: Universidad Central de Venezuela, 1985.

Pino Iturrieta, Elías, ed. *Juan Vicente Gómez y su época.* Caracas: Monte Avila, 1988.

Powell, John Duncan. *Political Mobilization of the Venezuelan Peasant.* Cambridge, Mass.: Harvard University Press, 1971.

Price, Marie Daly. "Hands for the Coffee: Migration, Settlement, and Trade in Western Venezuela, 1870–1930." Ph.D. diss., Syracuse University, 1990.

———. "Hands for the Coffee: Migrants and Western Venezuela's Coffee Production, 1870–1930." *Journal of Historical Geography* 20.1 (1994): 62–80.

Quintero, Inés. *El ocaso de una estirpe: La centralización restauradora y el fin los caudillos históricos.* Caracas: Fondo Editorial Acta Científica Venezolana, 1989.

———. "La muerte del caudillismo en tres actos." *Tierra Firme* 29 (1990): 41–53.

Ríos de Hernández, Josefina. *La hacienda venezolana (una visión a través de la historia oral).* Caracas: Tropykos, 1988.

Rodríguez, Luis Cipriano. *Gómez: Agricultura, petróleo, y dependencia.* Caracas: Tropykos, 1983.

Rodríguez Marrufo, Luisa. "Aportes para el estudio del movimiento agrario en el Estado Lara, 1936–1948." Master's thesis, Universidad Central de Venezuela, Caracas, 1986.

———. "Controversia entre AD y el PCV por el control del movimiento sindical agrario en el Estado Lara, 1945–1948." *Tierra Firme* 30 (1990): 279–87.

Rojas, Reinaldo. "Aproximaciones a la comprensión histórica del régimen de la encomienda en Barquisimeto colonial, 1530–1810." Master's thesis, Universidad Santa María, Caracas, 1986.

Roseberry, William. *Anthropologies and Histories: Essays in Culture, History, and Political Economy.* New Brunswick, N.J.: Rutgers University Press, 1989.

———. *Coffee and Capitalism in the Venezuelan Andes.* Austin: University of Texas Press, 1983.

———. "La falta de brazos: Land and Labor in the Coffee Economies of Nineteenth-Century Latin America." *Theory and Society* 20 (1991): 351–82.

———. "Something About Peasants, History, and Capitalism." *Critique of Anthropology* 5.3 (1985): 69–76.

Roseberry, William, Lowell Gudmundson, and Mario Samper, eds. *Coffee, Society, and Power in Latin America.* Baltimore: Johns Hopkins University Press, 1995.

Samper, Mario. *Generations of Settlers: Rural Households and Markets on the Costa Rican Frontier, 1850–1935.* Boulder, Colo.: Westview Press, 1990.

Sanoja, Mario, and Iraída Vargas. *Antiguas formaciones y modos de producción venezolanos.* Caracas: Monte Avila Editores, 1974.

Scott, James C. *The Moral Economy of the Peasant: Rebellion and Subsistence in Southeast Asia.* New Haven: Yale University Press, 1976.

———. *Weapons of the Weak: Everyday Forms of Peasant Resistance.* New Haven: Yale University Press, 1985.

Segnini, Yolanda. *La consolidación del régimen de Juan Vicente Gómez.* Caracas: ANH, 1982.

Segnini, Yolanda, et al., eds. *Los hombres del Benemérito: Epistolario inédito.* 2 vols. Caracas: Universidad Central de Venezuela, 1985.

Silva Uzcátegui, R. D. *Enciclopedia larense.* Caracas: Ediciones de la Presidencia de la República, [1941] 1981; 2nd ed. Barquisimeto, n.p., 1969.

Skocpol, Theda. *States and Social Revolutions.* Cambridge: Cambridge University Press, 1979.

Smith, Carol A. "Anthropology and History: A Look at Peasants and Capitalism." *Critique of Anthropology* 5.3 (1985): 87–94.

Smith, Gavin. *Livelihood and Resistance: Peasants and the Politics of Land in Peru.* Berkeley and Los Angeles: University of California Press, 1989.

Stein, Stanley J. *Vassouras, a Brazilian Coffee County, 1850–1900: The Roles of Planter and Slave in a Plantation Society.* Princeton: Princeton University Press, 1985 [orig. publ. 1958].

Stolke, Verena. *Coffee Planters, Workers, and Wives: Class Conflict and Gender Relations on São Paulo Plantations.* London: Macmillan, 1988.

Thompson, E. P. *Customs in Common.* Harmondsworth, England: Penguin Books, 1993.

———. "The Moral Economy of the English Crowd in the Eighteenth Century." *Past and Present* 50 (1970): 76–136.

———. *Whigs and Hunters: The Origin of the Black Act.* New York: Pantheon Books, 1975.

Tutino, John. *From Insurrection to Revolution in Mexico: Social Bases of Agrarian Violence, 1750–1940.* Princeton: Princeton University Press, 1986.

Urbaneja, Diego Bautista. "Caudillismo y pluralismo en el siglo xix venezolano." *Politeia* (Caracas), no. 4 (1975): 133–51.

———. "El sistema política gomecista." In *Juan Vicente Gómez y su época,* ed. Elías Pino Iturrieta. Caracas: Monte Avila, 1985.

Van Young, Eric. "Mexican Rural History Since Chevalier: The Historiography of the Colonial Hacienda." *Latin American Research Review* 18 (1983): 5–62.

Vásquez, Francisco de Paula. *Apuntaciones para la historia del Estado Lara.* Barquisimeto: Tipografía Nicolás Vásquez, 1940.

Velásquez, Ramón J. *La caída del liberalismo amarillo: Tiempo y drama de Antonio Paredes.* 6th ed. Caracas: Ediciones de la Presidencia de la República, 1988.

Venezuela, Ministerio de Fomento. *Apuntes estadísticos del Estado Barquisimeto.* Caracas: La Opinión Nacional, 1876.

———. *Censos agrícola y pecuario, 1937, Estado Lara.* Caracas: Ministerio de Agricultura y Cría, 1968.

———. *Memoria.* Caracas: Imprenta y Litografía del Gobierno Nacional, 1888.

———. *Memoria.* Caracas: Imprenta y Litografía del Gobierno Nacional, 1890.

———. *Segundo censo agropecuario.* Caracas: Ministerio de Fomento, 1959.

———. *Tercer censo de la república.* Vol. 2. Caracas: Imprenta y Litografía del Gobierno Nacional, 1891.

Verna, Paul. *Las minas del Libertador: Tres siglos y medio de historia venezolana.* Caracas: Imprenta Nacional, 1975.

Vila, Marco Aurelio. *Aspectos geográficos del Estado Lara*. Caracas: Corporación Venezolana de Fomento, 1966.

———. *Notas sobre geoeconomía prehispánica de Venezuela*. Caracas: Universidad Central
de Venezuela, 1976.

Vincent, Joan. "Political Anthropology: Manipulative Strategies." *Annual Reviews in
Anthropology* 7 (1978): 175–94.

Williams, Robert G. *States and Social Evolution: Coffee and the Rise of National Governments in Central America*. Chapel Hill: University of North Carolina Press, 1994.

Wolf, Eric R. "San José: Subcultures of a 'Traditional' Coffee Municipality." In *The People of Puerto Rico: A Study in Social Anthropology,* ed. Julian Steward et al. Urbana:
University of Illinois Press, 1956.

———. "Types of Latin American Peasantry: A Preliminary Discussion." *American
Anthropologist* 57 (1955): 452–71.

Yarrington, Douglas K. "Duaca in the Age of Coffee: Land, Society, and Politics in a
Venezuelan District, 1830–1936." Ph.D. diss., University of Texas, Austin, 1992.

Ziems, Angel. *El gomecismo y la formación del ejército nacional*. Caracas: Editorial Ateneo
de Caracas, 1979.

Index